Few Christians have exercised such an enormous international influence on evangelicalism as John Stott. From the articulate proclamation and defense of Christ's redeeming work to the advancement of world missions, Dr. Stott's mission to relate apostolic truth to contemporary challenges and opportunities has shaped a generation. Timothy Dudley-Smith has rendered us an invaluable service by collecting the best words of wisdom that will deepen our faith, inflame our passion and embolden us for witness and service.

MICHAEL HORTON
president
Christians United for Reformation

No one sets a higher standard in popular Christian writing than John R. W. Stott. Anyone who cares about the progress of the gospel—even those who may disagree with him here and there—must surely admire his wonderful clarity, his abundance of insight and his fair-minded fervor in expounding the Word of God for our time. This marvelous collection gives us a rare overview of the lifework produced by one of the most respected, prolific and influential evangelical voices of our century.

GEORGE HUNSINGER
Center of Theological Inquiry
Princeton, New Jersey

Since I consider John Stott the sanest, clearest and most solidly biblical living writer on theological topics in the English language, I am of course enthusiastic about this book. It is a thoughtful distillation of many of Stott's signally concise expositions of important Christian teachings. Timothy Dudley-Smith has done a good job in his work as collector, editor and sorter. I'm sure that Dudley-Smith would not mind my adding that what makes me even more enthusiastic about this book is the stimulus it will provide for securing and reading John Stott's books in their entirety. And that is a consummation devoutly to be wished.

MARK A. NOLL
McManis Professor of Christian Thought
Wheaton College

No modern author has been more helpful to me than John Stott. For more than thirty years I have eagerly learned from his example, demeanor and teaching, and I warmly welcome this resource.

D. STUART BRISCOE
pastor
Elmbrook Church, Brookfield, Wisconsin

Authentic Christianity is more than an anthology of John Stott's writings drawn from a lifetime of faithful Bible exposition and pastoral ministry. It is a sixty-seven-part survey of theology, from thoughts on the doctrine of God to the believer's hope of glory. If you are familiar with Stott's writings, you will welcome this addition to your collection. If you are not yet familiar with Stott, begin to get acquainted now. *Authentic Christianity* is a splendid place to start.

JAMES M. BOICE
minister
Tenth Presbyterian Church, Philadelphia, Pennsylvania

These 970 well-chosen selections display the range, forthrightness and fertility of John Stott's magisterial mind to fullest advantage. Here is a very remarkable treasure-house of wisdom. Buy, browse, enjoy and be built up!

J. I. PACKER
Sangwoo Youtong Chee Professor of Theology
Regent College

Authentic Christianity—
the Christianity of Christ and his apostles—
is supernatural Christianity.
It is not a tame and harmless ethic,
consisting of a few moral platitudes,
spiced with a dash of religion.
It is rather a resurrection religion,
a life lived by the power of God.

(see no. 731)

AUTHENTIC CHRISTIANITY

FROM THE WRITINGS OF

JOHN STOTT

Chosen and introduced by
Timothy Dudley-Smith

InterVarsity Press
Downers Grove, Illinois

Acknowledgments for the use of copyrighted material may be found beginning on page 417.

InterVarsity Press® is the book-publishing division of InterVarsity Christian Fellowship®, a student movement active on campus at hundreds of universities, colleges and schools of nursing in the United States of America, and a member movement of the International Fellowship of Evangelical Students. For information about local and regional activities, write Public Relations Dept., InterVarsity Christian Fellowship, 6400 Schroeder Rd., P.O. Box 7895, Madison, WI 53707-7895.

Cover illustration: Scala/Art Resource, NY: Leonardo da Vinci. Last Supper. *S. Maria delle Grazie, Milan, Italy*
ISBN 0-8308-1620-8

Printed in the United States of America ∞

Library of Congress Cataloging-in-Publication Data

Stott, John R. W.
    Authentic Christianity/from the writings of John Stott:
[compiled by] Timothy Dudley-Smith.
        p.   cm.
    Includes bibliographical references.
    ISBN 0-8308-1620-8 (alk. paper)
    1. Theology, Doctrinal—Quotations, maxims, etc.
2. Evangelicalism.   I. Dudley-Smith, Timothy.   II. Title.
BT78.S845   1996
230'.044—dc20   95-48952
                                                  CIP

17	16	15	14	13	12	11	10	9	8	7	6	5	4	3	2	1
10	09	08	07	06	05	04	03	02	01	00	99	98	97	96		

Foreword _____ 9

I. The living God _____ 15
1. The one eternal God _____ 17
2. Creator and Father _____ 22
3. Righteousness and love _____ 26

II. The Lord Jesus Christ _____ 31
4. The Word made flesh _____ 33
5. Teacher and Lord _____ 39
6. The kingdom of heaven _____ 43
7. The uniqueness of Christ _____ 47
8. The cross of Jesus _____ 50
9. Risen and ascended _____ 59
10. The return in glory _____ 64
11. Christ our contemporary _____ 66

III. The Holy Spirit _____ 69
12. The coming of the Spirit _____ 71
13. The Spirit and the Son _____ 74
14. The work of the Spirit _____ 76
15. Baptism and fullness _____ 79
16. The Spirit-filled Christian _____ 81

IV. Revelation and Scripture _____ 85
17. The divine self-disclosure _____ 87
18. 'God has spoken . . .' _____ 92
19. Biblical authority _____ 96
20. Listening and interpreting _____ 105
21. Scripture, reason and tradition _____ 114
22. The study of theology _____ 118
23. Truth and error _____ 123
24. A living Word _____ 130

V. What it is to be human _____ 135
25. Who am I? _____ 137
26. Human worth and dignity _____ 140

27. Our fallen nature —————————————————— 146
28. Self-love ————————————————————— 155
29. Mere religion —————————————————— 158

VI. Such great salvation ————————————— 161
30. The Christian gospel ———————————— 163
31. Full salvation ————————————————— 168
32. Justification ————————————————— 171
33. Faith ———————————————————————— 176
34. Grace, mercy and peace ———————————— 181
35. Law and judgment ————————————— 184

VII. Becoming a Christian —————————————— 189
36. Chosen and called ———————————————— 191
37. Turning to Christ ————————————————— 198
38. The new birth ————————————————— 203

VIII. Living as a Christian ——————————————— 209
39. Christian assurance ———————————————— 211
40. Growing and continuing ——————————— 214
41. Life in the Spirit ————————————————— 219
42. Prayer and the Bible ———————————————— 225
43. Morality and holiness ———————————————— 230
44. Humility and obedience ——————————— 237
45. Vocation and service ———————————————— 244
46. Freedom and authority ————————————— 253
47. The Christian mind ———————————————— 256

IX. The church of God ———————————————— 261
48. God's new society ————————————————— 263
49. Word, worship and sacrament ————————— 271
50. Ministers and ministry ———————————————— 282
51. The unity of the church ————————————— 296
52. Reforming the church ———————————————— 301
53. The evangelical tradition ——————————— 308

X. Into all the world ————————————————— 313
54. Christian mission ———————————————— 315
55. A servant church ————————————————— 320
56. The call to evangelize ————————————— 323
57. Proclaiming the gospel ——————————————— 332

XI. Christian thinking on social issues _____ 339
58. Evangelism and social action _____ 341
59. Christianity, religion and culture _____ 345
60. Politics and the state _____ 351
61. War, violence and peacemaking _____ 357
62. Work, wealth, poverty and human rights _____ 362
63. Gender, sexuality, marriage and divorce _____ 369

XII. Things temporal and things eternal _____ 377
64. Time, history and prophecy _____ 379
65. Miracles, healing and suffering _____ 386
66. The reality of evil _____ 393
67. The hope of glory _____ 398

List of sources _____ 407
Acknowledgments _____ 417
Index _____ 419

FOREWORD

John Stott has been writing for publication for over fifty years: his first article appeared in January 1945 when he was still a student. Before then his only contributions had been to school magazines: since then his writings have multiplied to include well over thirty books and some hundreds of pamphlets, articles, and chapters in symposia. It would be a Herculean task to trace in full the publishing history of translations of his work: *Basic Christianity* alone has appeared in some fifty languages, with a further twenty-two in preparation.

It is not difficult to see why his books are in demand. Indeed, with the single change of the fifth word in the following quotation from 'letters' to 'writings', one could apply to himself and his readers John Stott's description in his Tyndale Commentary of the author and students of the Johannine letters:

> Those students of John's letters who are likely to profit from them most, are those who share with the author his own combination of theological and ethical concerns. For John is above all else a pastor, entrusted with the care of a group of local churches, and anxious to help their members to learn how to think and live Christianly. At the foundation of their Christian thinking must be a right grasp of the unique divine-human person of Jesus, and at the foundation of their Christian living a transparent integrity of righteousness and love.

That need for 'Christian thinking' is a recurring theme in John Stott's teaching ministry, whether at the London Institute, on his travels, or in his books. *Thinking Christianly* was a possible title for this anthology, borrowing from Harry Blamires' seminal book *The Christian Mind*. The title actually chosen combines key words from the titles of two of his own books, *The Authentic Jesus* and *Basic Christianity*; and asserts the proposition that Christianity is authentic only when it is truly biblical. No-one can read far in John Stott's writings, even in such a collection as this, without being aware that his concern is to teach and expound a revealed faith, and to interpret the

authoritative and timeless Scriptures for a contemporary
world.

The idea for this book owes something to Clyde Kilby's C. S.
Lewis anthology, *A Mind Awake*. Like Kilby, I have gathered
quotations under an orderly arrangement of headings, the
better to reveal my author's mind. It is important, however, to
make clear that this book is neither a systematic theology nor
even a full and balanced exposition of John Stott's thought and
teaching. The extracts I quote are drawn from a variety of
different times and circumstances, often addressed to quite
different readerships; and I have not been at all concerned to
see that something is included on every topic that might
reasonably come within an individual chapter. Nor have I felt it
necessary always to include every qualification, or even every
balancing argument. For these, as indeed for a proper understanding of the author, I must refer the reader to his original
published writings. My sole criterion in reading or re-reading –
no doubt with unimportant exceptions – everything that John
Stott has written, has been to select the telling or instructive or
(above all) *thought-provoking* quotation. All I would ask is that
if something in these pages provokes disagreement, the reader
should not hold John Stott himself responsible until the
passage has been read in full, and in context, in the original
work from which it has been extracted.

C. S. Lewis, himself an anthologist (of the writings of George
Macdonald, for example), had pertinent things to say on the
subject when writing in 1941 for the *Review of English Studies* on
the newly published *Oxford Book of Christian Verse*:

> With the exception of textual criticism there is perhaps
> no scholarly activity in which the work is so dispropor-
> tionate to the reward as in the compiling of an
> anthology. The labour of reading through all, or nearly
> all, our sacred poets from Rolle to Ruth Pitter; of
> flogging into activity a critical faculty which must,
> before the end of the task, become as jaded as that of an
> examiner; of seeking – what is never attained – perfect
> accuracy in transcription and proof-reading, is very
> great; the reward is usually to have one's final choice
> criticized by reviewers who have not given a hundredth
> part of the editor's thought to the subject and who,
> perhaps, take for granted considerations which he has

had to abandon after serious reflection. I find myself just
such a reviewer.

I think it possible that you may find yourself just such a reader.
But this book will have served its purpose if it sends the
browser back to look again at such works by John Stott as may
be on his or her shelves – and to add to them.

There are a few further necessary words of explanation. For
instance, the importance of a particular truth or doctrine in the
spectrum of theological understanding may bear little relation
to the space here given to it. John Stott wrote a major book
(arguably his best) on *The Cross of Christ*, and this is well
represented. His writing on the incarnation, or on the resurrection, is more diverse. Again, some of these extracts may appear
longer than a reader with a taste for brevity might wish. This is
because John Stott's gifts (and concern) are more for sustained
and reasoned exposition and analysis than for epigram –
though there are memorable epigrams in these pages. Not only
is the content therefore determined to some extent by those
themes on which the author has written frequently or at length
– the Scriptures, preaching, the gospel and social responsibility,
for example – but some of his most valued and lasting writing
can only be hinted at here (for example, in the series *The Bible
Speaks Today*), because for the most part it needs to be read at
length, in its full context, alongside the passage it expounds. A
further characteristic of this author is largely absent from these
pages: his ability to quote tellingly from a variety of writers,
and notably from secular commentators on the contemporary
world. In making this selection, though, I have tried to offer
John Stott's original writing, rather than his power of quotation, however apt. When Walter de la Mare came to write
Winged Chariot, his reflection on the nature of time, he adorned
the book with what seemed to be quotations from a wide range
of sources, though in fact many had been devised by himself to
suit his purpose. I hope my List of Sources is sufficient
guarantee that though there are not in this anthology many
instances of John Stott's use of quotation, yet all the passages
here included are from his own pen!

No doubt, too, the classification adopted in these twelve
sections is bound at times to appear somewhat arbitrary:
many extracts could equally well be included under a number
of headings. Sometimes, where the point is relevant and

important, and occurs more than once in John Stott's writings, it will be found in slightly different words in differing chapters of this book. For the 'bedtime reader' I judge this is no loss; and for someone making reference to the book for a particular purpose, it should be gain. Indeed, it is difficult to describe exactly the reader for whom this anthology is intended. I have tried to select items which may be less than self-evident to the general reader – but of course we all start from different levels of background and understanding, and there are inevitably a number of specific topics which relate more to the study of theology than to day-by-day discipleship. If some appear too self-evident to be worth repeating, I cannot do better than call once more on C. S. Lewis. Writing in 1939 to Dom Bede Griffiths, he made this point, which was to be repeated in *The Screwtape Letters* a couple of years later:

> The process of living seems to consist in coming to realize truths so ancient and simple that, if stated, they sound like barren platitudes. They cannot sound otherwise to those who have not had the relevant experience: that is why there is no real teaching of such truths possible and every generation starts from scratch . . .

Nevertheless, I dare to hope that this book may have a part to play for somebody in the learning of such truths. We all need to be put in mind from time to time of basic principles in the spiritual life which we fondly believe we have long outgrown. But if a given extract has nothing to say to you – why, read on!

The quotations are drawn from the original editions of the books, except in cases where a new and revised edition has superseded the original. Style in matters such as the use of capital letters for pronouns of deity has been standardized; but biblical quotations are cited from a variety of different translations, usually depending on the date of publication. Similarly since these extracts span over fifty years of writing, they show a considerable difference of usage in matters such as inclusive language of persons; and this variety has been retained in faithfulness to the original. The source of each extract is given in abbreviated form based on its year of publication, and may be interpreted by reference to the List of Sources on pp. 407ff. In the case of extract 1, for example, the source is given as '1971a:11'. The reader is thus referred to the sub-heading '1971' in the List, and to title 'a' under that sub-heading, namely *Basic Christianity*. The final number, 11, is the page reference.

Footnotes have been kept to a minimum and biblical references generally omitted except where they are necessary for the understanding of a passage. Indeed, a major reason for referring the interested reader to the original is that in all his books John Stott's thinking is shown to depend on, and to be buttressed by, a formidable weight of reference to Scripture.

Since this is a popular work, I have felt free to make minor adjustments to the exact form of the extracts, with no intrusive use of brackets, *etc.*, to denote the change. For the most part such alterations consist of removing unnecessary references to preceding arguments, or to the specific local context from which an extract has been drawn. But I have (I believe) been scrupulously careful that such editing, designed to secure easier reading, does not misrepresent the original. Fuller references to John Stott's published writings may be found in my book *John R. W. Stott: A Comprehensive Bibliography*, published simultaneously with this anthology.

I owe a debt of thanks to John Stott himself, to the various publishers who have given permissions, and to the publishers of this book (Jo Bramwell of IVP undertook much detailed editorial work), for making this anthology possible. My hope is that it may serve to introduce some new readers to the books and articles here quoted.

Ford, 1994   *Timothy Dudley-Smith*

I. THE LIVING GOD

1. The one eternal God
2. Creator and Father
3. Righteousness and love

1. THE ONE ETERNAL GOD

1. In the beginning

You can never take God by surprise. You can never anticipate him. He always makes the first move. He is always there 'in the beginning'. Before man existed, God acted. Before man stirs himself to seek God, God has sought man. In the Bible we do not see man groping after God; we see God reaching after man.

(1971a:11)

2. The divine vision

The vision we need is the vision of God himself, the God of the whole biblical revelation, the God of creation who made all things fair and good, and made man male and female to bear his image and subdue his world, the God of the covenant of grace who in spite of human rebellion has been calling out a people for himself, the God of compassion and justice who hates oppression and loves the oppressed, the God of the incarnation who made himself weak, small, limited and vulnerable, and entered our pain and alienation, the God of resurrection, ascension and Pentecost, and so of universal authority and power, the God of the church or the kingdom community to whom he has committed himself for ever, and whom he sends into the world to live, serve, suffer and die, the God of history who is working according to a plan and towards a conclusion, the God of the *eschaton*, who one day will make all things new.

There is no room for pessimism here, or for apathy either. There is room only for worship, for expectant faith, and for practical obedience in witness and service. For once we have seen something of the glory of our God, and of the greatness of his commission, we can only respond, 'I was not disobedient to the heavenly vision.'

(1978c:182)

3. Sovereign, ceaseless, purposeful activity

Perhaps the dominant theme of the whole Bible is the sovereign, ceaseless, purposeful activity of Almighty God. In contrast to the idols, which had eyes, ears, mouths and hands but could neither see nor hear, neither speak nor act, our God is a living and a busy God.

In its own dramatic and figurative way the Bible leaves us in no doubt of this. The breath of all living creatures is in his hand. The thunder is his voice and the lightning his fire. He causes the sun to shine and the rain to fall. He feeds the birds of the air and clothes the lilies of the field. He makes the clouds his chariot and the winds his messengers. He causes the grass to grow. His trees are well watered. He calms the raging of the sea. He also guides the affairs of people and nations. The mighty empires of Assyria and Babylonia, of Egypt and Persia, of Greece and Rome, were under his overruling control. He called Abraham from Ur. He delivered the Israelites from Egypt, led them across the desert and settled them in the Promised Land. He gave them judges and kings, priests and prophets. Finally he sent his only Son into the world to live, to teach, to die and to rise again.

(1991d:59)

4. The God of rationality

All scientific research is based on the convictions that the universe is an intelligible, even meaningful, system; that there is a fundamental correspondence between the mind of the investigator and the data being investigated; and that this correspondence is rationality. In consequence, 'a scientist faced with an apparent irrationality does not accept it as final . . . He goes on struggling to find some rational way in which the facts can be related to each other . . . Without that passionate faith in the ultimate rationality of the world, science would falter, stagnate and die . . .'[1] It is therefore no accident that the pioneers of the scientific revolution were Christians. They believed that the rational God had stamped his rationality both upon the world and upon them.

(1992b:115)

[1] Lesslie Newbigin, *Foolishness to the Greeks* (SPCK, 1986), p. 70.

5. Imperturbable sovereignty

'He who sits in the heavens laughs; the LORD has them in derision' (Ps. 2:4). There is no need for us to be offended by this anthropomorphism. God's 'laughter' and 'contempt' are highly dramatic imagery for his imperturbable sovereignty against which all the violent antagonism of men is ridiculous in its impotence. **(1966b:65)**

6. Too religious a God?

Our God is often too small because he is too religious. We imagine that he is chiefly interested in religion – in religious buildings (churches and chapels), religious activities (worship and ritual) and religious books (Bibles and prayer books). Of course he is concerned about these things, but only if they are related to the whole of life. According to the Old Testament prophets and the teaching of Jesus, God is very critical of 'religion', if by that is meant religious services divorced from real life, loving service and the moral obedience of the heart.

(1990a:15)

7. God in his fullness

The Areopagus address reveals the comprehensiveness of Paul's message. He proclaimed God in his fullness as Creator, Sustainer, Ruler, Father and Judge. He took in the whole of nature and of history. He passed the whole of time in review, from the creation to the consummation. He emphasized the greatness of God, not only as the beginning and the end of all things, but as the One to whom we owe our being and to whom we must give account. He argued that human beings already know these things by natural or general revelation, and that their ignorance and idolatry are therefore inexcusable. So he called on them with great solemnity, before it was too late, to repent. **(1990b:290)**

8. Unity and Trinity

God is both one and three. He is *the one . . . God . . ., Father, Son and Holy Spirit.* There can be no question of his unity. The Christian affirms this as strongly as any Jew or Muslim. 'The LORD our God is one LORD (Dt. 6:4). He says, 'I am the LORD, and there is no other, beside me there is no God' (Is. 45:5). The unity of the Godhead is fundamental to all evangelism. It is because 'there is one God' that he demands and deserves the total allegiance of all mankind. Yet this one God revealed himself in three stages (first as the God of Israel, then as the incarnate Lord, then as the Holy Spirit) in such a way as to show that he exists eternally in these three personal modes of being. So the risen Jesus has commanded us to baptize converts 'in the name (note the singular) of the Father and of the Son and of the Holy Spirit' (Mt. 28:19). **(1975d:5)**

9. A trinitarian Bible

The Christian understanding of the Bible is essentially a trinitarian understanding. The Bible comes from God, centres on Christ and is inspired by the Holy Spirit. So the best definition of the Bible is also trinitarian: 'the Bible is the witness of the Father to the Son through the Holy Spirit'.

(1982b:36)

10. A Christ-centred faith

It is true that the Christian faith is a trinitarian faith. We believe in God as Creator, Sustainer and Father. We also believe in the Holy Spirit as the Spirit of truth who spoke through the prophets and apostles, and who sanctifies the people of God. But above all our testimony is directed to Jesus Christ, Son of the Father and giver of the Spirit, who was conceived and born, suffered, and was crucified, died, was buried, and went to the dead, rose again, ascended, reigns and will come back to judge. The disproportion of clauses in the Apostles' Creed clearly exhibits the Christ-centred nature of the Christian faith; it contains only three relating to the work of the Spirit, but thirteen which speak of the Son. **(1985:9)**

11. God is light

Of the statements about the essential being of God, none is more comprehensive than *God is light*. It is his nature to reveal himself, as it is the property of light to shine; and the revelation is of perfect purity and unutterable majesty. We are to think of God as a personal being, infinite in all his perfections, transcendent, 'the high and lofty One . . . he who lives for ever, whose name is holy' (Is. 57:15), yet who desires to be known and has revealed himself. **(1988g:75)**

12. Why God is not always known

Just as it is the nature of light to shine, so it is the nature of God to reveal himself. True, he hides himself from the wise and clever, but only because they are proud and do not want to know him; he reveals himself to 'babies', that is, to those humble enough to receive his self-disclosure . . . The chief reason why people do not know God is not because he hides from them, but because they hide from him. **(1982a:93)**

13. God's self-consistency

Scripture has several ways of drawing attention to God's self-consistency, and in particular of emphasizing that when he is obliged to judge sinners, he does it because he must, if he is to remain true to himself. **(1986a:124)**

14. Seeking God

We must cast aside apathy, pride, prejudice and sin, and seek God in scorn of the consequences. Of all these hindrances to effective search the last two are the hardest to overcome, intellectual prejudice and moral self-will. Both are expressions of fear, and fear is the greatest enemy of the truth. Fear paralyses our search. We know that to find God and to accept Jesus Christ would be a very inconvenient experience. It would involve the rethinking of our whole outlook on life and the readjustment of our whole manner of life. And it is a combination of intellectual and moral cowardice which makes us hesitate. We do not find because we do not seek. We do not seek because we do not want to find, and we know that the way to be certain of not finding is not to seek. **(1971a:18)**

2. CREATOR AND FATHER

15. God the Creator

God the Creator is lord of his creation. He has not abdicated his throne. He rules what he has made. No Christian can have a mechanistic view of nature. The universe is not a machine which operates by inflexible laws, nor has God made laws to which he is himself now a slave . . . He is living and active in his universe . . . **(1988e:101)**

16. The divine constancy

Natural law is not an alternative to divine action, but a useful way of referring to it. So-called natural laws simply describe a uniformity which scientists have observed. And Christians attribute this uniformity to the constancy of God. Further, to be able to explain a process scientifically is by no means to explain God away; it is rather (in the famous words of the astronomer Kepler) to 'think God's thoughts after him' and to begin to understand his ways of working. **(1970b:59)**

17. The creative word

God created all things by *his sovereign will*. This is all that I would care to say dogmatically about the *mode* of creation, the means employed by God to bring things into existence. Christians still differ from one another in their views about creation and evolution, but all Christians must agree that, whatever precise mode God employed, all things came into being by the power of his will. One of the most significant refrains of the first chapter of Genesis is '*And God said . . .*' 'And God said, "let there be light", and there was light', '*And God said, "let there be a firmament"*, and it was so.' Now this creative word of God was an expression of his will, so that the heavenly hosts are represented in the Revelation as worshipping God partly for this reason, 'for thou didst create all things, and *by thy will* they existed and were created'. **(1962a:9)**

18. Creation and stewardship

The living God of the Bible is the God of both creation and redemption, and is concerned for the totality of our well-being. Put another way, the older theologians used to say that God

22

has written two books, one called 'nature' and the other called 'Scripture', through which he has revealed himself. Moreover, he has given us these two books to study. The study of the natural order is 'science', and of the biblical revelation 'theology' . . .

Christian people should surely have been in the vanguard of the movement for environmental responsibility, because of our doctrines of creation and stewardship. Did God make the world? Does he sustain it? Has he committed its resources to our care? His personal concern for his own creation should be sufficient to inspire us to be equally concerned. **(1993b:ix)**

19. The God of the gaps

The God of the biblical Christian has sometimes been termed the 'God of the gaps' because it is supposed that we resort to him only when we cannot fill the *lacunae* in our knowledge. Now that scientific discovery is steadily reducing the number of these gaps, the argument runs, God is being squeezed out. One day there will be no gaps left, and we shall then be able to dispense with him altogether. Long before the current fashion of the 'death of God' theology had been thought of, this notion had been expressed. In a manifesto adopted by the Secularist League at Liège in 1865 it was said: 'science has made God unnecessary.'

What is utterly bogus about this confident claim to have closed the gaps and dispensed with God is that at least two gaps are as wide as ever and will never be filled by human ingenuity. The first is the gulf between God and man caused by man's sin and God's judgment upon it, and the second is the gulf between man as he is and man as God meant him to be. Technology cannot span these gaps, nor can secular education teach us to build our own bridges. Only God can cross this great divide. And he has taken the initiative in Christ to do so. **(1967e:44)**

20. Creator, King and Father

The doctrine of God as a universal Father was not taught by Christ nor by his apostles. God is indeed the universal Creator, having brought all things into existence, and the universal King, ruling and sustaining all that he has made. But he is the Father only of our Lord Jesus Christ and of those whom he adopts into his family through Christ. If we would be the sons of God, then we must be 'in Christ Jesus . . . through faith' (Gal. 3:26), which is a better rendering than the familiar 'by faith in Christ Jesus' (AV). It is through faith that we are in Christ, and through being in Christ that we are sons of God.

(1968c:99)

21. A potential fatherhood

The universal fatherhood of God and the universal brotherhood of man, of which we hear much, is potential, not actual. It cannot come into being until all men and women submit to Jesus Christ and are born again.　　　　　　**(1991d:60)**

22. The God of the covenants

An understanding of the Bible is impossible without an understanding of the two covenants. After all, our Bibles are divided in half, into the Old and New Testaments, meaning the Old and New 'Covenants'. A covenant is a solemn agreement between God and men, by which he makes them his people and promises to be their God. God established the old covenant through Moses and the new covenant through Christ, whose blood ratified it. The old (Mosaic) covenant was based on law; but the new (Christian) covenant, foreshadowed through Abraham and foretold through Jeremiah, is based on promises. In the law God laid the responsibility on men and said 'thou shalt . . . thou shalt not . . .' but in the promise God keeps the responsibility himself and says 'I will . . . I will . . .' **(1968c:124)**

23. A jealous God?

It is written that Yahweh, 'whose name is Jealous, is a jealous God' (Ex. 34:14). Now jealousy is the resentment of rivals, and whether it is good or evil depends on whether the rival has any business to be there. To be jealous of someone who threatens to outshine us in beauty, brains or sport is sinful, because we cannot claim a monopoly of talent in those areas. If, on the other hand, a third party enters a marriage, the jealousy of the injured person, who is being displaced, is righteous, because the intruder has no right to be there. It is the same with God, who says, 'I am the LORD, that is my name! I will not give my glory to another or my praise to idols' (Is. 42:8). Our Creator and Redeemer has a right to our exclusive allegiance, and is 'jealous' if we transfer it to anyone or anything else.　　　　　　**(1990b:278)**

24. *God and our human predicament*

'Man come of age' in a technological world is still man in sin and under judgment, man the slave of his passions and helpless to save himself.

Contrary to what is often asserted nowadays, many people are still aware of this their human predicament. Let me give you an example. A friend of mine during the Second World War was the Sub-Lieutenant serving as navigator on the destroyer HMS *Eclipse*. He tells me that he could not escape from four realities. First, he made great resolves to break free from sin, only to be humiliated by repeated failure. Secondly, he knew he had broken God's laws. It used to strike him that if the 'King's Regulations and Admiralty Instructions' were held in great honour, with various unalterable penalties, God must be at least as just as the King and the Lords of the Admiralty. Thirdly, his sense of accountability to God increased when he was on watch by himself and remembered the unwelcome fact that death was possibly very near. Fourthly, his sense of sin and need was heightened by the awe-inspiring sights of the creation. 'If the God with whom I had to do had made the vast Atlantic rollers which carried us up and down with such irresistible power, then how great was he against whom I knew I had sinned. On watch at night the serenity and eternity of the stars also spoke of this same indescribably powerful God.'

(1967e:45)

3. RIGHTEOUSNESS AND LOVE

25. The righteousness of God

'The righteousness of God' can be thought of as a divine attribute (our God is a righteous God), or activity (he comes to our rescue), or achievement (he bestows on us a righteous status). All three are true and have been held by different scholars, sometimes in relation to each other. For myself, I have never been able to see why we have to choose, and why all three should not be combined . . . it is at one and the same time a quality, an activity and a gift.   **(1994:63)**

26. God's holiness and human sinfulness

That God is holy is foundational to biblical religion. So is the corollary that sin is incompatible with his holiness. His eyes are 'too pure to look on evil' and he 'cannot tolerate wrong'. Therefore our sins effectively separate us from him, so that his face is hidden from us and he refuses to listen to our prayers (Hab. 1:13; Is. 59:1ff.).   **(1986a:102)**

27. Fellowship with God

God's self-revelation is ethical, and there can be no fellowship with him without righteousness.   **(1988g:47)**

28. Consistent omnipotence

The idea that there may be something which God 'cannot' do is entirely foreign to some people. Can he not do anything and everything? Are not all things possible to him? Is he not omnipotent? Yes, but God's omnipotence needs to be understood. God is not a totalitarian tyrant that he should exercise his power arbitrarily and do absolutely anything whatsoever. God's omnipotence is the freedom and the power to do absolutely anything he chooses to do. But he chooses only to do good, only to work according to the perfection of his character and will. God can do everything consistent with being himself. The one and only thing he cannot do, because he will not, is to deny himself or act contrary to himself. So God remains for ever himself, the same God of mercy and of justice, fulfilling his promises (whether of blessing or of judgment), giving us life if we die with Christ and a kingdom if we endure, but denying us if we deny him, just as he warned, because he cannot deny himself. **(1973b:64)**

29. The proof of love

The objective ground for believing that God loves us is historical. It concerns the death of his Son on the cross: 'Christ died for us while we were yet sinners, and that is God's own proof of his love towards us' (Rom. 5:8). The subjective ground for believing that God loves us is experimental. It is not in history but in experience. It concerns not the death of Christ, but the gift of the Holy Spirit within us. **(1966c:22)**

30. Love and wrath

Man is, in fact, the object of God's love and wrath concurrently. The God who condemns man for his disobedience has already planned how to justify him. Three verses in the first chapter of Romans summarize this. 'The gospel', Paul writes, 'is the power of God for salvation . . . For in it the righteousness of God is revealed (that is, God's way of putting sinners right with himself) . . . For the wrath of God is revealed from heaven against all ungodliness and wickedness . . .' (Rom. 1:16–18). Precisely how God's wrath is being revealed from heaven against sin is not explained; Paul is probably referring to the fearful process of moral deterioration which works in wilful sinners whom God gives up to their own wilfulness, and which he describes at the end of the chapter. But if God's wrath is seen in the corruption of man and of society, his remedy for sin is seen in the gospel. There are thus two revelations of God. His righteousness (or way of salvation) is revealed in the gospel, because his wrath is revealed from heaven against all unrighteousness. So the God of the Bible is a God of love and wrath, of mercy and judgment. And all the restlessness, pleasure-seeking and escapism that mark the life of man in every age, and all the world over, are symptomatic of his judicial estrangement from God. **(1967e:42)**

31. The character of God

God's wrath is not incompatible with his love. The contrast between verses 3 and 4 of Ephesians 2 is notable: *we were by nature children of wrath . . . But God, who is rich in mercy, out of the great love with which he loved us . . .* Thus Paul moves from the wrath of God to the mercy and love of God without any sense of embarrassment or anomaly. He is able to hold them together in his mind because he believed that they were held together in God's character. **(1979e:75)**

32. *The Judge and the Lover*

God is not at odds with himself, however much it may appear to us that he is. He is 'the God of peace', of inner tranquillity not turmoil. True, we find it difficult to hold in our minds simultaneously the images of God as the Judge who must punish evil-doers and of the Lover who must find a way to forgive them. Yet he is both, and at the same time. **(1986a:131)**

33. *The nature of wrath*

God's wrath is not arbitrary or capricious. It bears no resemblance to the unpredictable passions and personal vengefulness of the pagan deities. Instead, it is his settled, controlled, holy antagonism to all evil. **(1988g:88)**

34. *Deliverance from judgment*

God's wrath is neither an impersonal process of cause and effect (as some scholars have tried to argue), nor a passionate, arbitrary or vindictive outburst of temper, but his holy and uncompromising antagonism to evil, with which he refuses to negotiate. One day his judgment will fall. It is from this terrible event that Jesus is our deliverer. **(1991c:42)**

35. *Christian propitiation*

Of course the wrath of God is not like human wrath, nor is the propitiation of Christ like heathen propitiations. But once all unworthy elements have been eliminated, namely the concept of the arbitrary wrath of a vengeful deity being placated by the paltry offerings of men, we are left with the Christian propitiation in which God's own love sent his own dear Son to appease his own holy wrath against sin (1 Jn. 2:2; 4:10).
(1975c:103)

36. *Propitiation and the cross*

We should not be shy of using the word 'propitiation' in relation to the cross, any more than we should drop the word 'wrath' in relation to God. Instead, we should struggle to reclaim and reinstate this language by showing that the Christian doctrine of propitiation is totally different from pagan or animistic superstitions. The need, the author and the nature of the Christian propitiation are all different.

First the need. Why is a propitiation necessary? The pagan answer is because the gods are bad-tempered, subject to moods and fits, and capricious. The Christian answer is because God's holy wrath rests on evil. There is nothing unprincipled, unpredictable or uncontrolled about God's anger; it is aroused by evil alone.

Secondly, the author. Who undertakes to do the propitiating? The pagan answer is that we do. We have offended the gods; so we must appease them. The Christian answer, by contrast, is that we cannot placate the righteous anger of God. We have no means whatever by which to do so. But God in his undeserved love has done for us what we could never do by ourselves. *God presented him* (*sc.* Christ) as a sacrifice of atonement. John wrote similarly: 'God . . . loved us and sent his Son as an atoning sacrifice (*hilasmos*) for our sins' (1 Jn. 4:10). The love, the idea, the purpose, the initiative, the action and the gift were all God's.

Thirdly, the nature. How has the propitiation been accomplished? What is the propitiatory sacrifice? The pagan answer is that we have to bribe the gods with sweets, vegetable offerings, animals, and even human sacrifices. The Old Testament sacrificial system was entirely different, since it was recognized that God himself has 'given' the sacrifices to his people to make atonement (*e.g.* Lv. 17:11). And this is clear beyond doubt in the Christian propitiation, for God gave his own Son to die in our place, and in giving his Son he gave himself (Rom. 5:8; 8:32).

In sum, it would be hard to exaggerate the differences between the pagan and the Christian views of propitiation. In the pagan perspective, human beings try to placate their bad-tempered deities with their own paltry offerings. According to the Christian revelation, God's own great love propitiated his own holy wrath through the gift of his own dear Son, who took our place, bore our sin and died our death. Thus God himself gave himself to save us from himself.　　　　　　**(1994:114)**

II. THE LORD JESUS CHRIST

4. *The Word made flesh*
5. *Teacher and Lord*
6. *The kingdom of heaven*
7. *The uniqueness of Christ*
8. *The cross of Jesus*
9. *Risen and ascended*
10. *The return in glory*
11. *Christ our contemporary*

4. THE WORD MADE FLESH

37. Jesus of Nazareth

If you find it hard to believe in God, I strongly advise you to
begin your search not with philosophical questions about the
existence and being of God, but with Jesus of Nazareth. Most
people, like myself, feel on more solid ground when we are
thinking and talking about Jesus Christ. The concept of God as
he is in himself is beyond us. But with Jesus of Nazareth we are
dealing with a historical person. Besides, we believe that this
was God's purpose. God himself is infinite in his being and
altogether beyond our reach and comprehension. That is why
he has taken the initiative to reveal himself – for we could
never come to know him otherwise. And the climax of his self-
revelation was the coming of his Son in human flesh. God
means us to approach him through Jesus Christ, not the other
way round. So if you can't believe in God, let me urge you to
read the four gospels which tell the story of Jesus. I'm
astonished how many intelligent people haven't read the
gospels since they were kids at school. But if you read again
the story of Jesus, and read it as an honest and humble seeker,
Jesus Christ is able to reveal himself to you, and thus make
God the Father real to you.   **(1962c)**

38. The divine Wisdom

In our search for wisdom we cannot stay in the Old Testament,
or even in the wisdom literature. We have to move on to its
fulfilment in Jesus Christ. For he is made unto us wisdom, and
in him all the treasures of wisdom and knowledge are to be
found. Especially the cross, which is foolishness to the proud, is
the wisdom and the power of God. For the two chief blessings
of Jesus' death and resurrection are the knowledge of God and
deliverance from evil. And so we are back where we started:
the fear of the Lord, that is wisdom; and to depart from evil is
understanding.   **(1988c:26)**

39. The mediator of God

Instinctively we know that we cannot box God up in any
conceptual framework of our own devising, and that if we
think we have succeeded in doing so, then what we have in our

box is not God. Our little minds cannot conceive him, let alone contain him. ' "For my thoughts are not your thoughts, neither are your ways my ways" declares the LORD. "As the heavens are higher than the earth, so are my ways higher than your ways and my thoughts than your thoughts" ' (Is. 55:8–9).

Even the fleeting glimpses we catch of him as he passes by in moments of ecstasy or pain, of beauty or wonder, of goodness or love, leave us tantalized by the fullness of the Reality beyond. Yet these glimpses are themselves a form of 'mediation'. For they are declarations of God through the glories of heaven and earth, through the intricate mechanisms of nature, through the complexities of the human situation in its combination of nobility and degradation, and through the whole range of our responses to it. These 'mediations' leave us dissatisfied, however. They point to heights we cannot scale, to depths we cannot fathom. We need a mediation that is at once more concrete, more personal, more genuinely human. In a word, we need Jesus Christ. For however rich the reality we have ever seen or felt or thought or suspected, apart from Jesus Christ, God remains the Infinitely Beyond. Only once has this Beyond come personally into our midst, when the Eternal Word of God actually became a human being and lived among us. Only then did human eyes behold true 'glory' in human form, the radiance of ultimate personal reality, 'the glory of the One and Only, who came from the Father' (Jn. 1:14).

(1991b:10)

40. God's self-revelation

It is impossible to distinguish between Jesus and the Christ, the historical and the eternal. They are the same person, who is both God and man. Such an emphasis on the historical revelation of the invisible and intangible is still needed today, not least by the scientist trained in the empirical method, the radical who regards much in the gospels as 'myths' (but you cannot 'demythologize' the incarnation without thereby contradicting it) and the mystic who becomes preoccupied with his subjective religious experience to the neglect of God's objective self-revelation in Christ. **(1988g:66)**

41. The authentic Jesus

Which Jesus are we talking about? Even Paul in his day recognized the possibility of teachers proclaiming 'another

Jesus' than the Jesus he preached (2 Cor. 11:4). And there are many Jesuses abroad today. There is Jesus the Bultmannian myth and Jesus the revolutionary firebrand, Jesus the failed superstar and Jesus the circus clown. It is over against these human reinterpretations that we need urgently to recover and reinstate the authentic Jesus, the Jesus of history who is the Jesus of Scripture. **(1975c:48)**

42. *A Christmas anthem*

The singing of the Easter Anthem in place of the *Venite* makes a magnificent introduction to our congregational worship at Morning Prayer on Easter Day, particularly when it is sung with the triumphant dignity of Pelham Humfrey's seventeenth-century chant. One wishes that our Prayer Book provided other seasonal variations, at least on the major festivals. I venture to suggest one for Christmas Day . . .

A CHRISTMAS ANTHEM

Behold a virgin shall conceive and bear a ' son: and shall ' call his ' name Imm'anuel.   *Isaiah 7:14*

2 And thou shalt call his ' name ' Jesus: for he shall ' save his ' people from their ' sins.   *Matthew 1:21*

3 When the fullness of the time was come, God sent ' forth his ' Son: made of a ' woman made ' under the ' law,

4 To redeem them that were ' under the ' law: that we might re'ceive the ad'option of ' sons.   *Galatians 4:4–5*

5 And the Word was made flesh and ' dwelt am'ong us: (and we beheld his glory, the glory as of the only begotten of the Father) ' full of ' grace and ' truth.

6 No man hath seen ' God at ' any time: the only begotten Son which is in the bosom of the Father ' he ' hath de'clared him.   *John 1:14, 18*

7 For unto us a child is born; unto us a ' son is ' given: and the government shall ' be up'on his ' shoulder;

8 And his name shall be called wonderful counsellor, the ' mighty ' God: the everlasting ' Father the ' Prince of ' Peace.

9 Of the increase of his government and peace there shall ' be no ' end: upon the throne of David ' and up'on his ' kingdom;

10 To order it and to establish it with ' judgment and with ' justice: from ' henceforth ' even for ' ever.   *Isaiah 9:6–7*
                                        (1966b:25)

43. *The ultimate question*

The real issue is neither linguistic (whether the word incarnation is mythical, metaphorical, or literal), nor cultural (how far the biblical or Chalcedonian formulations reflect the concepts of their day). The ultimate question is absolutely plain, even to the man in the street to whom semantics, culture, and theology are all closed books. It is this: is Jesus to be worshipped or only to be admired? If he is God, then he is worthy of our worship, faith, and obedience; if he is not God, then to give him such devotion is idolatry. **(1978a)**

44. *Altogether beyond our reach*

Jesus renounced the joys of heaven for the sorrows of earth, exchanging an eternal immunity to the approach of sin for painful contact with evil in this world. He was born of a lowly Hebrew mother in a dirty stable in the insignificant village of Bethlehem. He became a refugee baby in Egypt. He was brought up in the obscure hamlet of Nazareth, and toiled at a carpenter's bench to support his mother and the other children in their home. In due time he became an itinerant preacher, with few possessions, small comforts and no home. He made friends with simple fishermen and publicans. He touched lepers and allowed harlots to touch him. He gave himself away in a ministry of healing, helping, teaching and preaching.

He was misunderstood and misrepresented, and became the victim of men's prejudices and vested interests. He was despised and rejected by his own people, and deserted by his own friends. He gave his back to be flogged, his face to be spat upon, his head to be crowned with thorns, his hands and feet to be nailed to a common Roman gallows. And as the cruel spikes were driven home, he kept praying for his tormentors, 'Father, forgive them; for they know not what they do.'

Such a man is altogether beyond our reach. He succeeded just where we invariably fail. He had complete self-mastery. He never retaliated. He never grew resentful or irritable. He had such control of himself that, whatever men might think or say or do, he would deny himself and abandon himself to the will of God and the welfare of mankind. 'I seek not my own will', he said, and 'I do not seek my own glory'. As

Paul wrote, 'For Christ did not please himself.'

This utter disregard of self in the service of God and man is what the Bible calls love. **(1971a:44)**

45. Observant love

True love is always observant, and the eyes of Jesus never missed the sight of need. Nobody could accuse him of being like the priest and Levite in his parable of the Good Samaritan. Of both it is written, 'he saw him'. Yet each saw him without seeing, for he looked the other way, and so 'passed by on the other side'. Jesus, on the other hand, truly 'saw'. He was not afraid to look human need in the face, in all its ugly reality. And what he saw invariably moved him to compassion, and so to compassionate service. Sometimes, he spoke. But his compassion never dissipated itself in words; it found expression in deeds. He saw, he felt, he acted. The movement was from the eye to the heart, and from the heart to the hand. His compassion was always aroused by the sight of need, and it always led to constructive action. **(1975f:6)**

46. Uncontested deity

The New Testament letters contain no hint that the divine honours given to Jesus were the subject of controversy in the church, as was the case, for example, with the doctrine of justification. There can be only one explanation of this. Already by the middle of the first century, the deity of Jesus was part of the faith of the universal church. **(1981f)**

47. Christ's sinless humanity

The sending of the divine Son involved his becoming incarnate, a human being, which is expressed by the words *in the likeness of sinful man*, or better 'in the likeness of sinful flesh' (Rom. 8:3, RSV). This somewhat roundabout phrase, which has puzzled commentators mainly because of its use of 'likeness', was doubtless intended to combat false views of the incarnation. That is, the Son came neither 'in the likeness of flesh', only seeming to be human, as the docetists taught, for his humanity was real; nor 'in sinful flesh', assuming a fallen nature, for his humanity was sinless, but 'in the likeness of sinful flesh', because his humanity was both real and sinless simultaneously. **(1994:219)**

37

48. 'And was made man . . .'

Of the Son's 'identification' with the world into which he was sent, there can be no shadow of doubt. He did not remain in heaven; he came into the world. The word was not spoken from the sky; 'the Word was made flesh'. And then he 'dwelt among us'. He did not come on a fleeting visit and hurry back home again. He stayed in the world into which he came. He gave men a chance to behold his glory. Nor did he only let them gaze from a distance. He scandalized the church leaders of his day by mixing with the riff-raff they avoided. 'Friend of publicans and sinners', they dubbed him. To them it was a term of opprobrium; to us it is a title of honour. He touched untouchable lepers. He did not recoil from the caresses of a prostitute. And then he, who at his birth had been 'made flesh', was in his death 'made sin' and 'made a curse'. He had assumed our nature; he now assumed our transgressions, our doom, our death. His self-identification with man was utter and complete.

Therefore when he says to us 'Go', this is what he means.

(1967e:65)

5. TEACHER AND LORD

49. *Under the yoke*

Every Christian is a pupil in the school of Jesus Christ. We sit at the feet of our Master. We want to bring our minds and our wills, our beliefs and our standards, under his yoke. In the Upper Room he said to the apostles: 'You call me "Teacher" and "Lord", and rightly so, for that is what I am' (Jn. 13:13). That is, 'Teacher' and 'Lord' were no mere courtesy titles; they bore witness to a reality. Jesus Christ is our Teacher to instruct us and our Lord to command us. All Christian people are under the instruction and the discipline of Jesus Christ. It should be inconceivable for a Christian ever to disagree with, or to disobey, him. Whenever we do, the credibility of our claim to be converted Christians is in doubt. For we are not truly converted if we are not intellectually and morally converted, and we are not intellectually and morally converted if we have not subjected our minds and our wills to the yoke of Jesus Christ.   **(1991b:57)**

50. *'That is what I am'*

Looking round at his disciples, Jesus said, *'You call me Teacher and Lord, and you are right; that is what I am'* (Jn. 13:13).

The Christian is under both instruction and authority. He looks to Jesus as his Teacher to instruct him, and as his Lord to command him. He believes what he believes because Jesus taught it, and he does what he does because Jesus told him to do it.

He is our Teacher to instruct us, and we learn to submit and to subordinate our minds to his mind. We do not presume to have views or ideas or opinions which are in contradiction to the views and ideas of Jesus Christ. Our view of Scripture is derived from Christ's view of Scripture, just as our view of discipleship, of heaven and hell, of the Christian life, and of everything else, is derived from Jesus Christ. Any question about the inspiration of Scripture and its authority therefore resolves itself to: 'What did Jesus Christ teach about these points?'

We would say, without any doubt, that he gave reverent

assent to the authority and inspiration of the Old Testament. There is no indication anywhere in his teachings that he disagreed with the Old Testament writers. He regarded the words of the Old Testament writings as being the words of God. He submitted to them in his own life, he believed them, he accepted their statements, and sought to apply their principles. He regarded Scripture as the great arbiter in dispute. He said to his contemporaries, 'You make many mistakes, because you don't know the Scriptures.'

We find in the New Testament that he invested the apostles with authority to teach in his Name. He said that the Holy Spirit would lead them into all truth, would bring to their remembrance what he had spoken to them, and would show them things to come. He evidently expected that in the providence of God there would be others to interpret, expound, and bear witness to the revelation given in himself, just as there were prophets raised up by God and inspired to bear witness to what he did in Old Testament days.

To sum up, the authority of Scripture is due to the inspiration of Scripture. The Old and New Testaments are authoritative in our lives, because they are in fact inspired.

And therefore, since Jesus Christ is our Teacher as well as our Lord, the authority of Christ and the authority of Scripture stand or fall together. **(1965:)**

51. Christ the controversialist

The popular image of Christ as 'gentle Jesus, meek and mild' simply will not do. It is a false image. To be sure, he was full of love, compassion and tenderness. But he was also uninhibited in exposing error and denouncing sin, especially hypocrisy . . . The evangelists portray him as constantly debating with the leaders of contemporary Judaism . . . Christ was a controversialist. **(1970b:49)**

52. Scripture and tradition

The Pharisees came to Jesus and said: 'Why do your disciples not live according to the tradition of the elders, but eat with hands defiled?' [In reply] he had something to say about their views on purification, and . . . then went on to say something about their view of tradition . . . In opposition to the opinions of the Pharisees he enunciated three important principles. First, that Scripture is divine, while tradition is human. Secondly, that Scripture is obligatory, while tradition is optional. Thirdly, that Scripture is supreme, while tradition is subordinate.

(1970b:69)

53. Radical and conservative

It is not sufficiently understood that our Lord Jesus Christ was at one and the same time a conservative and a radical although in different spheres. There is no question that he was conservative in his attitude to Scripture. 'The Scripture cannot be broken', he said, 'I did not come to abolish the law and the prophets, but to fulfil them.' Again, 'not an iota, not a dot, will pass from the law until all is accomplished' (Jn. 10:35; Mt. 5:17–18). One of Jesus' chief complaints against contemporary Jewish leaders concerned their disrespect for Old Testament Scripture and their lack of a true submission to its divine authority.

But Jesus may also be truly described as a radical. He was a keen, fearless critic of the Jewish Establishment, not only because of their insufficient loyalty to God's Word, but also because of their exaggerated loyalty to their own human traditions. Jesus had the temerity to sweep away centuries of inherited traditions ('the traditions of the elders') in order that God's Word might again be seen and obeyed. He was also very daring in his breaches of social convention. He insisted on caring for those sections of the community who were normally despised. He spoke to women in public, which in his day was not done. He invited children to come to him, although in Roman society unwanted children were commonly 'exposed' or dumped, and his own disciples took it for granted that he would not want to be bothered with them. He allowed prostitutes to touch him (Pharisees recoiled from them in horror) and himself actually touched an untouchable leper (Pharisees threw stones at them to make them keep their distance). In these and other ways Jesus refused to be bound by human custom; his mind and conscience were bound by God's Word alone.

Thus Jesus was a unique combination of the conservative and the radical, conservative towards Scripture and radical in his scrutiny (his *biblical* scrutiny) of everything else. **(1975a:29)**

54. Words and works

Jesus' words explained his works, and his works dramatized his words. Hearing and seeing, voice and vision, were joined.

Each supported the other. For words remain abstract until they are made concrete in deeds of love, while works remain ambiguous until they are interpreted by the proclamation of the gospel. Words without works lack credibility; works without words lack clarity. So Jesus' works made his words visible; his words made his works intelligible. **(1992b:345)**

55. Three times Lord

Jesus is Lord three times over: first, by right of his Godhead, sharing the throne of God; second, by right of his historical ministry, ushering in the kingdom of God; and third, by right of his supreme exaltation, sitting at the right hand of God. Jesus is three times Lord, and thus deserves our full homage and our worship. **(1977h:21)**

56. Lord for a lifetime

Christian commitment has a *vocational dimension*. That is to say, it includes our life work. To say 'Jesus is Lord' commits us to a lifetime of service. **(1992b:93)**

6. THE KINGDOM OF HEAVEN

57. *Where Christ rules*

The kingdom itself exists only where Christ rules by bestowing salvation and receiving homage. **(1979c:23)**

58. *The message of the New Testament*

The message of the New Testament is first and foremost a declaration. It is good news about God. It is the story of what God has done in and through his Son Jesus Christ, our Lord and Saviour. He has established his kingdom. True, the full manifestation of the kingdom is yet to come. We await the final consummation. But the kingdom of God has been inaugurated. The time has been fulfilled. The dreams of ancient visionaries have come true. God has kept his promise to Abraham. Long centuries of Old Testament expectation have at last materialized. The new age has dawned. The new covenant has been ratified through the bloodshedding of Jesus. Those who repent of their sins, renounce themselves and believe in Christ hear the covenant promise '. . . I will be their God, and they shall be my people . . . for I will forgive their iniquity, and I will remember their sin no more' (Je. 31:33–4). **(1954c:176)**

59. *A spiritual conquest*

The kingdom of God in the teaching of Jesus is a spiritual conquest of men and women. It also has material benefits, since the King's subjects are the Father's children . . . **(1954c:9)**

60. *Total blessing and total demand*

When Jesus spoke of the kingdom of God he was not referring to the general sovereignty of God over nature and history, but to that specific rule over his own people which he himself had inaugurated, and which begins in anybody's life when he humbles himself, repents, believes, submits and is born again. God's kingdom is Jesus Christ ruling over his people in total blessing and total demand. To 'seek first' this kingdom is to desire as of first importance the spread of the reign of Jesus Christ. Such a desire will start with ourselves, until every single department of our life – home, marriage and family, personal morality, professional life and business ethics, bank balance, tax returns, lifestyle, citizenship – is joyfully and freely submissive to Christ. It will continue in our immediate environment, with the acceptance of evangelistic responsibility towards our relatives, colleagues, neighbours and friends. And it will also reach out in global concern for the missionary witness of the church. **(1978f:170)**

61. Present and yet future

That Jesus regarded and described the kingdom as a present phenomenon is indubitable. He taught that the time of fulfilment had arrived; that 'the strong man' was now bound and disarmed, facilitating the plundering of his goods, as was evident from his exorcisms; that the kingdom was already either 'within' or 'among' people; that it could now be 'entered' or 'received'; and that, since the time of John the Baptist his forerunner, who had announced its imminent arrival, 'forceful men' had in fact been 'laying hold' of it or 'forcing their way' into it.

Yet in Jesus' perspective the kingdom was a future expectation as well. It would not be perfected until the last day. So he looked forward to the end, and taught his disciples to do so also. They were to pray 'Your kingdom come' and to 'seek' it first, giving priority to its expansion. At times he also referred to the final state of his followers in terms of 'entering' the kingdom or 'receiving' it.

In particular, his agricultural parables (*e.g.* those of the seed growing secretly, the mustard seed, and the wheat and the tares) bring together the processes of planting, growth and harvest. Like seed the kingdom had already been planted in the world; now it would grow by invisible divine activity until the end. This seems to be what Jesus meant by 'the mystery (or secret) of the kingdom'. Its presence was unobtrusive, yet also revolutionary, as the power of God would cause it to grow until finally it would become manifest to all. **(1992b:379)**

62. No one moment

There was no one moment in the triumphant progress of our saving Lord from his cradle in Bethlehem to his final glory at the Father's right hand, at which it may be said 'the kingdom came or will come then.' The kingdom was coming all the time. It is still growing. Its progress is twofold, first as God gives it, and second as man receives it. **(1954c:13)**

63. The law of the kingdom

Jesus performed miracles exhibiting his power over nature by stilling a storm on the lake, walking on water and multiplying loaves and fishes. But his commonest miracles were healing miracles, effected, now by a touch of the hand, now by a bare word of command. From one point of view, the sufficient explanation of his healing ministry is his love, for he was moved to compassion by the sight of every form of suffering. But, in addition, his miracles were 'signs' both of God's kingdom and of his own deity. They signified that the Messiah's reign had begun, as the Scriptures had foretold. It was with this evidence that Jesus sought to reassure the doubts of John the Baptist in prison:

> Go back and report to John what you have seen and heard: The blind receive their sight, the lame walk, those who have leprosy are cured, the deaf hear, the dead are raised, and the good news is preached to the poor (Lk. 7:22).

Similarly, the miracles were signs that the forces of evil were in full retreat before the advancing kingdom of God:

> But if I drive out demons by the finger of God, then the kingdom of God has come to you (Lk. 11:20).

The miracles were also signs that Jesus was the Son of God, for each was an acted parable, dramatizing one of his divine claims. The feeding of the 5,000 set forth visibly his claim to be the bread of life, his healing of the man born blind his claim to be the light of the world, and his raising of the dead his claim to be the resurrection and the life.   **(1984d:95)**

64. Greatness in the kingdom

Greatness in the kingdom of God is measured in terms of obedience.   **(1962e:92)**

65. A threefold misunderstanding

On the Mount of Olives the disciples asked him, 'wilt thou at this time restore the kingdom to Israel?' (Acts 1:6). As Calvin wrote, there are almost as many errors as words in their question! They revealed a threefold misunderstanding about the kingdom. First, they were mistaken about the *time* of its manifestation. They were not to know. The Father had fixed the times and the seasons by his own authority (1:7). Secondly, they were mistaken about its *sphere*. They asked if he would restore the kingdom to Israel. He replied that they would be witnesses unto the uttermost parts of the earth (1:8). Thirdly, they were mistaken about its *character*. They appear still to have been thinking in terms of a material domain. He told them of a spiritual dominion. The kingdom would spread as the Spirit gave them power for witness to Christ (1:8). The same Spirit who cast out demons in the ministry of Jesus would cause the kingdom to spread as he bore witness through the apostles to the unbelieving world.   (1954c:16)

66. An international community

Christ's kingdom, while not incompatible with patriotism, tolerates no narrow nationalisms. He rules over an international community in which race, nation, rank and sex are no barriers to fellowship. And when his kingdom is consummated at the end, the countless redeemed company will be seen to be drawn 'from every nation, tribe, people and language' (Rev. 7:9).   (1990b:43)

7. THE UNIQUENESS OF CHRIST

67. Through Jesus alone

God is partly revealed in the ordered loveliness of the created universe. He is partly revealed in history and in experience, in the human conscience and the human consciousness, and above all in Scripture, which is the Father's testimony to the Son. Nevertheless, God's full and final self-revelation, his revelation as the Father who saves and adopts us into his family, has been given in and through Jesus alone. Therefore, 'he who has seen me', said Jesus, 'has seen the Father'. That is the reason why every enquiry into the truth of Christianity must begin with the historic Jesus, who without any fanfare of trumpets quietly and unobtrusively claimed that only he knew the Father and only he could make him known.   **(1988b:90)**

68. Held in high honour

Even in other religions and ideologies Jesus is held in high honour. Hindus would gladly recognize him as an 'avatar' (descent) of Vishnu, and so assimilate him into Hinduism, if only he would renounce his exclusive claims. Jews who reject Jesus as their Messiah have never lost interest in him. Their scholars write books about him, and their hostility has often been more to Gentile anti-Semitism than to Jesus himself. Muslims acknowledge him as one of the great prophets, whose virgin birth, sinlessness, miracles, inspiration and future return are all affirmed in the Qur'an. Marxists, while fiercely critical of 'religion' as an opium which drugs the oppressed into tolerating the injustices of the *status quo*, nevertheless respect Jesus for his confrontation with the Establishment and his compassionate solidarity with the poor.   **(1991b:7)**

69. Jesus the Great?

To relegate Christianity to one chapter in a book of the world's religions is to Christian people intolerable. Jesus Christ to us is not one of many spiritual leaders in the history of the world. He is not one of Hinduism's 330 million gods. He is not one of the forty prophets recognized in the Qur'an. He is not even, to quote Carnegie Simpson, 'Jesus, the Great', as you might say Napoleon the Great or Alexander the Great . . . To us, he is the only. He is simply Jesus. Nothing could be added to that. He is unique. **(1978g)**

70. *The uniqueness of Christianity*

If the uniqueness of Christianity is the uniqueness of Christ, wherein does his uniqueness lie? Historically speaking, it is found in his birth, death and resurrection. As for his birth, he was 'conceived by the Holy Spirit, born of the Virgin Mary', and therefore is both God and man. As for his death, he died for our sins, in our place, to secure our salvation. As for his resurrection, he thereby conquered death and possesses universal authority. Or, to express these historical events theologically, the uniqueness of Jesus lies in the incarnation, the atonement and the exaltation. Each is unparalleled.

(1985:73)

71. *The source of all goodness*

We should not hesitate to claim that everything good, beautiful and true, in all history and in all the earth, has come from Jesus Christ, even though men are ignorant of its origin. **(1975c:68)**

72. *'Only to Christ . . .'*

The uniqueness to which Christians bear witness does not refer to Christianity in any of its numerous empirical manifestations, but only to Christ. He has no peers, no rivals, no successors. And his uniqueness is most evident in relation to the incarnation, the atonement and the resurrection. He is the one and only God-man, who died for our sins and was then raised from the dead to authenticate his person and work. And it is this threefold, historical uniqueness which qualifies him to be the Saviour of the world, the only mediator between God and humankind. No-one else has these qualifications. **(1988d:323)**

73. *Inerrant and sinless*

It is very dangerous to begin with such a presupposition as 'to err is human', and then to add, 'therefore to be human Jesus must have erred'. Could we not equally well argue that 'to sin is human, and therefore Jesus must have sinned'? But the unanimous testimony of the Scriptures, which the church has always accepted, is that our Lord was sinless. Of course sin and error are part of our fallen human nature, but they are no necessary part of the perfect human nature which God made and Christ assumed. The evidence of Scripture is that the man Christ Jesus, through the perfect surrender of his mind to the revelation of God, was inerrant, and through the perfect surrender of his will to the will of God, was sinless. **(1956a:20)**

74. *Qualified to redeem*

The divinity of Christ, the humanity of Christ and the righteousness of Christ uniquely qualified him to be man's redeemer. If he had not been man, he could not have redeemed men. If he had not been a righteous man, he could not have redeemed unrighteous men. And if he had not been God's Son, he could not have redeemed men for God or made them the sons of God. **(1968c:106)**

75. *No other Saviour*

Because in no other person but the historic Jesus of Nazareth has God become man and lived a human life on earth, died to bear the penalty of our sins, and been raised from death and exalted to glory, there is no other Saviour, for there is no other person who is qualified to save. **(1985:78)**

76. *God's full revelation*

We have much more to learn, but God has no more to reveal than he has revealed in Jesus Christ. **(1991b:20)**

77. *The ultimate issue*

The ultimate issue in relation to Jesus Christ is not one of semantics (the meaning of words) but of homage (the attitude of the heart), not whether our tongue can subscribe to an orthodox formulation of the person of Jesus, but whether our knee has bowed before his majesty. Besides, reverence always precedes understanding. We shall know him only if we are willing to obey him. **(1985:24)**

8. THE CROSS OF JESUS

78. A universal symbol

A universally acceptable Christian emblem would obviously need to speak of Jesus Christ, but there was a wide range of possibilities. Christians might have chosen the crib or manger in which the baby Jesus was laid, or the carpenter's bench at which he worked as a young man in Nazareth, dignifying manual labour, or the boat from which he taught the crowds in Galilee, or the apron he wore when washing the apostles' feet, which would have spoken of his spirit of humble service. Then there was the stone which, having been rolled from the mouth of Joseph's tomb, would have proclaimed his resurrection. Other possibilities were the throne, symbol of divine sovereignty, which John in his vision of heaven saw that Jesus was sharing, or the dove, symbol of the Holy Spirit sent from heaven on the day of Pentecost. Any of these seven symbols would have been suitable as a pointer to some aspect of the ministry of the Lord. But instead the chosen symbol came to be a simple cross. Its two bars were already a cosmic symbol from remote antiquity of the axis between heaven and earth. But its choice by Christians had a more specific explanation. They wished to commemorate as central to their understanding of Jesus neither his birth nor his youth, neither his teaching nor his service, neither his resurrection nor his reign, nor his gift of the Spirit, but his death, his crucifixion.   **(1986a:21)**

79. To the undeserving

The repeated promises in the Qur'an of the forgiveness of a compassionate and merciful Allah are all made to the meritorious, whose merits have been weighed in Allah's scales, whereas the gospel is good news of mercy to the undeserving. The symbol of the religion of Jesus is the cross, not the scales.
(1975c:51)

80. A public portrayal

The gospel is Christ crucified, his finished work on the cross. And to preach the gospel is publicly to portray Christ as crucified. The gospel is not good news primarily of a baby in a manger, a young man at a carpenter's bench, a preacher in the fields of Galilee, or even an empty tomb. The gospel concerns Christ upon his cross. Only when Christ is 'openly displayed upon his cross' (Gal. 3:1) is the gospel preached. **(1968c:74)**

81. Unsullied love

Only one act of pure love, unsullied by any taint of ulterior motive, has ever been performed in the history of the world, namely the self-giving of God in Christ on the cross for undeserving sinners. That is why, if we are looking for a definition of love, we should look not in a dictionary, but at Calvary. **(1986a:212)**

82. 'Mission accomplished'

The story begins on the evening of Maundy Thursday. Jesus had already seen the sun set for the last time. Within about fifteen hours his limbs would be stretched out on the cross. Within twenty-four hours he would be both dead and buried. And he knew it. Yet the extraordinary thing is that he was thinking of his mission as still future, not past. He was a comparatively young man, almost certainly between thirty and thirty-five years of age. He had lived barely half the allotted span of human life. He was still at the height of his powers. At his age most people have their best years ahead of them. Muhammad lived until he was sixty, Socrates until he was seventy, and Plato and the Buddha were over eighty when they died. If death threatens to cut a person's life short, a sense of frustration plunges him or her into gloom. But not Jesus, for this simple reason: he did not regard the death he was about to die as bringing his mission to an untimely end, but as actually necessary to accomplish it. It was only seconds before he died (and not till that moment) that he would be able to shout, 'Finished!' So then, although it was his last evening, and although he had but a few more hours to live, Jesus was not looking *back* at a mission he had completed, still less that had failed; he was still looking *forward* to a mission which he was about to fulfil. The mission of a lifetime of thirty to thirty-five years was to be accomplished in its last twenty-four hours, indeed, its last six. **(1986a:66)**

83. We were there

The blaming of the Jewish people for the crucifixion of Jesus is extremely unfashionable today. Indeed, if it is used as a justification for slandering and persecuting the Jews (as it has been in the past), or for anti-Semitism, it is absolutely indefensible. The way to avoid anti-Semitic prejudice, however, is not to pretend that the Jews were innocent, but, having admitted their guilt, to add that others shared in it. This was how the apostles saw it. Herod and Pilate, Gentiles and Jews, they said, had together 'conspired' against Jesus (Acts 4:27). More important still, we ourselves are also guilty. If we were in their place, we would have done what they did. Indeed, we *have* done it. For whenever we turn away from Christ, we 'are crucifying the Son of God all over again and subjecting him to public disgrace' (Heb. 6:6). We too sacrifice Jesus to our greed like Judas, to our envy like the priests, to our ambition like Pilate. 'Were you there when they crucified my Lord?' the old negro spiritual asks. And we must answer, 'Yes, we were there.' Not as spectators only but as participants, guilty participants, plotting, scheming, betraying, bargaining, and handing him over to be crucified. We may try to wash our hands of responsibility like Pilate. But our attempt will be as futile as his. For there is blood on our hands. Before we can begin to see the cross as something done *for* us (leading us to faith and worship), we have to see it as something done *by* us (leading us to repentance). **(1986a:59)**

84. The mystery of the cross

I cannot begin to unfold the meaning of the death of Christ without first confessing that much remains a mystery. Christians believe that the cross is the pivotal event in history. Small wonder that our puny minds cannot fully take it in! One day the veil will be altogether removed, and all riddles will be solved. We shall see Christ as he is and worship him through eternity for what he has done. 'Now we see in a mirror dimly, but then face to face. Now I know in part; then I shall understand fully, even as I have been fully understood.' So said the great apostle Paul with his massive intellect and his many revelations; and if he said it, how much more should we?

(1971a:88)

85. The world's anger

What is there about the cross of Christ which angers the world and stirs them up to persecute those who preach it? Just this: Christ died on the cross for us sinners, becoming a curse for us

(Gal. 3:13). So the cross tells us some very unpalatable truths about ourselves, namely that we are sinners under the righteous curse of God's law and we cannot save ourselves. Christ bore our sin and curse precisely because we could gain release from them in no other way. If we could have been forgiven by our own good works, by being circumcised and keeping the law, we may be quite sure that there would have been no cross. Every time we look at the cross Christ seems to say to us, 'I am here because of you. It is your sin I am bearing, your curse I am suffering, your debt I am paying, your death I am dying.' Nothing in history or in the universe cuts us down to size like the cross. All of us have inflated views of ourselves, especially in self-righteousness, until we have visited a place called Calvary. It is there, at the foot of the cross, that we shrink to our true size.

And of course men do not like it. They resent the humiliation of seeing themselves as God sees them and as they really are. They prefer their comfortable illusions. So they steer clear of the cross. They construct a Christianity without the cross, which relies for salvation on their works and not on Jesus Christ's. They do not object to Christianity so long as it is not the faith of Christ crucified. But Christ crucified they detest. And if preachers preach Christ crucified, they are opposed, ridiculed, persecuted. Why? Because of the wounds which they inflict on men's pride. **(1968c:179)**

86. Christ died our death

What did Christ do? He died. To say this is not simply to state a fact, but to explain it, because human death in Scripture is never a meaningless phenomenon. On the contrary, death is always a fact of theological significance, the dreadful penalty for human sin. From the second chapter of Genesis ('in the day that you eat of it you shall die') to the penultimate chapter of Revelation (in which impenitent sinners die 'the second death') the same theme is consistently emphasized: 'the wages of sin is death'. Since Jesus had no sin either in his nature or in his conduct, he need never have died, either physically or spiritually. He could have been 'translated' like Enoch and Elijah. He nearly was – at the transfiguration. But he deliberately stepped back into this world, in order voluntarily to lay down his life. Then why did he do it? What was the rationale of his death? There is only one possible, logical, biblical answer. It is that he died for *our* sins, not his own. The death he died was our death, the penalty which our sins had richly deserved. For these sins he died, not only in body but in soul, in the awful God-forsaken darkness. The evidence for this is not simply in isolated proof texts but in the whole scriptural witness to the relation between sin and death.   **(1967e:39)**

87. 'Saved by his death'

There can be no question that, although Christ's saving career is one, it is principally by his *death* that men may be saved. We read in 1 Corinthians 15:3ff. . . . that 'Christ *died* for our sins', not that 'Christ *rose* for our sins'. Certainly the apostle goes on in this primitive statement of the gospel to say 'he was raised' and that 'he appeared' to various chosen witnesses, but his resurrection did not in itself accomplish our salvation, but rather gave public evidence of its accomplishment by Christ's death, with which the Father was well pleased. That is why Paul can write later in the same chapter: 'if Christ has not been raised, then our preaching is in vain and your faith is in vain . . . If Christ has not been raised, your faith is futile and you are still in your sins' (verses 14, 17). If Jesus never rose from the dead, men are still unsaved sinners, not because the resurrection would have saved them, but because without the resurrection, the death of Jesus is shown to have been without saving efficacy.   **(1961:35)**

88. God in Christ

If we speak only of Christ suffering and dying, we overlook the initiative of the Father. If we speak only of God suffering and dying, we overlook the mediation of the Son. The New Testament authors never attribute the atonement either to Christ in such a way as to disassociate him from the Father, or to God in such a way as to dispense with Christ, but rather to God and Christ, or to God acting in and through Christ with his whole-hearted concurrence.   **(1986a:156)**

89. Objective finality

In his death Jesus did something objective, final, absolute and decisive; something which enabled him to cry on the cross, 'It is accomplished'; something which was described by the author of the epistle to the Hebrews as 'one sacrifice for sins for ever'; something which turns Christianity from pious good advice into glorious good news; which transforms the characteristic mood of Christianity from the imperative (do) into the indicative (done); which makes evangelism not an invitation for men to do something, but a declaration of what God has already done in Christ. **(1962f:4)**

90. Dead to sin

Consider Christ. 'The death he died he died to sin, once for all' (Rom. 6:10). What does this mean? It can mean only one thing; that Christ died to sin in the sense that he bore sin's penalty. He died for our sins, bearing them in his own innocent and sacred person. He took upon himself our sins and their just reward. The death that Jesus died was the wages of sin – our sin. He met its claim, he paid its penalty, he accepted its reward, and he did it 'once', once and for all. As a result sin has no more claim or demand on him. So he was raised from the dead to prove the satisfactoriness of his sin-bearing, and he now lives for ever to God.

If this is the sense in which Christ died to sin, it is equally the sense in which we, by union with Christ, have died to sin. We have died to sin in the sense that in Christ we have borne its penalty. Consequently our old life has finished; a new life has begun. **(1966c:43)**

91. A divine substitute

How could God express simultaneously his holiness in judgment and his love in pardon? Only by providing a divine substitute for the sinner, so that the substitute would receive the judgment and the sinner the pardon. We sinners still of course have to suffer some of the personal, psychological and social consequences of our sins, but the penal consequence, the deserved penalty of alienation from God, has been borne by Another in our place, so that we may be spared it. **(1986a:134)**

92. A substitutionary sacrifice

When we review so much Old Testament material (the shedding and sprinkling of blood, the sin offering, the Passover, the meaning of 'sin-bearing', the scapegoat and Isaiah 53), and consider its New Testament application to the death of Christ, we are obliged to conclude that the cross was a substitutionary sacrifice. Christ died for us. Christ died instead of us. **(1986a:149)**

93. Satisfaction and substitution

We strongly reject, therefore, every explanation of the death of Christ which does not have at its centre the principle of 'satisfaction through substitution', indeed divine self-satisfaction through divine self-substitution. The cross was not a commercial bargain with the devil, let alone one which tricked and trapped him; nor an exact equivalent, a *quid pro quo* to satisfy a code of honour or technical point of law; nor a compulsory submission by God to some moral authority above him from which he could not otherwise escape; nor a punishment of a meek Christ by a harsh and punitive Father; nor a procurement of salvation by a loving Christ from a mean and reluctant Father; nor an action of the Father which bypassed Christ as Mediator. Instead, the righteous, loving Father humbled himself to become in and through his only Son flesh, sin and a curse for us, in order to redeem us without compromising his own character. The theological words 'satisfaction' and 'substitution' need to be carefully defined and safeguarded, but they cannot in any circumstances be given up.   **(1986a:159)**

94. God and ourselves

Any notion of penal substitution in which three independent actors play a role – the guilty party, the punitive judge and the innocent victim – is to be repudiated with the utmost vehemence. It would not only be unjust in itself but would also reflect a defective christology. For Christ is not an independent third person, but the eternal Son of the Father, who is one with the Father in his essential being.

What we see, then, in the drama of the cross is not three actors but two, ourselves on the one hand and God on the other. Not God as he is in himself (the Father), but God nevertheless, God–made-man-in-Christ (the Son).   **(1986a:158)**

95. Atonement for us

I am not saying that substitution is *the* one and only meaning of the cross, for the cross speaks also of victory over evil, the revelation of love and glory through suffering. But if you are talking of atonement, the means by which we sinners can be reconciled to the God of holy love, why then, yes, I don't think we can escape the truth of the divine substitution. **(1988d:165)**

56

96. 'Through Christ'

Five times in one brief paragraph (Rom. 5:1–11) Paul repeats the preposition 'through' in relation to Jesus Christ. It is through the death of Christ that we were reconciled to God. So it is through Christ that we have received our reconciliation, that we have obtained access into the state of grace, that we enjoy peace with God, and that we rejoice in God. Reconciliation, access, peace and joy – these are all blessings which become ours only through the finished sacrifice and the present mediation of Jesus Christ. No wonder our prayers are offered to God through him, for there is no other way to the Father except through his Son, our Lord and Saviour, Jesus Christ (Jn. 14:6).   **(1991b:18)**

97. To every generation

It is highly significant that the only regular ritual act instituted and commanded by Jesus sets forth supremely his death. It is his *death*, his body given and blood shed, which the bread and wine were intended to signify. In issuing the command to 'do this in remembrance' of him, he intended that his atoning death should be kept before every generation, indeed 'placarded' before their very eyes. This according to Paul is the function of preaching. It is one of the functions of communion also. The ministry of both Word and sacrament makes Christ's death contemporary, presenting it anew not to God (for the sacrifice itself was offered on the cross once for all) but to men (for its benefits are always freshly available).   **(1970b:119)**

98. God the reality

When we look at the cross we see the justice, love, wisdom and power of God. It is not easy to decide which is the most luminously revealed, whether the justice of God in judging sin, or the love of God in bearing the judgment in our place, or the wisdom of God in perfectly combining the two, or the power of God in saving those who believe. For the cross is equally an act, and therefore a demonstration, of God's justice, love, wisdom and power. The cross assures us that this God is the reality within, behind and beyond the universe.   **(1986a:226)**

99. The power of the cross

There is wonderful power in the cross of Christ. It has power to wake the dullest conscience and melt the hardest heart; to cleanse the unclean; to reconcile him who is afar off and restore him to fellowship with God; to redeem the prisoner from his bondage and lift the pauper from the dunghill; to break down the barriers which divide men from one another; to transform our wayward characters into the image of Christ and finally make us fit to stand in white robes before the throne of God.

(1961:102)

100. How love is kindled

The cross is the blazing fire at which the flame of our love is kindled, but we have to get near enough to it for its sparks to fall on us. **(1990c:27)**

101. Enemies of the cross

To be an enemy of the cross is to set ourselves against its purposes. Self-righteousness (instead of looking to the cross for justification), self-indulgence (instead of taking up the cross to follow Christ), self-advertisement (instead of preaching Christ crucified) and self-glorification (instead of glorying in the cross) – these are the distortions which make us 'enemies' of Christ's cross. **(1986a:351)**

102. Three lessons

There are three final lessons which I learned from the cross.

First, that my sin is foul beyond words. If there were no way for our sins to be cleansed and forgiven but that the Son of God should die for them, then our sins must be sinful indeed.

Secondly, I learn that God's love is great beyond all understanding. He could have abandoned us to our just fate and left us to perish in our sins. But he didn't. He loved us, and he pursued us even to the desolate agony of the cross.

Thirdly, I learn that salvation is a free gift. I do not deserve it. I cannot earn it. I do not need to attempt to procure it by my own merit or effort. Jesus Christ on the cross has done everything that is necessary for us to be forgiven. He has borne our sin and curse. What, then, must we do? Nothing! Nothing but fall on our knees in penitence and faith, and stretch out an open, empty hand to receive salvation as a gift that is entirely free. **(1962d)**

9. RISEN AND ASCENDED

103. From death to life
We live and die. Christ died and lived!   (1990c:36)

104. The supernatural power of God
The *natural* process which God has established, partly by creation and partly by judgment, is birth, growth, decay, death and dissolution. This is the cycle of nature. It includes man: 'you are dust, and to dust you shall return.' The very concept of 'resurrection' is therefore *supernatural*. At Christ's resurrection the natural process of physical decomposition was not only arrested, nor even reversed, but actually superseded. Instead of dissolving into dust, his body was transfigured into a new and glorious vehicle for his soul. Indeed, the resurrection of Jesus is presented in the New Testament as the supreme manifestation of the supernatural power of God.   (1970b:61)

105. An objective historical event
The resurrection was *an objective, historical event*. Indeed, it was datable; it happened 'on the third day'. Bishop David Jenkins has called it 'not an event, but a series of experiences'. But no, it became a series of experiences only because it was first an event. And in God's providence the words 'on the third day' witness to the historicity of Jesus' resurrection, much as the words 'under Pontius Pilate' in the Apostles' Creed witness to the historicity of his sufferings and death.   (1992b:77)

106. The mainstay of assurance
What we have to ask about the resurrection is not only whether it happened, but whether it really matters whether it happened. For if it happened, it happened nearly 2,000 years ago. How can an event of such remote antiquity have any great importance for us today? Why on earth do Christians make such a song and dance about it? Is it not irrelevant? No; my argument now is that the resurrection resonates with our human condition. It speaks to our needs as no other distant event does or could. It is the mainstay of our Christian assurance.   (1992b:80)

107. *A verdict reversed*

It is hard for us to grasp, let alone to feel, how completely the verdict seemed to have gone against Jesus when he died, and how in consequence the apostles' past hopes had been extinguished. Jesus had been condemned in a Jewish court for blasphemy by duly authorized legal procedures. He was then sentenced and executed for sedition by the Romans. Worse, he had been 'hanged on a tree' and therefore (according to Dt. 21:22–23) had died under the curse of God. After that, he was taken down from the cross and buried, which was the final touch in disposing of him. The public rejection of Jesus could not have been more thorough. At every dimension he was finished – judicial, political, spiritual and physical. Religion, law, God, man and death had all conspired to wipe him off the face of the earth. It was all over now. The verdict was as decisive as it could possibly have been. No power on earth could ever rescue or reinstate him.

But the apostles had left out of account the resurrection power of God. Small wonder that their earliest proclamation could be summarized in the words, 'you killed him, but God raised him'. And in raising him, God reversed the verdict which had been passed on him . . . In other words, by raising Jesus, God was making a declaration about him, and in particular was turning all human opinions about him upside down. Condemned for blasphemy, he was now designated Son of God by the resurrection. Executed for sedition, for claiming to be a king, God made him 'both Lord and Christ'. Hanged on a tree under the curse of God, he was vindicated as the Saviour of sinners, the curse he bore being due to us and not to him.

(1985:45)

108. *Victory endorsed*

We are not to regard the cross as defeat and the resurrection as victory. Rather, the cross was the victory won, and the resurrection the victory endorsed, proclaimed and demonstrated. **(1986a:235)**

109. *Demonstrations of power*

We are given in Scripture two major paradigms of the power of God, the creation of the universe and the resurrection of Jesus. In his letter to the Romans Paul even brings them together, describing the living God as the one 'who gives life to the dead and calls things that are not as though they were' (Rom. 4:17). In other words, God's power has been put forth above all in creation out of nothing and resurrection out of death. And both are objective and historical displays of power. For creation and resurrection have happened in time, and their results are visible. Otherwise they would not do as demonstrations of power. God's invisible power is clearly seen in what he has made. Similarly, although nobody saw the resurrection take place (any more than anybody saw the creation), yet the risen Lord himself was seen, heard and touched, so that the chosen eye-witnesses were able to testify to what they had seen and heard. **(1984:48)**

110. A reversal and a vindication

The resurrection was not only the sequel to the death of Jesus; it was the reversal of the human verdict passed on him and the public vindication of the divine purpose in his death.

(1992b:60)

111. A studied variety

An investigation of the ten appearances reveals an almost studied variety in the circumstances of person, place and mood in which they occurred. He was seen by individuals alone (Mary Magdalene, Peter and James), by small groups and by more than five hundred people together. He appeared in the garden of the tomb, near Jerusalem, in the upper room, on the road to Emmaus, by the lake of Galilee, on a Galilee mountain and on the Mount of Olives.

If there was variety in person and place, there was variety in mood also. Mary Magdalene was weeping; the women were afraid and astonished; Peter was full of remorse, and Thomas of incredulity. The Emmaus pair were distracted by the events of the week and the disciples in Galilee by their fishing. Yet through their doubts and fears, through their unbelief and preoccupation the risen Lord made himself known to them.

(1971a:57)

112. The evidence of history

Perhaps the transformation of the disciples of Jesus is the greatest evidence of all for the resurrection, because it is entirely artless. They do not invite us to look at themselves, as they invite us to look at the empty tomb and the collapsed graveclothes and the Lord whom they had seen. We can see the change in them without being asked to look. The men who figure in the pages of the gospels are new and different men in the Acts. The death of their Master left them despondent, disillusioned, and near to despair. But in the Acts they emerge as men who hazard their lives for the name of the Lord Jesus Christ and who turn the world upside down. **(1971a:58)**

113. The beginning of God's new creation

We should insist, against the denials by one or two church leaders, that 'resurrection' means 'bodily resurrection' (1) because of the evangelists' witness that the tomb was empty, (2) because the apostolic tradition affirmed that Jesus 'died, was buried, was raised and was seen' (1 Cor. 15:3–5) so that what was raised was what had been buried, *i.e.* his body, and (3) because the resurrected body of Jesus was and is the first bit of the material universe which has been redeemed, and is therefore the beginning and the pledge of God's new creation.

(1991d:70)

114. Affirming the resurrection

To affirm the living presence of Jesus by his Spirit in our hearts is not the same as to affirm his resurrection. His indwelling presence is a continuing experience; his resurrection was an historical event. By it his body was transformed, his tomb became empty and the power of death was defeated. **(1985:37)**

115. The 'principle of analogy'

Miracles do not need precedents to validate them. The classical argument of the eighteenth-century deists was that we can believe strange happenings outside our experience only if we can produce something analogous to them within our experience. This 'principle of analogy', if correct, would be enough in itself to disprove many of the biblical miracles, for we have no experience (for example) of somebody walking on water, multiplying loaves and fishes, rising from the dead or ascending into heaven. An ascension, in particular, would defy the law of gravity, which in our experience operates always and everywhere. The principle of analogy, however, had no relevance to the resurrection and ascension of Jesus, since both were *sui generis*. We are not claiming that people frequently (or even occasionally) rise from the dead and ascend into heaven, but that both events have happened once. The fact that we can produce no analogies before or since confirms their truth, rather than undermining it. **(1990b:47)**

116. The exaltation of Jesus

It is a pity that we call it 'Ascension Day', for the Bible speaks more of Christ's exaltation than of his ascension. This is an interesting avenue to explore. The four great events in the saving career of Jesus are described in the Bible both actively and passively, as deeds done both by Jesus and to Jesus. Thus, we are told with reference to his birth both that he came and that he was sent; with reference to his death both that he gave himself and that he was offered; with reference to his resurrection both that he rose and that he was raised; with reference to his ascension both that he ascended and that he was exalted. If we look more closely, we shall find that in the first two cases, the active phrase is commoner: he came and died, as a deliberate, self-determined choice. But in the last two cases, the passive phrase is more common: he was raised from the tomb and he was exalted to the throne. It was the Father's act. **(1954a:12)**

117. A sign of finality

There is no need to doubt the literal nature of Christ's ascension, so long as we realize its purpose. It was not necessary as a mode of departure, for 'going to the Father' did not involve a journey in space and presumably he could simply have vanished as on previous occasions. The reason he ascended before their eyes was rather to show them that this departure was final. He had now gone for good, or at least until his coming in glory. So they returned to Jerusalem with great joy and waited – not for Jesus to make another resurrection appearance, but for the Holy Spirit to come in power, as had been promised. **(1984d:103)**

118. Saviour and Lord

The symbolic statement that Jesus is 'at God's right hand' comprises the two great gospel affirmations that he is Saviour (with authority to bestow salvation) and that he is Lord (with authority to demand submission). **(1975c:50)**

10. THE RETURN IN GLORY

119. The Lord's return

We are confidently looking forward to the personal return, in power and glory, of our Lord Jesus Christ, and this Christian hope strongly motivates us. Not that we should make the mistake in 2000 AD which many made in 1000 AD, and predict that date (or any other date) as marking his return, for we do not know when he will come. Nor should we make our expectation of his coming an excuse for social inaction. On the contrary, the eschatological vision of the new world of righteousness and peace, which Christ will usher in, shows us what kind of society pleases God, and therefore gives us a strong incentive to seek at least an approximation to it now.

(1983e:viii)

120. Personal and visible

Two aspects of the return of Jesus are really beyond question. His advent will involve the personal presence of one now absent, the visible presence of one now unseen. Beyond this we shall be wise to exercise caution. The actual manner of his personal, visible return will no doubt transcend both the categories in which the prophecy has been made and the measure of our own understanding. It will be a dramatic, cataclysmic event terminating the whole process of history. But, although we may not wish to dogmatize beyond this point, we cannot stop short of it if we would be true to the New Testament revelation. The return of Jesus may indeed be *more* glorious, but it cannot be *less* than fully personal and visible.

(1962b)

121. A universal coming

It is not clear how literally we are to understand our being *caught up . . . in the clouds* (1 Thes. 4:17). We know from Jesus himself that his coming will be personal, visible and glorious, but we also know from him that it will not be local ('There he is!' 'Here he is!') but universal ('like the lightning, which flashes and lights up the sky from one end to the other'; Lk. 17:23–24). Presumably, therefore, our going to meet him will also transcend space. As for *the clouds*, they are to every Bible reader a familiar and easily recognized symbol of the immediate presence of God – at the Exodus, on Mount Sinai, filling the tabernacle, during the wilderness wanderings, at the transfiguration of Jesus, at his ascension, and at his glorious appearing. **(1991c:104)**

122. A transcendent event

An example of the importance of considering each part of Scripture's teaching on any subject in the light of the whole is the second coming of Christ. It would be easy (and dangerous) to be selective in the texts from which we build up our doctrine. Thus, some passages indicate that Christ's return will be personal and visible, indeed that he will come 'in the same way' as he went (Acts 1:11). But before we press this into meaning that the return will be a kind of ascension in reverse, like a film played backwards, and that Christ will set his feet on the precise spot on the Mount of Olives from which he was taken up, we need to consider something Jesus said to counter those who wanted to localize his return:

> For the Son of Man in his day will be like the lightning, which flashes and lights up the sky from one end to the other (Lk. 17:24).

The truly biblical Christian, anxious to be faithful to all Scripture, will want to do equal justice to both these strands of teaching. The coming of the Lord will indeed be personal, historical and visible; but it will also be 'in power and great glory', as universal as the lightning, a transcendent event of which the whole human population of both hemispheres will be simultaneously aware. **(1984d:179)**

123. The Lord and his own

The Christian hope, however, is more than the expectation that the King is coming; it is also the belief that when he comes, the Christian dead will come with him, and the Christian living will join them. **(1991c:97)**

11. CHRIST OUR CONTEMPORARY

124. To every culture, every age

Jesus Christ is timeless. Though born into a first-century Palestinian culture, he belongs to every culture. He is not dated. He speaks to all people in their vernacular. Christ is our contemporary. **(1981g:4)**

125. 'Alive for evermore . . .'

The Jesus who was born into our world, and who lived and died in first-century Palestine, also rose from the dead, is now alive for ever, and is available and accessible to his people. Jesus Christ is not to be relegated, like other religious leaders, to history and the history books. He is not dead and gone, finished or fossilized. He is alive and active. He calls us to follow him, and he offers himself to us as our indwelling and transforming Saviour. **(1992b:313)**

126. The man Christ Jesus

The incarnation was a historical and unrepeatable event with permanent consequences. Reigning at God's right hand today is the man Christ Jesus, still human as well as divine, though now his humanity has been glorified. Having assumed our human nature, he has never discarded it, and he never will.
(1984:74)

127. The divine person

Confidence in the divine-human person of Jesus is the one weapon against which neither the error, nor the evil, nor the force of the world can prevail. **(1988g:177)**

128. Lord of creation, Lord of the church

Often, our Christianity is mean because our Christ is mean. We impoverish ourselves by our low and paltry views of him. Some speak of him today as if he were a kind of hypodermic to be carried about in our pocket, so that when we are feeling depressed we can give ourselves a fix and take a trip into fantasy. But Christ cannot be used or manipulated like that. The contemporary church seems to have little understanding of the greatness of Jesus Christ as Lord of creation and Lord of the church, before whom our place is on our faces in the dust. Nor do we seem to see his victory as the New Testament portrays it, with all things under his feet, so that if we are joined to Christ, all things are under our feet as well.

(1984d:iii)

129. To touch reality

The One we preach is not Christ-in-a-vacuum, nor a mystical Christ unrelated to the real world, nor even only the Jesus of ancient history, but rather the contemporary Christ who once lived and died, and now lives to meet human need in all its variety today. To encounter Christ is to touch reality and experience transcendence. He gives us a sense of self-worth or personal significance, because he assures us of God's love for us. He sets us free from guilt because he died for us, from the prison of our own self-centredness by the power of his resurrection, and from paralysing fear because he reigns, all the principalities and powers of evil having been put under his feet. He gives meaning to marriage and home, work and leisure, personhood and citizenship. He introduces us into his new community, the new humanity he is creating. He challenges us to go out into some segment of the world which does not acknowledge him, there to give ourselves in witness and service for him. He promises us that history is neither meaningless nor endless, for one day he will return to terminate it, to destroy death and to usher in the new universe of righteousness and peace. **(1982a:154)**

130. The fundamental test

The fundamental doctrinal test of the professing Christian concerns his view of the person of Jesus. If he is a Unitarian, or a member of a sect denying the deity of Jesus, he is not a Christian. Many strange cults which have a popular appeal today can be easily judged and quickly repudiated by this test. The extreme seriousness of the lie is that a second denial is implicit in the first: he *denies the Father and the Son* (1 Jn. 2:23).

(1988g:116)

131. Love for the Name

The early Christians, who were proud 'to suffer indignity for the sake of the Name', were eager to evangelize in the same cause. Even love for the commands of Christ and love for the lost sheep of Christ are subordinate to and dependent on this love for the name of Christ.

Love for his name is not a sentimental attachment either to his personal name 'Jesus' or to his official title 'Christ' or to any of his designations in Scripture. Instead, it is a concern for his honour in the world, an ardent desire for the fulfilment of our prayer: 'Not to us, O LORD, not to us, but to thy name give glory' (Ps. 115:1). It is a recognition that God the Father has exalted him 'far above . . . every name that is named' (Eph. 1:21) and indeed 'bestowed on him the name which is above every name', with a view to securing 'that at the name of Jesus', before his supreme rank and dignity, 'every knee should bow . . . and every tongue confess that Jesus Christ is Lord . . .' (Phil. 2:9–11). **(1967e:20)**

III. THE HOLY SPIRIT

12. *The coming of the Spirit*
13. *The Spirit and the Son*
14. *The work of the Spirit*
15. *Baptism and fullness*
16. *The Spirit-filled Christian*

12. THE COMING OF THE SPIRIT

132. The day of Pentecost

There are at least four ways in which we may think of the day of Pentecost. First, it was the final act of the saving ministry of Jesus before the parousia. He who was born into our humanity, lived our life, died for our sins, rose from the dead and ascended into heaven, now sent his Spirit to his people to constitute them his body and to work out in them what he had won for them. In this sense the day of Pentecost is unrepeatable. Christmas Day, Good Friday, Easter Day, Ascension Day and Whit Sunday are annual celebrations, but the birth, death, resurrection, ascension and Spirit-gift they commemorate happened once and for all. Secondly, Pentecost brought to the apostles the equipment they needed for their special role. Christ had appointed them to be his primary and authoritative witnesses, and had promised them the reminding and teaching ministry of the Holy Spirit (Jn. 14 – 16). Pentecost was the fulfilment of that promise. Thirdly, Pentecost was the inauguration of the new era of the Spirit. Although his coming was a unique and unrepeatable historical event, all the people of God can now always and everywhere benefit from his ministry. Although he equipped the apostles to be the primary witnesses, he also equips us to be secondary witnesses. Although the inspiration of the Spirit was given to the apostles alone, the fullness of the Spirit is for us all. Fourthly, Pentecost has been called – and rightly – the first 'revival', using this word to denote one of those altogether unusual visitations of God, in which a whole community becomes vividly aware of his immediate, overpowering presence. **(1990b:60)**

133. A Spirit-filled people

It is incorrect to call the day of Pentecost 'the birthday of the church'. For the church as the people of God goes back at least 4,000 years to Abraham. What happened at Pentecost was that the remnant of God's people became the Spirit-filled body of Christ. **(1990b:81)**

134. A universal blessing

The evidence from the New Testament in general, and in particular from Peter's sermon in Acts 2 and Paul's teaching in 1 Corinthians 12:13, indicates that the 'baptism' of the Spirit is identical with the 'gift' of the Spirit, that it is one of the *distinctive* blessings of the new covenant, and, because it is an *initial* blessing, is also a *universal* blessing for members of the covenant. It is part and parcel of belonging to the new age. The Lord Jesus, the mediator of the new covenant and the bestower of its blessings, gives both the forgiveness of sins and the gift of the Spirit to all who enter his covenant. Further, baptism with water is the sign and seal of baptism with the Spirit, as much as it is of the forgiveness of sins. Water-baptism is the initiatory Christian rite, because Spirit-baptism is the initiatory Christian experience.　　　　　　　　　　　　　　　　　　　**(1975b:43)**

135. The age of the Spirit

It is the unanimous conviction of the New Testament authors that Jesus inaugurated the last days or messianic age, and that the final proof of this was the outpouring of the Spirit, since this was the Old Testament promise of promises for the end-time. This being so, we must be careful not to re-quote Joel's prophecy as if we are still awaiting its fulfilment, or even as if its fulfilment has been only partial, and we await some future and complete fulfilment. For this is not how Peter understood and applied the text. The whole messianic era, which stretches between the two comings of Christ, is the age of the Spirit in which his ministry is one of abundance. Is not this the significance of the verb 'pour out'? The picture is probably of a heavy tropical rainstorm, and seems to illustrate the generosity of God's gift of the Spirit (neither a drizzle nor even a shower but a downpour), its finality (for what has been 'poured out' cannot be gathered again) and its universality (widely distributed among the different groupings of human-kind).　　　　　　　　　　　　　　　　　　　　　　**(1990b:73)**

136. Babel undone

Ever since the early church fathers, commentators have seen the blessing of Pentecost as a deliberate and dramatic reversal of the curse of Babel. At Babel human languages were confused and the nations were scattered; in Jerusalem the language barrier was supernaturally overcome as a sign that the nations would now be gathered together in Christ, prefiguring the great day when the redeemed company will be drawn 'from every nation, tribe, people and language' (Gn. 11:1–9; Rev. 7:9). Besides, at Babel earth proudly tried to ascend to heaven, whereas in Jerusalem heaven humbly descended to earth.

(1990b:68)

137. No need to wait

There is no need for us to wait, as the one hundred and twenty had to wait, for the Spirit to come. For the Holy Spirit did come on the day of Pentecost, and has never left his church. Our responsibility is to humble ourselves before his sovereign authority, to determine not to quench him, but to allow him his freedom. For then our churches will again manifest those marks of the Spirit's presence, which many young people are specially looking for, namely biblical teaching, loving fellowship, living worship, and an ongoing, outgoing evangelism.

(1990b:87)

138. A missionary Spirit

Pentecost was a missionary event. It was the fulfilment of God's promise through the prophet Joel to pour out his Spirit 'on all people' (Joel 2:28; Acts 2:17), irrespective of their race, sex, age or social standing. And the foreign languages which the disciples spoke (which seems clearly to have been what the 'tongues' were, at least on the day of Pentecost) were a dramatic sign of the international nature of the Messiah's kingdom which the Holy Spirit had come to establish.

The rest of the Acts is a logical unfolding of that beginning. We watch enthralled as the missionary Spirit creates a missionary people and thrusts them out on their missionary task. **(1992b:330)**

13. THE SPIRIT AND THE SON

139. A better ministry

During his last evening with the Twelve in the upper room Jesus astonished them by saying: 'It is for your good that I am going away. Unless I go away, the Counsellor will not come to you; but if I go, I will send him to you' (Jn. 16:7). In what ways was the ministry of the Spirit better than that of the Son? In two ways. First, the Holy Spirit *universalizes* the presence of Jesus. On earth the disciples could not enjoy uninterrupted fellowship with their Master, for when they were in Galilee, he might be in Jerusalem, or *vice versa*. His presence was limited to one place at one time. But no longer. Now through his Spirit Jesus is with us everywhere and always. Secondly, the Holy Spirit *internalizes* the presence of Jesus. He said to the disciples: 'You know him [the Spirit of truth, the Counsellor], for he lives with you and will be in you. I will not leave you as orphans; I will come to you' (Jn. 14:17–18). On earth Jesus was with them and could teach them, but he could not enter their personality and change them from within. Now, however, through the Holy Spirit Christ dwells in our hearts by faith and does his transforming work there. **(1991d:78)**

140. The Spirit's witness

How do people come to acknowledge the divine-human person of Jesus? The apostolic testimony is necessary, but it does not compel assent. It is only by the Spirit of God that anybody ever confesses that Jesus is the Christ come in the flesh (1 Jn. 4:2). **(1988g:170)**

141. Change from within

There is a sense in which we may say that the teaching ministry of Jesus had proved a failure. Several times he had urged his disciples to humble themselves like a little child, but Simon Peter remained proud and self-confident. Often he had told them to love one another, but even John seems to have deserved his nickname 'son of thunder' to the end. Yet when you read Peter's first letter you cannot fail to notice its references to humility, and John's letters are full of love. What made the difference? The Holy Spirit. Jesus taught them to be

74

humble and loving; but neither quality appeared in their lives until the Holy Spirit entered their personality and began to change them from within. **(1971a:100)**

142. Status and experience

God's purpose was not only to secure our sonship by his Son, but to assure us of it by his Spirit. He sent his Son that we might have the *status* of sonship, and he sent his Spirit that we might have an *experience* of it. **(1968c:107)**

143. Glorifying Christ

Christian experience is experience of God: Father, Son and Holy Spirit. There really is no such thing as 'an experience of the Holy Spirit' from which the Father and the Son are excluded. In any case, the Holy Spirit is a reticent Spirit. He does not willingly draw attention to himself. Rather he prompts us to pray 'Abba! Father!' and thus witnesses to our filial relationship to God. And above all he glorifies Christ. He turns the bright beams of his searchlight upon the face of Jesus Christ. He is never more satisfied than when the believer is engrossed in Jesus Christ. **(1975b:69)**

14. THE WORK OF THE SPIRIT

144. Word and Spirit

We must never divorce what God has married, namely his Word and his Spirit. The Word of God is the Spirit's sword. The Spirit without the Word is weaponless; the Word without the Spirit is powerless. **(1991c:34)**

145. The indwelling Spirit

Romans 8:9 is of great importance in relation to our doctrine of the Holy Spirit for at least two reasons. First, it teaches that the hallmark of the authentic believer is the possession or indwelling of the Holy Spirit. Indwelling sin (Rom. 7:17, 20) is the lot of all the children of Adam; the privilege of the children of God is to have the indwelling Spirit to fight and subdue indwelling sin. As Jesus had promised, 'he lives with you and will be in you' (Jn. 14:17). Now in fulfilment of this promise every true Christian has received the Spirit, so that our body has become 'a temple of the Holy Spirit' in which he dwells (1 Cor. 6:19). Conversely, if we do not have Christ's Spirit in us, we do not belong to Christ at all. This makes it plain that the gift of the Spirit is an initial and universal blessing, received when we first repent and believe in Jesus. Of course there may be many further and richer experiences of the Spirit, and many fresh anointings of the Spirit for special tasks, but the personal indwelling of the Spirit is every believer's privilege from the beginning. To know Christ and to have the Spirit are one. Bishop Handley Moule was wise to write that 'there is no *separable* "Gospel of the Spirit"'. Not for a moment are we to advance, as it were, from the Lord Jesus Christ to a higher or deeper region, ruled by the Holy Ghost.'[1] **(1994:224)**

[1] H. C. G. Moule, *The Epistle of St Paul to the Romans*, The Expositor's Bible (Hodder and Stoughton, 2nd edn. 1894), p. 206.

146. A variety of gifts

Paul specifically says in 1 Corinthians 12:4: 'Now there are varieties of gifts'. It is important to recall this because many today have a very restricted view of *charismata*. For example, some people speak and write of 'the nine gifts of the Spirit', presumably to make a neat but artificial parallel with the Spirit's ninefold fruit. Others seem to be preoccupied, even obsessed, with only three of the more spectacular gifts ('tongues', 'prophecy' and 'healing'). In fact, however, the five lists given in the New Testament mention between them at least twenty distinct gifts, some of which are very prosaic and unsensational (like 'doing acts of mercy', Rom 12:8). Moreover, each list diverges widely from the others, and gives its selection of gifts in an apparently haphazard fashion. This suggests not only that no one list is complete, but that even all five together do not represent an exhaustive catalogue. Doubtless there are many more which are unlisted.   **(1979e:159)**

147. *Spiritual gifts*

The list of seven spiritual gifts in Romans 12 is much less well-known than either the two overlapping lists in 1 Corinthians 12 (nine in the first list and eight in the second) or the short list of five in Ephesians 4:11. It is important to note both the similarities and the dissimilarities between them. First, all the lists agree that the *source* of the gifts is God and his grace, although in Romans it is God the Father, in Ephesians God the Son and in 1 Corinthians God the Holy Spirit. Being gifts of trinitarian grace (*charismata*), both boasting and envying are excluded. Secondly, all agree that the *purpose* of the gifts is related to the building up of the body of Christ, although Ephesians 4:12 is the most explicit, and 1 Corinthians 14:12 says that we should evaluate the gifts according to the degree to which they edify the church. Thirdly, all the lists emphasize the *variety* of the gifts, each seeming to be a random selection of them. But, whereas students of the 1 Corinthians lists tend to focus on the supernatural (tongues, prophecy, healing and miracles), in Romans 12 all the gifts apart from prophecy are either general and practical (service, teaching, encouragement and leadership) or even prosaic (giving money and doing acts of mercy). It is evident that we need to broaden our understanding of spiritual gifts.   **(1994:328)**

148. *The Spirit and the sinner*

We need to recapture our belief that one of the God-appointed functions of the Holy Spirit is to make us know, feel, mourn, loathe, and forsake our sins; and if we are conscious of a superficial view of sin our proper course of action is to cry to the Holy Spirit, not to flee to the confessional.   **(1964:72)**

149. Faith in the Spirit's power

Some of us are not leading holy lives for the simple reason that we have too high an opinion of ourselves. No man ever cries aloud for deliverance who has not seen his own wretchedness. In other words, the only way to arrive at faith in the power of the Holy Spirit is along the road of self-despair. **(1966c:74)**

150. Fruits and gifts

What are the marks of a person filled with the Spirit of God today? There can be no doubt that the chief evidence is moral not miraculous, and lies in the Spirit's fruit not the Spirit's gifts.
(1975b:54)

15. BAPTISM AND FULLNESS

151. The baptism of the Spirit

The teaching of the pentecostal churches, and of many people in the charismatic or neo-pentecostal movement, is that we receive the 'gift' of the Spirit when we first believe, but then need a second and subsequent experience called the 'baptism' of the Spirit, usually evidenced by 'speaking in tongues'. What the New Testament teaches, however, is not a stereotype of two stages, but rather the initial blessing of regeneration by the Spirit, followed by a process of growth into maturity, during which we may indeed be granted many deeper and richer experiences of God. These often bring a fresh experience of the reality of God and a more vivid awareness of his love. But they should not be called 'the baptism of the Spirit'. The expression to be 'baptized with the Spirit' occurs only seven times in the New Testament. Six of them are quotations of John the Baptist's words 'I baptize with water, but he will baptize with the Spirit', a promise which was fulfilled on the day of Pentecost. The seventh (1 Cor. 12:13) emphasizes that all of us have been 'baptized' with the Spirit and been made to 'drink' of the Spirit – two graphic pictures of our having received him. **(1991d:80)**

152. Already baptized

The apostles urge upon us ethical conduct, often in considerable detail. They appeal to us to live out in the concrete realities of daily life what God has already done for us in Christ. They command us to grow in faith, love, knowledge and holiness. They warn us of judgment and challenge us with the expectation of the Lord's return. Meanwhile, they beg us not to grieve the Spirit, but rather to walk in the Spirit and to go on being filled with the Spirit . . . But never, not once, do they exhort and instruct us to 'be baptized with the Spirit'. There can be only one explanation of this, namely that they are writing to Christians, and Christians have already been baptized with the Holy Spirit. **(1975b:45)**

153. The one and the many

The New Testament teaching may be summed up as 'one baptism, many fillings'. **(1975b:68)**

154. Not optional but obligatory

'Be filled' (Eph. 5:18) is not a tentative suggestion, a mild recommendation, a polite piece of advice. It is a command which comes to us from Christ with all the authority of one of his chosen apostles. We have no more liberty to escape this duty than we have the ethical duties which surround the text, *e.g.* to speak the truth, to do honest work, to be kind and forgiving to one another, or to live lives of purity and love. The fullness of the Holy Spirit is not optional for the Christian, but obligatory. **(1975b:60)**

155. Recovering the fullness

The failure and poor performance of many Christians are evidence *not of their need to be baptized with the Spirit* (even the proud, loveless, quarrelsome and sin-tolerant Corinthian Christians had been baptized with the Spirit), *but of their need to recover the fullness of the Spirit* which they have lost through sin or unbelief. **(1975b:66)**

16. THE SPIRIT-FILLED CHRISTIAN

156. Sealed with the Spirit

A seal is a mark of ownership . . . and God's seal, by which he brands us as belonging for ever to him, is the Holy Spirit himself. The Holy Spirit is the identity tag of the Christian. If the Holy Spirit dwells within you, you are a Christian. If the Holy Spirit doesn't, you are not a Christian. For God has sealed us if we believed in Jesus, with the seal of the Holy Spirit himself who dwells within us.   **(1972c:207)**

157. Our common possession

Every Christian believer has an experience of the Holy Spirit from the very first moments of his Christian life. For the Christian life begins with a new birth, and the new birth is a birth 'of the Spirit' (Jn. 3:3–8). He is 'the Spirit of life', and it is he who imparts life to our dead souls. More than this, he comes himself to dwell within us, and the indwelling of the Spirit is the common possession of all God's children.

(1975b:19)

158. Filled with the Spirit

When Paul says to us, 'Be filled with the Spirit', he uses a present imperative, implying that we are to go on being filled. For the fullness of the Spirit is not a once-for-all experience which we can never lose, but a privilege to be renewed continuously by continuous believing and obedient appropriation. We have been 'sealed' with the Spirit once and for all; we need to be filled with the Spirit and go on being filled every day and every moment of the day.

(1979e:209)

159. Self-control

It is a serious mistake to suppose that to be filled with the Spirit of Jesus Christ is a kind of spiritual inebriation in which we lose control of ourselves. On the contrary, 'self-control' (*enkrateia*) is the final quality named as 'the fruit of the Spirit' in Galatians 5:22–23. Under the influence of the Holy Spirit we do not lose control; we gain it.   **(1979e:204)**

160. The Spirit of truth

One of the clearest evidences of a Spirit-filled Christian is his hunger for Scripture and his humble submissiveness to the authority of Scripture as God's written Word. But show me a person who claims to be a Christian yet is not devoting himself to the apostles' teaching, who rather neglects and even disregards it, and you give me cause to question whether he has received the Holy Spirit at all. For the Holy Spirit is the Spirit of truth (as Jesus called him). He is given us to be our teacher, and those who are filled with him have a keen appetite for his instruction. **(1977d:74)**

161. The greatest gift

God gives the Spirit; we receive him. Indeed, the greatest gift the Christian has ever received, ever will or could receive, is the Spirit of God himself. He enters our human personality and changes us from within. He fills us with love, joy and peace. He subdues our passions and transforms our characters into the likeness of Christ. Today there is no man-made temple in which God dwells. Instead, his temple is his people. He inhabits both the individual believer and the Christian community. 'Do you not know', asks Paul, 'that your body is a temple of the Holy Spirit, who is in you?' Again: 'Do you not know that you yourselves [plural, corporately] are God's temple and that God's Spirit lives in you?' (1 Cor. 6:19; 3:16).

(1990c:86)

162. The Spirit's fruit

The expression 'the fruit of the Spirit' comes from Paul's letter to the Galatians. These are his words:

> But the fruit of the Spirit is love, joy, peace, patience, kindness, goodness, faithfulness, gentleness, self-control (Gal. 5:22–23a).

The mere recital of these Christian graces should be enough to make the mouth water and the heart beat faster. For this is a portrait of Jesus Christ. No man or woman has ever exhibited these qualities in such balance or to such perfection as the man Christ Jesus. Yet this is the kind of person that every Christian longs to be.

This, then, is the portrait of Christ, and so – at least in the ideal – of the balanced, Christlike, Spirit-filled Christian. We have no liberty to pick and choose among these qualities. For it is together (as a bunch of fruit or a harvest) that they constitute Christlikeness; to cultivate some without the others is to be a lopsided Christian. The Spirit gives different Christians different gifts . . . but he works to produce the same fruit in all. He is not content if we display love for others, while we have no control of ourselves; or interior joy and peace without kindness to others; or a negative patience without a positive goodness; or gentleness and pliability without the firmness of Christian dependability. The lopsided Christian is a carnal Christian; but there is a wholeness, a roundness, a fullness of Christian character which only the Spirit-filled Christian ever exhibits. **(1975b:76)**

163. Unconditional surrender

Our attitude to our fallen nature should be one of ruthless repudiation. For 'those who belong to Christ Jesus have crucified the sinful nature with its passions and desires' (Gal. 5:24). That is, we have taken this evil, slimy, slippery thing called 'the flesh' and nailed it to the cross. This was our initial repentance. Crucifixion is dramatic imagery for our uncompromising rejection of all known evil. Crucifixion does not lead to a quick or easy death; it is an execution of lingering pain. Yet it is decisive; there is no possibility of escaping from it.

Our attitude to the Holy Spirit, on the other hand, is to be one of unconditional surrender. Paul uses several expressions for this. We are to 'live by the Spirit', to be 'led by the Spirit' and to 'keep in step with the Spirit' (Gal. 5:16, 18, 25). That is, we are to allow him his rightful sovereignty over us, and follow his righteous promptings.

Thus both our repudiation of the flesh and our surrender to the Spirit need to be repeated daily, however decisive our original repudiation and surrender may have been. In Jesus' words, we are to 'take up (our) cross daily' and follow him (Lk. 9:23). We are also to go on being filled with the Spirit (Eph. 5:18), as we open our personality to him daily. Both our repudiation and our surrender are also to be worked out in disciplined habits of life. It is those who 'sow to the Spirit' (Gal. 6:8) who reap the fruit of the Spirit. And to 'sow to the Spirit' means to cultivate the things of the Spirit, for example, by our wise use of the Lord's Day, the discipline of our daily prayer and Bible reading, our regular worship and attendance at the Lord's Supper, our Christian friendships and our involvement in Christian service. An inflexible principle of all God's dealings, both in the material and in the moral realm, is that we reap what we sow. The rule is invariable. It cannot be changed, for 'God cannot be mocked' (Gal. 6:7). We must not therefore be surprised if we do not reap the fruit of the Spirit when all the time we are sowing to the flesh. Did we think we could cheat or fool God? **(1992b:154)**

IV. REVELATION AND SCRIPTURE

17. *The divine self-disclosure*
18. *'God has spoken . . .'*
19. *Biblical authority*
20. *Listening and interpreting*
21. *Scripture, reason and tradition*
22. *The study of theology*
23. *Truth and error*
24. *A living Word*

17. THE DIVINE SELF-DISCLOSURE

164. The mind of God

God's mind, being infinite, is impenetrable by finite beings. His thoughts are as much higher than our thoughts as the heavens are higher than the earth (Is. 55:9). How then can we know them? By ourselves we cannot. They are beyond us. There is no ladder by which we may climb to the heights of heaven, no way by which we may delve into the mind of God. But God has disclosed his thoughts to us by speaking. The Isaiah 55 passage continues: 'As the rain and the snow come down from heaven, . . . so is my word that goes out from my mouth' (verses 10–11). God has clothed his thoughts in words. His mouth has declared what is in his mind. Theologically we may say that revelation has come to us through the means of inspiration.   **(1981g:8)**

165. An inherent authority

It is a basic tenet of the Christian religion that we believe what we believe not because human beings have invented it but because God has revealed it. In consequence, there is an authority inherent in Christianity which can never be destroyed.   **(1982a:57)**

166. Revelation and illumination

The human mind is both finite and fallen, and will neither understand nor believe without the gracious work of the Holy Spirit. It is not only necessary that he should have given an objective revelation. We need his subjective illumination too. If I were to take a blindfold man to the ceremony of unveiling of some stone tablet, two processes would be necessary before he could read the inscription. First, the tablet must be unveiled (and of course 'revelation' means unveiling). Second, the bandage must be taken from his eyes. Similarly, it is not enough that God through his Spirit has unveiled the truth in Christ. The veil must be removed from our eyes as well.

(1956a:26)

167. General revelation

Because Romans 1:19–20 is one of the principal New Testament passages on the topic of 'general revelation ', it may be helpful to summarize how 'general' differs from 'special' revelation. God's self-revelation through 'what has been made' has four main characteristics. First, it is 'general' because made to everybody everywhere, as opposed to 'special' because made to particular people in particular places, through Christ and the biblical authors. Secondly, it is 'natural' because made through the natural order, as opposed to 'supernatural', involving the incarnation of the Son and the inspiration of the Scriptures. Thirdly, it is 'continuous' because since the creation of the world it has gone on 'day after day . . . night after night' (Ps. 19:2), as opposed to 'final' and finished in Christ and in Scripture. And fourthly it is 'creational', revealing God's glory through creation, as opposed to 'salvific', revealing God's grace in Christ. **(1994:73)**

168. Progressive revelation

The concept of progressive revelation (God teaching his people in many parts and many ways) is a notion quite different from that of progressive religious evolution (man groping in a darkness which becomes gradually less dark). A biblical understanding of progressive revelation does not imply an adverse judgment on any of the biblical material involved at any stage in the process. It is all God's truth, so far as it goes; the only difference is that some parts go further than others.

(1967b:54)

169. The divine autobiography

The Bible is God's self-disclosure, the divine autobiography. In the Bible the subject and the object are identical, for in it God is speaking about God. He makes himself known progressively in the rich variety of his being: as the Creator of the universe and of human beings in his own image, the climax of his creation; as the living God who sustains and animates everything he has made; as the covenant God who chose Abraham, Isaac, Jacob and their descendants to be his special people; and as a gracious God who is slow to anger and quick to forgive, but also as a righteous God who punishes idolatry and injustice among his own people as well as in the pagan nations. Then in the New Testament he reveals himself as the Father of our Lord and Saviour Jesus Christ, who sent him into the world to take our nature upon him, to be born and grow, live and teach, work and suffer, die and rise, occupy the throne and send the Holy Spirit; next as the God of the new covenant community, the church, who sends his people into the world as his witnesses and his servants in the power of the Holy Spirit; and finally as the God who one day will send Jesus Christ in power and glory to save, to judge and to reign, who will create a new universe, and who in the end will be everything to everybody. **(1982b:69)**

170. Worship, faith and obedience

In the Bible God gives us revelations of himself which lead us to worship, promises of salvation which stimulate our faith, and commandments expressing his will which demand our obedience. This is the meaning of Christian discipleship. Its three essential ingredients are worship, faith and obedience. And all three are called forth by the Word of God. **(1982b:74)**

171. Revealed truths

God's Word is designed to make us Christians, not scientists, and to lead us to eternal life through faith in Jesus Christ. It was not God's intention to reveal in Scripture what human beings could discover by their own investigations and experiments. So the first three chapters of Genesis reveal in particular four spiritual truths which could never be discovered by the scientific method. First, that God made everything. Secondly, that he made it out of nothing. There was no original raw material as eternal as himself on which he could work. Thirdly, that he made man male and female in his own image. Fourthly, that everything which he made was 'very good'. When it left his hand it was perfect. Sin and suffering were foreign invasions into his lovely world, and spoiled it. **(1991d:58)**

172. The limits of knowledge

Although God's revelation is final and complete in Christ, this does not mean that it is exhaustive. In Christ God has revealed all of himself that it is possible for him to reveal through human flesh, and all that it is his pleasure to reveal to man in this age. But we do not mean that we now know everything. On the contrary, there are many indications in the New Testament itself that our knowledge, though immeasurably increased in Christ, is still strictly limited. Did not Christ say that he himself was ignorant of the day of his return (Mk. 13:32), and later add that it was not for us to know (Acts 1:7)?

Did not the great apostle Paul liken his understanding to that of a child's and his sight to the reflections of a mirror, and add that our knowledge now is imperfect and partial (1 Cor. 13:9–12)? Did not the saintly, philosophical St John concede with regard to the next life that 'it doth not yet appear what we shall be' (1 Jn. 3:2)? Let Moses have the last word in this matter. 'The secret things belong unto the Lord our God: but those things which are revealed belong unto us' (Dt. 29:29).

(1956a:12)

173. Christian assurance

Christian dogmatism has, or should have, a limited field. It is not tantamount to a claim to omniscience. Yet in those things which are clearly revealed in Scripture, Christians should not be doubtful or apologetic. The corridors of the New Testament reverberate with dogmatic affirmations beginning 'We know', 'We are sure', 'We are confident'. If you question this, read the First Epistle of John in which verbs meaning 'to know' occur about forty times. They strike a note of joyful assurance which is sadly missing from many parts of the church today and which needs to be recaptured.   (1970b:15)

174. Babes and fools

To God's revealed message men must humbly submit. 'If any one among you thinks that he is wise in this age, let him become a fool that he may become wise' (1 Cor. 3:18). I believe that this 'let him become a fool' is one of the hardest words of Scripture to the proud hearts and minds of men. Like the brilliant intellectuals of ancient Greece our contemporaries have unbounded confidence in the human reason. They want to think their way to God by themselves, and to gain credit for discovering God by their own effort. But God resists such swellings of pride on the part of the finite creature. Of course men have been given minds to use, and they are never to stifle or smother them, but they must humble them reverently before the revelation of God, becoming in Paul's word 'fools' and in Christ's word 'babes'. It is only babes to whom God reveals himself and only fools whom he makes wise.   (1961:99)

175. Stewards of truth

All revealed truth is held in stewardship. It is given to be shared, not monopolized. If men cannot keep their scientific

90

discoveries to themselves, how much less should we keep to ourselves the divine disclosures? **(1979e:120)**

176. Revelation and responsibility

God has not revealed his truth in such a way as to leave us free at our pleasure to believe or disbelieve it, to obey or disobey it. Revelation carries with it responsibility, and the clearer the revelation, the greater the responsibility to believe and obey it.
(1988g:208)

18. 'GOD HAS SPOKEN . . .'

177. A God who speaks

God is the supreme communicator. **(1979d:ix)**

178. Thoughts into words

The assertion that God has 'spoken' (Heb. 1:1), that he has put his thoughts into words, must be taken with full seriousness. It is impossible for us human beings to read even each other's thoughts if we remain silent. Only if I speak to you can you know what is in my mind; only if you speak to me can I know what is in your mind. If, then, men and women remain strangers to each other until and unless they speak to one another, how much more will God remain a stranger to us unless he speaks or has spoken? His thoughts are not our thoughts, as we have seen. It is impossible for human beings to read the mind of God. If we are ever to know his mind he must speak; he must clothe his thoughts in words. This, we believe, is precisely what he has done. **(1991b:12)**

179. 'God-breathed'

The Bible is the Word of God. He spoke it. It issued from his mouth. The term *inspiration* means neither that God breathed into the human authors in order to heighten their perception of truth, nor that he breathed into their writings in order somehow to change human prose into divine poetry, but rather that the words they spoke were actually breathed out of his mouth. The emphasis is not on the transformation of truths which were already there (in the minds or words of the prophets), but on the origination of truths which were not there until God thought and spoke them. We cannot escape this. It is the plain teaching of 2 Timothy 3:16 that 'all Scripture is God-breathed' – *theopneustos* – breathed out from his mouth. Hence the familiar prophetic formulas – 'the word of the Lord came to me, saying' or 'thus says the Lord' – and the comparable claim of the apostles to be bearers or speakers of God's word. **(1981g:6)**

180. Deeds and words

Scripture affirms that God has spoken both through historical deeds and through explanatory words, and that the two belong indissolubly together. Even the Word made flesh, the climax of God's progressive self-revelation, would have remained enigmatic if it were not that he also spoke and that his apostles both described and interpreted him. **(1982a:95)**

181. Christians or Athenians?

'Revelation' describes the initiative God took to unveil or disclose himself. It is a humbling word. It presupposes that in his infinite perfections God is altogether beyond the reach of our finite minds. Our mind cannot penetrate his mind. We have no ability to read his thoughts. Indeed, his thoughts are as much higher than our thoughts as the heavens are higher than the earth (Is. 55:9). Consequently, we would know nothing about God if he had not chosen to make himself known. Without revelation we would not be Christians at all but Athenians, and all the world's altars would be inscribed 'TO AN UNKNOWN GOD' (Acts 17:23). But we believe God has revealed himself, not only in the glory and order of the created universe, but supremely in Jesus Christ his incarnate Word, and in the written Word which bears a comprehensive and variegated witness to him. **(1992b:209)**

182. God's powerful Word

We are not to think of the Word as existing apart from God or as possessing power apart from God. The Word is powerful only and precisely because it is *God's* Word, the Word which God has spoken and therefore continues to speak. And God's Word, when God speaks it, has God's authority and power.

(1968a:6)

183. Written for our learning

We live in very subjective days in which existentialism distinguishes sharply between 'authentic' living, and uses purely subjective criteria by which to assess what is 'authentic', namely whether it seems authentic to me at the moment. But Christians, especially evangelical Christians, are convinced that God has spoken historically and objectively, that his Word culminated in Christ and in the apostolic witness to Christ, and that Scripture is precisely God's Word written for our learning. All our traditions, all our opinions and all our experiences must therefore be submitted to the independent and objective test of biblical truth. **(1975b:9)**

184. A rational revelation

The Christian doctrine of revelation, far from making the human mind unnecessary, actually makes it indispensable and assigns to it its proper place. God has revealed himself in *words* to *minds*. His revelation is a rational revelation to rational creatures. Our duty is to receive his message, to submit to it, to seek to understand it, and to relate it to the world in which we live.

That God needs to take the initiative to reveal himself shows that our minds are finite and fallen; that he chooses to reveal himself to babies (Mt. 11:25) shows that we must humble ourselves to receive his Word; that he does so at all, and in words shows that our minds are capable of understanding it. One of the highest and noblest functions of man's mind is to listen to God's Word, and so to read his mind and think his thoughts after him, both in nature and in Scripture.

(1972d:18)

185. Self-disclosure progressive and completed

The self-disclosure of God through the Old Testament was not only varied in form, but also partial in content. Christians believe in progressive revelation, that God revealed himself bit by bit and stage by stage, each new stage building on those which had preceded it. But over against the 'many parts' of the Old Testament revelation is set God's Son who, it is implied, is the grand finale of the drama, since in and through him God's self-disclosure was brought to completion.

(1991b:14)

186. More than speech

The biblical understanding of God's Word is not just that he speaks it, but that he acts through it. His words are not merely speech; they are deeds as well. This is clear of creation, which was effected by God's words of command. 'God said . . . and it was so'; 'He spoke, and it came to be; he commanded, and it stood forth' (Gn. 1:6–7; Ps. 33:9). The same is true of salvation, which indeed is a new creation. For the same God who said 'Let light shine out of darkness' has shone in our hearts, revealing Christ to us (2 Cor. 4:6). His Word was creative; it brought to us both light and life.

(1976b:40)

187. God still speaks

When once we have grasped the truth that 'God still speaks through what he has spoken', we shall be well protected against two opposite errors. The first is the belief that, though it was heard in ancient times, God's voice is silent today. The second is the claim that God is indeed speaking today, but that his Word has little or nothing to do with Scripture. The first leads to Christian antiquarianism, the second to Christian existentialism. Safety and truth are found in the related convictions that God has spoken, that God speaks, and that his two messages are closely connected to one another, because it is *through* what he spoke that he speaks. He makes his Word living, contemporary and relevant, until we find ourselves back on the Emmaus Road with Christ himself expounding the Scriptures to us, and with our hearts on fire. Another way of putting the same truth is to say that we must keep the Word of God and the Spirit of God together. For apart from the Spirit the Word is dead, while apart from the Word the Spirit is alien.

(1982a:102)

19. BIBLICAL AUTHORITY

188. The sceptre of Christ's authority

There is no doubt where supreme authority resides, for God has given it to the risen and exalted Lord Jesus. 'All authority has been given to me', he said, 'in heaven and on earth' (Mt. 28:18) . . .

So how does Jesus Christ exercise his authority and rule his church today? It is here that Christians and churches part company. Put simply, there are three main views. The Roman Catholic Church believes that Christ rules through the teaching authority of the Pope with the College of Bishops. Theological liberals believe that Christ teaches through the individual's reason and conscience, and through the contemporary climate of educated opinion. But the reformed and evangelical conviction is that Christ exercises his authority by his Spirit through his Word. Although both tradition and reason are important, Scripture is the sceptre by which Christ rules the church.

(1992c:5)

189. Jesus and Scripture

The first and foremost reason why Christians believe in the divine inspiration and authority of Scripture is not because of what the churches teach, the writers claimed or the readers sense, but because of what Jesus Christ himself said. Since he endorsed the authority of Scripture, we are bound to conclude that his authority and Scripture's authority either stand or fall together . . . All the available evidence confirms that Jesus Christ assented in his mind and submitted in his life to the authority of Old Testament Scripture. Is it not inconceivable that his followers should have a lower view of it than he?

(1984d:145, 147)

190. Christ's view must become ours

The disciple is not above his teacher. It is inconceivable that a Christian who looks to Jesus as his Teacher and Lord should have a lower view of the Old Testament than he had. What is the sense in calling Jesus 'Teacher' and 'Lord', and then disagreeing with him? We have no liberty to disagree with him. His view of Scripture must become ours. **(1982b:29)**

191. All Christ's teaching

Where is all the teaching of Jesus Christ to be found? The correct answer is not 'in his discourses in the gospels', but 'in the whole Bible'. Properly understood, the teaching of Jesus Christ includes the Old Testament (for he set his seal upon its truth and its authority), the gospels (in which his own words are recorded), and the rest of the New Testament (which contains the teaching of the apostles through whom, we believe, he continued to speak, in order to complete his self-revelation). **(1967d:48)**

192. Jesus and the Old Testament

It was the consistent teaching of Jesus that Old Testament Scripture was God's Word bearing witness to him. For example, he said, 'Abraham rejoiced . . . to see my day' (Jn. 8:56). Or in John 5:46 he says, 'Moses . . . wrote of me', and again, 'the scriptures . . . bear witness to me' (verse 39). At the beginning of his ministry, when he went to worship in the synagogue at Nazareth, you will remember, he read from Isaiah 61 about the Messiah's mission and message of liberation, and added: 'Today this scripture has been fulfilled in your hearing' (Lk. 4:21). In other words, 'If you want to know whom the prophet was writing about, he was writing about me.' Jesus continued to say this kind of thing throughout his ministry. Even after the resurrection he had not changed his mind, for 'he interpreted to them in all the scriptures the things concerning himself' (Lk. 24:27). Thus from the beginning to the end of his ministry Jesus declared that the whole prophetic testimony of the Old Testament, in all its rich diversity, converged upon him. 'The scriptures . . . bear witness to me.' **(1982b:24)**

193. Paul and the Old Testament

Paul's reference in Romans 14 to Christ's fulfilment of Psalm 69:9 leads him into a brief digression about the nature and purpose of Old Testament Scripture. *For everything that was written in the past was written to teach us, so that through endurance and the encouragement of the Scriptures we might have hope* (verse 4). From this thoughtful statement it is legitimate to derive five truths about Scripture, which we would do well to remember.

First, its *contemporary intention*. The books of Scripture were of course primarily intended for those to and for whom they were written in the past. Yet the apostle is persuaded that they were also *written to teach us*.

Secondly, its *inclusive value*. Having quoted only half a verse from one psalm, Paul declares that *everything* written in the past is for us, although obviously not everything is of equal value. Jesus himself spoke of 'the more important matters of the law' (Mt. 23:23).

Thirdly, its *christological focus*. Paul's application of Psalm 69 to Christ is a fine example of how the risen Lord could explain to his disciples 'what was said in all the Scriptures concerning himself' (Lk. 24:27).

Fourthly, its *practical purpose*. Not only is it able to make us 'wise for salvation through faith in Christ Jesus' (2 Tim. 3:15), but it can bring us *encouragement* with a view to *endurance*, so that *we might have hope*, looking beyond time to eternity, beyond present sufferings to future glory.

Fifthly, its *divine message*. The striking fact that 'endurance and encouragement', which in verse 4 are attributed to Scripture, in verse 5 are attributed to God, can only mean that it is God himself who encourages us through the living voice of Scripture. For God continues to speak through what he has spoken. **(1994:370)**

194. No actual autograph

It is true that no actual autograph of Scripture has survived. The loss is presumably due to a deliberate providence of God, which may have been to prevent us giving superstitious reverence to pieces of paper. Nevertheless, we know something of the scrupulous care with which scribes copied the sacred Hebrew text, and the same would have been true of the New Testament documents. Further, we possess a great many more early copies of the original text than of any other ancient literature. By comparing these with each other, with the early 'versions' (*i.e.* translations) and with biblical quotations in the writings of the church fathers, scholars (called 'textual critics') have been able to establish the authentic text (especially of the New Testament) beyond any reasonable doubt. The uncertainties which remain are almost entirely trivial; no doctrine of any importance hangs upon them.

(1984d:143)

195. Biblical inspiration

Inspiration is the word traditionally used to describe God's activity in the composition of the Bible. Indeed, the Bible's divine inspiration is the foundation of its divine authority. It is authoritative because – and only because – it is inspired. This statement needs immediately to be qualified, however. To say 'the Bible is the Word of God' is true, but it is only a half-truth, even a dangerous half-truth. For the Bible is also a human word and witness.

This, in fact, is the account which the Bible itself gives of its origins. The law, for instance, is termed by Luke both 'the law of Moses' and 'the law of the Lord', and that in consecutive verses (Lk. 2:22–23). Similarly, at the beginning of Hebrews it is stated that 'God spoke . . . through the prophets', and in 2 Peter 1:21 that 'men spoke from God'. Thus God spoke and men spoke. Both statements are true, and neither contradicts the other. **(1981g:5)**

196. God's authority

'Authority' is the power or weight which Scripture possesses because of what it is, namely a divine revelation given by divine inspiration. If it is a word from God, it has authority over men. For behind every word that anybody utters stands the person who speaks it. It is the speaker himself (his character, knowledge and position) who determines how people regard his words. So God's Word carries God's authority. It is because of who he is that we should believe what he has said. **(1984d:139)**

197. The word of power

There is no saving power in the words of men. The devil does not relinquish his grasp upon his prisoners at the bidding of mere mortals. No word has authority for him but the Word of God. **(1961:100)**

198. Inspired by God

I am very thankful for the New International Version translation of 2 Timothy 3:16, 'All Scripture is God-breathed.' That is undoubtedly the correct translation. The Authorized Version, 'given by inspiration of God', was always a little cumbersome because it took five words to translate one Greek word that means 'God-breathed'. And the New English Bible, I am afraid, is mistaken because it says that, 'every inspired Scripture has its use', as much as to say every inspired one is useful, but there are others that are not inspired and are therefore not useful. Now that is not only a contradiction in terms, because Scripture means inspired writing, but it also omits a very important little word there called 'also' in the Greek text. Paul says not only one thing, every inspired Scripture is useful, but two things – every Scripture is inspired or God-breathed and it is useful, and indeed useful for us, because it has been inspired by God. **(1989c:3)**

199. Out of whose mouth?

'God-breathed' is not the only account which Scripture gives of itself, since God's mouth was not the only mouth involved in its production. The same Scripture which says 'the mouth of the LORD has spoken' (Is. 1:20) also says that God spoke 'by the mouth of his holy prophets' (Acts 3:18, 21). Out of whose mouth did Scripture come, then? God's or man's? The only biblical answer is 'both'. Indeed, God spoke through the human authors in such a way that his words were simultaneously their words, and their words were simultaneously his. This is the double authorship of the Bible. Scripture is equally the Word of God and the words of human beings. Better, it is the Word of God through the words of human beings.
(1992b:168)

200. Verbal inspiration

'Verbal inspiration' means that what the Holy Spirit has spoken and still speaks through the human authors, understood according to the plain, natural meaning of the words used, is true and without error. There is no need at all to be embarrassed by this Christian belief, or to be ashamed or afraid of it. On the contrary, it is eminently reasonable, because words are the units of which sentences are made up. Words are the building-blocks of speech. It is therefore impossible to frame a precise message without constructing precise sentences composed of precise words . . .

This is the apostolic claim, that the same Holy Spirit of God, who searches the depths of God and revealed his researches to the apostles, went on to communicate them through the apostles in words with which he himself supplied them. He spoke his words through their words, so that they were equally the words of God and the words of men. This is the double authorship of Scripture and the meaning of 'inspiration'. The inspiration of Scripture was not a mechanical process. It was intensely personal, for it involved a Person (the Holy Spirit) speaking through persons (prophets and apostles) in such a way that his words were theirs, and their words were his, simultaneously. **(1982b:44)**

201. Dual authorship

The dual authorship of Scripture is an important truth to be carefully guarded. On the one hand, *God* spoke, revealing the truth and preserving the human authors from error, yet without violating their personality. On the other hand, *men* spoke, using their own faculties freely, yet without distorting the divine message. Their words were truly their own words. But they were (and still are) also God's words, so that what Scripture says, God says. **(1984d:141)**

202. Inspiration and incarnation

A number of writers both ancient and modern have detected an analogy between the double authorship of the one book and the two natures of the one Christ. Now all arguments from analogy are perilous, and the parallel between the inspiration of the written Word and the incarnation of the living Word is far from being exact. For example, the Bible possesses no inherent deity as we believe Jesus had and has. Nevertheless, in the blend of the divine with the human there is clearly some similarity. Two particular points strike me as worthy of comment. The first is that orthodoxy affirms the two without confusing them, and without allowing either to detract from the other. We must not speak of the deity of Jesus in such a way as to deny his real humanity, nor of his real humanity in such a way as to imply that it was imperfect through sin or error. Similarly, we must not speak of the divine origin of the Bible in such a way as to deny its human authorship, nor of the human authors in such a way as to imply that they were marred by error.

The second point I would make about this analogy is that in both cases we more conservative Christians have tended to overemphasize the divine at the expense of the human. In referring to the incarnation of the Word we sometimes speak

101

only of the deity of Jesus, and forget that he was also a man of flesh and blood. This is the heresy of docetism. Similarly, in referring to the inspiration of Scripture we sometimes speak only of its divine origin and forget that it was also written by human authors. This is the heresy of fundamentalism. It is as misleading to say, 'The Bible is the Word of God' without adding that it is also the words of men, as it is to say, 'Jesus is the Son of God' without adding that he is also the Son of man. Both errors are understandable because in both Christ and the Bible it is the divine element not the human which is usually under attack. **(1981g:13)**

203. *How we read*

The double authorship of the Bible will affect the way in which we read it. Because it is the word of men, we shall study it like *every* other book, using our minds, investigating its words and syntax, its historical origins and its literary composition. But because it is also the Word of God, we shall study it like *no* other book, on our knees, humbly, crying to God for illumination and for the ministry of the Holy Spirit, without whom we can never understand his Word. **(1982b:18)**

204. *Apostolic authority*

When in the fourth century the church came finally to settle which books should be included in the New Testament canon and which excluded, the test they applied was whether a book came from the apostles. That is, was it written by an apostle? If not, did it nevertheless emanate from the circle of the apostles and carry the endorsement of their authority? It is important to add this, for not every New Testament book was written by an apostle. But it seems to have been recognized that if a non-apostolic document nevertheless carried a kind of apostolic imprimatur, it should be recognized as 'apostolic'. For example, Luke was known to have been a regular companion and colleague of Paul, and Mark was described by the early church fathers Papias and Irenaeus as 'the interpreter of Peter' who faithfully recorded Peter's memories of Christ and the substance of his preaching. Thus, the church was in no sense conferring authority on the canonical books; it was simply recognizing the authority they already possessed. **(1984d:152)**

205. The finality of Scripture

Just as the Old Testament canon is closed because it witnesses prophetically to Christ, and Christ has come; so the New Testament canon is closed because it witnesses historically to Christ, and Christ has come. The finality of Scripture is thus due to – is, indeed, one aspect of – the finality of Jesus Christ.

(1967b:59)

206. A parable of freedom

Let me develop a little parable. It uses flight as a picture of freedom (memories of *Jonathan Livingstone Seagull!*) and seeks to characterize (not, I hope, caricature) the essential difference between the fundamentalist, the liberal and the evangelical.

The fundamentalist seems to me to resemble a caged bird, which possesses the capacity for flight, but lacks the freedom to use it. For the fundamentalist mind is confined or caged by an over-literal interpretation of Scripture, and by the strict traditions and conventions into which this has led him. He is not at liberty to question these, or to explore alternative, equally faithful ways of applying Scripture to the modern world, for he cannot escape from his cage.

The liberal seems to me to resemble (no offence meant!) a gas-filled balloon, which takes off and rises into the air, buoyant, free, directed only by its own built-in navigational responses to wind and pressure, but entirely unrestrained from earth. For the liberal mind has no anchorage; it is accountable only to itself.

The evangelical seems to me to resemble a kite, which can also take off, fly great distances and soar to great heights, while all the time being tethered to earth. For the evangelical mind is held by revelation. Without doubt it often needs a longer string, for we are not renowned for creative thinking. Nevertheless, at least in the ideal, I see evangelicals as finding true freedom under the authority of revealed truth, and combining a radical mindset and lifestyle with a conservative commitment to Scripture.

(1988d:106)

207. Authority and relevance

The modern world detests authority but worships relevance. So to bracket these two words in relation to the Bible is to claim for it one quality (authority) which people fear it has but wish it had not, and another (relevance) which they fear it has not but wish it had.

Our Christian conviction is that the Bible has both authority and relevance – to a degree quite extraordinary in so ancient a book – and that the secret of both is in Jesus Christ. Indeed, we should never think of Christ and the Bible apart. 'The Scriptures . . . bear witness to me,' he said (Jn. 5:39), and in so saying also bore his witness to them. This reciprocal testimony between the living Word and the written Word is the clue to our Christian understanding of the Bible. For his testimony to it assures us of its authority, and its testimony to him of its relevance. The authority and the relevance are his.   **(1981g:3)**

208. Submission to Scripture

Submission to Scripture is for us evangelicals a sign of our submission to Christ, a test of our loyalty to him. We find it extremely impressive that our incarnate Lord, whose own authority amazed his contemporaries, should have subordinated himself to the authority of the Old Testament Scriptures as he did, regarding them as his Father's written Word.

(1988d:85)

20. LISTENING AND INTERPRETING

209. Obedience and understanding

Obedience is a precondition of understanding. We need to repent of the haughty way in which we sometimes stand in judgment upon Scripture and must learn to sit humbly under its judgment instead. If we come to Scripture with our minds made up, expecting to hear from it only an echo of our own thoughts and never the thunderclap of God's, then indeed he will not speak to us and we shall only be confirmed in our own prejudices. We must allow the Word of God to confront us, to disturb our security, to undermine our complacency and to overthrow our patterns of thought and behaviour.   **(1981g:33)**

210. The meaning of exposition

'Exposition' means to bring out of Scripture what is there. Its opposite is 'imposition', which is to read into Scripture what is not there, but what one would like to find there if only one could . . .   **(1978e:168)**

211. The Bible's human authors

The biblical historians were not historians in the modern sense, writing with scientific detachment. They were theologians too, writing from a divine perspective. They were not morally and spiritually neutral; they were deeply committed to God's cause. The Old Testament history books were regarded as prophecy, and the four lives of Jesus are not biographies but gospels written by evangelists, who were bearing witness to Jesus. Consequently, they selected and arranged their material according to their theological purpose. Moreover, their purpose arose naturally – though also in God's providence – from their temperament, their background and their God-given responsibilities to the people of God. Man and message were related to each other. It was no accident that Amos was the prophet of God's justice, Isaiah of his sovereignty and Hosea of his love; or that Paul was the apostle of grace, James of works, John of love and Peter of hope; or that Luke, the only Gentile contributor to the New Testament, stressed the worldwide embrace of the gospel. The Holy Spirit communicated through each a distinctive and appropriate emphasis.   **(1981g:10)**

212. Revelation and culture

There can be no gainsaying the fact that in the purpose of God his revelation reached its culmination in the first century AD, in Christ and in the apostolic witness to Christ, and therefore in what to us is an ancient culture of mixed Hebrew, Greek and Roman ingredients. Nor can there be any doubt that, in order to grasp his revelation, we have to think ourselves back into that culture. But the fact that God disclosed himself in terms of a particular culture gives us not a justification for rejecting his revelation, but rather the right principle by which to interpret it, and also the solemn responsibility to reinterpret it in terms meaningful to our own culture. **(1975c:42)**

213. No cultural vacuum

No word of the Bible was spoken in a cultural vacuum. Every part of it was culturally conditioned. This is not to say that its message was controlled by the local culture in such a way as to be distorted by it, but rather that the local culture was the medium through which God expressed himself. This is a fact which we neither can nor should deny. But we must be careful what deductions we draw from it. Extreme positions are being taken up on both sides of the debate. Some, whenever they find biblical teaching couched in cultural terms other than their own, declare the teaching irrelevant because the culture is alien. Others make the opposite mistake and invest both the kernel of the teaching and the cultural shell with equal normative authority. The more judicious way, however, is to preserve the inner substance of what God is teaching or commanding, while claiming the liberty to reclothe it in modern cultural dress.

For example, Jesus commanded us to wash one another's feet. We should not discard this instruction on the ground that foot-washing is no part of the contemporary culture of the West. Nor should we ignore the cultural factor and with wooden unimaginative literalism go round asking people to take their shoes and socks off in order to let us wash their feet. No, the right response is to discern the inner reality of our Lord's command, which is that if we love one another we will serve one another, even by doing dirty and menial jobs for one another. Then, if we do not wash each other's feet, we will gladly clean each other's shoes. The purpose of such cultural transposition, it will be seen, is not to dodge the awkward commands of Jesus, but rather to make our obedience contemporary. **(1981g:28)**

214. Cultural transposition

To transpose a piece of music is to put it into a different key from that in which it was originally written. To transpose a biblical text is to put it into a different culture from that in which it was originally given. In musical transposition the tune and harmonization remain the same; only the key is different. In biblical transposition the truth of the revelation remains the same; only the cultural expression is different.

(1992b:196)

215. Our cultural bias

It is essential to give up the illusion that we come to the biblical text as innocent, objective, impartial, culture-free investigators, for we are nothing of the kind. No, the spectacles through which we look at the Bible have cultural lenses. And the mind with which we think about the Bible, however open we keep it, is not empty. On the contrary, it is filled with cultural prejudices. So, though we cannot altogether rid ourselves of our cultural inheritance, we should be aware of our cultural bias. **(1982a:185)**

216. Scripture and culture

We all need to discern more clearly between Scripture and culture. For Scripture is the eternal unchanging Word of God. But culture is an amalgam of ecclesiastical tradition, social convention and artistic creativity. Whatever 'authority' culture may have is derived only from church and community. It cannot claim an immunity to criticism or reform. On the contrary, culture changes from age to age and from place to place. Moreover we Christians, who say we desire to live under the authority of God's Word, should subject our own contemporary culture to continuous biblical scrutiny. Far from resenting or resisting cultural change, we should be in the forefront of those who propose and work for its progressive modification in order to make it more truly expressive of the dignity of man and more pleasing to the God who created us.

(1975a:30)

217. Scripture through the world's eyes

Throughout its long and variegated career, the church has seldom cultivated a humble, sensitive attitude of listening to God's Word. Instead, it has frequently done what it has been forbidden to do, namely, become conformist. It has accommodated itself to the prevailing culture, leaped on board all the trendiest bandwagons and hummed all the popular tunes. Whenever the church does this, it reads Scripture through the world's eyes and rationalizes its own unfaithfulness. Church history is replete with tragic examples. How was it that the Christian conscience not only approved but actually glamourized those terrible Crusades to recover the holy places from Islam – an unholy blunder which Muslims have never forgotten and which continues to obstruct the evangelization of the Muslim world? How is it that torture could ever have been employed in the name of Jesus Christ to combat heresy and promote orthodoxy? How is it that for centuries Protestant churches were so inward-looking and so disobedient to Christ's Great Commission that William Carey's proposal of a mission to India was greeted with that patronizing retort, 'Sit down, young man. When God wants to convert the heathen, he'll do it without your help'? How is it that the cruel degradations of slavery and of the slave trade were not abolished in the so-called Christian West until eighteen hundred years after Christ? How is it that racial discrimination and environmental pollution have become widely recognized as the evils they are only since World War 2? Such is a catalogue of some of the worst blind spots which have marred the church's testimony down the ages. None of them can be defended from Scripture. All are due to a misreading of Scripture, or to an unwillingness to sit under its authority.

(1981g:34)

218. Principles of interpretation

The principles of biblical interpretation are not arbitrary. They are derived from the character of the Bible itself as God's Word written, and from the character of God as revealed in it.

We look for the *natural* meaning because we believe that God intended his revelation to be a plain and readily intelligible communication to ordinary human beings.

We look for the *original* meaning because we believe that

God addressed his word to those who first heard it, and that it can be received by subsequent generations only in so far as they understand it historically. Our understanding may be fuller than that of the first hearers (*e.g.* of the prophecies of Christ); it cannot be substantially different.

We look for the *general* meaning because we believe that God is self-consistent, and that his revelation is self-consistent also.

So our three principles (of simplicity, history and harmony) arise partly from the nature of God and partly from the nature of Scripture as a plain, historical, consistent communication from God to men. **(1984d:182)**

219. The intention of the author

Among many points which evangelicals would want to make, in regard to alleged discrepancies in the gospels, are the following, which all relate to the intention of the author and the unfairness of criticizing him for not doing what he never set out to do. Thus, it is possible to condense speeches, paraphrase them, and translate them into a different cultural idiom, without thereby falsifying their meaning; to change the sequence of events, deliberately subordinating chronology to theology, without by this practice committing an error; to give round figures and make free quotations, according to the literary conventions of the pre-computer age, without being accused of making mistakes (imprecision is not a synonym for inaccuracy); and to quote the Old Testament in such a way as to draw attention to a principle, parallel or pattern, rather than to the detailed fulfilment of a specific prophecy, without being guilty of misquotation. **(1988d:99)**

220. A sure interpreter

The safest of all principles of biblical interpretation is to allow Scripture to explain Scripture. **(1979e:65)**

221. The four gospels

The gospels are not biography; they are testimony. **(1971b:43)**

222. Problems or errors?

A number of old problems, which decades ago were confidently pronounced 'biblical errors', have subsequently proved not to have been. They have yielded to patient study and further light. I will give only one example. In Acts 17:6 and

8 Luke calls the city rulers or magistrates in Thessalonica 'politarchs', a word which occurs nowhere else in the New Testament and has not been found in any other Greek literature. So earlier critical scholars accused Luke of either ignorance or carelessness. But since then a number of inscriptions have been found, dating from the second and third centuries AD, several in Thessalonica itself, which have vindicated Luke's use of the title. It is now known that the city council in Macedonian towns consisted of a group of politarchs, and that there were five or six of them in Thessalonica. This seems to me to illustrate the wisdom of referring to 'unresolved problems' rather than 'proven errors'.

(1988d:102)

223. Analogy and metaphor

Scripture is very rich in metaphorical language, and in every metaphor it is essential to ask at what point the analogy is being drawn. We must avoid arguing from analogy, that is, elaborating the correspondence beyond the limits which Scripture sets. Thus, God is our Father and we are his children. As our Father, he has begotten us, he loves us and cares for us. As his children, we depend on him and must love and obey him. But we have no liberty to argue, for example, that since God is our heavenly Father, we must also have a heavenly mother, on the ground that no child can have a father without a mother. Nor can we argue that because we are called 'children', we can avoid the responsibility of adult thought and action. For the same Scripture which commends to us the humility of a little child also condemns in us a child's immaturity.

(1984d:169)

224. Christ in the Old Testament

The Old Testament is a book of hope, of unfulfilled expectation. From beginning to end it looks forward to Christ. Its many promises through Abraham, Moses and the prophets find their fulfilment in Christ. Its law, with its unbending demands, was man's 'custodian until Christ came', keeping him confined and under restraint, even in bondage, until Christ should set him free (Gal. 3:23 – 4:7). Its sacrificial system, teaching day after day that without the shedding of blood there could be no forgiveness, prefigured the unique bloodshedding of the Lamb of God. Its kings, for all their imperfections, foreshadowed the

Messiah's perfect reign of righteousness and peace. And its prophecies are all focused upon him. Thus Jesus Christ is the seed of the woman who would bruise the serpent's head, the posterity of Abraham through whom all the families of the earth would be blessed, the star that would come forth out of Jacob and the sceptre that would rise out of Israel. Jesus Christ is also the priest after the order of Melchizedek, the king of David's line, the servant of the Lord God who would suffer and die for the sins of the people, the Son of God who would inherit the nations, and the Son of man, coming with the clouds of heaven, to whom would be given dominion, glory and a kingdom, that all peoples, nations and languages should serve him for ever. Directly or indirectly Jesus Christ is the grand theme of the Old Testament. Consequently he was able to interpret to his disciples 'in all the scriptures the things concerning himself' (Lk. 24:27). **(1970b:98)**

225. The garden of Eden

It is fashionable nowadays to regard the biblical story of Adam and Eve as 'myth' (whose truth is theological but not historical), rather than 'significant event' (whose truth is both). Many people assume that evolution has disproved and discarded the Genesis story as having no basis in history. Since 'Adam' is the Hebrew word for 'man', they consider that the author of Genesis was deliberately giving a mythical account of human origins, evil and death.

We should certainly be open to the probability that there are symbolical elements in the Bible's first three chapters. The narrative itself warrants no dogmatism about the six days of creation, since its form and style suggest that it is meant as literary art, not scientific description. As for the identity of the snake and the trees in the garden, since 'that old serpent' and 'the tree of life' reappear in the book of Revelation, where they are evidently symbolic, it seems likely that they are meant to be understood symbolically in Genesis as well.

But the case with Adam and Eve is different. Scripture clearly intends us to accept their historicity as the original human pair. For the biblical genealogies trace the human race back to Adam; Jesus himself taught that 'at the beginning the Creator "made them male and female" ' and then instituted marriage (Mt. 19:4ff., quoting Gn. 1:27). Paul told the Athenian philosophers that God had made every nation 'from one man'

111

(Acts 17:26); and in particular Paul's carefully constructed analogy between Adam and Christ depends for its validity on the equal historicity of both. He affirmed that Adam's disobedience led to condemnation for all, as Christ's obedience led to justification for all (Rom. 5:18).

Moreover, nothing in modern science contradicts this. Rather the reverse. All human beings share the same anatomy, physiology and chemistry, and the same genes. Although we belong to different so-called 'races' (Caucasoid, Negroid, Mongoloid and Australoid), each of which has adjusted to its own physical environment, we nevertheless constitute a single species, and people of different races can intermarry and interbreed. This homogeneity of the human species is best explained by positing our descent from a common ancestor. 'Genetic evidence indicates', writes Dr Christopher Stringer of London's Natural History Museum, 'that all living people are closely related and share a recent common ancestor.' He goes on to express the view that this common ancestor 'probably lived in Africa' (though this is not proved) and that from this ancestral group 'all the living peoples of the world originated'.[1]

(1994:162)

[1] From his article 'Evolution of Early Humans', in Steve Jones et al. (eds.), The Cambridge Encyclopedia of Human Evolution (Cambridge University Press, 1992), p. 249.

226. Not obscurantism but faith

We need to learn to face problems relating to the Bible as we face problems surrounding other Christian doctrines. If somebody comes to us with a biblical problem (a discrepancy, for example, between theology and science, or between two gospel accounts, or a moral dilemma), what should we do? We should not (from a mistaken integrity) suspend our belief in the truth of Scripture until we have solved the problem. Nor should we place the problem either on a shelf (indefinitely postponing its challenge) or under a carpet (permanently concealing it, even from ourselves). Instead, we should struggle conscientiously with the problem in thought, discussion and prayer. As we do so, some difficulties will be either wholly or partly cleared up, but then, in spite of those which remain, we should retain our belief about Scripture on the ground that Jesus himself taught and exhibited it.

If a critic says to me, 'You are an obscurantist to believe the Bible to be the Word of God in defiance of the problems,' I nowadays return the compliment and say, 'OK, if you like, I am. But then you are an obscurantist to believe in the love of God in defiance of the problems.' Actually, however, to believe a Christian doctrine in spite of its problems, because of the acknowledged lordship of Jesus Christ, is not obscurantism (preferring darkness to light) but faith (trusting him who said he was the light of the world). It is more than faith; it is the sober, intellectual integrity of confessing Jesus as Lord.

(1992b:179)

21. SCRIPTURE, REASON AND TRADITION

227. Understanding Scripture

It is by receiving the illumination of the Spirit, by using our own reason and by listening to the teaching of others in the church that we grow in our understanding of Scripture. I am anxious not to be misunderstood. I am emphatically not saying that Scripture, reason and tradition are a threefold authority of equal importance by which we come to know God's truth. No. Scripture alone is God's Word written, and the Holy Spirit its ultimate interpreter. The place of the individual's reason and of the church's tradition lies in the elucidation and application of Scripture. But both are subordinate to God himself as he speaks to us through his word. **(1984d:164)**

228. Reason and revelation

The old Deist attempt to replace revelation by reason was wrong-headed from the beginning. Reason has a vital role in the understanding and application of revelation, but it can never be a substitute for it. Without revelation reason gropes in the dark and flounders in the deep. **(1988d:83)**

229. Nature and Scripture

Nature and Scripture are both divine revelation ('general and special', 'natural and supernatural', to use the traditional terms), since God has revealed himself both in the world he has made and in Christ and the biblical witness to Christ. Science is the fallible human interpretation of nature, while theology (or 'tradition', which is theological reflection) is the fallible human interpretation of Scripture. You and I believe (I think) that in nature and Scripture there are certain given things, *data* (although they relate to largely different spheres), which, if they truly come from God, cannot contradict one another. The contradictions have not been between nature and Scripture, but between science and theology, that is, between different human interpretations of God's double revelation. If, therefore, we are to learn lessons from the past, it is neither for conservatives to deny the evidence of nature, nor for liberals to deny the evidence of Scripture, but for all of us to re-examine our interpretations of both. **(1988d:335)**

230. Scripture and tradition

Protestants do not deny the importance of tradition, and some of us should have more respect for it, since the Holy Spirit has taught past generations of Christians and did not begin his instruction only with us! Nevertheless, when Scripture and tradition are in collision, we must allow Scripture to reform tradition, just as Jesus insisted with the 'traditions of the elders' (*cf.* Mk. 7:1–13). If the Church of Rome were to have the courage to renounce unbiblical traditions (*e.g.* its dogmas about the immaculate conception and bodily assumption of the Virgin Mary), immediate progress would be made towards agreement under the Word of God. **(1982b:49)**

231. Anglican teaching

Although it is sometimes said in Anglican circles that Scripture, tradition and reason form a 'threefold cord' which restrains and directs the church, and although there are not lacking those who regard these three as having equal authority, yet official pronouncements continue to uphold the primary, the supreme authority of Scripture, while accepting the important place of tradition and reason in the elucidation of Scripture. Thus, the report on the Bible issued by the 1958 Lambeth Conference contained this heartening statement: 'The Church is not "over" the Holy Scriptures, but "under" them, in the sense that the process of canonization was not one whereby the Church conferred authority on the books but one whereby the Church acknowledged them to possess authority. And why? The books were recognized as giving the witness of the Apostles to the life, teaching, death, and resurrection of the Lord and the interpretation by the Apostles of these events. To that apostolic authority the Church must ever bow.'[1]

(1970b:83)

[1] *The Lambeth Conference 1958* (SPCK, 1958), part 2, p. 5.

232. The 'two-source' theory

We cannot rely on church tradition for our message, for we cannot accept the 'two-source' theory of divine revelation, namely that Holy Scripture and holy tradition are independent, equal, and authoritative sources of doctrine. Rather we see tradition standing alongside Scripture as a fallible interpretation of an infallible revelation. We feel obliged to affirm the supremacy of Scripture over tradition, as Jesus did, when he called the traditions of the elders 'the traditions of *men*' and subordinated them to the judgment of Scripture as the Word of *God* (Mk. 7:1–13). **(1981b)**

233. 'With all the saints . . .'

In rejecting every attempt to interpose the church or any other authoritative teaching body between God and his people, we must not deny that the church has a place in God's plan to give his people a right understanding of his Word. The individual Christian's humble, prayerful, diligent and obedient study of Scripture is not the only way the Holy Spirit makes clear what he has revealed. It would hardly be humble to ignore what the Spirit may have shown to others. The Holy Spirit is indeed our teacher, but he teaches us indirectly through others as well as directly to our own minds. It was not to one man that he revealed the truths now enshrined in Scripture, but to a multiplicity of prophets and apostles; his work of illumination is given to many also. It is not as individuals merely, but 'with all the saints' that we are given 'power . . . to grasp how wide and long and high and deep is the love of Christ . . . that surpasses knowledge' (Eph. 3:18–19). **(1984d:162)**

234. Fallible interpreters

God's word is infallible, for what he has said is true. But no Christian individual, group or church has ever been or will ever be an infallible interpreter of God's Word. Human interpretations belong to the sphere of tradition, and an appeal may always be made against tradition to the Scripture itself which tradition claims to interpret. **(1984d:156)**

235. Resisting false teaching

The apostolic traditions are the foundation of Christian faith and life, while subsequent ecclesiastical traditions are the superstructure which the church has erected on it. The primary traditions, to which we should hold fast, are those which the apostles received from Christ (either the historic Christ or the living Spirit of Christ), which they taught the early church by word or letter, and which are now preserved in the New Testament. To 'stand firm and hold to the teachings' means in our case to be biblical or evangelical Christians, to be uncompromisingly loyal to the teaching of Christ and his apostles. This is the road to stability. The only way to resist false teaching is to cling to the true teaching.   **(1991c:178)**

236. The place of tradition

When we seek to follow Christ in distinguishing between Scripture and tradition, we must be careful not to overstate the case. Jesus did not reject all human traditions out of hand, forbidding his disciples to cherish or follow any. What he did was to put tradition in its place, namely a secondary place, and then, provided that it was not contrary to Scripture, to make it optional.   **(1970b:71)**

237. The supremacy of Scripture

The supremacy of Scripture carries with it a radical calling into question of all human traditions and conventions, however ancient and sacred.   **(1988d:88)**

22. THE STUDY OF THEOLOGY

238. Intellectual exploration

The fact that God has revealed himself in Christ and in Scripture does not rule out intellectual exploration. The theologian is no more inhibited from theological research because God has revealed himself in Scripture than the scientist is inhibited from scientific research because God has revealed himself in nature. Both are limited to the data (which, to oversimplify, are nature on the one hand, Scripture on the other), but within the limits that the data themselves impose, the Creator encourages us to use our minds freely and creatively.

If, therefore, by the myth of God incarnate were meant the mystery of the incarnation, we would have no quarrel with the concept. The church has always acknowledged that the incarnation is a mystery beyond the full comprehension of human minds. A humble, reverent exploration of what God has revealed of himself in Christ is the essence of true christological scholarship. **(1978a)**

239. The biblical doctrine of Scripture

We take our stand on the divine origin of the Bible, because we believe the Bible itself requires us to do so. Indeed, it is a strange fact that theologians who are prepared to accept the biblical doctrine of God, of Christ, of the Holy Spirit, of man and of the church, are often not willing to accept the biblical doctrine of Scripture. But if the Bible is authoritative and accurate when speaking about other matters, there is no reason why it should not be equally so when speaking about itself.

(1956a:13)

240. Echoes of our own prejudice?

We have to open our minds wide enough to risk hearing what we do not want to hear. For we have been taught to come to the Bible for solace. Does not Paul himself write of 'the encouragement of the Scriptures' (Rom. 15:4)? So naturally we cherish the hope that through our Bible reading we shall be comforted; we have no wish to be disturbed. Hence we tend to come to it with our minds made up, anxious to hear only the reassuring echoes of our own prejudice. **(1982a:186)**

241. Contradiction, not interpretation

If the apostles were not deliberately using a mythical framework, but were rather intending to describe events which they believed to be both historically true and theologically significant (*e.g.* when they wrote about Jesus' birth of a virgin or resurrection from death), then we have no right to demythologize their testimony, attempting to preserve the theology while rejecting the history. For this would not be to reinterpret them, but to contradict them. **(1985:39)**

242. The fount of reformation

The English Reformation may be said to have begun in the White Horse Inn in Cambridge, where from 1519 a group met in secret to study the Greek Testament which Erasmus had published three years previously. It was this that Tyndale translated into English, determined (as he put it) that the ploughboy should know the Scriptures better than the Pope. And once the Bible was available to the people in the vernacular, the leaders of the Reformation urged the clergy to expound it to their people. So from the time of the second Prayer Book onwards (1552), the symbol of office presented to the newly ordained presbyter was no longer the chalice but the Bible.

There can be no continuing reformation of the church without a return to the Bible. **(1983c:xii)**

243. Theology as gospel

In one sense the whole Bible is gospel, for its fundamental purpose is to bear witness to Jesus Christ and to proclaim the good news of a new life to those who come to him. Now if the Bible (which is God's Word through men's words) is gospel, then all theologies (which are human formulations of biblical truth) must be framed as gospel also. Too much contemporary theology fails at this point. It is incommunicable. But any theology which cannot be communicated as gospel is of minimal value. For one thing, the task of formulating truth is fruitless if, once formulated, it cannot then be more readily communicated. If it cannot, why bother to formulate it? For another, Jesus taught that only those who pass on to others the truth they have received will receive any more. 'Take heed what you hear,' he warned, 'the measure you give will be the measure you get, and still more will be given you' (Mk. 4:24). **(1981g:38)**

119

244. Scripture and systems

I do not believe that the Bible provides 'a complete system of theology' or 'a comprehensive guide' to ethics. Systematic theology is certainly a legitimate and even necessary academic discipline, but God did not choose to reveal himself in systematic form, and all systems are exposed to the same temptation, namely to trim God's revelation to fit our system instead of adapting our system to accommodate his revelation.

(1988d:37)

245. What theology should be

It is sometimes said that you can make the Bible teach anything you like. I quite agree! You *can* make the Bible teach anything you like – if you are unscrupulous enough! But if we are scrupulous in using proper canons of interpretation (for example, looking for the natural, the original, and the general meaning), far from our being free to manipulate Scripture, we find that Scripture controls us. And theology becomes what it should always be, the result of applying to the text of Scripture the ordinary rules of grammar and logic. **(1967b:61)**

246. The 'new theology'

The evangelical quarrel with the modern fashion of radical theology, which boasts of a 'new reformation', a 'new theology', a 'new morality', even a 'new Christianity' is precisely this that, alas, it is what it claims to be! It is 'new'. It is not a legitimate reinterpretation of old first-century Christianity, for from this it deviates at many vital points. It is an invention of the twentieth century. **(1970b:41)**

247. Truth and heresy

There is something patently spurious about heresy, and something self-evidently true about the truth. Error may spread and be popular for a time. But it 'will not get very far'. In the end it is bound to be exposed, and the truth is sure to be vindicated. This is a clear lesson of church history. Numerous heresies have arisen, and some have seemed likely to triumph. But today they are largely of antiquarian interest. God has preserved his truth in the church. **(1973b:91)**

248. Contemporary heretics

What should the contemporary church do with heretics? Is that a harsh word? I think not. A humble and reverent probing into the mystery of the incarnation is the essence of true christological scholarship. But attempted reconstructions that effectively destroy that which is supposed to be being reconstructed is christological heresy.

Let me defend my question further. It is based on three convictions: there is such a thing as heresy, that is, a deviation from fundamental, revealed truth; heresy 'troubles' the church, while truth edifies it, and therefore if we love the truth and the church we cannot fold our arms and do nothing.

The purity of the church (ethical and doctrinal) is as much a proper Christian quest as its unity. Indeed we should be seeking its unity and purity simultaneously.

I do not myself think a heresy trial is the right way to approach this. Heretics are slippery creatures. They tend to use orthodox language to clothe their heterodox views. Besides, in our age of easy tolerance, the arraigned heretic becomes in the public mind first the innocent victim of bigoted persecutors, then a martyr, and then a hero or saint. But there are other ways to proceed. The New Testament authors are concerned not so much about false brethren as about false teachers, who act like wolves and scatter or destroy Christ's flock . . . Is it too much to hope and pray that some bishop sometime will have the courage to withdraw his licence from a presbyter who denies the incarnation? This would not be an infringement of civil or academic liberty. A man may believe, say, and write what he pleases in the country and the university. But in the church it is reasonable and right to expect all accredited teachers to teach the faith that the church in its official formularies confesses and that (incidentally) they have themselves promised to uphold. **(1977b)**

249. Reputation and revelation

We need the humility of Mary. She accepted God's purpose, saying, 'May it be to me as you have said' . . . We also need Mary's courage. She was so completely willing for God to fulfil his purpose, that she was ready to risk the stigma of being an unmarried mother, of being thought an adulteress herself and of bearing an illegitimate child. She surrendered her reputation to God's will. I sometimes wonder if the major cause of much theological liberalism is that some scholars care more about their reputation than about God's revelation. Finding it hard to be ridiculed for being naïve and credulous enough to believe in miracles, they are tempted to sacrifice God's revelation on the altar of their own respectability. I do not say that they always do so. But I feel it right to make the point because I have myself felt the strength of this temptation. **(1985:66)**

250. Theological devotion

It is important to note from Romans 1 – 11 that theology (our belief about God) and doxology (our worship of God) should never be separated. On the one hand, there can be no doxology without theology. It is not possible to worship an unknown god. All true worship is a response to the self-revelation of God in Christ and Scripture, and arises from our reflection on who he is and what he has done. It was the tremendous truths of Romans 1 – 11 which provoked Paul's outburst of praise in verses 33–36 of chapter 11. The worship of God is evoked, informed and inspired by the vision of God. Worship without theology is bound to degenerate into idolatry. Hence the indispensable place of Scripture in both public worship and private devotion. It is the Word of God which calls forth the worship of God.

On the other hand, there should be no theology without doxology. There is something fundamentally flawed about a purely academic interest in God. God is not an appropriate object for cool, critical, detached, scientific observation and evaluation. No, the true knowledge of God will always lead us to worship, as it did Paul. Our place is on our faces before him in adoration.

As I believe Bishop Handley Moule said at the end of the last century, we must 'beware equally of an undevotional theology and of an untheological devotion'. **(1994:311)**

23. TRUTH AND ERROR

251. Distinguishing tolerances

It is very easy to tolerate the opinions of others if we have no strong opinions of our own. But we should not acquiesce in this easy-going tolerance. We need to distinguish between the tolerant mind and the tolerant spirit. Tolerant in spirit a Christian should always be, loving, understanding, forgiving and forbearing others, making allowances for them, and giving them the benefit of the doubt, for true love 'bears all things, believes all things, hopes all things, endures all things' (1 Cor. 13:7). But how can we be tolerant in mind of what God has plainly revealed to be either evil or erroneous?

(1970b:17)

252. The evil of error

The devil disturbs the church as much by error as by evil. When he cannot entice Christian people into sin, he deceives them with false doctrine. **(1968c:24)**

253. 'The latest ideas'

Christians should always be 'conservative' in their theology. To have 'itching ears', ever running after new teachers, listening to anybody and never arriving at a knowledge of the truth, is a characteristic of the 'terrible times' which shall come 'in the last days' (2 Tim. 3:1, 7; 4:3). The continuous obsession for 'the latest ideas' is a mark of the Athenian not the Christian (Acts 17:21). Christian theology is anchored not only to certain historical events, culminating in the saving career of Jesus, but to the authoritative apostolic witness to, and interpretation of, these events. The Christian can never weigh anchor and launch out into the deep of speculative thought. Nor can he forsake the primitive teaching of the apostles for subsequent human traditions. The apostolic testimony is directed essentially to the Son. That is why it will keep Christians true to him if they remain true to it. **(1988g:117)**

254. From truth to truth

The principle of harmony does not deny that there has been progression in God's revelation of himself and of his purposes, but emphasizes rather that the progression has not been from error to truth, but from truth to more truth.   **(1984d:180)**

255. Two safeguards

There are two safeguards against error – the apostolic Word and the anointing Spirit (*cf.* Is. 59:21). Both are received at conversion . . .

The Word is an objective safeguard, while the anointing of the Spirit is a subjective experience; but both the apostolic teaching and the heavenly teacher are necessary for continuance in the truth. And both are to be personally and inwardly grasped. This is the biblical balance which is too seldom preserved. Some honour the Word and neglect the Spirit who alone can interpret it; others honour the Spirit but neglect the Word out of which he teaches. The only safeguard against lies is to have remaining within us both the Word that we *heard from the beginning* and the *anointing* that we *received* from him. It is by these old possessions, not by new teachings or teachers, that we shall remain in the truth.   **(1988g:119)**

256. The test of ideology

A good test of every ideology is whether it exalts God and humbles man, or whether it exalts man and dethrones God.
(1975d:31)

257. The balanced Christian

It seems that there is almost no pastime the devil enjoys more than tipping Christians off balance. Although I claim neither close acquaintance with his person nor inside information into his strategy, I guess that this is one of his favourite hobbies. My conviction is that we should love balance as much as the devil hates it, and seek to promote it as vigorously as he seeks to destroy it.

By our 'imbalance' I mean that we seem to enjoy inhabiting one or other of the polar regions of truth. If we could straddle both poles simultaneously, we would exhibit a healthy biblical balance. Instead, we tend to 'polarize'. Like Abraham and Lot we separate from one another. We push other people over to one pole, while keeping the opposite pole as our preserve.
(1975a:13)

258. Bondage to falsehood

Freedom to disagree with the Bible is an illusory freedom; in reality it is bondage to falsehood. **(1988d:37)**

259. Affirming and denying

It is bad enough to be dogmatic we are told. But 'if you must be dogmatic', our critics continue, 'do at least keep your dogmatism to yourself. Hold your own definite convictions (if you insist), but leave other people alone in theirs. Be tolerant. Mind your own business, and let the rest of the world mind theirs.'

Another way in which this point of view is expressed is to urge us to be always positive, if necessary dogmatically positive, but to eschew being negative. 'Speak up for what you believe,' we are urged, 'but don't speak against what other people believe.' Those who advocate this line have not remembered the double duty of the presbyter-bishop which is 'to give instruction in sound doctrine' and 'to confute those who contradict it' (Tit. 1:9). Nor have they heeded what C. S. Lewis wrote in a letter to Dom Bede Griffiths: 'Your Hindus certainly sound delightful. But what do they *deny*? That has always been my trouble with Indians – to find any proposition they would pronounce false. But truth must surely involve exclusions?'[1] **(1970b:17)**

[1] *Letters of C. S. Lewis*, edited by W. H. Lewis (Bles, 1966), p. 267.

260. Blurring the issues

False prophets are adept at blurring the issue of salvation. Some so muddle or distort the gospel that they make it hard for seekers to find the narrow gate. Others try to make out that the narrow way is in reality much broader than Jesus implied, and that to walk it requires little if any restriction on one's belief or behaviour. Yet others, perhaps the most pernicious of all, dare to contradict Jesus and to assert that the broad road does not lead to destruction, but that as a matter of fact all roads lead to God, and that even the broad and the narrow roads, although they lead off in opposite directions, ultimately both end in life. No wonder Jesus likened such false teachers to *ravenous wolves*, not so much because they are greedy for gain, prestige or power (though they often are), but because they are 'ferocious', that is, extremely dangerous. They are responsible for leading some people to the very destruction which they say does not exist. **(1978f.:199)**

261. A love of truth

They *all will be condemned who have not believed the truth but have delighted in wickedness* (2 Thes. 2:12). It is of great importance to observe that the opposite of 'believing the truth' is 'delighting in wickedness'. This is because the truth has moral implications and makes moral demands. Evil, not error, is the root problem. The whole process is grimly logical. First, they delight in wickedness, or 'make sinfulness their deliberate choice' (NEB). Secondly, they refuse to believe and love the truth (because it is impossible to love evil and truth simultaneously). Thirdly, Satan gets in and deceives them. Fourthly, God himself 'sends' them a strong delusion, giving them over to the lie they have chosen. Fifthly, they are condemned and perish. This is extremely solemn teaching. It tells us that the downward slippery path begins with a love for evil, and then leads successively to a rejection of truth, the deception of the devil, a judicial hardening by God, and final condemnation. The only way to be protected from being deceived is to love goodness and truth. **(1991c:173)**

262. False teachers

In telling people to *beware of false prophets* (Mt. 7:15), Jesus obviously assumed that there were such. There is no sense in putting on your garden gate the notice 'Beware of the dog' if all you have at home is a couple of cats and a budgerigar! No. Jesus warned his followers of false prophets because they already existed. We come across them on numerous occasions in the Old Testament, and Jesus seems to have regarded the Pharisees and the Sadducees in the same light. 'Blind leaders of the blind', he called them. He also implied that they would increase, and that the period preceding the end would be characterized not only by the worldwide spread of the gospel but also by the rise of false teachers who would lead many astray. We hear of them in nearly every New Testament letter. They are called either 'pseudo-prophets' as here ('prophets' presumably because they claimed divine inspiration), or 'pseudo-apostles' (because they claimed apostolic authority) or 'pseudo-teachers' or even 'pseudo-Christs' (because they made messianic pretensions or denied that Jesus was the Christ come in the flesh). But each was 'pseudo', and *pseudos* is the Greek word for a lie. The history of the Christian church has been a long and dreary story of controversy with false teachers. Their value, in the overruling providence of God, is that they have presented the church with a challenge to think out and define the truth, but they have caused much damage. I fear there are still many in today's church.

In telling us to beware of false prophets Jesus made another assumption, namely that there is such a thing as an objective standard of truth from which the falsehood of the false prophets is to be distinguished. The very notion of 'false' prophets is meaningless otherwise. **(1978f.:197)**

263. Clear-sighted contrasts

The apostle John's black and white contrasts are healthily clear-sighted. Opposing views are not to him 'complementary insights' but 'truth and error' (*cf.* 1 Jn. 2:21, 27). If we claim to enjoy fellowship with God while we walk in darkness, 'we lie' (1:6). He who says he knows God but disobeys his commands 'is a liar' (*pseustēs*, 2:4). So is the person who claims to love God but hates his brother (4:20). But what shall be said of him who denies that Jesus is the Christ? We must pronounce him 'the' liar . . . the liar *par excellence*. **(1988g:116)**

264. The 'unsophisticated'

One of the most distressing features of some recent statements by church leaders is the patronizing, even arrogant, way in which they have dismissed opposing views as being held only by the 'unsophisticated'. The essential condition of receiving light from heaven is not sophistication, however, but simplicity. For the Lord of the universe has 'hidden these things from the wise and learned', Jesus said, 'and revealed them to little children' (Mt. 11:25). **(1985:17)**

265. The witness of Scripture

Scripture bears an unwavering testimony to the power of ignorance and error to corrupt, and the power of truth to liberate, ennoble and refine. **(1979e:176)**

266. True freedom

Many suppose that intellectual freedom is identical with 'free thought', that is, the liberty to think and believe absolutely anything you want to think and believe. But this is not freedom.

To believe nothing is to be in bondage to meaninglessness. To believe lies is to be in bondage to falsehood. True intellectual freedom is found in believing the truth and living by it.

Archbishop Michael Ramsey in a series of sermons which he preached in Lent 1970 before the University of Cambridge (published now in the little book called *Freedom, Faith and the Future*) spoke of intellectual freedom. The Christian creed involves 'a certain yoke of specific belief', but is also, he said, 'a means of intellectual liberty'. 'It frees you into the large room of the family of Christ's followers across the ages. There is a timelessness about such a faith. It is not first century or 16th century or 20th century. It can free you from one of the most horrible of tyrannies, the dominance of the contemporary.' I would add, it can free you from a great deal else besides, including the shifting sands of subjectivity.

(1972b:14)

267. Prophecy today

We should certainly reject any claim that there are prophets today comparable to the biblical prophets. For they were the 'mouth' of God, special organs of revelation, whose teaching belongs to the foundation on which the church is built. There may well, however, be a prophetic gift of a secondary kind, as when God gives some people special insight into his Word and his will. But we should not ascribe infallibility to such communications. Instead, we should evaluate both the character and the message of those who claim to speak from God.

The principal way in which God speaks to us today is through Scripture, as the church in every generation has recognized. **(1992b:104)**

268. The nature of error

Two tendencies of heresy are most revealing. We would be wise to ask ourselves regarding every kind of teaching both what its attitude is towards God and what effect it has upon men. There is invariably something about error which is dishonouring to God and damaging to men. The truth, on the other hand, always honours God, promoting godliness (*cf.* Tit. 1:16), and always edifies its hearers. **(1973b:70)**

269. Christian discernment

Jesus warned his disciples of false prophets. So did Paul and Peter. Still today there are many voices clamouring for our attention, and many cults gaining widespread popular support. Some of them claim a special revelation or inspiration to authenticate their particular doctrine. There is need for Christian discernment. For many are too gullible, and exhibit a naïve readiness to credit messages and teachings which purport to come from the spirit-world. There is such a thing, however, as a misguided tolerance of false doctrine. Unbelief (*do not believe every spirit*, 1 Jn. 4:1) can be as much a mark of spiritual maturity as belief. We should avoid both extremes, the superstition which believes everything and suspicion which believes nothing. **(1988g:156)**

270. Truth, the true criterion

Experience must never be the criterion of truth; truth must always be the criterion of experience. **(1975b:15)**

271. Doing the truth

Everywhere in the New Testament God's truth is something to be *done*, not something only to be believed. It carries with it demands, duties, obligations. The evangelical faith radically transforms those who believe and embrace it. **(1983b:12)**

272. Truth and fire

It is when we reflect on the truth that our heart catches fire. Think of the Emmaus disciples on the afternoon of Easter Day. The risen Lord joined them on their walk and explained to them out of the Scriptures how the Messiah had to suffer before entering his glory. Later, after he had left them, they said to each other: 'Were not our hearts burning within us while he talked with us on the road and opened the Scriptures to us?' (Lk. 24:32). This inner burning of the heart is a profound emotional experience, but it was Jesus' biblical teaching which prompted it. Nothing sets the heart ablaze like fresh vistas of truth. **(1992b:126)**

24. A LIVING WORD

273. A word for our day

In response to the common feeling that Christianity is hopelessly out of date, we need to re-state our fundamental Christian conviction that God continues to speak through what he has spoken. His Word is not a prehistoric fossil, to be exhibited under glass, but a living message for the contemporary world. It belongs to the market place, not the museum. Through his ancient Word God addresses the modern world, for, as Dr J. I. Packer has said, 'the Bible is God preaching'. Even granted the historical particularities of the Bible, and the immense complexities of the modern world, there is still a fundamental correspondence between them, and God's Word remains a lamp to our feet and a light for our path.   **(1992b:11)**

274. More than a museum

Scripture is far more than a collection of ancient documents in which the words of God are preserved. It is not a kind of museum in which God's Word is exhibited behind glass like a relic or fossil. On the contrary, it is a living word to living people from the living God, a contemporary message for the contemporary world.   **(1982a:100)**

275. God's people and God's Word

We can recognize God's Word because God's people listen to it, just as we can recognize God's people because they listen to God's Word.   **(1988g:161)**

276. Love for the Scriptures

A man who loves his wife will love her letters and her photographs because they speak to him of her. So if we love the Lord Jesus we shall love the Bible because it speaks to us of him. The husband is not so stupid as to prefer his wife's letters to her voice, or her photographs to herself. He simply loves them because of her. So, too, we love the Bible because of Christ. It is his portrait. It is his love-letter.

(1956a:22)

277. A book of salvation

The Bible is essentially a handbook of salvation. Its over-arching purpose is to teach not facts of science (*e.g.* the nature of moon rock) which men can discover by their own empirical investigation, but facts of salvation, which no space exploration can discover but only God can reveal. The whole Bible unfolds the divine scheme of salvation – man's creation in God's image, his fall through disobedience into sin and under judgment, God's continuing love for him in spite of his rebellion, God's eternal plan to save him through his covenant of grace with a chosen people, culminating in Christ; the coming of Christ as the Saviour, who died to bear man's sin, was raised from death, was exalted to heaven and sent the Holy Spirit; and man's rescue first from guilt and alienation, then from bondage, and finally from mortality in his progressive experience of the liberty of God's children. **(1973b:102)**

278. Soul language

The Psalter speaks the universal language of the soul. 'The Book of Psalms', wrote Prothero, 'contains the whole music of the heart of man.' Again, echoing a phrase used by Athanasius and later by Calvin, it is 'a mirror in which each man sees the motions of his own soul'. Its theology is rich and full. It reveals a God who is both the Creator of the world and the redeemer of his people. Moreover, he sustains what he has created and shepherds whom he has redeemed. It is this past and present activity of God, in nature and in grace, which provides the constant theme for the psalmists' praise. Jehovah is not like dead, dumb idols; he is the living God, the Most High God, eternal and omnipresent. He is king. He reigns over the elements and over the nations. He is also a constant refuge, a fortress, and a strong tower where his people may find safety. He has entered into a covenant with them, and he is faithful to his covenant. He has given them his law, and expects them to be faithful to it. But, in contrast to God's eternity and greatness, man's life is transitory and his size diminutive. Further, he is sinful, and liable to sickness, persecution and death. He needs to cry to God for the forgiveness of his sins and for deliverance from all evil. Then one day God will send his Messiah to fulfil the ideals of kingship set forth in the royal psalms and of innocent suffering set forth in the passion psalms. It would be necessary for the Christ to suffer and to enter into his glory (Lk. 24:26). **(1966b:12)**

279. Witness to Christ

'Bible' and 'gospel' are almost alternative terms, for the major function of the Bible in all its length and breadth is to bear witness to Jesus Christ. **(1975c:43)**

280. A universal Word

On the one hand, *the message of the Bible* is exactly the same for all men in all places and at all times. Its relevance is not limited to any particular generation or any particular culture. On the contrary, it is *addressed to all mankind*. This is because *God's revelation in Christ and in Scripture is unchangeable*. As Jesus said, it 'cannot be broken' (Jn. 10:35). It has been delivered to us 'once for all' unalterably (Jude 3). And being God's truth it possesses a marvellous universality. As *through it the Holy Spirit still speaks today*, it has a message for everybody everywhere.

On the other hand, its unalterability is not a dead, wooden, colourless uniformity. For as the Holy Spirit used the personality and culture of the writers of his Word in order to convey through each something fresh and appropriate, so today *he illumines the minds of God's people in every culture to perceive its truth freshly through their own eyes*. It is he who opens the eyes of our hearts, and these eyes and hearts belong to young and old, Latin and Anglo-Saxon, African, Asian and American, male and female, poetic and prosaic. It is this 'magnificent and intricate mosaic of mankind' (to borrow a phrase of Dr Donald McGavran's) which the Holy Spirit uses to disclose from Scripture *ever more of the many-coloured wisdom of God* (a literal translation of Eph. 3:10). Thus *the whole church* is needed to receive God's whole revelation in all its beauty and richness (*cf.* Eph. 3:18, 'with all the saints'). **(1975d:8)**

281. The two-edged sword

The Word of God is said by the apostle Paul to be 'the sword of the Spirit', and in the letter to the Hebrews to be 'living and active'. Indeed, 'Sharper than any double-edged sword, it penetrates even to dividing soul and spirit, joints and marrow; it judges the thoughts and attitudes of the heart' (Eph. 6:17; Heb. 4:12). Whether or not we agree with Tertullian and Augustine that the two edges of the sword represent the Old

and New Testaments, the Bible has many sword-like qualities.
It pricks the conscience, and wounds the pride of sinners. It
cuts away our camouflage and pierces our defences. It lays
bare our sin and need, and kills all false doctrine by its deft,
sharp thrusts. **(1990c:54)**

282. Our personal agenda

We come to our reading of the Bible with our own agenda, bias,
questions, preoccupations, concerns and convictions, and,
unless we are extremely careful, we impose these on the
biblical text. We may sincerely pray before we read, 'Open my
eyes that I may see wonderful things in your law' (Ps. 119:18),
but still the same non-communication may persist. For even
that introductory prayer, though to be sure it is taken from the
Psalter, is suspect because it lays down the kind of message we
want to hear.

'Please, Lord, I want to see some "wonderful thing" in your
word.'

But he may reply, 'What makes you think I have only
"wonderful things" to show you? As a matter of fact, I have
some rather "disturbing things" to show you today. Are you
prepared to receive them?'

'Oh no, Lord, please not', we stammer in reply. 'I come to
Scripture only to be comforted; I really do not want to be
challenged or disturbed.' **(1992b:190)**

283. Submission to Christ

Our primary authority is Jesus Christ our Teacher and our
Lord, and our submission to Scripture is only the logical
outcome and necessary expression of our submission to him. It
is to Christ that we come; but Christ sends us to a book. Not
that the book to which he sends us is a dead and wooden letter,
or an authoritarian ogre. He bids us listen rather to his own
voice as he speaks to our particular situation by his Spirit and
through his written Word. **(1967b:64)**

V. WHAT IT IS TO BE HUMAN

25. Who am I?
26. Human worth and dignity
27. Our fallen nature
28. Self-love
29. Mere religion

25. WHO AM I?

284. The basic question

The nature of man (*i.e.* what it means to be human) is arguably the basic political issue of the twentieth century. It is certainly one of the chief points of conflict between Marx and Jesus, and therefore between the East and the West, namely whether human beings have any absolute value because of which they must be respected, or whether their value is only relative to the community, for the sake of which they may be exploited. More simply, are the people the servants of the institution, or is the institution the servant of the people? **(1990a:39)**

285. Jekyll and Hyde

Who am I? What is my 'self'? The answer is that I am a Jekyll and Hyde, a mixed-up kid, having both dignity, because I was created and have been re-created in the image of God, and depravity, because I still have a fallen and rebellious nature. I am both noble and ignoble, beautiful and ugly, good and bad, upright and twisted, image and child of God, and yet sometimes yielding obsequious homage to the devil from whose clutches Christ has rescued me. My true self is what I am by creation, which Christ came to redeem, and by calling. My false self is what I am by the fall, which Christ came to destroy. **(1986a:285)**

286. Self-denial and self-discovery

We are the product on the one hand of the fall, and on the other of our creation by God and re-creation in Christ. This theological framework is indispensable to the development of a balanced self-image and self-attitude. It will lead us beyond self-acceptance to something better still, namely self-affirmation. We need to learn both to affirm all the good within us, which is due to God's creating and re-creating grace, and ruthlessly to deny (*i.e.* repudiate) all the evil within us, which is due to our fallenness.

Then, when we deny our false self in Adam and affirm our true self in Christ, we find that we are free not to love ourselves, but rather to love him who has redeemed us, and our neighbour for his sake. At that point we reach the ultimate paradox of Christian living that when we lose ourselves in the selfless loving of God and neighbour we find ourselves (Mk. 8:35). True self-denial leads to true self-discovery. **(1978b)**

287. The paradox of humanness

It is part, I think, of the paradoxical nature of our humanness that we are both breath of God and dust of earth, godlike and bestial, created and fallen, noble and ignoble. That seems to be why we both seek God and run away from him, both practise righteousness and suppress the truth in our unrighteousness, both recognize the claims of the moral law upon us and refuse to submit to it, both erect altars in God's honour and need to repent of our ignorance and sin. **(1988d:322)**

288. Alienation

It was Karl Marx who popularized the word 'alienation', having himself taken it from the German theologian, Ludwig Feuerbach. Marx understood the plight of the proletariat in terms of economic alienation. Every worker puts into his craftsmanship a part of himself. When his employer then sells his product, he is guilty, at least in part, of alienating the worker from himself. This according to Marx was the basis of the class struggle . . .

But long before Feuerbach and Marx the Bible spoke of human alienation. It describes two other and even more radical alienations than the economic and the political. One is alienation from God our Creator, and the other alienation from one another, our fellow creatures. Nothing is more dehumanizing than this breakdown of fundamental human relationships. It is then that we become strangers in a world in which we should feel at home, and aliens instead of citizens. **(1979e:89)**

289. A philosophy of meaninglessness

Our generation is busy developing a philosophy of meaninglessness. It is fashionable nowadays to believe (or to say you believe) that life has no meaning, no purpose. There are many who admit that they have nothing to live for. They do not feel that they belong anywhere, or, if they belong, it is to the group known as 'the unattached'. They class themselves as 'outsiders', 'misfits'. They are without anchor, security or home. In biblical language, they are 'lost'.

To such people comes the promise that in Christ we find ourselves. The unattached become attached. They find their place in eternity (related first and foremost to God as his sons and daughters), in society (related to each other as brothers and sisters in the same family) and in history (related also to the succession of God's people down the ages).   **(1968c :101)**

290. Our likeness to God

Those who regard a human being as nothing but a programmed machine (behaviourists) or an absurdity (existentialists) or a naked ape (humanistic evolutionists) are all denigrating our creation in God's image. True, we are also rebels against God and deserve nothing at his hand except judgment, but our fallenness has not entirely destroyed our God-likeness. More important still, in spite of our revolt against him, God has loved, redeemed, adopted, and re-created us in Christ.   **(1978b)**

291. In our element

If fish were made for water, what are human beings made for? I think we have to answer that, if water is the element in which fish find their fishiness, then the element in which humans find their humanness is love, the relationships of love.   **(1992b:54)**

26. HUMAN WORTH AND DIGNITY

292. A Christian perspective

First, we affirm human dignity. Because human beings are created in God's image to know him, serve one another and be stewards of the earth, therefore they must be respected. Secondly, we affirm human equality. Because human beings have all been made in the same image by the same Creator, therefore we must not be obsequious to some and scornful to others, but behave without partiality to all. Thirdly, we affirm human responsibility. Because God has laid it upon us to love and serve our neighbour, therefore we must fight for his rights, while being ready to renounce our own in order to do so.

(1990a:161)

293. People matter

Only Christians believe in the intrinsic worth of human beings, because of the doctrines of creation and redemption. God made man male and female in his own image and gave them a responsible dominion over the earth and its creatures. He has endowed them with unique rational, moral, social, and creative faculties, which make them like him and unlike the animals. Human beings are godlike beings! True, they are fallen from their sublime origin, and their godlikeness has been severely distorted. But it has not been destroyed. The Bible is clear on this.

Christian teaching on the dignity, nobility, and worth of human beings is of the utmost importance today, partly for the sake of their own self-image and partly for the welfare of society. When human beings are devalued, everything in society goes sour. Women and children are despised; the sick are regarded as a nuisance, and the elderly as a burden; ethnic minorities are discriminated against; capitalism displays its ugliest face; labour is exploited in the mines and factories; criminals are brutalized in prison; opposition opinions are stifled; Belsen is invented by the extreme right and Gulag by the extreme left; unbelievers are left to die in their lostness; there is no freedom, dignity, or carefree joy; human life seems not worth living, because it is scarcely human any longer.

140

But when human beings are valued, because of their intrinsic worth, everything changes: women and children are honoured; the sick are cared for and the elderly allowed to live and die with dignity; dissidents are listened to; prisoners rehabilitated, and minorities protected; workers are given a fair wage, decent working conditions, and a measure of participation in the enterprise; and the gospel is taken to the ends of the earth. Why? Because people matter, because every man, woman, and child has significance as a human person made in the image of God. **(1988a:129)**

294. *The dignity of accountability*

Scripture recognizes both our ignorance ('they do not know what they are doing') and our weakness ('he remembers that we are dust'), but it dignifies us by holding us accountable for our thoughts and actions. **(1988d:321)**

295. *Humans and animals*

In the unfolding narrative of Genesis 1 it is clear that the divine image or likeness is what distinguishes humans (the climax of creation) from animals (whose creation is recorded earlier). A continuity between humans and animals is implied. For example, they share 'the breath of life' and the responsibility to reproduce. But there was also a radical discontinuity between them, in that only human beings are said to be 'like God'. This emphasis on the unique distinction between humans and animals keeps recurring throughout Scripture. The argument takes two forms. We should be ashamed both when human beings behave like animals, descending to their level, and when animals behave like human beings, doing better by instinct than we do by choice. As an example of the former, men and women are not to be 'senseless and ignorant' and behave like 'a brute beast', or 'like the horse or the mule, which have no understanding'. As an example of the latter, we are rebuked that oxen and donkeys are better at recognizing their master than we are, that migratory birds are better at returning home after going away, and that ants are more industrious and more provident. **(1992b:36)**

296. *A God-given dominion*

In human research, discovery and invention, in biology, chemistry, physics and other spheres, and in all the triumphs of technology, human beings have been obeying God and exercising their God-given dominion. There is no question (at least in principle) of their having behaved like Prometheus, who stole fire from the gods. In their progressive control of the earth, they have not been invading God's private sphere and wresting power from him, still less imagining that they have stopped up the gaps in which God used to lurk, so that they can now dispense with him. It is foolish to draw these deductions. Human beings may not have known it, or humbly acknowledged it, but in all their research and resourcefulness, far from usurping God's prerogatives or power, they have been exercising the dominion God gave them. Developing tools and technology, farming the land, digging for minerals, extracting fuels, damming rivers for hydro-electric power, harnessing atomic energy – all are fulfilments of God's primeval command. God has provided in the earth all the resources of food, water, clothing, shelter, energy and warmth which we need, and he has given us dominion over the earth in which these resources have been stored. **(1990a:119)**

297. The divine likeness

I myself believe in the historicity of Adam and Eve, as the original couple from whom the human race is descended . . . But my acceptance of Adam and Eve as historical is not incompatible with my belief that several forms of pre-Adamic 'hominid' seem to have existed for thousands of years previously. These hominids began to advance culturally. They made their cave drawings and buried their dead. It is conceivable that God created Adam out of one of them. You may call them *homo erectus*. I think you may even call some of them *homo sapiens*, for these are arbitrary scientific names. But Adam was the first *homo divinus*, if I may coin the phrase, the first man to whom may be given the specific biblical designation 'made in the image of God'. Precisely what the divine likeness was, which was stamped upon him, we do not know, for Scripture nowhere tells us. But it seems to have included those rational, moral, social and spiritual faculties which make man unlike all other creatures and like God the Creator, and on account of which he was given 'dominion' over the lower creation.

(1984d:49)

298. The image of God

Whatever mode God employed in creation (and the mode is eclipsed in importance by the fact), God made man in his own image or likeness. Although the Bible nowhere spells out in so many words what this means, the implications are clear. For everywhere Scripture assumes man's qualitative difference from the animals, and rebukes or ridicules man when his behaviour is more bestial than human in its irrationality of godlessness or selfishness.

The divine image in man is a complex of qualities, which might be summarized as follows:

(a) Man has an intelligence, a capacity to reason and even to evaluate and criticize himself.
(b) Man has a conscience, a capacity to recognize moral values and make moral choices.
(c) Man has a society, a capacity to love and to be loved in personal, social relationships.
(d) Man has a dominion, a capacity to exercise lordship over creation, to subdue the earth and to be creative.
(e) Man has a soul, a capacity to worship, to pray and live in communion with God.

These capacities (mental, moral, social, creative and spiritual) constitute the divine image, because of which man is unique.

(1971c)

299. God's moral law

The same moral law which God has revealed in Scripture he has also stamped on human nature. He has in fact written his law twice, once on stone tablets and once on human hearts. In consequence, the moral law is not an alien system, which it is unnatural to expect human beings to obey. The opposite is the case. God's moral law perfectly fits us, because it is the law of our own created being. There is a fundamental correspondence between God's law in the Bible and God's law in our hearts. Hence we can discover our authentic humanness only in obeying it. **(1980a:57)**

300. Right and wrong

In every human community there is a basic recognition of the difference between right and wrong, and an accepted set of values. True, conscience is not infallible, and standards are influenced by cultures. Nevertheless, a substratum of good and evil remains, and love is always acknowledged as superior to selfishness. This has important social and political implications. It means that legislators and educators can assume that God's law is good for society and that at least to some degree people know it. It is not a case of Christians trying to force their standards on an unwilling public, but of helping the public to see that God's law is 'for our own good at all times' (Dt. 6:24), because it is the law of human being and of human community. If democracy is government by consent, consent depends on consensus, consensus on argument, and argument on ethical apologists who will develop a case for the goodness of God's law. **(1994:89)**

301. Moral responsibility

Scripture invariably treats us as morally responsible agents. It lays upon us the necessity of choice . . . Why is it that people do not come to Christ? Is it that they cannot, or is it that they will not? Jesus taught both. And in this 'cannot' and 'will not' lies the ultimate antinomy between divine sovereignty and human responsibility. But however we state it, we must not eliminate either part. Our responsibility before God is an inalienable aspect of our human dignity. Its final expression will be on the day of judgment. **(1986a:95)**

302. The origin of human rights

The origin of human rights is creation. Man has never 'acquired' them. Nor has any government or other authority conferred them. We have had them from the beginning. We received them with our life from the hand of our Maker. They are inherent in our creation. They have been bestowed on us by our Creator. **(1990a:154)**

303. God and the individual

Psalm 139 is arguably the most radical statement in the Old Testament of God's personal relationship to the individual. Personal pronouns and possessives occur in the first person (I, me, my) forty-six times and in the second person (you, yours) thirty-two times. Further, the basis on which God knows us intimately (verses 1–7) and attaches himself to us so that we cannot escape from him (verses 7–12) is that he formed us in the womb and established his relationship with us then (verses 13–16). **(1980d)**

304. Men and women

Because men and women are equal (by creation and in Christ), there can be no question of the inferiority of either to the other. But because they are complementary, there can be no question of the identity of one with the other. Further, this double truth throws light on male–female relationships and roles. Because they have been created by God with *equal* dignity, men and women must respect, love, serve, and not despise one another. Because they have been created *complementary* to each other, men and women must recognize their differences and not try to eliminate them or usurp one another's distinctives.

(1990a:263)

305. To become human

To become Christian is in a real sense to become human because nothing dehumanizes more than rebellion against God or humanizes more than reconciliation to God and fellowship with God. But to assert joyfully that salvation includes humanization is not at all the same thing as saying that humanization (rescuing men from the dehumanizing process of modern society) equals salvation. **(1975c:105)**

27. OUR FALLEN NATURE

306. The teaching of Jesus

It is difficult to understand those who cling to the doctrine of the fundamental goodness of human nature, and do so in a generation which has witnessed two devastating world wars and especially the horrors which occasioned and accompanied the second. It is even harder to understand those who attribute this belief to Jesus Christ. For he taught nothing of the kind.

Jesus taught that within the soil of every man's heart there lie buried the ugly seeds of every conceivable sin – 'evil thoughts, acts of fornication, of theft, murder, adultery, ruthless greed, and malice; fraud, indecency, envy, slander, arrogance, and folly.' All thirteen are 'evil things', and they come out of the heart of 'the man' or 'the men', every man. This is Jesus Christ's estimate of fallen human nature. **(1970b:139, 141)**

307. The dim twilight of nature

Scripture teaches clearly that man in his natural state, unredeemed and unregenerate, is blind. 'The god of this world has blinded the minds of the unbelievers, to keep them from seeing the light of the gospel of the glory of Christ, who is the likeness of God'. How then can any man see and believe? In order to answer this question, Paul draws an analogy between the old creation and the new. He sends our thoughts racing back millions of years to the primeval chaos, when 'the earth was without form and void, and darkness was upon the face of the deep'. All was shapeless, lifeless, cheerless, dark and void, until God's creative word brought light and warmth, shape and beauty. So it is with the Christless heart of the natural man. The dim twilight of nature (his reason and conscience) just relieves the otherwise impenetrable gloom, but all is dark, void and chill until God's dramatic *fiat* causes a new creation. 'For it is the God who said, "Let light shine out of darkness", who has shone in our hearts to give the light of the knowledge of the glory of God in the face of Christ.' **(1961:95)**

308. The origin of human evil

Jesus taught *the inward origin of human evil*. Its source has to be traced neither to a bad environment nor to a faulty education (although both these can have a powerful conditioning influence on impressionable young people), but rather to our 'heart', our inherited and twisted nature. One might almost say that Jesus introduced us to Freudianism before Freud. At least what he called the 'heart' is roughly equivalent to what Freud called the 'unconscious'. It resembles a very deep well. The thick deposit of mud at the bottom is usually unseen, and even unsuspected. But when the waters of the well are stirred by the winds of violent emotion, the most evil-looking, evil-smelling filth bubbles up from the depths and breaks the surface – rage, hate, lust, cruelty, jealousy and revenge. In our most sensitive moments we are appalled by our potentiality for evil.

(1992b:41)

309. The assumption of human sinfulness

Much that we take for granted in a 'civilized' society is based upon the assumption of human sin. Nearly all legislation has grown up because human beings cannot be trusted to settle their own disputes with justice and without self-interest. A promise is not enough; we need a contract. Doors are not enough; we have to lock and bolt them. The payment of fares is not enough; tickets have to be issued, inspected and collected. Law and order are not enough; we need the police to enforce them. All this is due to man's sin. We cannot trust each other. We need protection against one another. It is a terrible indictment of human nature. **(1971a:62)**

310. The work of conscience

The conscience of fallen human beings is often mistaken (it needs to be educated by the Word of God) and often sleepy (it needs to be awakened by the Spirit of God). True also, some people deny that they have any sense of sin, insisting at the same time that everything is relative now, for there are no moral absolutes anymore. Do not believe them. For by creation God still endows all human beings with a moral sense, which our inherited fallenness has distorted but not destroyed. Unless and until people so violate and smother their conscience as to 'cauterize' it (a word Paul uses in 1 Tim. 4:2) or render it insensitive, it continues to trouble them. They know they are sinful and guilty, however much they may protest the contrary.

(1980a:57)

311. When conscience drives

A guilty conscience is a great blessing, but only if it drives us to come home. **(1986a:98)**

312. 'Total depravity'

The biblical doctrine of 'total depravity' means neither that all humans are equally depraved, nor that nobody is capable of any good, but rather that no part of any human person (mind, emotions, conscience, will, *etc.*) has remained untainted by the fall. **(1979e:79)**

313. Five aspects of sin

The New Testament uses five main Greek words for sin, which together portray its various aspects, both passive and active. The commonest is *hamartia*, which depicts sin as a missing of the target, the failure to attain a goal. *Adikia* is 'unrighteousness' or 'iniquity', and *ponēria* is evil of a vicious or degenerate kind. Both these terms seem to speak of an inward corruption or perversion of character. The more active words are *parabasis* (with which we may associate the similar *paraptōma*), a 'trespass' or 'transgression', the stepping over a known boundary, and *anomia*, 'lawlessness', the disregard or violation of a known law. In each case an objective criterion is implied, either a standard we fail to reach or a line we deliberately cross. **(1986a:89)**

314. Prisoners of a corrupt nature

It is when we see ourselves as we are, on the one hand rebels against God and under the judgment of God, and on the other prisoners of a corrupt nature, that we come, like David in Psalm 51, to despair of ourselves and to cry to God for mercy. **(1988e:63)**

315. The divided self

What we are (our self or personal identity) is partly the result of the Creation (the image of God), and partly the result of the fall (the image defaced). The self we are to deny, disown, and crucify is our fallen self, everything within us that is incompatible with Jesus Christ (hence Christ's command, 'let him deny himself and follow me'). The self we are to affirm and value is our created self, everything within us that is compatible with Jesus Christ (hence his statement that if we lose ourselves by self-denial we shall find ourselves). True self-denial (the denial of our false, fallen self) is not the road to self-destruction, but the road to self-discovery.

So, then, whatever we are by creation, we must affirm: our rationality, our sense of moral obligation, our masculinity and femininity, our aesthetic appreciation and artistic creativity, our stewardship of the fruitful earth, our hunger for love and community, our sense of the transcendent mystery of God, and our inbuilt urge to fall down and worship him. All this is part of our created humanness. True, it has all been tainted and twisted by sin. Yet Christ came to redeem and not destroy it. So we must affirm it.

But whatever we are by the fall, we must deny or repudiate: our irrationality; our moral perversity; our loss of sexual distinctives; our fascination with the ugly; our lazy refusal to develop God's gifts; our pollution and spoliation of the environment; our selfishness, malice, individualism, and revenge, which are destructive of human community; our proud autonomy; and our idolatrous refusal to worship God. All this is part of our fallen humanness. Christ came not to redeem this but to destroy it. So we must deny it.

(1984a)

316. The gravity of sin

Our sin must be extremely horrible. Nothing reveals the gravity of sin like the cross. For ultimately what sent Christ there was neither the greed of Judas, nor the envy of the priests, nor the vacillating cowardice of Pilate, but our own greed, envy, cowardice and other sins, and Christ's resolve in love and mercy to bear their judgment and so put them away. It is impossible for us to face Christ's cross with integrity and not to feel ashamed of ourselves. Apathy, selfishness and complacency blossom everywhere in the world except at the cross. There these noxious weeds shrivel and die. They are seen for the tatty, poisonous things they are. For if there was no way by which the righteous God could righteously forgive our unrighteousness, except that he should bear it himself in Christ, it must be serious indeed. It is only when we see this that, stripped of our self-righteousness and self-satisfaction, we are ready to put our trust in Jesus Christ as the Saviour we urgently need. **(1986a:83)**

317. Sin and forgiveness

The proper Christian attitude to sin is not to deny it but to admit it, and then to receive the forgiveness which God has made possible and promises to us. *If we confess our sins,* acknowledging before God that we are sinners not only by nature (*sin*) but by practice also (*our sins*), God will both *forgive us our sins and purify us from all unrighteousness* (1 Jn. 1:9). In the first phrase sin is a debt which he remits and in the second a stain which he removes. **(1988g:82)**

318. God's inaccessibility to sinners

We learn to appreciate the access to God which Christ has won for us only after we have first seen God's inaccessibility to sinners. We can cry 'Hallelujah' with authenticity only after we have first cried 'Woe is me, for I am lost'. In Dale's words, 'it is partly because sin does not provoke our own wrath, that we do not believe that sin provokes the wrath of God'.[1]

(1986a:109)

[1] R. W. Dale, *The Atonement* (Congregational Union, 1894), pp. 338–339.

319. Confessing our sins

The principle which we have sought to establish is that sin must be confessed only to the person or persons who have been offended and from whom forgiveness is therefore desired. Confession is never to a third party, both because he has not been offended, and because he is not in a position to forgive the sin. This is the simple reason why auricular confession is a practice to be deplored. It is not an answer to say that auricular confession is not 'to a priest', but either to God through the priest or in the presence of the priest, or to the church represented by the priest. Such representative confession is neither recognized nor recommended in Scripture. If the sin has been committed against God, it should be confessed to God secretly; if it has been committed against the church it should be confessed to the church publicly. Confessing such sins to a priest is not right, since it makes secret confession not secret through including another person and public confession not public through excluding the church. **(1964:84)**

320. Confessing and forsaking

It is important, when we bring our sins into the open before God, not to stop there, but to go on to adopt a right attitude towards both God and the sin itself. First, we confess the sin, humbling ourselves with a contrite heart before God. Secondly, we forsake it, rejecting and repudiating it. This is a vital part of what is meant by 'mortification' in the New Testament. It is taking up towards sin an attitude of resolute antagonism. The uncovering of sin is in itself of little value; it must lead us to an attitude both of humility towards God and of hostility towards sin. 'Ye that love the Lord hate evil', or 'the Lord loves those who hate evil' (Ps. 97: 10, AV and RSV); and it is this holy hatred of evil which is promoted by the faithful, systematic uncovering and confession of our sins. **(1964:20)**

321. Spiritual death

Biblical statements about the 'deadness' of non-Christian people raise problems for many because this does not seem to square with the facts of everyday experience. Lots of people who make no Christian profession whatever, who even openly repudiate Jesus Christ, appear to be very much alive. One has the vigorous body of an athlete, another the lively mind of a scholar, a third the vivacious personality of a film star. Are we to say that such people, if Christ has not saved them, are dead? Yes, indeed, we must and do say this very thing. For in the sphere which matters supremely (which is neither the body, nor the mind, nor the personality, but the soul) they have no life. And you can tell it. They are blind to the glory of Jesus Christ, and deaf to the voice of the Holy Spirit. They have no love for God, no sensitive awareness of his personal reality, no leaping of their spirit towards him in the cry, 'Abba, Father', no longing for fellowship with his people. They are as unresponsive to him as a corpse. So we should not hesitate to affirm that a life without God (however physically fit and mentally alert the person may be) is a living death, and that those who live it are dead even while they are living. To affirm this paradox is to become aware of the basic tragedy of fallen human existence. It is that people who were created by God and for God should now be living without God. Indeed, that was our condition until the Good Shepherd found us. **(1979e:72)**

322. God's holiness and human sin

All divine judgment seems and sounds unjust until we see God as he is and ourselves as we are, according to Scripture. As for God, Scripture uses the pictures of light and fire to set forth his perfect holiness.

He dwells in unapproachable light, dazzling, even blinding in its splendour, and is a consuming fire. Human beings who have only glimpsed his glory have been unable to bear the sight, and have turned away or run away or swooned. As for ourselves, I often want to say to my contemporaries what Anselm said to his, 'You have not yet considered the seriousness of sin.' **(1988d:321)**

323. No perfect society

Although it is right to campaign for social justice and to expect to improve society further, in order to make it more pleasing to God, we know that we should never perfect it. Christians are not utopians. Although we know the transforming power of the gospel and the wholesome effects of Christian salt and light, we also know that evil is ingrained in human nature and human society. We harbour no illusions. Only Christ at his second coming will eradicate evil and enthrone righteousness for ever. For that day we wait with eagerness. **(1992b:390)**

324. The only exit

Death is the only exit to the prison house of sin. 'He who has died has been justified from his sin' (Rom. 6:7, literally). This death Christ died for us. He died our death. If, then, we are united to Christ, it is as true to say, 'I died in Christ' as it is to say, 'He died for me.' Since Christ died my death and I am in him, God sees me as if I had died myself. Having died and risen with Christ, the law's demands are met, and I am set free. **(1954c:61)**

325. The origin of death

We read in Genesis 5:5 that 'Adam . . . died.' Why did he die? What was the origin of death? Was it there from the beginning? Certainly vegetable death was. God created 'seed-bearing plants . . . that bear fruit with seed in it' (Gn. 1:1ff.). That is, the cycle of blossom, fruit, seed, death and new life was established in the created order. Animal death existed too, for many fossils of predators have been found with their prey in their stomach. But what about human beings? Paul wrote that death entered the world through sin (Rom. 5:12). Does that mean that, if he had not sinned, he would not have died? Many ridicule this notion. 'Obviously', writes C. H. Dodd with great self-confidence, 'we cannot accept such a speculation as an account of the origin of death, which is a natural process inseparable from organic existence in the world we know . . .'[1]

We have already agreed that death is 'a natural process' in the vegetable and animal kingdoms. But we must not think of human beings as merely rather superior animals, who on that account die like animals. On the contrary, it is because we are not animals that Scripture regards human death as unnatural, an alien intrusion, the penalty for sin, and not God's original intention for his human creation. Only if Adam disobeyed, God warned him, would he 'surely die' (Gn. 2:17). Since, however, he did not immediately die, some conclude that it was spiritual death, or separation from God, which was meant. But when God later pronounced his judgment on Adam, he said to him, 'Dust you are, and to dust you will return' (Gn. 3:19). So physical death was included in the curse, and Adam became mortal when he disobeyed. Certainly the Rabbis understood Genesis in this way. For example, 'God created man for incorruption, and made him an image of his own proper being; but by the envy of the devil death entered into the world . . .' (Wisdom 2:23f.). This is why the biblical authors lament death, and are outraged by it. They see it as demoting us, levelling us down to the animal creation, so that we (God's special creation) have become 'like the beasts that perish' (Ps. 49:12). The author of Ecclesiastes feels the indignity of it too: 'Man's fate is like that of the animals; the same fate awaits them both: As one dies, so dies the other. All have the same breath; man has no advantage over the animal' (Ec. 3:19).

It appears, therefore, that for his unique image-bearers God originally had something better in mind, something less degrading and squalid than death, decay and decomposition, something which acknowledged that human beings are not animals. Perhaps he would have 'translated' them like Enoch and Elijah, without the necessity of death. Perhaps he would have 'changed' them 'in a flash, in the twinkling of an eye', like those believers who will be alive when Jesus comes (1 Cor. 15:51f.). Perhaps too we should think of the transfiguration of

Jesus in this light. His face shone, his clothing became dazzling white, and his body translucent like the resurrection body he would later have. Because he had no sin, he did not need to die. He could have stepped straight into heaven without dying. But he deliberately came back in order of his own free and loving will to die for us. **(1994:165)**

[1] C. H. Dodd, *The Epistle of Paul to the Romans*, The Moffatt New Testament Commentary (Hodder and Stoughton, 11th edn. 1947), p. 81.

28. SELF-LOVE

326. The secular mind

Probably at no point does the Christian mind clash more violently with the secular mind than in its insistence on humility and its implacable hostility to pride. **(1990a:37)**

327. Envy, vanity and pride

Envy is the reverse side of a coin called vanity. Nobody is ever envious of others who is not first proud of himself. **(1986a:53)**

328. The urge to self-aggrandizement

It would be hard to improve on Luther's description of fallen man as *homo in se incurvatus*, 'man curved in on himself'. Human fallenness is human selfishness. Most ambition is selfish ambition. People who 'succeed', because they attain wealth, fame or power, do so mainly because they are driven by an inner urge to self-aggrandizement. This is not pessimism, but the sober realism of Christians who want to look facts in the face. **(1991b:86)**

329. Pharisaic ambition

The Pharisaic spirit still haunts every child of Adam today. It is easy to be critical of Christ's contemporaries and miss the repetition of their vainglory in ourselves. Yet deeply ingrained in our fallen nature is this thirst for the praise of men. It seems to be a devilish perversion of our basic psychological need to be wanted and to be loved. We hunger for applause, fish for compliments, thrive on flattery. It is the plaudits of men we want; we are not content with God's approval now or with his 'Well done, good and faithful servant' on the last day. Yet, as Calvin put it: 'What is more foolish, nay, what is more brutish, than to prefer the paltry approval of men to the judgment of God?'[1] **(1970b:205)**

[1] *The Gospel According to St John*. Comment on John 12:43.

330. Self-centredness

By 'sin' the Bible means self-centredness. God's order is that we love him first, our neighbour next and ourselves last. Sin is

155

precisely the reversal of this order. It is to put ourselves first, our neighbour next (when it suits our convenience) and God somewhere in the distant background. **(1991d:21)**

331. Self-love in Scripture

Self-love is the biblical understanding of sin. **(1986a:276)**

332. The vocabulary of 'self'

That self-centredness is a worldwide phenomenon of human experience is evident from the rich variety of words in our language which are compounded with 'self'. There are more than fifty which have a pejorative meaning – words like self-applause, self-absorption, self-assertion, self-advertisement, self-indulgence, self-gratification, self-glorification, self-pity, self-importance, self-interest and self-will. **(1992b:50)**

333. The primeval temptation

Every sin is a surrender to the primeval temptation to become like God. **(1970b:207)**

334. True freedom

True freedom is not freedom from all responsibility to God and man in order to live for myself, but the exact opposite. True freedom is freedom from myself and from the cramping tyranny of my own self-centredness, in order to live in love for God and others. Only in such self-giving love is an authentically free and human existence to be found. **(1977f.:28)**

335. Self-deification

Pride is more than the first of the seven deadly sins; it is itself the essence of all sin. For it is the stubborn refusal to let God be God, with the corresponding ambition to take his place. It is the attempt to dethrone God and enthrone ourselves. Sin is self-deification. **(1992a:111)**

336. '. . . our neighbours as ourselves . . .'

It is sometimes claimed that the command to love our neighbours as ourselves is implicitly a requirement to love ourselves as well as our neighbours. But this is not so. One can say this with assurance, partly because Jesus spoke of the first and second commandment, without mentioning a third; partly because *agapē* is selfless love which cannot be turned in on the self; and partly because according to Scripture self-love is the essence of sin. Instead, we are to affirm all of ourselves which stems from the creation, while denying all of ourselves which stems from the fall. What the second commandment requires is that we love our neighbours as much as we do in fact (sinners as we are) love ourselves. **(1994:350)**

29. MERE RELIGION

337. Religious experience

Mystical experience without moral commitment is false religion. **(1982c)**

338. Empty religion

We need to listen again to the biblical criticism of religion. No book, not even by Marx and his followers, is more scathing of empty religion than the Bible. The prophets of the eighth and seventh centuries BC were outspoken in their denunciation of the formalism and hypocrisy of Israelite worship. Jesus then applied their critique to the Pharisees of his day: 'These people . . . honour me with their lips, but their hearts are far from me' (Is. 29:13; Mk. 7:6). And this indictment of religion by the Old Testament prophets and by Jesus is uncomfortably applicable to us and our churches today. Too much of our worship is ritual without reality, form without power, fun without fear, religion without God. **(1992b:228)**

339. Religion and morality

In the history of mankind, although this is a shameful thing to confess, religion and morality have been more often divorced than married. **(1973b:87)**

340. The service of ourselves

Our fallen human nature is incurably self-centred, and pride is the elemental human sin, whether the form it takes is self-importance, self-confidence, self-assertion or self-righteousness. If we human beings were left to our own self-absorption, even our religion would be pressed into the service of ourselves. Instead of being the vehicle for the selfless adoration of God, our piety would become the base on which we would presume to approach God and to attempt to establish a claim on him. The ethnic religions all seem to degenerate thus, *and so does Christianity.* **(1994:29)**

341. Pharisaism

Pharisaism haunts the churches of the West . . . It ruins true religion, for reality is an indispensable condition of God's blessing. We must be more honest before God, more open with each other and more real in ourselves if we are to expect God to use us. **(1954b:xiii)**

342. Pluralism and syncretism

Both the pluralism which seeks to preserve all religions, each in its own integrity, and the syncretism which prefers to blend them, deny the uniqueness and the finality of Jesus. **(1981f)**

343. A body without breath

Christianity without Christ is a frame without a picture, a casket without a jewel, a body without breath. **(1991d:18)**

VI. SUCH GREAT SALVATION

30. *The Christian gospel*
31. *Full salvation*
32. *Justification*
33. *Faith*
34. *Grace, mercy and peace*
35. *Law and judgment*

30. THE CHRISTIAN GOSPEL

344. The fundamental questions

The fundamental questions in every religion are the same: By what authority do we believe and teach what we believe and teach? By what means can sinful men and women be reconciled to God, or 'saved'? **(1988d:332)**

345. A trinitarian gospel

At the beginning of Paul's letter to the Romans, where he uses the expression 'the gospel of God', it is plain that God is the subject not the object of the genitive. It is God who conceived, engineered and published the gospel, whereas the substance of the good news is Christ: 'Paul . . . called to be an apostle, set apart for the gospel of God . . . concerning his Son . . . Jesus Christ our Lord' (Rom. 1:1–4). The gospel of God concerns the Son of God; it is an announcement about Christ. The Holy Spirit bears witness 'concerning' Christ (Jn. 15:26), and the apostolic message could be summarized in the words, 'him we proclaim' (Col. 1:28).

The central truth of the good news, then, is Christ himself.
(1967e:35)

346. The essence of Christianity

Christianity is in its very essence a rescue religion. **(1985:75)**

347. Non-negotiable revelation

The gospel is a non-negotiable revelation from God. We may certainly discuss its meaning and its interpretation, so long as our purpose is to grasp it more firmly ourselves and commend it more acceptably to others. But we have no liberty to sit in judgment on it, or to tamper with its substance. For it is God's gospel not ours, and its truth is to be received not criticized, declared not discussed. **(1975c:59)**

348. The irreducible minimum

The three major constituents of the gospel of God are Jesus Christ and him crucified, the plight and peril of man in sin and under judgment, and the necessary response called 'obedience of faith'. Or, in simple monosyllables, 'sin – grace – faith'. This is the irreducible minimum. **(1967e:54)**

349. Not good advice

The gospel is not good advice to men, but good news about Christ; not an invitation to us to do anything, but a declaration of what God has done; not a demand, but an offer. **(1968c:70)**

350. Promise and condition: offer and demand

The gospel offer is not unconditional. It does not benefit its hearers willy nilly, 'whether they hear or refuse to hear'. It is clear that sinners cannot be forgiven if they persist in clinging to their sins. If they desire God to turn from their sins in remission, they must themselves turn from them in repentance. We are charged, therefore, to proclaim the condition as well as the promise of forgiveness. Remission is the gospel offer; repentance is the gospel demand. **(1967d:53)**

351. One gospel, many presentations

There is of course only one apostolic gospel, as Paul emphasized, so that he could call down God's judgment on anybody (NB himself included) who preaches 'a different gospel'. Yet the apostles presented it in a wide variety of ways – now sacrificial (the shedding and sprinkling of Christ's blood), now messianic (the breaking in of the new age or of God's promised rule), now mystic (receiving and enjoying eternal life, being 'in Christ'), now legal (the righteous Judge pronouncing the unrighteous righteous), now personal (the Father reconciling his wayward children), now salvific (the heavenly liberator coming to the rescue of his oppressed people, and leading them out in a new exodus) and now cosmic (the universal Lord claiming universal dominion over the powers). And these seven are only a selection! **(1988d:330)**

352. A new gospel?

Some modern theologians argue that we must have a new gospel for this new world. The old-fashioned gospel will no longer do. It is out of date, irrelevant. It must be discarded and replaced. In contrast to this, it is refreshing to read the view expressed in *Towards the Conversion of England*. At the head of chapter II is William Temple's statement: 'The Gospel is true always and everywhere, or it is not a Gospel at all, or true at all.' **(1967e:33)**

353. 'The unobjectionable residue'

The seventeenth-century Jesuits in China, in order not to upset the social sensitivities of the Chinese, excluded the crucifixion and certain other details from the gospel. But, Professor Hugh Trevor-Roper has written (in a letter to *The Times* on 1 December 1959), 'we do not learn that they made many lasting converts by the unobjectionable residue of the story'.

(1967e:49)

354. God's dilemma

God is not omnipotent in the sense that he can do anything. God can only do those things which are consistent with his nature. He cannot therefore readily pardon the sinner, because he is a God of infinite justice. But neither can he readily punish the sinner, because he is also a God of infinite mercy. Here, then, if we may use human language, was the divine dilemma. How could he pardon the sinner without compromising his justice? How could he judge the sinner without frustrating his love? How in the face of human sin could he be at the same time a God of love and of wrath? How could he both pardon the sinner and punish his sin? How could a righteous God forgive unrighteous men without involving himself in their unrighteousness?

(1967c:50)

355. The gospel according to Paul

As we read Paul's letters, he gives us a superb exposition of the gospel of God's grace. He tells us what God has done for guilty sinners like us who are without excuse and deserve nothing at his hand but judgment. He declares that God sent his Son to die for our sins on the cross and to rise again, and that if we are united to Jesus Christ, by faith inwardly and by baptism outwardly, then we die with him and rise again with him, and experience a new life in him. It is a magnificent gospel that Paul unfolds.

(1982b:42)

356. The key to the New Testament

'God made him who had no sin to be sin for us, so that in him we might become the righteousness of God' (2 Cor. 5:21). It is surely one of the most startling statements in the Bible, yet we must not on that account evade it. James Denney was not exaggerating when he wrote of it: 'Mysterious and awful as

this thought is, it is the key to the whole of the New Testament.'[1] For our sake God actually made the sinless Christ to be sin with our sins. The God who refused to reckon our sins to us reckoned them to Christ instead. Indeed, his personal sinlessness uniquely qualified him to bear our sins in our place.
(1986a:200)

[1] James Denney, *The Death of Christ* (Tyndale Press, 2nd edn. 1951), p. 88.

357. Sin and salvation

The concept of substitution may be said, then, to lie at the heart of both sin and salvation. For the essence of sin is man substituting himself for God, while the essence of salvation is God substituting himself for man. **(1986a:160)**

358. What must we do?

The gospel offers blessings; what must we do to receive them? The proper answer is 'nothing'! We do not have to *do* anything. We have only to *believe*. Our response is not 'the works of the law' but 'hearing with faith', that is, not obeying the law, but believing the gospel. For obeying is to attempt to do the work of salvation ourselves, whereas believing is to let Christ be our Saviour and to rest in his finished work. **(1968c:75)**

359. God's free offer

That Christ finished his work is certain. But some people thoughtlessly suppose that, through his death on the cross, forgiveness of sins is automatically conferred upon all men. God's solution to the fundamental problem of sin is, however, not mechanical and impersonal. He does not impose salvation on those who do not want it. He still respects his own gift of free will to mankind. He offers me salvation. He does not oblige me to accept it. **(1972a:8)**

360. Only through Christ

Self-salvation is impossible. We know that Jesus Christ is the only Saviour (because he alone has the necessary qualifications, as we have seen), and that salvation is by God's grace alone, on the ground of Christ's cross alone, by faith alone.

What we do not know, however, is exactly how much knowledge and understanding of the gospel people need before they can cry to God for mercy and be saved. In the Old Testament, people were certainly 'justified by grace through faith', even though they had little knowledge or expectation of Christ. Perhaps there are others today in a somewhat similar position. They know they are sinful and guilty before God, and that they cannot do anything to win his favour, so in self-despair they call upon the God they dimly perceive to save them. If God does save such, as many evangelical Christians tentatively believe, their salvation is still only by grace, only through Christ, only by faith. **(1992b:319)**

361. 'Refusing to let God be gracious'

There are large numbers of people who . . . are seeking to commend themselves to God by their own works. They think it noble to try to win their way to God and to heaven. But it is not noble; it is dreadfully ignoble. For, in effect, it is to deny both the nature of God and the mission of Christ. It is to refuse to let God be gracious. It is to tell Christ that he need not have bothered to die. For both the grace of God and the death of Christ become redundant, if we are masters of our own destiny and can save ourselves. **(1968c:66)**

362. Life and death redefined

Romans 8:13 suggests that we need to redefine both life and death. What the world calls life (a desirable self-indulgence) leads to alienation from God which in reality is death, whereas the putting to death of all perceived evil within us, which the world sees as an undesirable self-abnegation, is in reality the way to authentic life. **(1994:230)**

31. FULL SALVATION

363. 'Are you saved?'

Salvation is a big and comprehensive word. It embraces the totality of God's saving work, from beginning to end. In fact salvation has three tenses, past, present and future. I am myself always grateful to the good man who led me to Christ over forty years ago that he taught me, raw and brash young convert that I was, to keep saying: 'I have been saved (in the past) from the penalty of sin by a crucified Saviour. I am being saved (in the present) from the power of sin by a living Saviour. And I shall be saved (in the future) from the very presence of sin by a coming Saviour' . . .

If therefore you were to ask me, 'Are you saved?' there is only one correct biblical answer which I could give you: 'yes and no.' Yes, in the sense that by the sheer grace and mercy of God through the death of Jesus Christ my Saviour he has forgiven my sins, justified me and reconciled me to himself. But no, in the sense that I still have a fallen nature and live in a fallen world and have a corruptible body, and I am longing for my salvation to be brought to its triumphant completion.

(1980a:103)

364. God's eternal purpose

God's whole purpose, conceived in a past eternity, being worked out for and in his people in history, to be completed in the glory to come, may be encapsulated in this single concept: *God intends to make us like Christ.* Whether we are thinking about eternal predestination or initial conversion or continuing sanctification or final glorification, the same theme stands out. At each stage there is a reference to the 'image' or 'likeness' of Jesus Christ. The fullness of salvation is conformity to him.

(1991b:101)

365. Salvation accomplished

The New Testament gospel is good news about what God has done in Christ. It is the proclamation of an achievement. It is the heralding of an accomplished salvation. **(1956a:32)**

366. Christ's finished work

One of the essential differences between pre-Reformation religion and Reformation religion is that the former was in many respects man-centred, while the Reformers were determined to be God-centred. In the matter of authority they repudiated the traditions of *men*, because they held the supremacy and the sufficiency of *God's* Word written. In the matter of salvation they repudiated the merits of *men*, because they held the sufficiency of *Christ's* finished work. **(1970b:193)**

367. Bigger than forgiveness

Salvation and forgiveness are not convertible or interchangeable terms. Salvation is bigger than forgiveness . . . forgiveness and holiness and immortality are all aspects of our salvation.

Salvation is a good word; it denotes that comprehensive purpose of God by which he justifies, sanctifies, and glorifies his people: first pardoning their offences and accepting them as righteous in his sight; then progressively transforming them by his Spirit into the image of Christ, until finally they become like Christ in heaven, when they see him as he is, and their bodies are raised incorruptible like Christ's body of glory. I long to rescue salvation from the narrow concepts to which even evangelical Christians sometimes reduce it. **(1969a:51)**

368. The images of Scripture

'Images' of salvation (or of the atonement) is a better term than 'theories'. For theories are usually abstract and speculative concepts, whereas the biblical images of the atoning achievement of Christ are concrete pictures and belong to the data of revelation. They are not alternative explanations of the cross, providing us with a range to choose from, but complementary to one another, each contributing a vital part to the whole. As for the imagery, 'propitiation' introduces us to rituals at a shrine, 'redemption' to transactions in a market-place, 'justification' to proceedings in a lawcourt, and 'reconciliation' to experiences in a home or family. My contention is that 'substitution' is not a further 'theory' or 'image' to be set alongside the others, but rather the foundation of them all, without which each lacks cogency. If God in Christ did not die in our place, there could be neither propitiation, nor redemption, nor justification, nor reconciliation. **(1986a:168)**

369. Salvation is freedom

Salvation is freedom . . . It includes freedom from the just judgment of God on our sins, from our guilt and our guilty conscience, into a new relationship with him in which we become his reconciled, forgiven children and we know him as our Father. It is freedom from the bitter bondage of meaninglessness into a new sense of purpose in God's new society of love, in which the last are first, the poor rich and the meek heirs. It is freedom from the dark prison of our own self-centredness into a new life of self-fulfilment through self-forgetful service. And one day it will include freedom from the futility of pain, decay, death and dissolution into a new world of immortality, beauty and unimaginable joy. All this – and more! – is 'salvation'. **(1992b:310)**

370. Salvation concerns persons

To call socio-political liberation 'salvation' and to call social activism 'evangelism' – this is to be guilty of a gross theological confusion. It is to mix what Scripture keeps distinct – God the Creator and God the Redeemer, the God of the cosmos and the God of the covenant, the world and the church, common grace and saving grace, justice and justification, the reformation of society and the regeneration of men. For the salvation offered in the gospel of Christ concerns persons rather than structures. It is deliverance from another kind of yoke than political and economic oppression. **(1975c:95)**

371. The persons God meant us to be

The gospel is good news not only of what Jesus *did* (he died for our sins and was raised, according to the Scriptures) but also of what he *offers* as a result. He promises to those who respond to him both the forgiveness of sins (to wipe out the past) and the gift of the Spirit (to make us new people). Together these constitute the freedom for which many are searching, freedom from guilt, defilement, judgment and self-centredness, and freedom to be the persons God made and meant us to be. Forgiveness and the Spirit comprise 'salvation', and both are publicly signified in baptism, namely the washing away of sin and the outpouring of the Spirit. **(1990b:80)**

32. JUSTIFICATION

372. God loving . . . God giving

Justification is a gift of God's sheer grace, not a reward for any merit or works of ours. For God's 'grace' is his spontaneous generosity, his free and unmerited favour, his gracious kindness to the undeserving. Grace is God loving, God stooping, God coming, God giving. **(1980a:69)**

373. 'Not a religion but a gospel'

Justification (its source God and his grace, its ground Christ and his cross, and its means faith alone, altogether apart from works) is the heart of the gospel and unique to Christianity. No other system, ideology or religion proclaims a free forgiveness and a new life to those who have done nothing to deserve it but a lot to deserve judgment instead. On the contrary, all other systems teach some form of self-salvation through good works of religion, righteousness or philanthropy. Christianity, by contrast, is not in its essence a religion at all; it is a gospel, the gospel, good news that God's grace has turned away his wrath, that God's Son has died our death and borne our judgment, that God has mercy on the undeserving, and that there is nothing left for us to do, or even contribute. Faith's only function is to receive what grace offers. **(1994:118)**

374. The cross and justification

If God justifies sinners freely by his grace, on what ground does he do so? How is it possible for the righteous God to declare the unrighteous to be righteous without either compromising his righteousness or condoning their unrighteousness? That is our question. God's answer is the cross.

(1994:112)

375. Instant acceptance

Justification is a legal pronouncement which is instantaneous. As soon as any sinner turns from his sin and commits himself in absolute trust to Jesus Christ who died for him and rose again, God pronounces him righteous. He is 'accepted in the Beloved' (Eph. 1:6), or 'justified in Christ' (Gal. 2:17). **(1954c:65)**

171

376. Legally righteous

When God justifies sinners, he is not declaring bad people to be good, or saying that they are not sinners after all; he is pronouncing them legally righteous, free from any liability to the broken law, because he himself in his Son has borne the penalty of their law-breaking. **(1986a:190)**

377. Justification – the penalty paid

The only way to be justified from sin is that the wages of sin be paid, either by the sinner or by the God-appointed substitute. There is no way of escape but that the penalty be borne. How can a man be justified who has been convicted of a crime and sentenced to a term of imprisonment? Only by going to prison and paying the penalty of his crime. Once he has served his term, he can leave prison justified. He need have no more fear of police or magistrates, for the demands of the law have been satisfied. He has been justified from his sin.

The same principle holds good if the penalty is death. There is no way of justification except by paying the penalty. You may respond that in this case to pay the penalty is no way of escape. And you would be right if we were talking about capital punishment on earth. Once a murderer has been executed (in countries where the death penalty survives), his life on earth is finished. He cannot live again on earth justified, as can a person who has served a prison sentence. But the wonderful thing about our Christian justification is that our death is followed by a resurrection, in which we can live the life of a justified person, having paid the death penalty (in and through Christ) for our sin.

For us, then, it is like this. We deserved to die for our sins. And in fact we did die, though not in our own person, but in the person of Jesus Christ our substitute, who died in our place, and with whom we have been united by faith and baptism. And by union with the same Christ we have risen again. So the old life of sin is finished, because we died to it, and the new life of justified sinners has begun. Our death and resurrection with Christ render it inconceivable that we should go back. It is in this sense that our sinful self has been deprived of power and we have been set free. **(1994:177)**

378. Justification and reconciliation

Justification and reconciliation are not identical, though God never justifies sinners without reconciling them to himself, and never reconciles sinners to himself without justifying them. But justification is the verdict of a judge in a lawcourt; it does not necessarily involve him in any personal relationship with the prisoner he has acquitted. Reconciliation takes place, however, when the father welcomes the prodigal home and reinstates him in the family. There is no peace like peace with God. It is peace *with* God as an objective fact which is the foundation of the peace *of* God as a subjective experience. For our Judge has become our Father, and our Creator our Friend.

(1980a:92)

379. Justification and pardon

Some scholars maintain that 'justification' and 'pardon' are synonymous . . . But surely this cannot be so. Pardon is negative, the remission of a penalty or debt; justification is positive, the bestowal of a righteous status, the sinner's reinstatement in the favour and fellowship of God.   **(1994:110)**

380. Justification and sanctification

Justification describes the position of acceptance with God which he gives us when we trust in Christ as our Saviour. It is a legal term, borrowed from the lawcourts, and its opposite is condemnation. To justify is to acquit, to declare an accused person to be just, not guilty. So the divine judge, because his Son has borne our condemnation, justifies us, pronouncing us righteous in his sight. 'Therefore, there is now no condemnation for those who are in Christ Jesus' (Rom. 8:1).

Sanctification, on the other hand, describes the process by which justified Christians are changed into the likeness of Christ. When God justifies us, he *declares* us righteous through Christ's death for us; when he sanctifies us, he *makes* us righteous through the power of his Holy Spirit within us. Justification concerns our outward status of acceptance with God; sanctification concerns our inward growth in holiness of character. Further, whereas our justification is sudden and complete, so that we shall never be more justified than we were on the day of our conversion, our sanctification is gradual and incomplete. It takes a few moments only in court for a judge to pronounce his verdict and for the accused to be acquitted; it takes a lifetime even to approach Christlikeness. **(1991d:38)**

381. Forgiven every day

We can be justified only once; but we need to be forgiven every day. When Jesus washed the apostles' feet, he gave them an illustration of this. Peter asked him to wash his hands and his head as well as his feet. But Jesus replied: 'He who has bathed does not need to wash, except for his feet, but he is clean all over.' A man invited to a dinner party in Jerusalem would take a bath before going out. On arrival at his friend's house, he would not be offered another bath; but a slave would meet him at the front door and wash his feet. So when we first come to Christ in repentance and faith, we receive a 'bath' (which is justification, and is outwardly symbolized in baptism). It never needs to be repeated. But as we walk through the dusty streets of the world, we constantly need to 'have our feet washed' (which is daily forgiveness). **(1971a:135)**

382. An unpopular doctrine?

The real reason why the doctrine of justification by grace alone through faith alone is unpopular is that it is grievously wounding to our pride. **(1970b:129)**

383. The verdict now

Justification is a legal or forensic term, belonging to the law courts. Its opposite is condemnation. Both are the pronouncements of a judge. In a Christian context they are the alternative eschatological verdicts which God the judge may pass on judgment day. So when God justifies sinners today, he anticipates his own final judgment by bringing into the present what belongs properly to the last day. **(1994:110)**

384. Moses and Jesus

In his epistle to the Galatians Paul paints a vivid contrast between Moses and Jesus. Moses administers law, Jesus exhibits grace. Moses says 'Work'; Jesus says 'Believe'. Moses says that salvation is 'through the works of the law'; Jesus says it is 'in me, by grace through faith'. Moses holds us in bondage as slaves; Jesus sets us free and makes us sons. This contrast is drawn out in Galatians 3:23 – 4:11 (*cf.* Acts 13:38–9). It is the same contrast which Jesus drew in his parable of the Pharisee and the publican (Lk. 18:9–14); which was rediscovered at the Reformation; and which was incorporated in our Article 11, *Of Justification*: 'We are accounted righteous before God, only for the merit of our Lord and Saviour Jesus Christ by faith, and not for our own works or deservings: wherefore, that we are justified by faith only is a most wholesome doctrine, and very full of comfort . . .' There is perhaps no message which needs more to be recovered and proclaimed in our generation.

(1954c:63)

385. *Paul and James*

Paul and James have been thought to contradict one another. Abraham was justified not by works but by faith, Paul wrote in Romans 4:2–3. 'Was not Abraham our father justified by works . . .?' asks James in 2:21. It is well known that Martin Luther, living in an age of controversy when the great doctrine of justification by faith had just been rediscovered, repudiated the epistle of James, adding contemptuously that it was made of 'straw'. The contradiction between the two apostles is, however, purely imaginary. The New Testament represents them as recognizing each other's place in God's purpose for the church. James had welcomed Paul's mission to the Gentiles (Gal. 2:9), and Paul had respected James's concern for Jewish feeling (Acts 21:17–26). The two men were given a different ministry but not a different message. They proclaimed the same gospel, but with a different emphasis.

(1954c:104)

33. FAITH

386. Faith and reason

It is amazing how many people suppose that faith and reason are incompatible. But they are never set over against each other in Scripture. Faith and sight are contrasted (2 Cor. 5:7), but not faith and reason. For faith according to Scripture is neither credulity, nor superstition, nor 'an illogical belief in the occurrence of the improbable',[1] but a quiet, thoughtful trust in the God who is known to be trustworthy. **(1992b:116)**

[1] H. L. Mencken, who wrote for the *Baltimore Sun* and was sometimes called 'the sage of Baltimore'.

387. Faith's ladder

Faith goes beyond reason, but rests on it. Knowledge is the ladder by which faith climbs higher, the springboard from which it leaps further. **(1979e:67)**

388. A leap in the dark?

There is much misunderstanding about faith. It is commonly supposed to be a leap in the dark, totally incompatible with reason. This is not so. True faith is never unreasonable, because its object is always trustworthy. When we human beings trust one another, the reasonableness of our trust depends on the relative trustworthiness of the people concerned. But the Bible bears witness to Jesus Christ as absolutely trustworthy. It tells us who he is and what he has done, and the evidence it supplies for his unique person and work is extremely compelling. As we expose ourselves to the biblical witness to this Christ, and as we feel its impact – profound yet simple, varied yet unanimous – God creates faith within us. We receive the testimony. We believe. **(1984d:22)**

389. Belief on testimony

As the book Genesis is introduced by 'In the beginning God', affirming the Father's existence, so St John's gospel is introduced by 'In the beginning was the Word', affirming the Son's pre-existence. These eternal truths are a fit subject for dogma, not for demonstration, because they are the product of divine revelation, not of human speculation. They are to be accepted or rejected on testimony, for faith is not belief in spite of evidence but belief on testimony. **(1954c:118)**

390. No merit of ours

It is vital to affirm that there is nothing meritorious about faith, and that, when we say that salvation is 'by faith, not by works', we are not substituting one kind of merit ('faith') for another ('works'). Nor is salvation a sort of cooperative enterprise between God and us, in which he contributes the cross, and we contribute faith. No, grace is non-contributory, and faith is the opposite of self-regarding. The value of faith is not to be found in itself, but entirely and exclusively in its object, namely Jesus Christ and him crucified. To say 'justification by faith alone' is another way of saying 'justification by Christ alone'. Faith is the eye that looks to him, the hand that receives his free gift, the mouth that drinks the living water. **(1994:117)**

391. Confiding trust

Faith is variously described and illustrated in the New Testament. Essentially it is a confiding trust. **(1967e:50)**

392. A mysterious exchange

If we come to Christ and put our trust in him, a marvellous but mysterious exchange takes place. He takes away our sins, and clothes us with his righteousness instead. In consequence, we stand before God 'not trusting in our own righteousness, but in God's manifold and great mercies', not in the tattered rags of our own morality but in the spotless robe of the righteousness of Christ. And God accepts us not because we are righteous, but because the righteous Christ died for our sins and was raised from death. **(1991d:19)**

393. The gift of faith

We must never think of salvation as a kind of transaction between God and us in which he contributes grace and we contribute faith. For we were dead, and had to be quickened before we could believe. No, Christ's apostles clearly teach elsewhere that saving faith too is God's gracious gift.
(1979e:83)

394. God's unbreakable promises

I sometimes wonder if there is any more vital lesson for Christian living than this: that God has condescended to our weakness by making us promises, that he will never break them, and that faith reckons on his faithfulness by grasping hold of them. We sometimes smile at the Victorians' 'promise-boxes'. Biblical promises were printed on small pieces of paper, rolled up like miniature scrolls and stored in a wooden box for random selection in times of need. And, to be sure, that practice did wrench the divine promises from the context in which they were originally given. Nevertheless, I rather think that even such a naïve trust in detached promises was better than the present-day accurate but unbelieving knowledge of the promises in their context. So many of us complain of spiritual doubt, darkness, depression and lethargy, of besetting sins and unconquered temptations, of slow progress towards Christian maturity, of sluggishness in worship and in prayer, and of many other spiritual ills, while all the time we do not use the secret weapon which God has put into our hands.

(1991b:27)

395. In Christ by faith

All men are in Adam, since we are in Adam by birth, but not all men are in Christ, since we can be in Christ only by faith. In Adam by birth we are condemned and die. But if we are in Christ by faith we are justified and live . . . Peace, grace, glory (the three privileges of the justified) are not given to those who are in Adam, but only to those who are in Christ. **(1966c:27)**

396. The lordship of Christ

In saying that saving faith includes obedience, I mean that in true faith there is an element of submission. Faith is directed towards a Person. It is in fact a complete commitment to this Person involving not only an acceptance of what is offered but a humble surrender to what is or may be demanded. The bent knee is as much a part of saving faith as the open hand.

(1959b:17)

397. How to find faith

It is no use moaning that we seem to suffer from a chronic unbelief, or envying others ('I wish I had your faith'), as if our lack of faith were like our temperament, a congenital condition which cannot be changed. For God himself has given us the means to increase our faith:

> Faith comes from hearing the message, and the message is heard through the word of Christ (Rom. 10:17).

We have to take time and trouble to hear in order to believe.

(1984d:189)

398. A hostile will

Ostensibly Jerusalem rejected Christ on theological grounds, and outwardly the Pharisees condemned Jesus for blasphemy. But beneath these intellectual and doctrinal objections was a hostile will. Jesus had exposed their hypocrisy and unmasked their sins. Their pride was wounded. They felt humiliated. They hated him for his holiness. They were jealous of his influence on the common people. These things were at the root of their repudiation of Christ. But it was more respectable to find fault with his theology than to admit their moral embarrassment. Their doubts were a cloak for their sins.

It has often been so. I do not say it is always so, because of course many people have genuine theological problems. But frequently a man's deepest need is not intellectual but moral, and his supposed inability to believe is really an unwillingness to obey. **(1956a:29)**

399. The sin of unbelief

Unbelief is not a misfortune to be pitied; it is a sin to be deplored. Its sinfulness lies in the fact that it contradicts the word of the one true God and thus attributes falsehood to him.

(1988g:185)

400. 'By faith alone'

Three times in one paragraph Paul underlines the necessity of faith: *through faith in Jesus Christ to all who believe* (Rom. 3:22); *through faith in his blood* (25) or, more probably, 'by his blood, to be received by faith' (RSV); and God *justifies those who have faith in Jesus* (26). Indeed, justification is 'by faith alone', *sola fide*, one of the great watchwords of the Reformation. True, the word 'alone' does not occur in Paul's text of verse 28, where Luther added it. It is not altogether surprising, therefore, that the Roman Catholic Church accused Luther of perverting the text of Holy Scripture. But Luther was following Origen and other early Church Fathers, who had similarly introduced the word 'alone'. A true instinct led them to do so. Far from falsifying or distorting Paul's meaning, they were clarifying and emphasizing it. It was similar with John Wesley who wrote that he felt he 'did trust in Christ, in Christ alone, for salvation'. Justification is by grace alone, in Christ alone, through faith alone.

(1994:117)

34. GRACE, MERCY AND PEACE

401. Free grace

The gospel is the gospel of grace, of God's free and unmerited favour. To turn from him who called you in the grace of Christ is to turn from the true gospel. Whenever teachers start exalting man, implying that he can contribute anything to his salvation by his own morality, religion, philosophy or respectability, the gospel of grace is being corrupted. That is the first test. The true gospel magnifies the free grace of God.(1968c:27)

402. A special sort of love

No-one can understand the message of Scripture who does not know the meaning of grace. The God of the Bible is 'the God of all grace' (1 Pet. 5:10). Grace is love, but love of a special sort. It is love which stoops and sacrifices and serves, love which is kind to the unkind, and generous to the ungrateful and undeserving. Grace is God's free and unmerited favour, loving the unlovable, seeking the fugitive, rescuing the hopeless, and lifting the beggar from the dunghill to make him sit among princes (Ps. 113:7–8). (1984d:127)

403. 'The reign of grace'

Nothing could sum up better the blessings of being in Christ than the expression 'the reign of grace'. For grace forgives sins through the cross, and bestows on the sinner both righteousness and eternal life. Grace satisfies the thirsty soul and fills the hungry with good things. Grace sanctifies sinners, shaping them into the image of Christ. Grace perseveres even with the recalcitrant, determining to complete what it has begun. And one day grace will destroy death and consummate the kingdom. So when we are convinced that 'grace reigns', we will remember that God's throne is a 'throne of grace', and will come to it boldly to receive mercy and to find grace for every need (Heb. 4:16). (1994:157)

404. God's unfolding purpose

In 2 Timothy 1:9–10 we seem to detect five stages by which God's saving purpose unfolds. The first is the eternal gift to us in Christ of his grace. The second is the historical appearing of

181

Christ to abolish death by his death and resurrection. The third is the personal call of God to sinners through the preaching of the gospel. The fourth is the moral sanctification of believers by the Holy Spirit. And the fifth is the final heavenly perfection in which the holy calling is consummated. **(1973b:40)**

405. Common grace

Christians do certainly believe that God has revealed himself in Jesus Christ, as witnessed to in Scripture, in a unique and final way, so that, in this life, he has nothing more to reveal than he has revealed, although of course we have much more to learn. But we are not suggesting that outside the church we consider God inactive and truth absent. Not at all. God sustains all his creatures, and therefore 'is not far from any of them'. By creation they are his 'offspring', who 'live and move and have (their) being' in him (Acts 17:27–28). Also Jesus Christ, as the *logos* of God and the light of men (Jn. 1:1–5), is himself ceaselessly active in the world. Because he is described as 'the true light that gives light to every man' (Jn. 1:9), we dare to claim that all beauty, truth and goodness, wherever they are found among human beings, derive from him, whether people know it or not. This is an aspect of God's so-called 'common grace', his love shown to all humankind; it is not, however, his 'saving grace', which he extends to those who humbly cry to him for mercy. **(1992b:317)**

406. Grace and faith

Grace is 'the free and unmerited favour of God'. It is Paul's word to describe the loving, undeserved initiative of God in giving Christ to die, raising him from the dead and revealing him to sinners. His whole message became 'the word of his grace' (Acts 14:3) and 'the good news of the grace of God' (Acts 20:24). 'The grace of God has appeared for the salvation of all men' (Tit. 2:11). It is supremely manifested in the provision and offer of salvation. By 'salvation' Paul is using a word with the broadest possible concept. It includes the past, the present and the future. It describes God's liberation of man from all the ravages of sin in the conscience, the mind, the heart, the will and the body; in his relation to God, the world and himself. To use Paul's own words, it comprises the believer's justification (his acceptance before God), sanctification (his growth in holiness), edification (his life in the church) and glorification (his perfection in the eternal glory). Or more simply, it makes him a son and a saint, a brother and an heir. Such is the grace of Christ received by faith. The only function of faith is to respond to grace. Faith takes what grace offers.

(1954c:57)

407. The source of salvation

Although 'grace' and 'peace' are common monosyllables, they are pregnant with theological substance. In fact, they summarize Paul's gospel of salvation. The nature of salvation is peace, or reconciliation – peace with God, peace with men, peace within. The source of salvation is grace, God's free favour, irrespective of any human merit or works, his loving-kindness to the undeserving. And this grace and peace flow from the Father and the Son together. (1968c:16)

408. God's provision

Grace and mercy are both expressions of God's love, grace to the guilty and undeserving, mercy to the needy and helpless. Peace is that restoration of harmony with God, others and self which we call 'salvation'. Put together, peace indicates the character of salvation, mercy our need of it and grace God's free provision of it in Christ. (1988g:206)

409. Secure in grace

Justified believers enjoy a blessing far greater than a periodic approach to God or an occasional audience with the king. We are privileged to live in the temple and in the palace . . . Our relationship with God, into which justification has brought us, is not sporadic but continuous, not precarious but secure. We do not fall in and out of grace like courtiers who may find themselves in and out of favour with their sovereign, or politicians with the public. No, we *stand* in it, for that is the nature of grace. Nothing can separate us from God's love (Rom. 8:38f.). (1994:140)

410. 'What by grace we are . . .'

The overwhelming emphasis of the New Testament letters is not to urge upon Christian readers some entirely new and distinct blessing, but to remind us of what by grace we are, to recall us to it, and to urge us to live by it. (1975b:44)

35. LAW AND JUDGMENT

411. *The purpose of law*

The Sermon on the Mount as a kind of 'new law', like the old law, has two divine purposes . . . First, it shows the non-Christian that he cannot please God by himself (because he cannot obey the law) and so directs him to Christ to be justified. Secondly, it shows the Christian who has been to Christ for justification how to live so as to please God. More simply, as both the Reformers and the Puritans used to summarize it, the law sends us to Christ to be justified, and Christ sends us back to the law to be sanctified.   **(1978f.:36)**

412. *Law and gospel*

After God gave the promise to Abraham, he gave the law to Moses. Why? Simply because he had to make things worse before he could make them better. The law exposed sin, provoked sin, condemned sin. The purpose of the law was, as it were, to lift the lid off man's respectability and disclose what he is really like underneath – sinful, rebellious, guilty, under the judgment of God, and helpless to save himself.

And the law must still be allowed to do its God-given duty today. One of the great faults of the contemporary church is the tendency to soft-pedal sin and judgment. Like false prophets we 'heal the wound of God's people lightly' (Je. 6:14; 8:11). This is how Dietrich Bonhoeffer put it: 'It is only when one submits to the law that one can speak of grace . . . I don't think it is Christian to want to get to the New Testament too soon and too directly.'[1] We must never bypass the law and come straight to the gospel. To do so is to contradict the plan of God in biblical history.

Is this not why the gospel is unappreciated today? Some ignore it, others ridicule it. So in our modern evangelism we cast our pearls (the costliest pearl being the gospel) before swine. People cannot see the beauty of the pearl, because they have no conception of the filth of the pigsty. No man has ever appreciated the gospel until the law has first revealed him to himself. It is only against the inky blackness of the night sky that the stars begin to appear, and it is only against the dark background of sin and judgment that the gospel shines forth.

Not until the law has bruised and smitten us will we admit our need of the gospel to bind up our wounds. Not until the law has arrested and imprisoned us will we pine for Christ to set us free. Not until the law has condemned and killed us will we call upon Christ for justification and life. Not until the law has driven us to despair of ourselves will we ever believe in Jesus. Not until the law has humbled us even to hell will we turn to the gospel to raise us to heaven. **(1968c:93)**

[1] Dietrich Bonhoeffer, *Letters and Papers From Prison* (Fontana, 1959), p. 50.

413. Paul's attitude to the law

From Romans 7 we may summarize three possible attitudes to the law, the first two of which Paul rejects, and the third of which he commends. We might call them 'legalism', 'anti-nomianism' and 'law-fulfilling freedom'. *Legalists* are 'under the law' and in bondage to it. They imagine that their relationship to God depends on their obedience to the law, and they are seeking to be both justified and sanctified by it. But they are crushed by the law's inability to save them. *Antinomians* (or libertines) go to the opposite extreme. Blaming the law for their problems, they reject it altogether, and claim to be rid of all obligation to its demands. They have turned liberty into licence. *Law-fulfilling free people* preserve the balance. They rejoice both in their freedom from the law for justification and sanctification, and in their freedom to fulfil it. They delight in the law as the revelation of God's will (verse 22), but recognize that the power to fulfil it is not in the law but in the Spirit. Thus legalists fear the law and are in bondage to it. Antinomians hate the law and repudiate it. Law-abiding free people love the law and fulfil it. **(1994:191)**

414. Law-dodging

What is the righteousness to which Christians are summoned? It is a deep inward righteousness of the heart where the Holy Spirit has written God's law. It is new fruit exhibiting the newness of the tree, new life burgeoning from a new nature. So we have no liberty to try to dodge or duck the lofty demands of the law. Law-dodging is a pharisaic hobby; what is character-istic of Christians is a keen appetite for righteousness, hungering and thirsting after it continuously. And this righteousness, whether expressed in purity, honesty or charity, will show to whom we belong. Our Christian calling is to imitate not the world, but the Father. And it is by this imitation of him that the Christian counter-culture becomes visible. **(1978f:123)**

415. Letter and spirit

Is the law still binding upon the Christian? The answer to that is, No and Yes! 'No' in the sense that our acceptance before God does not depend on it. Christ in his death fully met the demands of the law, so that we are delivered from it. It no longer has any claims on us. It is no longer our lord. 'Yes' in the sense that our new life is still a bondage. We still 'serve'. We are still slaves, although discharged from the law. But the motive and the means of our service have altered.

Why do we serve? Not because the law is our master and we have to, but because Christ is our husband and we want to. Not because obedience to the law leads to salvation, but because salvation leads to obedience to the law. The law says, Do this and you will live. The gospel says, You live, so do this. The motive has changed.

How do we serve? Not in oldness of letter, but in newness of spirit. That is, not by obedience to an external code, but by surrender to an indwelling Spirit. **(1966c:65)**

416. Law and liberty

Christian liberty is not inconsistent with law any more than love is. True, Christians are not 'under law' in that our salvation does not depend on obedience to the law. Yet this does not relieve us of the obligation to keep the law. The freedom with which Christ has made us free is not freedom to break the law, but freedom to keep it. 'I will walk about in freedom, for I have sought your precepts' (Ps. 119:45).

(1988g:210)

417. Judged by our works

The whole New Testament teaches this; although we sinners can be 'justified' only by faith in Christ, yet we shall be 'judged' by our works. This is not a contradiction. It is because good works of love are the only available public evidence of our faith. Our faith in Jesus Christ is secret, hidden in our hearts. But if it is genuine, it will manifest itself visibly in good works. As James put it, 'I will show you my faith by what I do . . . faith without deeds is useless' (Jas. 2:18, 20). Since the judgment day will be a public occasion, it will be necessary for public evidence to be produced, namely the outworking of our faith in compassionate action. Jesus himself taught this many times. For example, 'The Son of man is going to come in his Father's glory with his angels, and then he will reward each person according to what he has done' (Mt. 16:27). It is not our salvation, but our judgment, which will be according to our works. **(1991b:82)**

418. Those who have never heard

I believe the most Christian stance is to remain agnostic on this question. When somebody asked Jesus, 'Lord, are only a few people going to be saved?', he refused to answer and instead urged them 'to enter through the narrow door' (Lk. 13:23–24). The fact is that God, alongside the most solemn warnings about our responsibility to respond to the gospel, has not revealed how he will deal with those who have never heard it. We have to leave them in the hands of the God of infinite mercy and justice, who manifested these qualities most fully in the cross. Abraham's question, 'will not the Judge of all the earth do right?' (Gn. 18:25) is our confidence too. **(1988d:327)**

VII. BECOMING A CHRISTIAN

36. Chosen and called
37. Turning to Christ
38. The new birth

36. CHOSEN AND CALLED

419. What is a Christian?

The New Testament definition of a Christian is a person 'in Christ'. It is necessary to insist, therefore, that according to Jesus and his apostles to be a Christian is not just to have been baptized, to belong to the church, to receive holy communion, to believe in the doctrines of the creed or to try to follow the standards of the Sermon on the Mount. Baptism and holy communion, church membership, creed and conduct are all part and parcel of living as a Christian, but they can form and have sometimes formed an empty casket from which the jewel has disappeared. The jewel is Jesus Christ himself. To be a Christian is primarily to live in union with Jesus Christ, as a result of which baptism, belief and behaviour slot naturally into place. **(1991b:37)**

420. 'What attracted you?'

In a questionnaire submitted to members of All Souls congregation I asked both: 'What first attracted you to Christ and the gospel?' and 'What mainly or finally brought you to Christ?' In their answers over half referred to something they had seen for themselves in Christian people, their parents, pastors, teachers, colleagues or friends. As one put it, these 'had something in their lives which I lacked but desperately longed for'. In several cases it was 'their external joy and inward peace'. To a student nurse it was 'the genuine and open friendship' offered by Christians; to an Oxford undergraduate studying law their 'sheer exuberance'; to a police constable the 'clear aim, purpose and idealism which Christian life offered' as seen in Christians; to a secretary in the BBC 'the reality of the warmth and inner resources which I observed in Christians'; and to a house surgeon 'the knowledge of Christ's working in another person's life'. **(1967e:71)**

421. The controlling citadel

I have always been impressed by Luke's description in Acts of how the apostles 'reasoned' with people out of the Scriptures and of how many people in consequence were 'persuaded'. Of course, God made us emotional as well as intellectual creatures. Nevertheless, our mind is the controlling citadel of our personality, and true evangelism never bypasses the mind. What the Holy Spirit does in conversion is to bring people to Christ, not in spite of the evidence, but because of the evidence when he opens their minds to attend to it. In the New Testament, conversion is not infrequently portrayed as a response not only to Christ but to 'the truth', even to a 'form of teaching' (Rom. 6:17).   **(1991a:9)**

422. God's eternal calling

'God chose you from the beginning for salvation . . . God called you through the gospel for glory.' There is nothing narrow-minded about the apostle Paul! His horizons are bounded by nothing less than the eternities of the past and of the future. In the eternity of the past God chose us to be saved. Then he called us in time, causing us to hear the gospel, believe the truth and be sanctified by the Spirit, with a view to our sharing Christ's glory in the eternity of the future. In a single sentence the apostle's mind sweeps from 'the beginning' to 'the glory'.   **(1991c:176)**

423. Only two ways

There are according to Jesus only two ways, hard and easy (there is no middle way), entered by two gates, broad and narrow (there is no other gate) trodden by two crowds, large and small (there is no neutral group), ending in two destinations, destruction and life (there is no third alternative). It is hardly necessary to comment that such talk is extremely unfashionable today. People like to be uncommitted. Every opinion poll allows not only for a 'yes' or 'no' answer, but for a convenient 'don't know'. Men are lovers of Aristotle and of his golden mean. The most popular path is the *via media*. To deviate from the middle way is to risk being dubbed an 'extremist' or a 'fanatic'. Everybody resents being faced with the necessity of a choice. But Jesus will not allow us to escape it.   **(1978f:196)**

424. The choice before us

If you suffer from moral anaemia, take my advice and steer clear of Christianity. If you want to live a life of easy-going self-indulgence, whatever you do, do not become a Christian. But if you want a life of self-discovery, deeply satisfying to the nature

God has given you; if you want a life of adventure in which you have the privilege of serving him and your fellow men; if you want a life in which to express something of the overwhelming gratitude you are beginning to feel for him who died for you, then I would urge you to yield your life, without reserve and without delay, to your Lord and Saviour, Jesus Christ. **(1971a:119)**

425. The cost of discipleship

'What can a man give in exchange for himself?' Nothing is valuable enough even to make an offer. Of course it costs to be a Christian; but it costs more not to be. It means losing oneself. **(1971a:118)**

426. 'Only the religious bit?'

The whole of our life belongs to God and is part of his calling, both before conversion and outside religion. We must not imagine that God first became interested in us when we were converted, or that now he is interested only in the religious bit of our lives. **(1992b:139)**

427. True freedom

True freedom is freedom to be our true selves, as God made us and meant us to be. **(1992b:53)**

428. The freedom of the forgiven

Nobody who is unforgiven is free. **(1980h:26)**

429. Free to be ourselves

Jesus Christ calls us to be different from the world around us and from what we ourselves once were. He endows us with gifts that equip us for different tasks and enrich our common life by their very diversity. He provides an authentic norm by which to evaluate alternative expressions of belief and behaviour. Above all, he sets us free, not by granting us a freedom without limits (limitless liberty is an illusion) but by enabling us to be the unique person he created and intends us to be. **(1984b:8)**

430. Sovereign grace

If we ask what caused Saul's conversion, only one answer is possible. What stands out from the narrative is the sovereign grace of God through Jesus Christ. Saul did not 'decide for Christ', as we might say. On the contrary, he was persecuting Christ. It was rather Christ who decided for him and intervened in his life. The evidence for this is indisputable . . . But sovereign grace is gradual grace and gentle grace. Gradually, and without violence, Jesus pricked Saul's mind and conscience with his goads. Then he revealed himself to him by the light and the voice, not in order to overwhelm him, but in such a way as to enable him to make a free response. Divine grace does not trample on human personality. Rather the reverse, for it enables human beings to be truly human. It is sin which imprisons; it is grace which liberates. The grace of God so frees us from the bondage of our pride, prejudice and self-centredness, as to enable us to repent and believe. One can but magnify the grace of God that he should have had mercy on such a rabid bigot as Saul of Tarsus, and indeed on such proud, rebellious and wayward creatures as ourselves.

(1990b:168, 173)

431. A Simon and a Barabbas

In one way, one might say, every Christian is both a Simon of Cyrene and a Barabbas. Like Barabbas we escape the cross, for Christ died in our place. Like Simon of Cyrene we carry the cross, for he calls us to take it up and follow him.   **(1986a:278)**

432. 'In Christ'

If we are in Christ, personally and organically united to him, God blesses us with enormous blessings – a new status (we are put right with him), a new life (we are renewed by the Holy Spirit) and a new community (we are members of God's family).

But how does it happen? We have to come in penitence and faith to Jesus Christ, and commit ourselves to him. It is thus that God unites us to Christ. And this union with him is publicly dramatized in baptism, for to be baptized, Paul wrote, is to be 'baptized into Christ' (Gal. 3:27).   **(1991b:46)**

433. The doctrine of election

To whatever denomination or tradition we may belong, the doctrine of election causes us difficulties and questions. To be sure, it is a truth which runs through Scripture, beginning with God's call of Abraham and later his choice of Israel 'out of all nations' to be his 'treasured possession . . . a kingdom of priests and a holy nation'. This vocabulary is deliberately transferred in the New Testament to the Christian community. Moreover, the topic of election is nearly always introduced for a practical purpose, in order to foster assurance (not presumption), holiness (not moral apathy), humility (not pride) and witness (not lazy selfishness). But still no explanation of God's election is given except God's love. This is clear in Deuteronomy: 'The LORD did not set his affection on you and choose you because you were more numerous than other peoples, for you were the fewest of all peoples. But it was because the LORD loved you . . .' (Dt. 7:7–8). Similarly in 1 Thessalonians 1:4 Paul unites the love of God and the election of God. That is, he chose us because he loves us, and he loves us because he loves us. He does not love us because we are lovable, but only because he is love. And with that mystery we must rest content. **(1991c:31)**

434. The mystery of election

Many mysteries surround the doctrine of election, and theologians are unwise to systematize it in such a way that no puzzles, enigmas or loose ends are left. At the same time, in addition to the arguments developed in the exposition of Romans 8:28–30, we need to remember two truths. First, election is not just a Pauline or apostolic doctrine; it was also taught by Jesus himself. 'I know those I have chosen,' he said. (Jn. 13:18). Secondly, election is an indispensable foundation of Christian worship, in time and eternity. It is the essence of worship to say: 'Not to us, O LORD, not to us, but to your name be the glory' (Ps. 115:1). If we were responsible for our own salvation, either in whole or even in part, we would be justified in singing our own praises and blowing our own trumpet in heaven. But such a thing is inconceivable. God's redeemed people will spend eternity worshipping him, humbling themselves before him in grateful adoration, ascribing their salvation to him and to the Lamb, and acknowledging that he alone is worthy to receive all praise, honour and glory. Why? Because our salvation is due entirely to his grace, will, initiative, wisdom and power. **(1994:268)**

435. The wonder of election

The wonder is not that some are saved and others not, but that anybody is saved at all. **(1994:269)**

436. The call to freedom

Our Christian life began not with our decision to follow Christ but with God's call to us to do so. He took the initiative in his grace while we were still in rebellion and sin. In that state we neither wanted to turn from sin to Christ, nor were we able to. But he came to us and called us to freedom.   **(1968c:139)**

437. God's purpose of grace

God's purpose of election is bound to be mysterious to men, for we cannot aspire to an understanding of the secret thoughts and decisions of the mind of God. However, the doctrine of election is never introduced in Scripture either to arouse or to baffle our carnal curiosity, but always for a practical purpose. On the one hand, it engenders deep humility and gratitude, for it excludes all boasting. On the other, it brings both peace and assurance, for nothing can quieten our fears for our own stability like the knowledge that our safety depends ultimately not on ourselves but on God's own purpose of grace.

(1973b:36)

438. Nominal Christianity

The Christian landscape is strewn with the wreckage of derelict, half-built towers – the ruins of those who began to build and were unable to finish. For thousands of people still ignore Christ's warning and undertake to follow him without first pausing to reflect on the cost of doing so. The result is the great scandal of Christendom today, so-called 'nominal Christianity'.   **(1971a:108)**

439. Called to be holy

Holiness is the very purpose of our election. So ultimately the only evidence of election is a holy life.   **(1979e:38)**

440. Whose decision?

A decision is involved in the process of becoming a Christian, but it is God's decision before it can be ours. This is not to deny that we 'decided for Christ', and freely, but to affirm that we did so only because he had first 'decided for us'. This emphasis on God's gracious, sovereign decision or choice is reinforced by the vocabulary with which it is associated. On the one hand, it is attributed to God's 'pleasure', 'will', 'plan' and 'purpose', and on the other it is traced back to 'before the creation of the world' or 'before time began'. **(1994:249)**

441. 'Your call is clear'

Your call is clear, cold centuries across;
You bid me follow you, and take my cross,
And daily lose myself, myself deny,
And stern against myself shout 'Crucify'.

My stubborn nature rises to rebel
Against your call. Proud choruses of hell
Unite to magnify my restless hate
Of servitude, lest I capitulate.

The world, to see my cross, would pause and jeer.
I have no choice, but still to persevere
To save myself – and follow you from far.
More slow than Magi – for I have no star.

And yet you call me still. Your cross
Eclipses mine, transforms the bitter loss
I thought that I would suffer if I came
To you – into immeasurable gain.

I kneel before you, Jesus, crucified,
My cross is shouldered and my self denied;
I'll follow daily, closely, not refuse
For love of you and man myself to lose.

(1971a:120)

37. TURNING TO CHRIST

442. Our need of Christ

Nothing keeps people away from Christ more than their inability to see their need of him or their unwillingness to admit it. As Jesus put it: 'It is not the healthy who need a doctor, but the sick. I have not come to call the righteous, but sinners' (Mk. 2:17). He was defending against the criticism of the Pharisees his policy of fraternizing with 'tax collectors and "sinners" '. He did not mean by his epigram about the doctor that some people *are* righteous, so that they do not need salvation, but that some people *think* they are. In that condition of self-righteousness they will never come to Christ. For just as we go to the doctor only when we admit that we are ill and cannot cure ourselves, so we will go to Christ only when we admit that we are guilty sinners and cannot save ourselves. The same principle applies to all our difficulties. Deny the problem, and nothing can be done about it; admit the problem, and at once there is the possibility of a solution. It is significant that the first of the 'twelve steps' of Alcoholics Anonymous is: 'We admitted we were powerless over alcohol – that our lives had become unmanageable.'

To be sure, some people insist with great bravado that they are neither sinful nor guilty, and that they do not need Christ. It would be quite wrong to seek to induce guilty feelings in them artificially. But if sin and guilt are universal (as they are), we cannot leave people alone in their false paradise of supposed innocence. The most irresponsible action of a doctor would be to acquiesce in a patient's inaccurate self-diagnosis. Our Christian duty is rather, through prayer and teaching, to bring people to accept the true diagnosis of their condition in the sight of God. Otherwise, they will never respond to the gospel.

(1994:67)

443. An irresistible offer

'Irresistible' is the word an Iranian student used when telling me of his conversion to Christ. Brought up to read the Qur'an, say his prayers and lead a good life, he nevertheless knew that he was separated from God by his sins. When Christian friends brought him to church and encouraged him to read the Bible, he learnt that Jesus Christ had died for his forgiveness. 'For me the offer was irresistible and heaven-sent,' he said, and he cried to God to have mercy on him through Christ. Almost immediately 'the burden of my past life was lifted. I felt as if a huge weight . . . had gone. With the relief and sense of lightness came incredible joy. At last it had happened. I was free of my past. I *knew* that God had forgiven me, and I felt clean. I wanted to shout, and tell everybody.' It was through the cross that the character of God came clearly into focus for him, and that he found Islam's missing dimension, 'the intimate fatherhood of God and the deep assurance of sins forgiven'. **(1986a:42)**

444. A twofold turn

Repentance and faith are in fact the constituent elements of conversion, when viewed from the standpoint of man's experience. For what is conversion but 'turning', and what is 'to be converted' but 'to turn'? The Greek verb is often used in the New Testament in secular, non-theological contexts to describe someone's action in turning round from one direction to another or turning from one place to another. When used in more technical, theological passages the verb has the same meaning. 'You turned to God from idols to serve the living and true God.' 'You were like sheep going astray, but have now returned to the Shepherd and Bishop of your souls' (1 Thes. 1:9; 1 Pet. 2:25).

Conversion therefore involves a twofold turn, a turn from idols and from sin on the one hand, and a turn to the living God and to the Saviour or Shepherd of souls on the other. The 'turn away' the New Testament calls repentance; the 'turn toward' the New Testament calls faith. So repentance plus faith equals conversion, and no man dare say he is converted who has not repented as well as believed. **(1959b:15)**

445. The shortest road

Memory is a precious and blessed gift. Nothing can stab the conscience so wide awake as memories of the past. The shortest road to repentance is remembrance. Let someone once recall what they used to be and reflect on what by God's grace they could be, and they will be led to repent, turning back from their sin to their Saviour. **(1990c:86)**

446. Nature fulfilled

Conversion, although supernatural in its origin, is natural in its effects. It does not distrust nature, but fulfils it, for it puts me where I belong. It relates me to God, to man and to history. It enables me to answer the most basic of all human questions, 'Who am I?' and to say, 'In Christ I am a son of God. In Christ I am united to all the redeemed people of God, past, present and future. In Christ I discover my identity. In Christ I find my feet. In Christ I come home.' **(1968c:102)**

447. The bondage of the old life

Our former life was one of bondage to sin, self, fear and guilt, and to the unseen powers of evil which, because of our estrangement from God, had enslaved us. Did we not sometimes sigh in those days: 'if only I could be liberated from my guilt, from the judgment of God upon my sins, and from the powers of evil which have control over me'? I did. Then I learned that the only way to be set free from sin was for its just penalty to be borne, and that God had done this himself in and through Jesus Christ who died for our sins on the cross. Next I learned that if we become personally united to Jesus Christ by faith, we die with him, his death becomes our death, so that the penalty is paid, the debt is settled, and we are set free from the bondage of the old life. **(1991b:67)**

448. The old life and the new

I find it helpful to think in these terms. Our biography is written in two volumes. Volume one is the story of the old man, the old self, of me before my conversion. Volume two is the story of the new man, the new self, of me after I was made a new creation in Christ. Volume one of my biography ended with the judicial death of the old self. I was a sinner. I deserved to die. I did die. I received my deserts in my Substitute with whom I have become one. Volume two of my biography opened with my resurrection. My old life having finished, a new life to God has begun. **(1966c:49)**

449. Revelation 3:20

Jesus Christ says he is standing knocking at the door of our lives, waiting. Notice that he is standing at the door, not pushing it; speaking to us, not shouting. This is the more remarkable when we reflect that the house is his in any case. He is the architect; he designed it. He is the builder; he made it. He is the landlord; he bought it with his life-blood. So it is his by right of plan, construction and purchase. We are only tenants in a house which does not belong to us. He could put his shoulder to the door; he prefers to put his hand to the knocker. He could command us to open to him; instead, he merely invites us to do so. He will not force an entry into anybody's life. He says (verse 18) 'I counsel you . . .' He could issue orders; he is content to give advice. Such are his condescension and humility, and the freedom he has given us.

(1971a:124)

450. Sudden conversion?

You can become a Christian in a moment, but not a mature Christian. Christ can enter, cleanse and forgive you in a matter of seconds, but it will take much longer for your character to be transformed and moulded to his will. It takes only a few minutes for a bride and bridegroom to be married, but in the rough-and-tumble of their home it may take many years for two strong wills to be dovetailed into one. So when we receive Christ, a moment of commitment will lead to a lifetime of adjustment. **(1971a:126)**

451. Baptism – the sign of entry

Of our saving union with Christ in his death and resurrection, baptism is the sign or 'sacrament'. But baptism is not the means of union. This is clear from a comparison between baptism and circumcision. Baptism is the sign of entry into the new covenant, as circumcision was the sign of entry into the old covenant. Now circumcision is defined by Paul as 'a sign or seal of the righteousness which he [*sc.* Abraham] had *by faith* while he was still uncircumcised' (Rom. 4:11). First Abraham received justification by faith. Then he received circumcision as a sign. It is by faith that we are joined to Christ and so justified and of this faith Abraham and David are the best Old Testament examples. **(1954c:62)**

452. United to Christ

When we become united to Christ by faith, something so tremendous happens that the New Testament cannot find language adequate to describe it. It is a new birth, yes, but also a new creation, a resurrection, light out of darkness, and life from the dead. We were slaves, now we are sons. We were lost, now we have come home. We were condemned and under the wrath of God, now we have been justified and adopted into his family. What subsequent experience can possibly compare with this in importance? We must be careful, in describing deeper experiences, not to denigrate regeneration or to cast a slur on this first, decisive and creative work of God's love.   **(1975b:71)**

453. A new person

A convert to Jesus Christ lives in the world as well as in the church, and has responsibilities to the world as well as to the church. I think it is the tendency of churches to 'ecclesiasticize' their members which has made so many modern Christians understandably wary of conversion and church membership. Conversion must not take the convert out of the world but rather send him back into it, the same person in the same world, and yet a new person with new convictions and new standards. If Jesus' first command was 'Come!', his second was 'Go!', that is, we are to go back into the world out of which we have come, and go back as Christ's ambassadors.   **(1975c:121)**

454. Only a beginning

In Acts 9 we see that conversion is only the beginning. The same grace which brings a person to new birth is able to transform him or her into Christ's image. Every new convert becomes a changed person, and has new titles to prove it, namely a 'disciple' (verse 26) or 'saint' (13), newly related to God, a 'brother' (17) or sister, newly related to the church, and a 'witness' (22:15; 26:16), newly related to the world. If these three relationships – to God, the church and the world – are not seen in professed converts, we have good reason to question the reality of their conversion. But whenever they are visibly present, we have good reason to magnify the grace of God.
(1990b:180)

455. The one reliable evidence

It is only the Lord who knows and recognizes his own people, and can tell the true from the spurious, for only he sees the heart. But though we cannot see the heart, we can see the life, which is the one reliable evidence of the heart's condition, and is apparent to all.   **(1973b:70)**

38. THE NEW BIRTH

456. Not when, but whether

It does not matter at all if, although you know you have turned to Christ, you do not know the date when you did so. Some do; others do not. What matters is not *when* but *whether* we have put our trust in Christ. Jesus called the beginning of our Christian life a second 'birth', and the analogy is helpful in many ways. For example, we are not conscious of our physical birth taking place, and would never have known our birthday if our parents had not told us. The reason we know we were born, even though we do not remember it, is that we are enjoying a life today which we know must have begun at birth. It is much the same with the new birth. **(1991d:24)**

457. The vision of God

The true Christian may be described both as being *from God* (*cf.* 1 Jn. 4:4, 6) and as having *seen God* (1 Jn. 3:6). Birth of God and the vision of God are to some extent equivalent. He who has been born of God has come, with the inner eye of faith, to see God. And this vision of God deeply affects his behaviour. To do good is to give evidence of a divine birth; to do evil is to prove that one has never seen God. **(1988g:232)**

458. The Holy Spirit's work

All four main stages in the great event we call conversion are the work of the Holy Spirit. First, *conviction of sin*. It is the Spirit, Jesus said, who would 'convince the world of sin and of righteousness and of judgment' (Jn. 16:8–11). Next, *faith in Christ*. It is the Spirit who opens the eyes of convicted sinners to see in Jesus their Saviour and Lord, and to believe in him, for 'no one can say "Jesus is Lord" except by the Holy Spirit' (1 Cor. 12:3). Thirdly, the *new birth* is a birth 'of the Spirit' (Jn. 3:6–8). Fourthly, *Christian growth* or sanctification is his work too (2 Cor. 3:18). So the power of the Holy Spirit in evangelism is not optional, but indispensable. **(1975d:34)**

459. Sudden or gradual?

Is conversion sudden or gradual? If by 'conversion' is really meant regeneration, the answer can only be 'sudden', for if words have meaning, 'birth' is a sudden and dramatic crisis. Of course, there are months of preparation before birth. Of course, too, there are years of growth after birth, but birth itself is an almost instantaneous experience.

So it is with the new birth. There may be months in which the Holy Spirit begins to convince a man of his sin and turn his thoughts to Christ as the Saviour of sinners. There may be months in which a man feels himself drawn by the magnetism of Christ. There will also be years of development in the Christian life after the new birth. 'As newborn babes, desire the sincere milk of the Word, that ye may grow thereby' (1 Pet. 2:2). The New Testament speaks of a growth in knowledge and holiness, in faith and love. A Christian's progress is likened to the gradual development of a child into maturity. But the months of pre-natal preparation and the years of post-natal growth must not be allowed to disguise the suddenness of birth itself.

Further, what growth is to birth, sanctification is to justification. Justification, like birth, is sudden. Sanctification, like growth, is gradual. Justification is a legal metaphor and indicates the judge's sentence when he pronounces the sinner righteous. The trial may take some time, and when it is over the justified sinner will take a lifetime to manifest in character the righteousness he has been accorded in standing, but the judge's sentence of justification is pronounced in a matter of seconds.

God's initial work in the soul then, whether we call it regeneration or justification, the experience of a new birth or the reception of a new status, is sudden. It cannot be anything else.   **(1956a:42)**

460. A birth 'from above'

Regeneration is the new birth, and it is absurd to imagine that anybody could ever give birth to himself, either physically or spiritually. The new birth is a birth 'from above', a birth 'of the Spirit', a birth 'of God'. It is God who 'begets' us, putting his Spirit within us, implanting life in our souls and making us partakers of his divine nature. All this is his work alone, making us in Christ a 'new creation'.   **(1967e:104)**

461. Baptism and regeneration

Let me cut the Gordian knot and declare that baptism and

regeneration are not the same thing, that the one neither conveys nor secures the other, that there are baptized people who are not spiritually regenerate, and also, although this is (to say the least) irregular, that there are some regenerate people who are not baptized. Let me emphasize, further, that neither Bible nor Prayer Book teaches that baptism effects regeneration. The expressions in the baptism service which have given rise to this view (for example 'seeing now . . . that this child/person is regenerate') can be properly interpreted only in the light of the whole service. To isolate a text from its context is as irresponsible in the Prayer Book as it is in the Bible, We need to ask ourselves: who is this person who is declared regenerate? It is not just somebody who has been baptized in the name of the Trinity, but somebody who, before being baptized, has publicly professed his repentance, faith and submission, either with his own mouth or (in the case of a child) through the lips of his sponsors. Whether the reformers were right to represent a child as thus speaking is another matter; the point here is that the only children baptized in the Church of England, and the only adults, are *professed believers*. And this is why they are declared regenerate. They are regenerate in the same sense in which they are penitent believers in Christ. This is the hypothetical language which is proper to the administration of sacraments, and which the New Testament itself uses when it attributes to baptism what it elsewhere attributes to grace and faith.

(1967e:110)

462. Sanctification and regeneration

To say that sanctification is a *natural* consequence of regeneration, is not to say that it is an *automatic* consequence. The truly regenerate Christian can still behave badly and thoughtlessly, sin grievously, fail in personal relationships and get into marriage problems. This is evident in the New Testament and in the lives of our fellow Christians, yes, and we know it in our own lives also. Hence the detailed moral instructions which are given in the epistles – about controlling the tongue, about the duty of working hard to earn our living, about being honest, just, hospitable, forgiving and kind, about sexual purity, and about the reciprocal duties between husbands and wives, parents and children, masters and servants. But were these not Christian people, regenerate people, to whom the apostles addressed these admonitions? Yes, they were! But the apostles did not take the holiness of the regenerate for granted; they worked for it by detailed instruction, by exhortation, example and prayer. **(1970b:145)**

463. Initiation into Christ

Initiation into Christ, according to the New Testament, is a single-stage experience, in which we repent, believe, are baptized, and receive both the forgiveness of sins and the gift of the Holy Spirit, after which by the indwelling power of the Spirit we grow into Christian maturity. During this period of growth there may indeed be many deeper, fuller, richer experiences of God; it is the insistence on a two-stage stereotype which we should reject. Moreover, no imposition of human hands is necessary for the accomplishment of the initial saving work of God. To be sure, the laying-on of hands is a significant gesture accompanying prayer for somebody, whether for blessing, comfort, healing or commissioning. And the Anglican Church has retained it in episcopal confirmation, although its purpose in this context is to assure candidates of God's acceptance of them and to introduce them into full church membership, and emphatically not to bestow the Holy Spirit on them. **(1990b:154)**

464. The norm of Christian initiation

The norm of Christian experience, then, is a cluster of four things: repentance, faith in Jesus, water baptism and the gift of the Spirit. Though the perceived order may vary a little, the four belong together and are universal in Christian initiation. The laying-on of apostolic hands, however, together with tongue-speaking and prophesying, were special to Ephesus, as to Samaria, in order to demonstrate visibly and publicly that particular groups were incorporated into Christ by the Spirit; the New Testament does not universalize them. There are no Samaritans or disciples of John the Baptist left in the world today. **(1990b:305)**

465. Evidence of new birth

If you know as a fact that God is righteous, John says, then you will perceive as a logical consequence *that everyone who does what is right has been born of him* (1 Jn. 2:29). The child exhibits the parent's character because he shares the parent's nature. A person's righteousness is thus the evidence of his new birth, not the cause or condition of it. **(1988g:122)**

466. *New birth, new behaviour*

The new birth results in new behaviour. Sin and the child of God are incompatible. They may occasionally meet; they cannot live together in harmony. **(1988g:194)**

467. *Faith, hope and love*

Every Christian without exception is a believer, a lover and a hoper (not necessarily an optimist, since 'optimism' is a matter of temperament, 'hope' of theology). Faith, hope and love are thus sure evidences of regeneration by the Holy Spirit. Together they completely reorientate our lives, as we find ourselves being drawn up towards God in faith, out towards others in love and on towards the parousia in hope. The new birth means little or nothing if it does not pull us out of our fallen introversion and redirect us towards God, Christ and our fellow human beings. **(1991c:30)**

468. *The indispensable sign*

At one of his weekly tea-parties somebody asked Simeon:[1] 'What, Sir, do you consider the principal mark of regeneration?' It was a probing question. With the current popularity of the 'born-again movement', one wonders how the average evangelical believer would reply today. This was Simeon's answer: 'the very first and indispensable sign is self-loathing and abhorrence. Nothing short of this can be admitted as an evidence of a real change . . . I want to see more of this humble, contrite, broken spirit amongst us. It is the very spirit that belongs to self-condemned sinners . . . This sitting in the dust is most pleasing to God . . . give me to be with a broken-hearted Christian, and I prefer his society to that of all the rest . . . Were I now addressing to you my dying words, I should say nothing else but what I have just said. Try to live in this spirit of self-abhorrence, and let it habitually mark your life and conduct.[2]

'Self-loathing', 'self-condemnation', 'self-abhorrence'. The words grate on modern ears. The contemporary craze is for a bigger and better self-image. We are exhorted on all sides to love ourselves, forgive ourselves, respect ourselves, assert ourselves. And to be sure, as in all heresies, there are a few grains of truth in this one. For we should gratefully affirm ourselves as creatures made in the image of God, and as children of God redeemed by Christ and indwelt by his Spirit. In this mercy of God our Creator and Saviour we are to rejoice greatly, and there is much exhortation to such joy in Simeon's sermons.

But to rejoice in God is one thing; to rejoice in ourselves is another. Self-congratulation and the worship of God are mutually incompatible. Those who have a high view of themselves always have a correspondingly low view of God.

(1986c:xxxix)

[1] Charles Simeon (1758–1836) Minister of Holy Trinity Church, Cambridge, 1783–1836.

[2] Quoted in William Carus (editor), *Memoirs of the Life of the Reverend Charles Simeon*, London 1848. pp. 651f.

VIII. LIVING AS A CHRISTIAN

39. Christian assurance
40. Growing and continuing
41. Life in the Spirit
42. Prayer and the Bible
43. Morality and holiness
44. Humility and obedience
45. Vocation and service
46. Freedom and authority
47. The Christian mind

39. CHRISTIAN ASSURANCE

469. Knowing and enjoying

Clearly one cannot enjoy a gift unless one knows that one possesses it. Therefore, if God means us to receive and enjoy eternal life, he must mean us to know we possess it.

(1954c:126)

470. The fundamental ground

The first and fundamental ground of our assurance, because it is the sole ground of our salvation, is 'the finished work of Christ'. Whenever our conscience accuses us, and we feel burdened with guilt, we need to look away from ourselves to Christ crucified. Then again we will have peace. For our acceptance with God depends not on ourselves and what we could ever do, but entirely on Christ and what he has done for all on the cross.

(1991d:29)

471. Father, Son and Spirit

God wants his children to be sure that they belong to him, and does not want us to remain in doubt and uncertainty. So much so, that each of the three persons of the Trinity contributes to our assurance. The witness of God the Holy Spirit confirms the word of God the Father concerning the work of God the Son. The three strong legs of this tripod make it very steady indeed.

(1991d:36)

472. Certainty and humility

Putting together the purposes of Gospel and letters, John's purpose is in four stages, namely that his readers may hear, hearing may believe, believing may live, and living may know. His emphasis is important because it is common today to dismiss any claim to assurance of salvation as presumptuous, and to affirm that no certainty is possible on this side of death. But certainty and humility do not exclude one another. If God's revealed purpose is not only that we should hear, believe and live, but also that we should know, presumptuousness lies in doubting his word, not in trusting it.

(1988g:187)

473. God's great forgiveness

There are some things which Scripture tells us to forget (like the injuries which others do to us). But there is one thing in particular which we are commanded to remember and never to forget. This is what we were before God's love reached down and found us. For only if we remember our former alienation (distasteful as some of it may be to us), shall we be able to remember the greatness of the grace which forgave and is transforming us. **(1979e:96)**

474. Dramatized promises

His Word of promise is not the only means of assurance which God has given us. He knows that our faith is 'brittle', to use Luther's word, and needs strengthening. Or, to change the metaphor, he knows how hard we find it to believe a 'naked' word; so he has graciously 'clothed' it for us to see, in the two sacraments of the gospel. Augustine called them *verba visibilia* (visible words), and Bishop Jewel added that 'the substance of all sacraments is the Word of God'. They dramatize the promises of the gospel in such a way as to evoke and confirm our faith. Baptism, being unique and unrepeatable, is the sacrament of our once-for-all justification; holy communion, being repeatedly enjoyed, is the sacrament of our daily forgiveness. By them we are assured, audibly and visibly, of our acceptance and forgiveness. **(1964:75)**

475. Unchanging grace

Paul is confident of the believer's eternal security, only because he is confident in God's unchanging grace. 'Whom he foreknew, he predestined . . . whom he predestined, he called; whom he called, he justified, he also glorified' (Rom. 8:29-30). This chain of divine grace cannot be broken at any of its links. **(1954c:73)**

476. A solid foundation

The solid foundation on which our hope of glory rests is the love of God. It is because God has set his love upon us that we know, beyond any question or doubt, that he is going to bring us to glory. We believe that we are going to persevere to the end, and we have good grounds for our confidence. It is partly because of the character God is forming in us through suffering that we can be confident ('suffering – endurance – character – hope'). If he is sanctifying us now, he will surely glorify us then. But it is chiefly because of 'the love that will not let us go'.

(1966c:16)

477. God's steadfastness

It is only because God is steadfast, that we can be steadfast too.

(1991c:175)

478. The promise of victory

Romans 8 contains five convictions about God's providence (verse 28), five affirmations about his purpose (29, 30) and five questions about his love (31–39), which together bring us fifteen assurances about him. We urgently need them today, since nothing seems stable in our world any longer. Insecurity is written across all human experience. Christian people are not guaranteed immunity to temptation, tribulation or tragedy, but we are promised victory over them. God's pledge is not that suffering will never afflict us, but that it will never separate us from his love.

(1994:259)

479. The perseverance of the saints

'He who stands firm to the end will be saved' (Mk. 13:13), not because salvation is the reward of endurance, but because endurance is the hallmark of the saved.

(1988g:110)

40. GROWING AND CONTINUING

480. God's grown-up children

God never ceases to be our Father, and we never cease to be his children. But he wants us to become his grown-up children. Dependent and obedient we must always be, yet the obedience we are to give to him must not be slavish, mechanical or grudging, but intelligent, glad and free . . . God treats his children as adults, and gives us the responsibility to discern and decide for ourselves. In this way our obedience becomes creative. It fosters and does not inhibit our growth.   **(1977f:26)**

481. A hearty appetite

There is perhaps no greater secret of progress in Christian living than in healthy, hearty spiritual appetite. Again and again Scripture addresses its promises to the hungry. God 'satisfies him who is thirsty, and the hungry he fills with good things' (Ps. 107:9). If we are conscious of slow growth, is the reason that we have a jaded appetite? It is not enough to mourn over past sin; we must also hunger for future righteousness.   **(1978f:45)**

482. A living relationship

The idea of spiritual growth is foreign to many people, not least in the areas of faith and love. We tend to speak of faith in static terms as something we either have or have not. 'I wish I had your faith,' we say, like 'I wish I had your complexion,' as if it were a genetic endowment. Or we complain 'I've lost my faith,' like 'I've lost my spectacles,' as if it were a commodity. But faith is a relationship of trust in God, and like all relationships is a living, dynamic, growing thing. There are degrees of faith, as Jesus implied when he said, 'You of little faith' and 'I have not found anyone in Israel with such great faith' (Mt. 8:26, 10). It is similar with love. We assume rather helplessly that we either love somebody or we do not, and that we can do nothing about it. But love also, like faith, is a living relationship, whose growth we can take steps to nurture.   **(1991c:144)**

483. What happens if I sin?

'But what happens if and when I sin?' you may ask. 'Do I then forfeit my sonship and cease to be God's child?' No. Think of the analogy of a human family. A boy is offensively rude to his parents. A cloud descends on the home. There is tension in the atmosphere. Father and son are not on speaking terms. What has happened? Has the boy ceased to be a son? No. Their relationship has not changed; it is their fellowship which has been broken. Relationship depends on birth; fellowship depends on behaviour. As soon as the boy apologizes, he is forgiven. And forgiveness restores fellowship. Meanwhile, his relationship has remained the same. He may have been temporarily a disobedient, and even a defiant, son; but he has not ceased to be a son.

So it is with the children of God. **(1971a:135)**

484. Temptation and trial

Although temptations are to be resisted, trials are to be welcomed (Jas. 1:2).The Greek word for 'temptation' and 'trial' is the same, but the meaning is different. A temptation is an enticement to sin which arises from within. A trial is a testing of faith which comes from some external circumstance such as persecution. The value of such trials is that they develop Christian character and 'produce steadfastness' (1:3-4).

(1954c:107)

485. Living the new life

We need to learn to talk to ourselves, and ask ourselves questions: 'Don't you know? Don't you know the meaning of your conversion and baptism? Don't you know that you have been united to Christ in his death and resurrection? Don't you know that you have been enslaved to God and have committed yourself to his obedience? Don't you know these things? Don't you know who you are?' We must go on pressing ourselves with such questions, until we reply to ourselves: 'Yes, I *do* know who I am, a new person in Christ, and by the grace of God I shall live accordingly.'

On 28th May 1972 the Duke of Windsor, the uncrowned King Edward VIII, died in Paris. The same evening a television programme rehearsed the main events of his life. Extracts from earlier films were shown, in which he answered questions about his upbringing, brief reign and abdication. Recalling his boyhood as Prince of Wales, he said: 'My Father [King George V] was a strict disciplinarian. Sometimes when I had done something wrong, he would admonish me saying, "My dear

boy, you must always remember who you are."' It is my conviction that our heavenly Father says the same to us every day: 'My dear child, you must always remember who are you.'
(1994:187)

486. Dead and risen

If Christ's death was a death to sin (which it was), and if his resurrection was a resurrection to God (which it was), and if by faith-baptism we have been united to Christ in his death and resurrection (which we have been), then we ourselves have died to sin and risen to God. We must therefore 'reckon' (AV), 'consider' (RSV), 'regard' (NEB), 'look upon' (JBP) or *count* (NIV) ourselves *dead to sin but alive to God in*, or by reason of our union with, *Christ Jesus* (Rom. 6:11).

This 'reckoning' is not make-believe. It is not screwing up our faith to believe what we do not believe. We are not to pretend that our old nature has died, when we know perfectly well it has not. Instead we are to realize and remember that our former self did die with Christ, thus putting an end to its career. We are to consider what in fact we are, *dead to sin and alive to God* (11), like Christ (10). Once we grasp this, that our old life has ended, with the score settled, the debt paid and the law satisfied, we shall want to have nothing more to do with it.   **(1994:179)**

487. The integrated Christian

Paul loved to liken the Christian life to a race in the arena. Notice that to 'run well' in the Christian race is not just to believe the truth (as if Christianity were nothing but orthodoxy), nor just to behave well (as it were just moral uprightness), but to 'obey the truth', applying belief to behaviour. Only he who obeys the truth is an integrated Christian. What he believes and how he behaves are all of a piece. His creed is expressed in his conduct; his conduct is derived from his creed.   **(1968c:135)**

488. In three dimensions

An integrated Christian is growing in faith, life, and mission as a three-dimensional responsibility.   **(1981c)**

489. Eternal life

To be 'in Christ' is Paul's characteristic description of the Christian. But John uses it too. To be (or to 'live', 1 Jn. 2:6) 'in' him is equivalent to the phrase to 'know' him (3, 4) and to 'love' him (5). Being a Christian consists in essence of a personal relationship to God in Christ, knowing him, loving him, and living in him as the branch lives in the vine (Jn. 15:1ff). This is the meaning of 'eternal life'. **(1988g:96)**

490. Looking back

Memory is a precious gift. To look back can be sinful; but it can also be sensible. To look back with lustful eyes, as Lot's wife did, to the sins of Sodom from which we have been delivered, is to court disaster. To look back wistfully to the easy-going comforts of the world once we have put our hands to the plough is to be unfit for the kingdom of God. But to look back along the way that God has led us is the least that gratitude can do, and to look back to the spiritual heights which once by the grace of God we occupied is to take the first step along the road of repentance. We must not live in the past. But to recall it, and to compare what we are with what we were, is a salutary, and often disturbing, experience. **(1990c:24)**

491. Affirming progress

What should our attitude be to Christians who are doing well in some aspect of their discipleship? Some people resort to congratulations: 'Well done! I think you're marvellous. I'm proud of you.' Others are uncomfortable with this and see its incongruity. It borders on flattery, promotes pride and robs God of his glory. So, although they may thank God privately in their prayers, they say nothing to the person concerned. They replace flattery with silence, which leaves him or her discouraged. Is there a third way, which affirms people without spoiling them? There is. Paul exemplifies it in 2 Thessalonians 1. He not only thanks God for the Thessalonians; he also tells them that he is doing so: 'we ought always to thank God for you. . . we boast about you'. If we follow his example, we will avoid both congratulations (which corrupts) and silence (which discourages). Instead, we can affirm and encourage people in the most Christian of all ways: 'I thank God for you, brother or sister. I thank him for the gifts he has given you, for his grace in your life, for what I see in you of the love and gentleness of Christ'. This way affirms without flattering, and encourages without puffing up. **(1991c:145)**

492. The call to be different

To me the key text of the Sermon on the Mount is Matthew 6:8: 'Do not be like them.' It is immediately reminiscent of God's word to Israel in olden days: 'You shall not do as they do' (Lv. 18:3). It is the same call to be different. **(1978f:18)**

41. LIFE IN THE SPIRIT

493. Fruit and fullness

For many years now I have recited to myself every day the ninefold fruit of the Spirit in Galatians 5:22–23, and have prayed for the fullness of the Spirit. For the chief mark of the fullness of the Spirit is the fruit of the Spirit: love, joy, peace, patience, kindness, goodness, faithfulness, meekness, and self-control. As I meditate every day on these graces, on this fruit of the Spirit, I have noticed recently that the first is love and the last is temperance. Now love is self-giving and temperance is self-control. So holiness concerns what we do with ourselves. It is seen in the mastery of self, and the giving of self.   **(1978d:10)**

494. Fruit by the Spirit

The Christian should resemble a fruit-tree, not a Christmas tree! For the gaudy decorations of a Christmas tree are only *tied* on, whereas fruit *grows* on a fruit-tree. In other words, Christian holiness is not an artificial human accretion, but a natural process of fruit-bearing by the power of the Holy Spirit.
(1970b:143)

495. Faith and love

Faith and love are signs of new birth (1 Jn. 5:1; 4:7). They are also commands. Some people object that faith and love are not amenable to discipline and are beyond the reach of any command. How can you tell me, they ask, to believe what I do not believe or love whom I do not love? The answer to this question lies in the nature of Christian faith and love. It is when faith is regarded as an intuition and love as an emotion that they appear to lie beyond the sphere of duty. But Christian faith is an obedient response to God's self-revelation in Christ. This revelation has a moral content. If people hate the light, it is because their deeds are evil (Jn. 3:19–21) . . . Similarly, Christian love belongs rather to the sphere of action than of emotion. It is not an involuntary, uncontrollable, passion, but unselfish service undertaken by deliberate choice.
(1988g:209)

496. A sign of authenticity

Love is as much a sign of Christian authenticity as is righteousness. **(1988g:164)**

497. God's love and ours

That 'the Father has sent his Son' is not only the chief test of doctrinal orthodoxy but also the supreme evidence of God's love and inspiration of ours. The divine-human person of Jesus Christ, God's love for us, and our love for God and neighbour cannot be separated. The theology which robs Christ of his Godhead, thereby robs God of the glory of his love, and robs us of the one belief that can generate a mature love within us.

(1988g:168)

498. The surest test

Great stress is laid in the New Testament on love as the pre-eminent Christian virtue, the first fruit of the Spirit (Gal. 5:22), the sign of the reality of faith (Gal. 5:6) and the greatest of the three abiding Christian graces, which never ends and without which we are 'nothing' (1 Cor. 13:2, 8, 13). Love is the surest test of having life . . . **(1988g:145)**

499. Love and law

Love is not the finish of the law (in the sense that it dispenses with it); love is the fulfilment of the law (in the sense that it obeys it). What the New Testament says about the law and love is not 'if you love you can break the law', but 'if you love you will keep it'. **(1970b:152)**

500. Love made new

The idea of love in general was not new, but Jesus Christ invested it in several ways with a richer and deeper meaning. First, it was new in the emphasis he gave it, bringing the love commands of Deuteronomy 6:5 and Leviticus 19:18 together and declaring that the whole teaching of the Law and the Prophets hung upon them. Secondly, it was new in the quality he gave it. A disciple was to love others not just as he loved himself but in the same measure as Christ had loved him, with selfless self-sacrifice even unto death. Thirdly, it was new in the extent he gave it, showing in the parable of the good Samaritan that the 'neighbour' we must love is anyone who needs our compassion and help, irrespective of race and rank, and includes our 'enemy' (*cf.* Mt. 5:44). It was also, fourthly, to continue new by our fresh apprehension of it, 'for though doctrinal Christianity is always old, experimental Christianity is always new'. In these ways it was 'a new command', and will always remain new. It is new teaching for the new age which has dawned, new . . . *because the darkness is passing and the true light is already shining* (1 Jn. 1:8).   **(1988g:98)**

501. Love is supreme

Knowledge is vital, faith indispensable, religious experience necessary, and service essential, but Paul gives precedence to love. Love is the greatest thing in the world. For 'God is love' in his innermost being. Father, Son and Spirit are eternally united to each other in self-giving love. So he who is love, and has set his love upon us, calls us to love him and others in return. 'We love because he first loved us' (1 Jn. 4:19). Love is the principal, the paramount, the pre-eminent, the distinguishing character-istic of the people of God. Nothing can dislodge or replace it. Love is supreme.   **(1992b:148)**

502. The servant of the will

There is much misunderstanding about the true nature of love. We may be sure that Jesus did not issue commands which cannot be obeyed. Since he commanded us to love each other (even, elsewhere, our enemies), we must conclude that the loving he meant is not the victim of our emotions, but the servant of our will. We may not feel like loving somebody, but we are commanded to do so. We have to learn deliberately to set our love on people whom we do not naturally like.

(1971b:59)

503. Personal relationships

In Colossians, chapter 3, St Paul gives us two general principles governing personal relationships. Here they are: 'Whatever you do in word or deed, do all in the name of the Lord Jesus.' The second is: 'Whatever you do, work at it heartily as to the Lord and not unto men' (verses 17 and 23). Now let me tell in my own words what I believe these two principles mean. Firstly, I have got to learn, if I am a Christian, to treat other people as if I were Jesus Christ. That is what it means to do everything *in the name of* the Lord Jesus. To do something in somebody else's name, is to do it as his representative. When David stood on the field of battle against Goliath, he said: 'I come to you in the name of the Lord of Hosts.' That is, I am not coming in my own name, I am coming as his representative. So to the Christian, to do everything in the name of Jesus Christ, is to do it as if he were Jesus Christ. I have got to learn, if I am a Christian, to treat other people with the respect and the consideration, the thoughtfulness and the graciousness with which Jesus Christ himself would treat them.

The second principle is the exact opposite. It is to learn to treat people as if *they* were Jesus Christ. I must learn to do everything as unto the Lord. The roles are now reversed and I must learn to treat every person with the graciousness, the humility, the understanding, and the courtesy, not now that he would give to them but that I would give to him . . .

I tell you that these two principles, to treat other people as if they were Christ and as if I were Christ, are as realistic as they are revolutionary. This is not idealist rubbish. This is practical advice about personal relationships.   (1959a:4)

504. Restrictive love

The attempt to restrict the spectrum of those we have to love and serve is a pastime of Pharisees, not Christians. Yet is there not sometimes a reluctance to help people of another faith, whether animist, Hindu, Buddhist or Muslim? Or at least a reluctance to serve them unless we use our aid as a lever to prize their hearts open to receive the gospel? Now of course we want to share the gospel with them, but unless we are motivated by genuine concern for the individual (which is clearly absent if we refuse to help him in other ways) our efforts will be worthless and even dishonouring to God. The love of Christ prompts us to share with people both our material blessings and our spiritual riches.   (1975f:15)

505. Unfailing love

The ground of the joy of believers is that God's *unfailing love* *surrounds* them. Human joy arises from God's love . . .
                 (1988e:44)

506. The pursuit of happiness

Those who pursue happiness never find it. Joy and peace are extremely elusive blessings. Happiness is a will-o'-the-wisp, a phantom. Even as we reach out a hand to grasp it, it vanishes into thin air. For joy and peace are not suitable goals to pursue; they are by-products of love. God gives them to us, not when we pursue *them*, but when we pursue *him* and *others* in love . . . The self-conscious pursuit of happiness will always end in failure. But when we forget ourselves in the self-giving service of love, then joy and peace come flooding into our lives as incidental, unlooked-for blessings. **(1992b:149, 150, 151)**

507. A vision of intimacy

What visions of intimacy with God the word 'sonship' conveys! Access to God and fellowship with God as Father – these are the privileges of his children. Not all human beings are God's children, however. Verse 14 of Romans 8 definitely and deliberately limits this status to those who are being led by the Spirit, who are being enabled by the Spirit to walk along the narrow path of righteousness. To be led by the Spirit and to be sons of God are virtually convertible terms. All who are led by the Spirit of God are the sons of God, and therefore all who are sons of God are led by the Spirit of God. **(1966c:93)**

508. Lift up your eyes!

Lift up your eyes! You are certainly a creature of time, but you are also a child of eternity. You are a citizen of heaven, and an alien and exile on earth, a pilgrim travelling to the celestial city.

I read some years ago of a young man who found a five-dollar bill on the street and who 'from that time on never lifted his eyes when walking. In the course of years he accumulated 29,516 buttons, 54,172 pins, 12 cents, a bent back and a miserly disposition.' But think what he lost. He could not see the radiance of the sunlight, the sheen of the stars, the smile on the face of his friends or the blossoms of springtime, for his eyes were in the gutter. There are too many Christians like that. We have important duties on earth, but we must never allow them to preoccupy us in such a way that we forget who we are and where we are going. **(1977d:90)**

509. Hungry for blessing

Hunger is still an indispensable condition of spiritual blessing, and complacent self-satisfaction its greatest enemy. The *rich* who are pleased with themselves as they are and have no consciousness of need, God sends empty away. **(1966b:48)**

510. The Christian and good works

Although we cannot be saved by works, we also cannot be saved without them. Good works are not the way of salvation, but its proper and necessary evidence. A faith which does not express itself in works is dead. **(1970b:127)**

511. Speaking in tongues

What, then, about the contemporary practice of private tongue-speaking as an aid to personal devotion? Many are claiming to discover through it a new degree of fluency in their approach to God. Others have spoken of a kind of 'psychic release' which they have found liberating and which one would not want to deny them. On the other hand, it needs to be said (from 1 Cor. 14) that if Paul completely forbids public tongue-speaking without interpretation, he strongly discourages private tongue-speaking if the speaker does not understand what he is saying. Verse 13 is often overlooked: 'He who speaks in a tongue should pray for the power to interpret'. Otherwise his mind will be 'unfruitful' or unproductive. So what is he to do? Paul asks himself. His reply is that he will pray and sing 'with the Spirit', but he will do so 'with the mind also'. It is clear that he simply cannot contemplate Christian prayer and praise in which the mind is not actively engaged. **(1975b:113)**

42. PRAYER AND THE BIBLE

512. *The road to maturity*
I do not hesitate to say that the Bible is indispensable to every Christian's health and growth. Christians who neglect the Bible simply do not mature. **(1982b:65)**

513. *Growth by the Word*
The greatest single secret of spiritual development lies in personal, humble, believing, obedient response to the Word of God. It is as God speaks to us through his Word that his warnings can bring us to conviction of sin, his promises to assurance of forgiveness, and his commands to amendment of life. We live and grow by his Word. **(1964:82)**

514. *Who and what we are*
We must keep reminding ourselves what we have and are in Christ. One of the great purposes of daily Bible reading, meditation and prayer is just this, to get ourselves correctly orientated, to remember who and what we are. We need to say to ourselves: 'Once I was a slave, but God has made me his son and put the spirit of his son into my heart. How can I turn back to the old slavery?' Again: 'Once I did not know God, but now I know him and have come to be known by him. How can I turn back to the old ignorance?' **(1968c:110)**

515. *Why read the Bible?*
There is no magic in the Bible or in the mechanical reading of the Bible. No, the written Word points to the Living Word and says to us 'Go to Jesus.' If we do not go to the Jesus to whom it points, we miss the whole purpose of the Bible reading.
(1982b:25)

516. *The battle of the threshold*
We need to win the battle of the prayer threshold. To help me persevere in prayer, I sometimes imagine a very high stone wall, with the living God on the other side of it. In this walled garden he is waiting for me to come to him. There is only one way into the garden – a tiny door. Outside that door stands the devil with a drawn sword, ready to stop me. It is at this point

that we need to defeat the devil in the name of Christ. That is the battle of the threshold.

I think there are many of us who give up praying before we have even tried to fight this battle. The best way to win, in my experience, is to claim the promises of Scripture, which the devil cannot undo. **(1992d:32)**

517. *An authentic activity*

Men and women are at their noblest and best when they are on their knees before God in prayer. To pray is not only to be truly godly; it is also to be truly human. For here are human beings, made by God like God and for God, spending time in fellowship with God. So prayer is an authentic activity in itself, irrespective of any benefits it may bring us. Yet it is also one of the most effective of all means of grace. I doubt if anybody has ever become at all Christlike who has not been diligent in prayer. **(1991d:118)**

518. *Why progress is slow*

I sometimes wonder if the comparatively slow progress towards world peace, world equity and world evangelization is not due, more than anything else, to the prayerlessness of the people of God. **(1991c:125)**

519. *The Lord's prayer*

The three petitions which Jesus puts upon our lips are beautifully comprehensive. They cover, in principle, all our human need – material (daily bread), spiritual (forgiveness of sins) and moral (deliverance from evil). What we are doing whenever we pray this prayer is to express our dependence upon God in every area of our human life. Moreover, a trinitarian Christian is bound to see in these three petitions a veiled allusion to the Trinity, since it is through the Father's creation and providence that we receive our daily bread, through the Son's atoning death that we may be forgiven and through the Spirit's indwelling power that we are rescued from the evil one. No wonder some ancient manuscripts (though not the best) end with the doxology, attributing 'the kingdom and the power and the glory' to this triune God to whom alone it belongs. **(1978f:150)**

520. Balanced devotion

For a healthy Christian life today it is of the utmost importance to follow Paul's example and keep Christian praise and Christian prayer together. Yet many do not manage to preserve this balance. Some Christians seem to do little but pray for new spiritual blessings, apparently oblivious of the fact that God has already blessed them in Christ with every spiritual blessing. Others lay such emphasis on the undoubted truth that everything is already theirs in Christ, that they become complacent and appear to have no appetite to know or experience their Christian privileges more deeply. Both these groups must be declared unbalanced. They have created a polarization which Scripture will not tolerate.   **(1979e:52)**

521. Giving thanks

We are to be 'always and for everything giving thanks' (Eph. 5:20). Most of us give thanks sometimes for some things; Spirit-filled believers give thanks always for all things. There is no time at which, and no circumstances for which, they do not give thanks. They do so 'in the name of our Lord Jesus Christ', that is because they are one with Christ and 'to God the Father', because the Holy Spirit witnesses with their spirit that they are God's children and that their Father is wholly good and wise. Grumbling, one of Israel's besetting sins, is serious because it is a symptom of unbelief. Whenever we start moaning and groaning, it is proof positive that we are not filled with the Spirit. Whenever the Holy Spirit fills believers, they thank their heavenly Father at all times for all things.

(1975b:58)

522. 'By God's will . . .'

Paul's reference to the will of God, in relation to prayer (Rom. 15:32) is very significant. He has prayed earlier that 'now at last by God's will the way may be opened' for him to come to Rome (1:10). Here he again prays that *by God's will* he may come to them. His use of this qualifying clause throws light on both the purpose and the character of prayer, on why and how Christians should pray.

The purpose of prayer is emphatically not to bend God's will to ours, but rather to align our will to his. The promise that our prayers will be answered is conditional on our asking 'according to his will' (1 Jn. 5:14). Consequently every prayer we pray should be a variation on the theme, 'Your will be done' (Mt. 6:10).

What about the character of prayer? Some people tell us, in spite of Paul's earlier statement that 'we do not know what we ought to pray for' (Rom. 8:26), that we should always be precise, specific and confident in what we pray for, and that to add 'if it be your will' is a cop-out and incompatible with faith. In response, we need to distinguish between the general and the particular will of God. Since God has revealed his general will for all his people in Scripture (*e.g.* that we should control ourselves and become like Christ), we should indeed pray with definiteness and assurance about these things. But God's particular will for each of us (*e.g.* regarding a life work and a life partner) has not been revealed in Scripture, so that, in praying for guidance, it is right to add 'by God's will'. If Jesus himself did this in the garden of Gethsemane ('Not my will, but yours be done'; Lk. 22:42), and if Paul did it twice in his letter to the Romans, we should do it too. It is not unbelief, but a proper humility. **(1994:389)**

523. 'Your will be done'

Prayer is not a convenient device for imposing our will upon God, or for bending his will to ours, but the prescribed way of subordinating our will to his. It is by prayer that we seek God's will, embrace it and align ourselves with it. Every true prayer is a variation on the theme, 'Your will be done.' Our Master taught us to say this in the pattern prayer he gave us, and added the supreme example of it in Gethsemane. **(1988g:188)**

524. A new dimension

Prevailing Christian prayer is wonderfully comprehensive. It has four universals, indicated in Ephesians 6:18 by the fourfold use of the word 'all'. We are to pray *at all times* (both regularly and constantly), *with all prayer and supplication* (for it takes many and varied forms), *with all perseverance* (because we need like good soldiers to *keep alert*, and neither give up nor fall asleep), *making supplication for all the saints* (since the unity of God's new society, which has been the preoccupation of this whole letter, must be reflected in our prayers). Most Christians pray sometimes, with some prayers and some degree of perseverance, for some of God's people. But to replace 'some' by 'all' in each of these expressions would be to introduce us to a new dimension of prayer. **(1979e:283)**

525. *The indispensable condition*

Obedience is the indispensable condition, not the meritorious cause, of answered prayer. **(1988g:152)**

43. MORALITY AND HOLINESS

526. Two-dimensional righteousness

It is important to acknowledge that according to Jesus Christian 'righteousness' has two dimensions, moral and religious. Some speak and behave as if they imagine their major duty as Christians lies in the sphere of religious activity, whether in public (church-going) or in private (devotional exercises). Others have reacted so sharply against such an overemphasis on piety that they talk of a 'religionless' Christianity. For them the church has become the secular city, and prayer a loving encounter with their neighbour. But there is no need to choose between piety and morality, religious devotion in church and active service in the world, loving God and loving our neighbour, since Jesus taught that authentic Christian 'righteousness' includes both.   **(1978f:125)**

527. The Christian and the law

What is the Christian's relation to the law? The so-called 'new morality' forces the question upon us with some urgency. It is quite true that Paul says to us, if we are Christians, that we have been set free from the law, that we are no longer under the law and that we must not submit again to the 'yoke of slavery' which is the law (Gal. 5:1). But we must take pains to grasp what he means by these expressions. Our Christian freedom from the law which he emphasizes concerns our relationship to God. It means that our acceptance depends not on our obedience to the law's demands, but on faith in Jesus Christ who bore the curse of the law when he died. It certainly does not mean that we are free to disregard or disobey the law.

On the contrary, although we cannot gain acceptance by keeping the law, yet once we have been accepted we shall keep the law out of love for him who has accepted us and has given us his Spirit to enable us to keep it. In New Testament terminology, although our justification depends not on the law but on Christ crucified, yet our sanctification consists in the fulfilment of the law (Rom. 8:3, 4).

Moreover, if we love one another as well as God, we shall find that we do obey his law because the whole law of God – at least the second table of the law touching our duty to our neighbour – is fulfilled in this one point: 'You shall love your neighbour as yourself', and murder, adultery, stealing, covetousness and false witness are all infringements of this law of love. Paul says the same thing in Galatians 6:2: 'Bear one another's burdens, and so fulfil the law of Christ.'

(1968c:142)

528. Daily living

Paul's epistles refer often to the Christian's private life in the home. He tells husbands to love their wives and wives to be submissive to their husbands; children to obey their parents and parents to discipline their children; slaves to serve their masters and masters to be fair to their slaves. He tells citizens to respect authority and to pay their taxes. He has some very practical and outspoken words to say about telling lies, losing one's temper, stealing, using bad language and being cantankerous; about impurity of deed and word; about wasting time and getting drunk; about being cheerful, appreciative and humble. He urges on his Philippian friends the Christian virtues of humility and unselfishness; of joy, prayer, peace and contentment. It is a Christian duty, he tells the Thessalonians, to work for your living and not be idle. He is quite clear that the Christian life is a life of moral purity. Above all, Christians are not to seek revenge, but to love each other, and all men, for love is the fulfilling of the law.   (1954c:66)

529. Scrupulous honesty

To steal is to rob a person of anything which belongs to him or is due to him. The theft of money or property is not the only infringement of this commandment. Tax evasion is robbery. So is dodging the customs. So is working short hours. What the world calls 'scrounging' God calls stealing. To overwork and underpay one's staff is to break this commandment. There must be few of us, if any, who have been consistently and scrupulously honest in personal and business affairs.

(1971a:68)

530. The bar of conscience

Scripture has a high view of the sacredness of conscience. Conscience is not infallible; it needs to be taught. But though consciences have to be educated, they are never to be violated, even when they are wrong.   (1991b:76)

231

531. A holy life

There is an urgent need for us, as pluralism and relativism spread worldwide, to follow Paul's example and give people plain, practical, ethical teaching. Christian parents must teach God's moral law to their children at home. Sunday school and day school teachers must ensure that their pupils know at least the Ten Commandments. Pastors must not be afraid to expound biblical standards of behaviour from the pulpit, so that the congregation grasps the relationship between the gospel and the law. And right from the beginning converts must be told that the new life in Christ is a holy life, a life bent on pleasing God by obeying his commandments.   **(1991c:77)**

532. The secret of holy living

The major secret of holy living is in the mind.   **(1994:180)**

533. Fruits of holiness

We would surely pursue holiness with greater eagerness if we were convinced that it is the way of life and peace. **(1994:224)**

534. A moral commitment

Love for God is not an emotional experience so much as a moral commitment.   **(1988g:176)**

535. Adorning the gospel

There are many pastors today who, for fear of being branded 'legalists', give their congregation no ethical teaching. How far we have strayed from the apostles! 'Legalism' is the misguided attempt to earn our salvation by obedience to the law. 'Pharisaism' is a preoccupation with the externals and the minutiae of religious duty. To teach the standards of moral conduct which adorn the gospel is neither legalism nor pharisaism but plain apostolic Christianity.   **(1982a:158)**

536. Christian righteousness

When Jesus said that Christian righteousness must exceed pharisaic righteousness (Mt. 5:20), he meant that Christian righteousness accepts the full implications of the law without trying to dodge them. It recognizes that the law's domain extends beyond the actual deed to the word, and beyond the word to the thoughts and motives of the heart. Pharisaic righteousness was an outward conformity to human traditions; Christian righteousness is an inward conformity of mind and heart to the revealed will of God. **(1970b:150)**

537. Holiness defined

Where today is the old evangelical emphasis on holiness? . . . I suspect it has been replaced by an emphasis on experience. Now experience is good, but holiness is better. For holiness is Christlikeness, and Christlikeness is God's eternal purpose for his children. **(1978d:8)**

538. Crucifixion and holiness

There are, in fact, two quite distinct ways in which the New Testament speaks of crucifixion in relation to holiness. The first is our death to sin through identification with Christ; the second is our death to self through imitation of Christ. On the one hand, we have been crucified with Christ. But on the other we have crucified (decisively repudiated) our sinful nature with all its desires, so that every day we renew this attitude by taking up our cross and following Christ to crucifixion (Lk. 9:23). The first is a legal death, a death to the penalty of sin; the second is a moral death, a death to the power of sin. The first belongs to the past, and is unique and unrepeatable; the second belongs to the present, and is repeatable, even continuous. I died to sin (in Christ) once; I die to self (like Christ) daily. **(1994:176)**

539. The need of knowledge

Growth in knowledge is indispensable to growth in holiness. Indeed, knowledge and holiness are even more intimately linked than as means and end. For the 'knowledge' for which Paul prays is more Hebrew than Greek in concept; it adds the knowledge of experience to the knowledge of understanding. **(1979e:54)**

540. No casual discipleship

Holiness is not a condition into which we drift. **(1979e:193)**

541. Sowing to the flesh

To 'sow to the flesh' is to pander to it, to cosset, cuddle and stroke it, instead of crucifying it. The seeds we sow are largely thoughts and deeds. Every time we allow our mind to harbour a grudge, nurse a grievance, entertain an impure fantasy, or wallow in self-pity, we are sowing to the flesh. Every time we linger in bad company whose insidious influence we know we cannot resist, every time we lie in bed when we ought to be up and praying, every time we read pornographic literature, every time we take a risk which strains our self-control, we are sowing, sowing, sowing to the flesh. Some Christians sow to the flesh every day and wonder why they do not reap holiness.

(1968c:170)

542. 'Dead to sin'

In every analogy we need to consider at what point the parallel or similarity is being drawn; we must not press a resemblance at every point. For instance, when Jesus told us to become like little children, he did not mean that we were to copy every characteristic of children (including their immaturity, way-wardness and selfishness), but only one, namely their humble dependence. In the same way, to say that we have 'died' to sin does not mean that we must exhibit every characteristic of dead people, including their insensibility to stimuli. We have to ask ourselves: at what point is the analogy of death being made?

If we answer these questions from Scripture rather than from analogy, from biblical teaching about death rather than from the properties of dead people, we shall find immediate help. Death is represented in Scripture more in legal than in physical terms; not so much as a state of lying motionless but as the grim though just penalty for sin. Whenever sin and death are coupled in the Bible, from its second chapter ('when you eat . . . [i.e. sin], you will surely die') to its last two chapters (where the fate of the impenitent is called 'the second death'), the essential nexus between them is that death is sin's penalty. This is plain also in Romans, in which we read that those who sin 'deserve death' (1:32), that death entered the world through sin (5:12) and that 'the wages of sin is death' (6:23).

Take Christ first: 'the death he died, he died to sin once for all' (Rom. 6:10). The natural and obvious meaning of this is that Christ bore sin's condemnation, namely death. He met its claim, he paid its penalty, he accepted its rewards and he did it 'once for all' (ephapax), an adverb which is many times applied to his atoning death in the New Testament. In consequence, sin has no more claim or demand on him. So God raised him from the dead, in order to demonstrate the satisfactoriness of his sin-bearing, and he now lives for ever to God.

What is true of Christ is equally true of Christians who are united to Christ. We too have 'died to sin', in the sense that through union with Christ we may be said to have borne its penalty. Some may object that we surely cannot speak of our bearing the penalty of our sins, even in Christ, since we cannot die for our own sins; he alone has done that. Is not the suggestion that we could a veiled form of justification by works? But no, it is nothing of the kind. Of course Christ's sin-bearing sacrifice was altogether unique, and we cannot share in its offering. But we can and do share in its benefits by being united to Christ. So the New Testament tells us not only that Christ died instead of us, as our substitute, so that we will never need to die for our sins, but also that he died for us, as our representative so that we may be said to have died in and through him. As Paul wrote elsewhere, for example, 'we are convinced that one died for all, and therefore all died' (2 Cor. 5:14). That is, by being united to him, his death became their death. **(1994:171)**

543. In the real world

Holiness is not a mystical condition experienced in relation to God but in isolation from human beings. You cannot be good in a vacuum but only in the real world of people. **(1979e:184)**

544. Called to be different

Every Christian is called to be different from the world. Indeed, if you do not like the word 'holy' because it sounds too pious to you, try the word 'different'. It is exactly what the word 'holy' means. Somebody who is holy is somebody who is different. He is set apart from the world unto God: his standards are not worldly but godly. He is different. **(1969a:112)**

545. The battle in the mind

It is not enough to *know* what we should be . . . We must go further and set our minds upon it. The battle is nearly always won in the mind. It is by the renewal of our mind that our character and behaviour become transformed. So Scripture calls us again and again to mental discipline in this respect. 'Whatever is true,' it says, 'whatever is honourable, whatever is just, whatever is pure, whatever is lovely, whatever is gracious, if there is any excellence, if there is anything worthy of praise, think about these things' (Phil. 4:8).

Again, 'If . . . you have been raised with Christ, seek the things that are above, where Christ is, seated at the right hand of God. Set your mind on things that are above, not on things that are on earth. For you have died, and your life is hid with Christ in God' (Col. 3:1–2).

Yet again, 'those who live according to the flesh set their minds on the things of the flesh, but those who live according to the Spirit set their minds on the things of the Spirit. To set the mind on the flesh is death, but to set the mind on the Spirit is life and peace' (Rom. 8:5–6).

Self-control is primarily mind-control. What we sow in our minds we reap in our actions. **(1972d:33)**

546. Sowing and reaping

Holiness is a harvest. True, it is 'the fruit (or 'harvest') of the Spirit', in that the Spirit is himself the chief farmer who produces a good crop of Christian qualities in the believer's life. But we have our part to play. We are to 'walk by the Spirit' and 'sow to the Spirit' (Gal. 5:16; 6:8), following his promptings and disciplining ourselves, if we would reap the harvest of holiness. Many Christians are surprised that they are not noticeably growing in holiness. Is it that we are neglecting to cultivate the field of our character? 'Whatever a man sows, that he will also reap' (Gal. 6:7). **(1973b:56)**

547. A paradox of Christian living

It is one of the great paradoxes of Christian living that the whole church is called (and every member of it) as much to involvement in the world as to separation from it, as much to 'worldliness' as to 'holiness'. Not to a worldliness which is unholy, nor to a holiness which is unworldly, but to 'holy worldliness', a true separation to God which is lived out in the world – the world which he made and sent his Son to redeem. **(1970b:191)**

44. HUMILITY AND OBEDIENCE

548. Christian humility

Humility is nothing but the truth. Humility is a synonym for honesty, not hypocrisy. It is not an artificial pretence about myself, but an accurate assessment of myself.   **(1970b:125)**

549. Submissive humility

Submission to the authority of Scripture is *the way of personal Christian humility.* Nothing is more obnoxious in us who claim to follow Jesus Christ than arrogance, and nothing is more appropriate or attractive than humility. And an essential element in Christian humility is the willingness to hear and receive God's Word. Perhaps the greatest of all our needs is to take our place again humbly, quietly and expectantly at the feet of Jesus Christ, in order to listen attentively to his Word, and to believe and obey it. For we have no liberty to disbelieve or disobey him.   **(1992b:184)**

550. A childlike dependence

In his public teaching ministry Jesus commended humility as the pre-eminent characteristic of the citizens of God's kingdom, and went on to describe it as the humility of a child . . .

Many people are puzzled by this teaching, since children are seldom humble in either character or conduct. Jesus must therefore have been alluding to their humility of status, not behaviour. Children are rightly called 'dependants'. They depend on their parents for everything. For what they know they depend on what they have been taught, and for what they have they depend on what they have been given. These two areas are, in fact, the very ones Jesus specifies when he develops the model of a child's humility.   **(1992a:118)**

551. Christ's example

Lowliness was much despised in the ancient world. The Greeks never used their word for humility (*tapeinotēs*) in a context of approval, still less of admiration. Instead they meant by it an abject, servile, subservient attitude, 'the crouching submissiveness of a slave'.[1] Not till Jesus Christ came was a true humility recognized. For he humbled himself. And only he among the world's religious and ethical teachers has set before us as our model a little child. **(1979e:148)**

[1] F. F. Bruce in E. K. Simpson and F. F. Bruce, *Commentary on the Epistles to the Ephesians and the Colossians*, The New International Commentary on the New Testament (Marshall, Morgan and Scott and Eerdmans, 1957), p. 88 note.

552. *The humility of dependence*

Humility to Bash [the Rev. E. J. H. Nash] was synonymous with dependence. He told me several times of the serious illness he had had when he was a young man. When he was at his lowest ebb, and was not at all sure that he would survive, he remembered being so helpless that he needed to be fed. This utter dependence which in a sense was for him the ultimate in humiliation, seems also to have been the beginning of humility. He learned then the inescapable fact of our human dependence on each other, and even more on God. The humility of a little child, to which Jesus several times alluded, is the humility of dependence. It is right to refer to children as 'dependants', for that is what they are, dependent on their parents for everything they possess. **(1992e:86)**

553. *A call to humility*

Nothing is more hostile to spiritual growth than arrogance, and nothing is more conducive to spiritual growth than humility. We need to humble ourselves before the infinite God, acknowledging the limitations of our human mind (that we could never find him by ourselves), and acknowledging our own sinfulness (that we could never reach him by ourselves).

Jesus called this the humility of a little child. God hides himself from the wise and clever, he said, but reveals himself to 'babies' (Mt. 11:25). He was not denigrating our minds, for God has given them to us. Rather was he indicating how we are to use them. The true function of the mind is not to stand in judgment on God's word, but to sit in humility under it, eager to hear it, grasp it, apply it and obey it in the practicalities of daily living. **(1982b:20)**

554. *Life in Christ*

No-one may dare to claim that he lives in Christ and Christ in him unless he is obedient to the three fundamental commands which John has been expounding (1 Jn. 4:24) which are belief in Christ, love for the brothers and moral righteousness. 'Living in Christ' is not a mystical experience which anyone may claim; its indispensable accompaniments are the confession of Jesus as the Son of God come in the flesh, and a consistent life of holiness and love. **(1988g:154)**

555. Pleasing God

Several points may be made in favour of 'pleasing God' as a guiding principle of Christian behaviour. First, it is a radical concept, for it strikes at the roots of our discipleship and challenges the reality of our profession. How can we claim to know and to love God if we do not seek to please him? Disobedience is ruled out. Secondly, it is a flexible principle. It will rescue us from the rigidities of a Christian Pharisaism which tries to reduce morality to a list of do's and don'ts . . . Thirdly, this principle is progressive. If our goal is to be perfectly pleasing to God, we shall never be able to claim that we have arrived . . . **(1991c:79)**

556. The proof of love

If we want to convince Jesus Christ that we love him, there is only one way to do so. It is neither to make protestations of our devotion, nor to work up feelings of affection toward him, nor to sing hymns of personal piety, nor even to give ourselves to the service of humanity. It is to obey his commandments. Jesus demonstrated his love for the Father by his obedience ('I do as the Father has commanded me', Jn. 14:31); we must demonstrate our love for Christ by our obedience. **(1971b:39)**

557. Words and deeds

John does not mince his words. If how a person behaves contradicts what he says, *he is a liar.* To claim to know God and have fellowship with God while we walk in the darkness of disobedience is to lie (1 Jn. 1:6; 2:4). To claim to possess the Father while denying the deity of the Son is to lie (2:22–23). To claim to love God while hating our brothers is also to lie. These are the three black lies of the letter: moral, doctrinal and social. We may insist that we are Christian, but habitual sin, denial of Christ or selfish hatred would expose us as liars. Only holiness, faith and love can prove the truth of our claim to know, possess and love God. **(1988g:173)**

558. Reputation and reality

The distinction between reputation and reality, between what human beings see and what God sees, is of great importance to every age and place. Although we have responsibilities to others, we are primarily accountable to God. It is before him that we stand, and to him that one day we must give an account. We should not therefore rate human opinion too highly, becoming depressed when criticized and elated when flattered. We need to remember that 'The LORD does not look at the things man looks at. Man looks at the outward appearance, but the LORD looks at the heart' (1 Sa. 16:7). He reads our thoughts and knows our motives. He can see how much reality there is behind our profession, how much life behind our façade. **(1990c:78)**

559. Integrated discipleship

There is no more integrating Christian principle than the affirmation 'Jesus Christ is Lord'. It is of the essence of integrated discipleship that we both confess his lordship with our lips and enthrone him as Lord in our hearts. We assume the easy yoke of his teaching authority. We seek to 'take captive every thought to make it obedient to Christ' (2 Cor. 10:5). And when Jesus is Lord of our beliefs, opinions, ambitions, standards, values and lifestyle, then we are integrated Christians, since then 'integrity' marks our life. Only when *he* is Lord do *we* become whole. **(1992b:177)**

560. Selective discipleship

'False Christs will arise,' Jesus prophesied. And it has been so. There have been religious quacks advancing great claims for themselves, and poor psychotics saying 'I am Jesus Christ.' There have also been misrepresentations of Christ, caricatures which depict him as fiery zealot, failed superstar or circus clown. And coming nearer home, there are our own distorted images of Jesus.

'Follow me,' he said. 'Yes, Lord,' comes our glib reply, 'we will follow you.' But which Christ are we following? The Christ some follow breathes love but never judgment, brings comfort but never challenge; while others among us are alert to his commission to evangelize, but have somehow never heard his call to care for the poor, the sick, the hungry and the deprived.

The apostles took up the theme of following Jesus. We are to 'imitate' him, they wrote, to 'follow in his steps'. What it will mean to do this depends on our understanding of the Jesus in whose shoes we are to walk. So let's look again for the *real* Jesus, the authentic Jesus of the Gospel records, over against the popular dreams which men have dreamed. Certainly our Christian lifestyle depends on the kind of Christ we envisage and believe in. **(1975f:3)**

561. *Present responsibilities*

We cannot tamper with God's clock. We have to be content to wait for his time. And meanwhile we are to pursue all the more conscientiously our duties on earth. Was it not a reluctance to do this on the part of the Gadarene demoniac which called forth such stern words from Jesus? This man, formerly naked, demented and uncontrollable but now 'dressed and in his right mind', begged Jesus that he might 'go *with him*'. It was an understandable appeal. He had been made whole. Jesus had transformed him into a new person. Naturally, he wanted to enjoy an uninterrupted, undistracted fellowship with his deliverer. He would certainly not return to the tombs or the mountains in which he had previously roamed, tormenting himself. Nor had he any particular wish to go to the nearby village in which presumably he had been born and brought up. No, he wanted to stay with Jesus. Who can blame him? But Jesus refused and said to him 'Go home to your family and tell them how much the Lord has done for you, and how he has had mercy on you' (see Mk. 5:1–20). He had responsibilities of witness and service which he must not shirk.

That man was the forerunner of millions of other followers of Jesus – pietistic, escapist Christians – who are anxious to be 'with Jesus' in the sense of opting out of the world. They want to telescope the stages of salvation and jump straight into heaven. It is understandable, but it is also reprehensible. We have to learn to be 'with Christ' now, by faith and not by sight, in the rough and tumble of earthly duty, before we are taken to be 'with Christ' in the everlasting peace of his heaven.

(1991b:63)

562. *Treasure upon earth*

It is important to face squarely and honestly the question: what was Jesus prohibiting when he told us not to lay up treasure for ourselves on earth? It may help if we begin by listing what he was (and is) not forbidding. First, there is no ban on possessions in themselves; Scripture nowhere forbids private property.

Secondly, 'saving for a rainy day' is not forbidden to Christians, or for that matter a life assurance policy which is only a kind of saving by self-imposed compulsion. On the contrary, Scripture praises the ant for storing in the summer the food it will need in the winter, and declares that the believer who makes no provision for his family is worse than an unbeliever (Pr. 6:6ff.; 1 Tim. 5:8). Thirdly, we are not to despise, but rather to enjoy, the good things which our Creator has given us richly to enjoy (1 Tim. 4:3–4; 6:17). So neither having possessions, nor making provision for the future, nor enjoying the gifts of a good Creator is included in the ban on earthly treasure-storage.

What then? What Jesus forbids his followers is the *selfish* accumulation of goods (NB 'Do not lay up *for yourselves* treasures on earth'); extravagant and luxurious living; the hardheartedness which does not feel the colossal need of the world's under-privileged people; the foolish fantasy that a person's life consists in the abundance of his possessions (Lk. 12:15); and the materialism which tethers our hearts to the earth. **(1978f:154)**

563. A simple lifestyle

What does it mean for the affluent to develop a simple style of living? . . . The truth is that concepts like 'poverty', 'simplicity' and 'generosity' are all relative and are bound to mean different things to different people. For example, running water, let alone constant hot water, is regarded as a wonderful luxury by those who have to queue for water at the village well, which sometimes dries up. But in other parts of the world it can hardly be regarded as incompatible with 'a simple lifestyle'. Scripture lays down no absolute standards. On the one hand, it gives no encouragement to an austere and negative asceticism, for it does not forbid the possession of private property, and it commands us to enjoy with gratitude the good gifts of our Creator. On the other hand, it implies that some measure of equality is more pleasing to God than disparity, and its appeal to believers to be generous is based on the grace of our Lord Jesus Christ, because grace means generosity (2 Cor. 8:8–15). **(1975d:24)**

564. 'Jesus is Lord'

The two-word affirmation *Kyrios Iēsous*[Jesus is Lord] sounded pretty harmless at first hearing. But it has far-reaching ramifications. Not only does it express our conviction that he is God and Saviour, but it also indicates our radical commitment to him. The dimensions of this commitment are intellectual (bringing our minds under Christ's yoke), moral (accepting his standards and obeying his commands), vocational (spending our lives in his liberating service), social (seeking to penetrate society with his values), political (refusing to idolize any human institution) and global (being jealous for the honour and glory of his name). **(1992b:98)**

45. VOCATION AND SERVICE

565. Called individually

In the New Testament the Greek verb to 'call' occurs about 150 times, and in most cases of God calling human beings. In the Old Testament God called Moses, Samuel and the prophets; in the New Testament Jesus called the Twelve and later Saul of Tarsus. Today, although we are neither prophets nor apostles, he still calls us into his service. It is a wonderful fact that God cares about us enough to call us personally and individually. In consequence, God is 'he who called you' (*e.g.* Gal. 5:8; 1 Pet. 1:15); and we are 'called according to his purpose' (*e.g.* Rom. 8:28; Heb. 9:15). **(1992b:132)**

566. Christian vocation

Vocation is one of many biblical words whose meaning over the passage of the years has shrunk. It is now used in a much narrower sense than its biblical meaning. If somebody asks you what your vocation is, it is a polite way of asking you what your job is and they expect the answer 'I am a doctor' or 'I am a teacher' or 'I am something else'. Vocational training, for example, normally means training for a particular career, but that is not the biblical meaning of the word. In biblical usage, vocation has a much broader, a much bigger and, I venture to say, a much nobler meaning than simply our job . . .

The point to make from Scripture about our calling or our vocation is that when God calls us he is not calling us primarily to do something but to be something. Our calling, according to Scripture, concerns much more our character and what kind of person we are than simply what our job is. **(1980g:13)**

567. Stretched in service

Every honourable work, whether manual or mental or both, whether waged or voluntary, however humble or menial, needs to be seen by Christians as some kind of cooperation with God, in which we share with him in the transformation of the world which he has made and committed to our care. This applies alike to industry and commerce, to public services and the professions, and to full-time home-making and motherhood. The great evil of unemployment is that some people are denied this privilege. As for the particular form which our partnership with God will take (*i.e.*, in more mundane terms, what career we will follow, what job we will take), this will depend more than anything else on our temperament and talents, education and training. We should want to be stretched in the service of God, so that everything we are and have is fulfilled, not frustrated. **(1991d:148)**

568. *Every Christian's calling*

I have suggested that the whole church is in a sense a 'diaconate' because it is called to *diakonia*, to service. 'I am among you as one who serves,' Jesus said (Lk. 22:27) and gave a visual demonstration of his words by girding himself with a servant's apron and washing his disciples' feet. Then, when he had resumed his place at supper, he said to them:

> if I . . . your Lord and Teacher, have washed your feet, you also ought to wash one another's feet. For I have given you an example, that you also should do as I have done to you. Truly, truly, I say to you, a servant is not greater than his master (Jn. 13:14–16).

So every Christian is called to service . . .

The opportunities for *diakonia*, for a ministry in which Christian people may serve both God and man, are extremely numerous. There is the vocation of parents, especially of the mother, to bring up the children 'in the discipline and instruction of the Lord' (Eph. 6:4), and to make the Christian home a place of love, hospitality and peace. There is a Christian's job, to be regarded primarily neither as a way to earn his living nor as a contribution to his country's economic stability, nor as a useful sphere of witness and evangelism – not in fact as a means to these or any other estimable ends – but as an end in itself, the *diakonia* of a Christian man, who is seeking to co-operate with the purpose of God in securing the welfare of men. There are also abundant openings for alert Christians in public service, through voluntary organizations, and among underprivileged and unwanted people in the neighbourhood.

But apart from the home, the job and the neighbourhood, most Christians will wish to be of service also in and through the local church to which they belong. It is fashionable nowadays, at least among more radical writers, to deride the notion of 'church service' as a regrettable kind of ecclesiastical self-centredness, and to insist that the proper sphere of a Christian's service is not the church but the world. I do not deny the truth contained in this assertion. No Christian should live out his entire spare-time life in the sheltered seclusion of the church; he has been sent by his Master into the world, there to serve others humbly in his name. Yet we must not become unbalanced in applying this principle, either by denying that some church service is rightly church-centred or by asserting that it is all of this kind.   **(1969b:48)**

569. No associate members

We must expect every Christian believer to be an active church member. We cannot afford to have associate members who want privileges without responsibilities.   **(1952:9)**

570. On fire for Christ

The idea of being on fire for Christ will strike some people as dangerous emotionalism. 'Surely,' they will say, 'we are not meant to go to extremes? You are not asking us to become hot-gospel fanatics?' Well, of course, it depends what you mean. If by 'fanaticism' you really mean 'wholeheartedness', then Christianity is a fanatical religion and every Christian should be a fanatic. But wholeheartedness is not the same as fanaticism. Fanaticism is an unreasoning and unintelligent wholeheartedness. It is the running away of the heart with the head. At the end of a statement prepared for a conference on science, philosophy and religion at Princeton University in 1940 came these words: 'Commitment without reflection is fanaticism in action; but reflection without commitment is the paralysis of all action.' What Jesus Christ desires and deserves is the reflection which leads to commitment and the commitment which is born of reflection. This is the meaning of wholeheartedness, of being aflame for God.   **(1990c:115)**

571. A twofold calling

In general terms, in spite of our specialist callings, every Christian is sent into the world as both a witness and a servant. Whenever we see someone in need, whether that need is spiritual or physical or social, if we have the wherewithal to meet it, we must do so; otherwise we cannot claim to have God's love dwelling in us (1 Jn. 3:16). Often people have more than one need, and if we love them with God's love we shall do our utmost to relieve their needs. It is then, too, that they are most likely to believe. Verbal witness is not enough. As Jesus said, it is when people 'see our good works' that our light shines most brightly and will give glory to our heavenly father (Mt. 5:16). **(1980e)**

572. A Christian life work

We often give the impression that if a young Christian man is really keen for Christ he will undoubtedly become a foreign missionary, that if he is not quite as keen as that he will stay at home and become a pastor, that if he lacks the dedication to be a pastor, he will no doubt serve as a doctor or a teacher, while those who end up in social work or the media or (worst of all) in politics are not far removed from serious backsliding! It seems to me urgent to gain a truer perspective in this matter of vocation. Jesus Christ calls all his disciples to 'ministry', that is, to service. He himself is the Servant *par excellence*, and he calls us to be servants too. This much then is certain: if we are Christians we must spend our lives in the service of God and man. The only difference between us lies in the nature of the service we are called to render. **(1975c:31)**

573. Christian penetration

Christians should seek to penetrate the world of the mass media, and equip themselves as television script writers, producers and performers. We can hardly complain of the low standard of many current programmes if we take no constructive initiatives to provide alternatives which are not only technically equal if not better, but more wholesome as well. In previous eras, as each new medium of communication has been developed (writing, painting, music, drama, print, film, radio), Christians have been among the first to discern its potential and to press it into the service of worship and evangelism. It must be the same with television. Indeed, in some parts of the world, it already is. **(1982a:75)**

574. Testing Christian vocation

It seems true to say that God seldom calls people to a wider ministry before they have first proved themselves in a narrower; and the best and most natural context in which to put to the test an incipient sense of vocation is the regular evangelistic outreach of the local church. **(1967e:88)**

575. Discovering the will of God

Jesus himself prayed, 'Not my will but yours be done,' and taught us to pray, 'May your will be done on earth as in heaven.' Nothing is more important in life than to discover and do the will of God. Moreover, in seeking to discover it, it is essential to distinguish between his 'general' and his 'particular' will. The former is so called because it relates to the generality of his people and is the same for all of us, *e.g.* to make us like Christ. His particular will, however, extending to the particularities of our life, is different for each of us, *e.g.* what career we shall follow, whether we should marry, and if so whom. Only after this distinction has been made can we consider how we may find out *what the will of the Lord is* (Eph. 5:17). His 'general' will is found in Scripture; the will of God for the people of God has been revealed in the Word of God. But we shall not find his 'particular' will in Scripture. To be sure we shall find general principles in Scripture to guide us, but detailed decisions have to be made after careful thought and prayer and the seeking of advice from mature and experienced believers. **(1979e:203)**

576. Divine guidance

Take our need of divine guidance. Too many people regard it as an alternative to human thought, even a convenient device for saving them the bother of thinking. They expect God to flash on to their inner screen answers to their questions and solutions to their problems, in such a way as to bypass their minds. And of course God is free to do this; perhaps occasionally he does. But Scripture gives us the warrant to insist that God's normal way of guiding us is rational, not irrational, namely through the very thought processes which he has created in us.

Psalm 32 makes this clear. Verse 8 contains a marvellous threefold promise of divine guidance, in which God says, 'I will instruct you and teach you in the way you should go; I will counsel you and watch over you' (RSV 'counsel you with my eye upon you'). But *how* will God fulfil his promise? Verse 9 continues: 'Do not be like the horse or the mule, which have no understanding, but must be controlled by bit and bridle or they will not come to you.' If we put together the promise and the prohibition, what God is saying to us is this: 'I promise that I will guide you, and show you the way to go. But do not expect me to guide you as you guide horses and mules (namely by force, not intelligence), for the simple reason that you are neither a horse nor a mule. They lack "understanding", but you don't. Indeed, I myself have given you the precious gift of understanding. Use it! Then I will guide you *through* your minds.' **(1992b:117)**

577. The choice of Matthias

It is instructive to note the cluster of factors which contributed to the discovery of God's will in this matter. First came the general leading of Scripture that a replacement should be made (Acts 1:16–21). Next, they used their common sense that if Judas' substitute was to have the same apostolic ministry he must also have the same qualifications, including an eye-witness experience of Jesus and a personal appointment by him. This sound deductive reasoning led to the nomination of Joseph and Matthias. Thirdly, they prayed. For though Jesus had gone, he was still accessible to them by prayer and was acknowledged as having a knowledge of hearts which they lacked. Finally, they drew lots, by which they trusted Jesus to make his choice known. Leaving aside this fourth factor, because the Spirit has now been given us, the remaining three (Scripture, common sense and prayer) constitute a wholesome combination through which God may be trusted to guide us today. **(1990b:58)**

578. Take time . . .

It is a mistake to be in a hurry or to grow impatient with God. It took him about 2,000 years to fulfil his promise to Abraham in the birth of Christ. It took him eighty years to prepare Moses for his life work. It takes him about twenty-five years to make a mature human being. So then, if we *have* to make a decision by a certain deadline, we must make it. But if not, and the way forward is still uncertain, it is wiser to wait. I think God says to us what he said to Joseph and Mary when sending them into Egypt with the child Jesus: 'Stay there until I tell you' (Mt. 2:13). In my experience, more mistakes are made by precipitate action than by procrastination. **(1992b:131)**

579. Love and service

If love and truth go together, and love and gifts go together, so do love and service, since true love always expresses itself in service. To love is to serve. We are left, then, with these four aspects of Christian life forming a ring or a circle which cannot be broken – love, truth, gifts and service. For love issues in service, service uses the gifts, the highest gift is the teaching of the truth, but truth must be spoken in love. Each involves the others, and wherever you begin all four are brought into operation. Yet 'the greatest of these is love' (1 Cor. 13:13).

(1975b:117)

580. No pains, no gains

Why should we *expect* our Christian life and service to be easy? The Bible never gives us any such expectation. Rather the reverse: the Bible says again and again, No cross, no crown; no rules, no wreath; no pains, no gains. It is this principle which took Christ through lowly birth and suffering death, to his resurrection and his reign in heaven. It is this principle that brought Paul his chains, and his prison cell, in order that the elect might obtain salvation in Jesus Christ. It is this principle which makes the soldier willing to endure hardship, the athlete discipline, the farmer toil. Do not expect Christian service to be easy. **(1969a:83)**

581. Only two ways

Ultimately there are only two controlling ambitions, to which all others may be reduced. One is our own glory, and the other God's. The fourth evangelist set them in irreconcilable opposition to each other, and in doing so disclosed Christ's fundamental quarrel with the Pharisees: 'they loved the glory of men', he wrote, 'more than the glory of God' (Jn. 12:43).

(1970b:192)

582. Contrasting ambitions

In the end, just as there are only two kinds of piety, the self-centred and the God-centred, so there are only two kinds of ambition: one can be ambitious either for oneself or for God. There is no third alternative. **(1978f:172)**

583. Nothing wasted, everything used

It seems to me fully compatible with our Christian doctrines of creation and redemption that we should talk to ourselves somewhat as follows: 'I am a unique person. (That is not conceit. It is a fact. If every snowflake and every blade of grass is unique, how much more is every human being?) My uniqueness is due to my genetic endowment, my inherited personality and temperament, my parentage, upbringing and education, my talents, inclinations and interests, my new birth and spiritual gifts. By the grace of God I am who I am. How then can I, as the unique person God has made me, be *stretched* in the service of Christ and of people, so that nothing he has given me is wasted, and everything he has given me is used?'

(1992b:144)

584. True greatness

Why did Jesus equate greatness with service? Must not our answer relate to the intrinsic worth of human beings, which was the presupposition underlying his own ministry of self-giving love, and which is an essential element of the Christian perspective? If human beings are Godlike beings, then they must be served not exploited, respected not manipulated.

(1990a:376)

585. 'As if Jesus Christ . . . '

A servant girl, who was once asked how she knew she was a converted Christian, replied: 'Well, you see, I used to sweep the dust under the mat, but now I don't.' It is possible to visit somebody else as if Jesus Christ lived there, to type a letter as if Jesus Christ were going to read it, to serve a customer as if Jesus Christ had come shopping that day, and to nurse a patient as if Jesus Christ were in that hospital bed. It is possible to cook a meal as if we were Martha in the kitchen, and Jesus Christ were going to eat it. **(1991b:79)**

586. Serving and waiting

'Serving' and 'waiting' go together in the experience of converted people. Indeed, this is at first sight surprising, since 'serving' is active, while 'waiting' is passive. In Christian terms 'serving' is getting busy for Christ on earth, while 'waiting' is looking for Christ to come from heaven. Yet these two are not incompatible. On the contrary, each balances the other. On the one hand, however hard we work and serve, there are limits to what we can accomplish. We can only improve society; we cannot perfect it. We shall never build a utopia on earth. For that we have to wait for Christ to come. Only then will he secure the final triumph of God's reign of justice and peace. On the other hand, although we must look expectantly for the coming of Christ, we have no liberty to wait in idleness, with arms folded and eyes closed, indifferent to the needs of the world around us. Instead, we must work even while we wait, for we are called to serve the living and true God.

Thus working and waiting belong together. In combination they will deliver us both from the presumption which thinks we can do everything and from the pessimism which thinks we can do nothing.   **(1991c:41)**

46. FREEDOM AND AUTHORITY

587. 'When we get freedom . . . '

Freedom is much misunderstood. Even those who talk loudest and longest about freedom have not always paused first to define what they are talking about. A notable example is the Marxist orator who was waxing eloquent on the street corner about the freedom we would all enjoy after the revolution. 'When we get freedom', he cried, 'you'll all be able to smoke cigars like that,' pointing at an opulent gentleman walking by.

'I prefer my fag,' shouted a heckler.

'When we get freedom,' the Marxist continued, ignoring the interruption and warming to his theme, 'you'll all be able to drive in cars like that,' pointing to a sumptuous Mercedes which was driving by.

'I prefer my bike,' shouted the heckler.

And so the dialogue continued until the Marxist could bear his tormentor no longer. Turning on him, he said: 'When we get freedom, you'll do what you're told.'   **(1992b:47)**

588. True freedom

True freedom is not freedom from responsibility to God and others in order to live for ourselves, but freedom from ourselves in order to live for God and others.   **(1991c:91)**

589. Salvation is freedom

To be saved by Jesus Christ is to be set free.   **(1992b:47)**

590. Illusory freedom

According to the first two chapters of Genesis, God created mankind male and female to be both morally responsible (receiving commandments) and free (invited but not coerced into loving obedience). We cannot therefore acquiesce either in licence (which denies responsibility) or in slavery (which denies freedom). Christians know from both Scripture and experience that human fulfilment is impossible outside some context of authority. Freedom unlimited is an illusion. The mind is free only under the authority of truth, and the will under the authority of righteousness. It is under Christ's yoke that we find the rest he promises, not in discarding it.   **(1982a:56)**

591. God's created norms

There can be no 'liberation' from God's created norms; true liberation is found only in accepting them. **(1990a:348)**

592. Inward freedom

Jesus Christ gives an inward freedom of the spirit which even the most oppressive tyrant cannot destroy. Think of Paul in prison: was he not free? **(1975c:100)**

593. The ennobling gift

'I counsel you . . . ' (Rev. 3:18). Perhaps we could first observe the fact that we have a God who is content to give advice to his creatures. I can never read this verse without being strangely moved. He is the great God of the expanding universe. He has countless galaxies of stars at his fingertips. The heaven and the heaven of heavens cannot contain him. He is the Creator and sustainer of all things, the Lord God Almighty. He has the right to issue orders for us to obey. He prefers to give advice which we need not heed. He could command; he chooses to counsel. He respects the freedom with which he has ennobled us.

(1990c:119)

594. The authority of truth

There is only one authority under which the mind is free, and that is the authority of truth. The mind is not free if it is believing lies. On the contrary, it is in bondage to fantasy and falsehood. It is free only when it is believing the truth, and this is so whether the truth in question is one of science or of Scripture. **(1991b:60)**

595. True and false authority

Christians distinguish between true and false authority, that is, between the tyranny which crushes our humanity and the rational, benevolent authority under which we find our authentic human freedom. **(1982a:52)**

596. Freedom and authority

Tyranny excludes freedom, and is therefore fundamentally opposed to authentic humanness. But authority is not identical with tyranny. And Christians want to add that if tyranny destroys freedom, a right authority guarantees it . . . A relationship of submission to Christ, far from crushing our personalities, enables them to develop. Just as children grow most naturally into maturity within the loving discipline of a secure and happy home, so Christians grow into maturity in Christ under his loving authority. To lose ourselves in the service of Christ is to find ourselves. His lordship in our lives spells not frustration but fulfilment and freedom. Such is the Christian conviction . . . **(1991b:48)**

47. THE CHRISTIAN MIND

597. Confidence and doubt

A Christian mind asks questions, probes problems, confesses ignorance, feels perplexity, but does these things within the context of a profound and growing confidence of the reality of God and of his Christ. We should not acquiesce in a condition of basic and chronic doubt, as if it were characteristic of Christian normality. It is not. It is rather a symptom of spiritual sickness in our spiritually sick age. **(1982a:86)**

598. The conversion of the mind

No man or woman is truly converted who is not intellectually converted. And nobody can claim to be intellectually converted who has not brought his or her mind into submission to the authority of Jesus as Lord. **(1977h:22)**

599. The yoke of Christ

To bring our minds under Christ's yoke is not to deny our rationality but to submit to his revelation. **(1991b:53)**

600. Full hearts and empty heads

Christianity lays great emphasis on the importance of knowledge, rebukes anti-intellectualism for the negative, paralysing thing it is, and traces many of our problems to our ignorance. Whenever the heart is full and the head is empty, dangerous fanaticisms arise. **(1991d:41)**

601. Accepted norms?

The morally 'disordering' influence of television is more subtle and insidious than direct incitement. What happens to all of us, unless our powers of moral judgment are acute and alert, is that our understanding of what is 'normal' begins to be modified. Under the impression that 'everybody does it', and that nobody nowadays believes much in God or in absolutes of truth and goodness, our defences are lowered and our values imperceptibly altered. We begin to assume that physical violence (when we are provoked), sexual promiscuity (when we are aroused) and extravagant consumer expenditure (when we are tempted) are the accepted norms of western society at the end of the twentieth century. We have been conned. (1982a:73)

602. Theological enquiry

We need to encourage Christian scholars to go to the frontiers and engage in the debate, while at the same time retaining their active participation in the community of faith. I know this is a delicate issue, and it is not easy to define the right relations between free enquiry and settled faith. Yet I have often been disturbed by the loneliness of some Christian scholars. Whether it is they who have drifted away from the fellowship, or the fellowship which has allowed them to drift, in either case their isolation is an unhealthy and dangerous condition. As part of their own integrity Christian scholars need both to preserve the tension between openness and commitment, and to accept some measure of accountability to one another and responsibility for one another in the body of Christ. In such a caring fellowship I think we might witness fewer casualties on the one hand and more theological creativity on the other. (1982a:87)

603. Anti-intellectualism

Anti-intellectualism and the fullness of the Spirit are mutually incompatible, because the Holy Spirit is the Spirit of truth.
(1990b:82)

604. The peril of isolation

The greatest peril to which any thinker is exposed is the isolation of his ivory tower. (1978c:180)

605. Knowing and reckoning

The secret of holy living is in *knowing* (Rom. 6:6) that our old self was crucified with Christ. It is in *knowing* (verse 3) that baptism into Christ is baptism into his death and resurrection. It is in *reckoning*, intellectually realizing (verse 11), that in Christ we have died to sin and we live to God. We are to know these things, to meditate on them, to realize that they are true. Our minds are so to grasp the fact and the significance of our death and resurrection with Christ, that a return to the old life is unthinkable. A born-again Christian should no more think of going back to the old life than an adult to his childhood, a married man to his bachelorhood, or a discharged prisoner to his prison cell. (1966c:50)

606. Hearts as well as minds

In order to urge people to use their minds, it is not necessary to urge them to suppress their feelings. I often say to our students at the Institute for Contemporary Christianity in London that we are not in the business of 'breeding tadpoles'. A tadpole is a little creature with a huge head and nothing much else besides. Certainly there are some Christian tadpoles around. Their heads are bulging with sound theology, but that is all there is to them. No, we are concerned to help people to develop not only a Christian mind, but also a Christian heart, a Christian spirit, a Christian conscience and a Christian will, in fact to become whole Christian persons, thoroughly integrated under the lordship of Christ. **(1992b:119).**

607. Mind and character

Faith has to be related to life. A Christian mind is ineffective without a Christian character. **(1981c)**

608. Falling in love

I want to urge you to beware of being swept off your feet by what is called falling in love and assuming that that in itself is an adequate basis for marriage. There are other considerations, such as intellectual compatibility. Is the person I find myself falling in love with a Christian, and a committed, mature and growing one? Is that person going to be a good father or mother to my children? Is that person going to be a good companion? Has that person my respect, as well as my physical desire? Now these are questions that the mind asks when the emotion of falling in love begins to well up inside me. Love is an unreliable emotion, it has to be checked by the Word of God. Several men have been to me in personal counselling, married men, and have said, 'I must divorce my wife, I have fallen in love with another woman and this woman is made for me and I am made for her and we fit perfectly. I made a mistake in marrying my present wife. I am so much in love with this other woman it must be right.' I say, 'On the contrary, it must be wrong. You already have a wife.' **(1980g:11)**

609. The last stronghold

I sometimes wonder if our minds are the last stronghold to capitulate to Jesus the Lord. Of course, major questions remain to be answered in the contemporary hermeneutical discussion. Yet we can safely say that no hermeneutical method or conclusion can be Christian which fails to honour Christ by enthroning him as Lord. **(1981f)**

IX. THE CHURCH OF GOD

48. God's new society
49. Word, worship and sacrament
50. Ministers and ministry
51. The unity of the church
52. Reforming the church
53. The evangelical tradition

48. GOD'S NEW SOCIETY

610. A people 'in Christ'

Fundamental to New Testament Christianity is the concept of the union of God's people with Christ. What constitutes the distinctness of the members of God's new society? Not just that they admire and even worship Jesus, not just that they assent to the dogmas of the church, not even that they live by certain moral standards. No, what makes them distinctive is their new solidarity as a people who are 'in Christ'. By virtue of their union with Christ they have actually shared in his resurrection, ascension and session. In the 'heavenly places', the unseen world of spiritual reality, in which the principalities and powers operate (Eph. 3:10; 6:12) and in which Christ reigns supreme (1:20), there God has blessed his people in Christ (1:3), and there he has seated them with Christ (2:6). For if we are seated with Christ in the heavenlies, there can be no doubt what we are sitting on: thrones! Moreover, this talk about solidarity with Christ in his resurrection and exaltation is not a piece of meaningless Christian mysticism. It bears witness to a living experience, that Christ has given us on the one hand a new life (with a sensitive awareness of the reality of God, and a love for him and for his people) and on the other a new victory (with evil increasingly under our feet). We are dead, but have been made spiritually alive and alert. We were in captivity, but have been enthroned.   **(1979e:81)**

611. Diversity and harmony

The church as a multi-racial, multi-cultural community is like a beautiful tapestry. Its members come from a wide range of colourful backgrounds. No other human community resembles it. Its diversity and harmony are unique. It is God's new society. And the many-coloured fellowship of the church is a reflection of the many-coloured (or 'many-splendoured', to use Francis Thompson's word) wisdom of God.   **(1979e:123)**

612. Promises fulfilled

The true fulfilment of the Old Testament promises is not literal but spiritual. They are fulfilled today not in the Jewish nation, as some dispensationalists hold, nor in the British or

Anglo-Saxon people, as the British Israelites teach, but in Christ and in the people of Christ who believe. We Christians are Abraham's seed, who inherit the blessing promised to his descendants . . . all the promises of God to his people in the Old Testament become ours if we are Christ's. **(1968c:128)**

613. A confessional church

The Christian church, whether universal or local, is intended by God to be a *confessional* church. The church is 'the pillar and foundation of the truth' (1 Tim. 3:15, literally). Revealed truth is thus likened to a building, and the church's calling is to be its 'foundation' (holding it firm so that it is not moved) and its 'pillar' (holding it aloft so that all may see it).

(1970b:26)

614. Love and acceptance

'Acceptance' is a popular word today, and rightly so. Theologically, God's acceptance of us is quite a good contemporary term for justification. But we should be cautious about modern talk of 'unconditional acceptance', as when the concept of an 'open church' is canvassed, in which membership is offered to everybody, with no questions asked and no conditions laid down. For though God's love is indeed unconditional, his acceptance of us is not, since it depends on our repentance and our faith in Jesus Christ. We need to bear this in mind when we consider that we are to accept the weak (Rom. 14:1) since 'God has accepted him' (14:3), and to accept one another 'just as Christ accepted' us (15:7). **(1994:359)**

615. An embodied gospel

If a local church is to become a gospel church, it must not only receive the gospel and pass it on, but also embody it in a community life of mutual love. **(1991c:135)**

616. God's church and God's gospel

It was natural for Paul to move on in his mind from God's church to God's gospel because he could not think of either without the other. It is by the gospel that the church exists and by the church that the gospel spreads. Each depends on the other. Each serves the other. **(1991c:32)**

617. Equality in Christ

What unites the church is a common faith in Christ and a common share in the Spirit. Apart from this essential, Christians may have nothing at all in common. We differ from one another in temperament, personality, education, colour, culture, citizenship, language and in a host of other ways. Thank God we do. The church is a wonderfully inclusive fellowship, in which 'there is neither Jew nor Greek, there is neither slave nor free, there is neither male nor female' (Gal. 3:28). In other words, in Christ we have equality.   **(1970b:183)**

618. Truth and love

Love is the first mark of a true and living church and truth is the second, because the Scriptures hold love and truth together in balance. Some Christians are so resolved to make love paramount, that they forget the sacredness of revealed truth. 'Let us drown our doctrinal differences', they urge, 'in the ocean of brotherly love!' Others are equally mistaken in their pursuit of truth at the expense of love. So dogged is their zeal for God's Word that they become harsh, bitter and unloving. Love becomes sentimental if it is not strengthened by truth, and truth becomes hard if it is not softened by love. We need to preserve the balance of the Bible which tells us to hold the truth in love, to love others in the truth, and to grow not only in love but in discernment.   **(1990c:44)**

619. Essentials and non-essentials

There are two particular principles which Paul develops in Romans 14, which, especially in combination, are applicable to all churches in all places at all times. The first is the principle of faith. Everything must be done 'from faith', he writes (14:23). Again, 'each one should be fully convinced in his own mind' (14:5). We need therefore to educate our consciences by the Word of God, so that we become strong in faith, growing in settled convictions and so in Christian liberty. Secondly, there is the principle of love. Everything must be done according to love (14:15). We need therefore to remember who our fellow Christians are, especially that they are our sisters and brothers for whom Christ died, so that we honour, not despise, them; serve, not harm, them; and especially respect their consciences.

One area in which this distinction between faith and love

should operate is in the difference between essentials and non-essentials in Christian doctrine and practice. Although it is not always easy to distinguish between them, a safe guide is that truths on which Scripture speaks with a clear voice are essentials, whereas whenever equally biblical Christians, equally anxious to understand and obey Scripture, reach different conclusions, these must be regarded as non-essentials. Some people glory in the so-called 'comprehensiveness' of certain denominations. But there are two kinds of comprehensiveness, principled and unprincipled.

Dr Alex Vidler has described the latter as the resolve 'to hold together in juxtaposition as many varieties of Christian faith and practice as are willing to agree to differ, so that the church is regarded as a sort of league of religions [a sort of 'United Religions', he might have said today]. I have nothing to say for such an unprincipled syncretism.' The true principle of comprehension, on the other hand, he writes, 'is that a church ought to hold the fundamentals of the faith, and at the same time allow for differences of opinion and of interpretation in secondary matters, especially rites and ceremonies . . .'[1]

In fundamentals, then, faith is primary, and we may not appeal to love as an excuse to deny essential faith. In non-fundamentals, however, love is primary, and we may not appeal to zeal for the faith as an excuse for failures in love. Faith instructs our own conscience; love respects the conscience of others. Faith gives liberty; love limits its exercise. No-one has put it better than Rupert Meldenius, a name which some believe was a *nom de plume* used by Richard Baxter:

> In essentials unity;
> In non-essentials liberty;
> In all things charity.

(1994:374)

[1] Alec Vidler, *Essays in Liberality* (SCM, 1957), p. 166.

620. The church's two homes

God's church was living in Thessalonica, and the Thessalonians' church was living in God. To be sure, the preposition 'in' has a different nuance in these statements, since the church is 'in' God as the source from which its life comes, whereas it is 'in' the world only as the sphere in which it lives. Nevertheless, it is still correct to say that every church has two homes, two environments, two habitats. It lives in God and it lives in the world.[1]   **(1991c:28)**

[1] *Cf.* 'in Christ at Philippi', Phil. 1:1, and 'in Christ at Colosse', Col. 1:2.

621. Ecclesiastical salt-cellars

When men reject what they know of God, God gives them up to their own distorted notions and perverted passions, until society stinks in the nostrils of God and of all good people.

Now Christians are set in secular society by God to hinder this process. God intends us to penetrate the world. Christian salt has no business to remain snugly in elegant little ecclesiastical salt cellars; our place is to be rubbed into the secular community, as salt is rubbed into meat, to stop it going bad. And when society does go bad, we Christians tend to throw up our hands in pious horror and reproach the non-Christian world; but should we not rather reproach ourselves? One can hardly blame unsalted meat for going bad. It cannot do anything else. The real question to ask is: where is the salt?

(1978f:65)

622. The Spirit and the church

Although we have no liberty to deny the validity of personal choice, it is safe and healthy only in relation to the Spirit and the church. There is no evidence that Barnabas and Saul 'volunteered' for missionary service; they were 'sent' by the Spirit through the church. Still today it is the responsibility of every local church (especially of its leaders) to be sensitive to the Holy Spirit, in order to discover whom he may be gifting and calling.   **(1990b:218)**

623. False independence

The Pharisees loved to be given deferential titles. It flattered them. It gave them a sense of superiority over other people. In contrast to them, Jesus said that there were three titles his disciples were not to assume or be given, 'Rabbi' (that is, teacher), 'father' and 'master'. What did Jesus mean by it? Well, the father exercises authority over his children by reason of the fact that they depend upon him. I suggest that what Jesus is saying is that we are never to adopt towards a fellow man in the church the attitude of dependence which a child has towards his father, nor are we to require others to be or become spiritually dependent upon us. That this is what Jesus intended is confirmed by the reason he gives, namely 'for you have one Father, who is in heaven'. **(1961:73)**

624. Theory is not enough

Biblical preaching and teaching on such topics as prayer and evangelism I take to be indispensable. But in such practical activities a grasp of the theory is not enough. We can learn to pray only by praying, especially in a prayer group. And we can learn to evangelize only by going out with a more experienced Christian either to witness on the street corner or to visit in some homes. Moreover, it is by active membership of the body of Christ that we learn the meaning of the church which is described in the New Testament. A fellowship meeting is a happening in which the individual is accepted, welcomed and loved. Then abstract concepts of forgiveness, reconciliation and fellowship take on a concrete form, and preached truth comes to life. **(1982a:79)**

625. Discipline in the church

The New Testament gives clear instructions about discipline, on the one hand its necessity for the sake of the church's holiness, and on the other its constructive purpose, namely, if possible, to 'win over' and 'restore' the offending member. Jesus himself made it abundantly plain that the object of discipline was not to humiliate, let alone to alienate, the person concerned, but rather to reclaim him. He laid down a procedure which would develop by stages. Stage one is a private, one-to-one confrontation with the offender, 'just between the two of you', during which, if he listens, he will be won over. If he refuses, stage two is to take several others along in order to establish the rebuke. If he still refuses to listen, the church is to be told, so that he may have a third chance to repent. If he still obstinately refuses to listen, only then is he to be excommunicated (Mt. 18:15–17). Paul's teaching was similar. A church member 'caught in a sin' is to be 'restored' in a spirit of gentleness and humility; this would be an example of bearing each other's burdens and so fulfilling Christ's law of love (Gal. 6:1–2). Even a 'handing over to Satan', by which presumably Paul was referring to the excommunication of a flagrant offender, had a positive purpose, either that he might be 'taught not to blaspheme' (1 Tim. 1:20), or at least that 'his spirit (might be) saved on the day of the Lord' (1 Cor. 5:5). Thus all disciplinary action was to exhibit the love and justice of the cross. **(1986a:297)**

626. The spiritually poor

The Church consists of the spiritually poor. The only condition of eligibility is destitution. The rich are sent away empty. We have to acknowledge our spiritual bankruptcy, that we have no merit to plead, no strings to pull, no power to save ourselves. To such Jesus says 'Blessed are the poor in spirit; the kingdom of God is theirs'. **(1981a)**

627. Teaching before experience

In two separate paragraphs of the Acts Luke tells us that the early Christians in Jerusalem sold many of their possessions, held the rest in common, and distributed goods and money 'as any had need' (2:44, 45; 4:32–37). Are we to deduce from this that they set a pattern which all Christians are meant to copy, and that private property is forbidden to Christians? Some groups have thought so. Certainly the generosity and mutual care of those early Christians are to be followed, for the New Testament commands us many times to love and serve one another, and to be generous (even sacrificial) in our giving. But to argue from the practice of the early Jerusalem church that all private ownership is abolished among Christians not only cannot be maintained from Scripture but is plainly contradicted by the apostle Peter in the same context (Acts 5:4) and by the apostle Paul elsewhere (*e.g.* 1 Tim. 6:17). This example should put us on the alert. We must derive our standards of belief and behaviour from the teaching of the New Testament, wherever it is given, rather than from the practices and experiences which it portrays. **(1975b:16)**

628. Inside-out people

Everything we have and are in Christ both comes from God and returns to God. It begins in his will and ends in his glory. For this is where everything begins and ends.

Yet such Christian talk comes into violent collision with the man-centredness and self-centredness of the world. Fallen man, imprisoned in his own little ego, has an almost boundless confidence in the power of his own will, and an almost insatiable appetite for the praise of his own glory. But the people of God have at least begun to be turned inside out. The new society has new values and new ideals. For God's people are God's possession who live by God's will and for God's glory. **(1979e:50)**

49. WORD, WORSHIP AND SACRAMENT

629. Form and power

True religion combines form and power. It is not external form without power. Nor, on the other hand, does it emphasize moral power in such a way as to despise or dispense with proper external forms. It combines them. It fosters a worship which is essentially 'spiritual', arising from the heart, but which expresses itself through public, corporate services, and which also issues in moral behaviour. Otherwise, it is not only valueless; it is actually an abomination to the Lord. **(1973b:88)**

630. The church's twofold task

The vocation of the church is to be occupied with God and with the world. God has constituted his church to be a worshipping and witnessing community. **(1967e:59)**

631. Christian exultation

Christian exultation in God begins with the shamefaced recognition that we have no claim on him at all, continues with wondering worship that while we were still sinners and enemies Christ died for us, and ends with the humble confidence that he will complete the work he has begun. So to exult in God is to rejoice not in our privileges but in his mercies, not in our possession of him but in his of us. **(1994:147)**

632. Worship and Scripture

The church needs constantly to hear God's Word. Hence the central place of preaching in public worship. Preaching is not an intrusion into it but rather indispensable to it. For the worship of God is always a response to the Word of God.
(1982b:57)

633. A religion of the Word

Preaching is indispensable to Christianity. Without preaching a necessary part of its authenticity has been lost. For Christianity is, in its very essence, a religion of the Word of God . . . The trinitarian statement of a speaking Father, Son and Holy Spirit, and so of a Word of God that is scriptural, incarnate and contemporary, is fundamental to the Christian religion. And it

271

is God's speech which makes our speech necessary. We must speak what he has spoken. **(1982a:15)**

634. The nature of exposition

Christian preaching is not the proud ventilation of human opinions: it is the humble exposition of God's Word. Biblical expositors bring out of Scripture what is there; they refuse to thrust into the text what is not there. They pry open what appears closed, make plain what seems obscure, unravel what is knotted, and unfold what is tightly packed. In expository preaching the biblical text is neither a conventional introduction to a sermon on a largely different topic, nor a convenient peg on which to hang a ragbag of miscellaneous thoughts, but a master which dictates and controls what is said. **(1981d)**

635. A bridge for truth

The expository preacher is a bridge builder, seeking to span the gulf between the Word of God and the mind of man. He must do his utmost to interpret the Scripture so accurately and plainly, and to apply it so forcefully, that the truth crosses the bridge. **(1961:25)**

636. The real secret

The real secret of expository preaching is not mastering certain techniques, but being mastered by certain convictions.
(1978e:159)

637. Study and pulpit

'There is no need for me to prepare before preaching', somebody argues; 'I shall rely on the Holy Spirit to give me the words. Jesus himself promised that it would be given us in that hour what we are to say.' Such talk sounds plausible, until we remember that the misquotation of Scripture is the devil's game. Jesus was referring to the hour of persecution not of proclamation, and to the prisoner's dock in a law court, not the pulpit in a church. Trust in the Holy Spirit is not intended to save us the bother of preparation. The Holy Spirit can indeed give us utterance if we are suddenly called upon to speak and there has been no opportunity to prepare. But he can also clarify and direct our thinking in our study. Indeed, experience suggests that he does a better job there than in the pulpit.
(1975c:126)

638. The prepared heart

There is no greater need for the preacher than that he should know God. I care not about his lack of eloquence and artistry, about his ill-constructed discourse or his poorly-enunciated message, if only it is evident that God is a reality to him and that he has learned to abide in Christ. The preparation of the heart is of far greater importance than the preparation of the sermon. The preacher's words, however clear and forceful, will not ring true unless he speaks from conviction born of experience. **(1961:68)**

639. The sparkle of authenticity

It seems to me that one might well single out freshness of spiritual experience as the first indispensable quality of the effective preacher. No amount of homiletical technique can compensate for the absence of a close personal walk with God. Unless he puts a new song in our mouth, even the most polished sermons will lack the sparkle of authenticity.

(1986c:xxix)

640. The need to listen

The best preachers are always diligent pastors, who know the people of their district and congregation, and understand the human scene in all its pain and pleasure, glory and tragedy. And the quickest way to gain such an understanding is to shut our mouth (a hard task for compulsive preachers) and open our eyes and ears. It has been well said that God has given us two ears and two eyes, but only one mouth, so that he obviously intends us to look and listen twice as much as we talk. **(1982a:192)**

641. 'He understands us'

Love will help the preacher to be understanding in his approach not only because he will then take trouble to get to know his people and their problems, but also because he will be the better able to appreciate them when he knows them. Love has a strange intuitive faculty. Jesus our Lord possessed it to perfection. Again and again it is said of him that he knew people's thoughts. Indeed, the apostle John writes, 'He knew all men and needed no one to bear witness of man; for he himself knew what was in man.' Men felt instinctively that he

273

understood them. He is the great *kardiognōstēs*, or heart-knower, who 'searches mind and heart', and we should seek from him insight to be and do the same. Love, the unselfish care which longs to understand and so to help, is one of the greatest secrets of communication. It is when the preacher loves his people, that they are likely to say of him, 'He understands us.'   **(1961:79)**

642. Authority and humility

We shall be wise, in our preaching, neither to say 'Thus says the Lord' (since we do not have the authority of an inspired Old Testament prophet) nor to declare 'I say to you' (since we do not have the authority of Jesus Christ and his apostles), but rather, at least most of the time, to use the 'we' form of address. For then it will be clear that we preach nothing to others which we do not also and first preach to ourselves, and that authority and humility are not mutually exclusive.   **(1982a:58)**

643. Text and pretext

Although there are, strictly speaking, no prophets or apostles today, I fear there are false prophets and false apostles. They speak their own words instead of God's Word. Their message originates in their own mind. These are men who like to ventilate their own opinions on religion, ethics, theology or politics. They may be conventional enough to introduce their sermon with a Scripture text, but the text bears little or no relation to the sermon which follows, nor is any attempt made to interpret the text in its context. It has been truly said that such a text without a context is a pretext.   **(1961:13)**

644. A touchstone of health

The health of every congregation depends more than anything else on the quality of its preaching ministry.   **(1982b:62)**

645. Holiness and humility

On what conditions may preachers hope to be vehicles of divine power? We must be faithful in handling the Word of God, expounding the Scriptures and preaching the cross, for there is power in God's Word and in Christ's cross. But how can we become channels for the power of the Holy Spirit? How can the promise of John be fulfilled that from our innermost being the 'rivers of living water' will flow into the lives of others? (Jn. 4:14). I believe there are two essential conditions: holiness and humility. **(1961:107)**

646. The glory of preaching

I pity the preacher who enters the pulpit with no Bible in his hands, or with a Bible which is more rags and tatters than the Word of God. He cannot expound Scripture, because he has no Scripture to expound. He cannot speak, for he has nothing worth saying. But to enter the pulpit with the confidence that God has spoken, that he has caused what he has spoken to be written, and that we have this inspired text in our hands – ah! then our head begins to swim, our heart to beat, our blood to flow, and our eyes to sparkle, with the sheer glory of having God's Word in our hands and on our lips. **(1992b:210)**

647. Preaching and worship

Word and worship belong indissolubly to each other. All worship is an intelligent and loving response to the revelation of God, because it is the adoration of his Name. Therefore acceptable worship is impossible without preaching. For preaching is making known the Name of the Lord, and worship is praising the Name of the Lord made known. Far from being an alien intrusion into worship, the reading and preaching of the Word are actually indispensable to it. The two cannot be divorced. Indeed, it is their unnatural divorce which accounts for the low level of so much contemporary worship. Our worship is poor because our knowledge of God is poor, and our knowledge of God is poor because our preaching is poor. But when the Word of God is expounded in its fullness, and the congregation begin to glimpse the glory of the living God, they bow down in solemn awe and joyful wonder before his throne. It is preaching which accomplishes this, the proclamation of the Word of God in the power of the Spirit of God. That is why preaching is unique and irreplaceable.

(1982a:82)

648. Form and freedom

Now public worship is a vital part of the life of the local church. It is even essential to its identity. Yet in the interests of 'spontaneity' worship services often lack both content and form, and so become slovenly, mindless, irreverent or dull. Most churches could afford to give more time and trouble to the preparation of their worship. It is a mistake to imagine either that freedom and form exclude one another, or that the Holy Spirit is the friend of freedom in such a way as to be the enemy of form. **(1991c:124)**

649. Unconditional praise?

The strange notion is gaining popularity in some Christian circles that the major secret of Christian freedom and victory is unconditional praise; that a husband should praise God for his wife's adultery and a wife for her husband's drunkenness; and that even the most appalling calamities of life should become subjects for thanksgiving and praise. Such a suggestion is at best a dangerous half-truth, and at worst ludicrous, even blasphemous. Of course God's children learn not to argue with him in their suffering, but to trust him, and indeed to thank him for his loving providence by which he can turn even evil to good purposes (*e.g.* Rom. 8:28). But that is praising God for being God; it is not praising him for evil. To do this would be to react insensitively to people's pain (when Scripture tells us to weep with those who weep) and to condone and even encourage evil (when Scripture tells us to hate it and to resist the devil). God abominates evil, and we cannot praise or thank him for what he abominates. **(1979e:207)**

650. Loss of a dimension

Some of our services are far too formal, respectable and dull. At the same time, in some modern meetings the almost total loss of the dimension of reverence disturbs me. It seems to be assumed by some that the chief evidence of the presence of the Holy Spirit is noise. Have we forgotten that a dove is as much an emblem of the Holy Spirit as are wind and fire? When he visits his people in power, he sometimes brings quietness, silence, reverence and awe. His still small voice is heard. Men bow down in wonder before the majesty of the living God and worship. 'The LORD is in his holy temple; let all the earth keep silence before him' (Hab. 2:20). **(1975a:39)**

651. Heart and mind

The first characteristic of heart-worship is that it is rational; the mind is fully involved in it. For the 'heart' in Scripture is not simply equivalent to the emotions, as it usually is in common parlance today. In biblical thought the 'heart' is the centre of the human personality and is often so used that the intellect is more emphasized than the emotions. Thus, the exhortation in Proverbs 23:26, 'My son, give me your heart,' has often been interpreted as an entreaty for our love and devotion. It has served as a convenient text for many sermons on whole-hearted discipleship. But in reality it is a command to listen, to pay attention, to sit up and take notice, an appeal more for concentration than for consecration. **(1970b:162)**

652. Scripture and sacrament

God speaks to his people through his Word both as it is read and expounded from Scripture and as it is dramatized in the two gospel sacraments, baptism and the Lord's Supper. Perhaps 'word and sacrament' is not the best or most accurate coupling, common though it is. For strictly speaking the sacrament itself is a word, a 'visible word' according to Augustine. What builds up the church more than anything else is the ministry of God's Word as it comes to us through Scripture and Sacrament (that is the right coupling), audibly and visibly, in declaration and drama. **(1990b:321)**

653. Sermon and sacrament

Strictly speaking, the sacraments are not themselves worship, any more than the sermon is worship. Sermon and sacrament are both manward rather than Godward in their direction. They set forth, the one audibly and the other visibly, the glory of God's grace in the salvation of sinners. Therefore, though not themselves acts of worship, they lead to worship – the adoration of the God who once gave himself for his people and now gives himself to them today. **(1970b:164)**

654. The eye and the ear

Both Word and sacrament bear witness to Christ. Both promise salvation in Christ. Both quicken our faith in Christ. Both enable us to feed on Christ in our hearts. The major difference between them is that the message of the one is directed to the eye, and of the other to the ear. So the sacraments need the Word to interpret them. The ministry of Word and sacrament is a single ministry, the Word proclaiming, and the sacrament dramatizing, God's promises. Yet the Word is primary, since without it the sign becomes dark in meaning, if not actually dumb. **(1982a:114)**

655. Signs and promises

The sacraments dramatize salvation and do not in themselves automatically convey it. Augustine called them *verba visibilia*, 'visible words', and Hooker 'signs to which are annexed promises'. Therefore it is not by the mere outward administration of water in baptism that we are cleansed and receive the Spirit, nor by the mere gift of bread and wine in communion that we feed on Christ crucified, but by faith in the promises of God thus visibly expressed, a faith which is itself meant to be illustrated in our humble, believing acceptance of these signs. But we must not confuse the signs with the promises which they signify. It is possible to receive the sign without receiving the promise, and also to receive the promise apart from the receiving of the sign. **(1970b:121)**

656. Baptism into Christ

Baptism signifies our union with Christ, especially with Christ crucified and risen. It has other meanings, including cleansing from sin and the gift of the Holy Spirit, but its essential significance is that it unites us with Christ. Hence the use of the preposition *eis*, 'into'. True, at its institution, baptism was said to be into the single name of Father, Son and Holy Spirit (Mt. 28:19). Elsewhere, however, it is 'into the name of the Lord Jesus' (Acts 8:16; 19:5) or simply 'into Christ' (Gal. 3:27; Rom. 6:3). And to be baptized into Christ means to enter into relationship with him. **(1994:173)**

657. Baptism – the evangelical doctrine

It is the claim of the evangelical churchman that his doctrine of baptism is *the biblical doctrine*. At all events, he could not contemplate the existence of an *evangelical* doctrine of baptism as distinct from a *biblical* doctrine; since his primary concern is to understand the biblical doctrine and to conform his thinking and practice to it. If the so-called 'evangelical' doctrine of baptism can be shown to be unbiblical, the evangelical churchman is ready to abandon it in favour of any doctrine which can be shown to be more biblical . . . We would all (I imagine) agree with the definition of a sacrament given in the Catechism: 'an outward and visible sign of an inward and spiritual grace given unto us . . . as a means whereby we receive the same, and a pledge to assure us thereof' . . .

The . . . evangelical view is that the sign not only signifies the gift, but seals or pledges it, and pledges it in such a way as to convey not indeed the gift itself, but a title to the gift – the baptized person receiving the gift (thus pledged to him) *by faith*, which may be before, during or after the administration of the sacrament. **(1963:87)**

658. Recipients of God's grace

The primary movement which the gospel sacraments embody is from God to man, not man to God. The application of water in baptism represents either cleansing from sin and the outpouring of the Spirit (if it is administered by affusion) or sharing Christ's death and resurrection (if by immersion) or both. We do not baptize ourselves. We submit to baptism, and the action done to us symbolizes the saving work of Christ. In the Lord's Supper, similarly, the essential drama consists of the taking, blessing, breaking and giving of bread, and the taking, blessing, pouring and giving of wine. We do not (or should not) administer the elements to ourselves. They are given to us; we receive them. And as we eat the bread and drink the wine physically, so spiritually by faith we feed on Christ crucified in our hearts. Thus, in both sacraments we are more or less passive, recipients not donors, beneficiaries not benefactors.

(1986a:259)

659. Our offering and Christ's

The New Testament authors never express the concept of our offering being united to Christ's. What they do is exhort us to give ourselves (as a sacrifice) in loving obedience to God in three ways. First, 'like' Christ: 'live a life of love, just as Christ loved us and gave himself up for us as a fragrant offering and sacrifice to God' (Eph. 5:2). His self-offering is to be the model of ours. Secondly, the spiritual sacrifices we offer to God are to be offered 'through' Christ (1 Pet. 2:5), our Saviour and Mediator. Since they are all tainted with self-centredness, it is only through him that they become acceptable. Thirdly, we are to give ourselves in sacrifice 'unto' or 'for' Christ, constrained by his love to live for him alone the new life-from-death which he has given us (2 Cor. 5:14–15). Thus, we are to offer ourselves 'like', 'through' and 'for' Christ. These are the prepositions which the New Testament uses; it never suggests that our offerings may be made 'in' or 'with' Christ. **(1986a:270)**

660. Spiritual sacrifices

The uniqueness of Christ's sacrifice does not mean, then, that we have no sacrifices to offer, but only that their nature and purpose are different. They are not material but spiritual, and their object is not propitiatory but eucharistic, the expression of a responsive gratitude. This is the second biblical undergirding of Cranmer's position. The New Testament describes the church as a priestly community, both a 'holy priesthood' and a 'royal priesthood', in which all God's people share equally as 'priests'. This is the famous 'priesthood of all believers', on which the Reformers laid great stress. In consequence of this universal priesthood, the word 'priest' (*hiereus*) is never in the New Testament applied to the ordained minister, since he shares in offering what the people offer, but has no distinctive offering to make which differs from theirs.   **(1986a:263)**

661. Justification and the Lord's Supper

The English Reformers were resolved, being consistent theologians, that their doctrines of justification and of the Lord's Supper should be compatible with one another. They strenuously denied transubstantiation ('the change is not in the nature, but the dignity' – Latimer), the real presence of Christ in the elements ('his true body is truly present to them that truly receive him, but spiritually' – Cranmer), and the notion that the mass could be a propitiatory sacrifice (for then 'doth this sacrament take upon it the office of Christ's passion, whereby it might follow that Christ died in vain' – Ridley). They were also consistent (as we should be) in their vocabulary, believing that the presbyter is a minister serving a sacramental supper from a table, not a priest offering a sacrifice on an altar.   **(1983c:xiv)**

662. Transignification

The sacraments have been given to us in order to stimulate our faith. In fact, they are means of grace mainly because they are means to faith. And the Lord's Supper is a means to faith because it sets forth in dramatic visual symbolism the good news that Christ died for our sins in order that we might be forgiven. Hugh Latimer, the great preacher of the English Reformation, explained this symbolism during his trial in Oxford, before going to the stake:

There is a change in the bread and wine, and such a change as no power but the omnipotency of God can make, in that that which before was bread should now have the dignity to exhibit Christ's body. And yet the bread is still bread, and the wine is still wine. For the change is not in the nature but the dignity.

This is sometimes called 'transignification', in distinction to 'transubstantiation', for the change which is in mind is one of significance, not of substance. As the officiant offers the bread and wine to our bodies, so Christ offers his body and blood to our souls. Our faith looks beyond the symbols to the reality they represent, and even as we take the bread and wine, and feed on them in our mouths by eating and drinking, so we feed on Christ crucified in our hearts by faith. The parallel is so striking, and the corresponding words of administration are so personal, that the moment of reception becomes to many communicants a direct faith-encounter with Jesus Christ.

(1991d:134)

663. Our participation

We participate in Christ's sacrifice only in the sense that we share in the benefits of it, not in the sense that we share in the offering of it. **(1991d:138)**

664. The image of a Christian

I confess that I love to see a communicant kneeling at the rail. This is my brand image of a Christian. Not a soldier brandishing a sword, not an athlete stripped for the race, not a farmer braving wind and rain, with his hand on the plough and never looking back – though all these are true. But a penitent sinner, with knees bent, head bowed and downcast eyes, but with open, empty hands uplifted to receive a gift. **(1970b:131)**

665. Worship and mission

Worship which does not beget mission is hypocrisy. We cannot acclaim the worth of God if we have no desire to proclaim it.

(1967e:28)

50. MINISTERS AND MINISTRY

666. God's church

In delegating his care or oversight to men, or exercising it through men, God does not himself relinquish it. The church is still his church, and the oversight is still his oversight. He created the church, bought it, owns it, supervises it. It remains the new Israel, God's inheritance, God's flock, a people for God's own possession. **(1966a:11)**

667. Guardians and heralds

It was Paul's firm assurance that his message came from God, and that 'his' gospel was in reality 'God's' gospel. He had not invented it. He was only a steward entrusted with it and a herald commissioned to proclaim it. He must above all else be faithful.

Every authentic Christian ministry begins here, with the conviction that we have been called to handle God's Word as its guardians and heralds. We must not be satisfied with 'rumours of God' as a substitute for 'good news from God'. For, as Calvin put it, 'the gospel . . . is as far removed from conjecture as heaven is from the earth'.[1] Of course we are not apostles of Christ like Paul. But we believe that in the New Testament the teaching of the apostles has been preserved and is now bequeathed to us in its definitive form. We are therefore trustees of this apostolic faith, which is the Word of God and which works powerfully in those who believe. Our task is to keep it, study it, expound it, apply it and obey it. **(1991c:68)**

[1] John Calvin, *The Epistles of Paul the Apostle to the Romans and to the Thessalonians*, tr. Ross Mackenzie (Oliver and Boyd, 1961), p. 347.

668. No other Christ

We have put our trust in Christ, and we have done it through the apostles' teaching. If the apostles had not borne their unique testimony to Jesus Christ and if their unique first-hand testimony had not been recorded and preserved in the New Testament, we could never have believed in Jesus. True, we probably came to believe in him through the witness of some contemporary Christian – a preacher or relative or friend – but theirs was a secondary testimony, an endorsement from personal experience of the apostles' testimony. The Christ they were witnessing to was the apostles' Christ, the Christ of the New Testament witness. There is no other.   **(1971b:82)**

669. Three meanings of 'apostle'

The word 'apostle' has three main meanings in the New Testament. Once only it seems to be applied to every individual Christian, when Jesus said: 'A servant is not greater than his master; nor is he who is sent (*apostolos*) greater than he who sent him' (Jn. 13:16). So every Christian is both a servant and an apostle. The verb *apostellō* means to 'send', and all Christian people are sent out into the world as Christ's ambassadors and witnesses, to share in the apostolic mission of the whole church.

Secondly, there were 'apostles of the churches', messengers sent out by a church either as missionaries or on some other errand. And thirdly there were the 'apostles of Christ', a very small and distinctive group, consisting of the Twelve (including Matthias who replaced Judas), Paul, James the Lord's brother, and possibly one or two others. They were personally chosen and authorized by Jesus, and had to be eyewitnesses of the risen Lord.   **(1979e:160)**

670. A fourfold uniqueness

The apostles of Jesus appear to have had a fourfold uniqueness. First, they had a personal call and authorization by Jesus. This was clear in the case of the Twelve, and Paul claimed something comparable. He vehemently asserted and defended his apostolic authority, insisting that he had received his commission to be an apostle 'not from men nor by man, but by Jesus Christ and God the Father' (Gal. 1:1) . . .

Secondly, they had an eye-witness experience of Christ. The Twelve were appointed, Mark says, to be 'with him, and that he might send them out to preach'. The verb 'sent out' is again *apostellein*, and their essential qualification for the work of apostleship was to be 'with him'. Similarly, shortly before he died, Jesus said to them:

> You also must testify, for you have been with me from the beginning (Jn. 15:27) . . .

Thirdly, they had an extraordinary inspiration of the Holy Spirit. We saw [in the previous chapter] that the in-dwelling and illumination of the Holy Spirit is the privilege of all God's children. This privilege was not restricted to the apostles. Nevertheless, the ministry of the Spirit which Christ promised the apostles was something quite unique, as should be clear from these words:

All this I have spoken while still with you. But the Counsellor, the Holy Spirit, whom the Father will send in my name, will teach you all things and will remind you of everything I have said to you . . .
I have much more to say to you, more than you can now bear. When he, the Spirit of truth, comes, he will guide you into all truth . . . (John 14:25–26; 16:12–13).

Fourthly, they had the power to work miracles. The book of Acts is rightly called 'The Acts of the Apostles', and Paul designates the 'signs and wonders and miracles' which he had performed 'the things that mark an apostle' (2 Cor. 12:12). Further, the purpose of the miraculous power given to the apostles was to authenticate their apostolic commission and message . . .
In these four ways the apostles seem to have been unique.
(1984d:149, 150)

671. A unique authority

It is extremely important to recover today an understanding of the unique authority of Christ's apostles. For there are no apostles in the contemporary church. To be sure, there are missionaries and church leaders of different kinds who may be described as having an 'apostolic' ministry, but there are no apostles like the Twelve and Paul who were eyewitnesses of the risen Lord. **(1982b:32)**

672. A unique witness

What we hold, therefore, is this. The witness of the apostles to Christ was accurate (not corrupt), authorized by Christ (not the church), and unique (not repeatable). The church needs to assert today the uniqueness not only of the Christ-event, but of the apostolic witness to the Christ-event. We know nothing of Christ but what the apostles have given us. We cannot know Christ or reach Christ in any other way, except through the apostles. It is through their witness that we have come to believe in Christ, and so receive life in his name.   **(1967b:58)**

673. Authority in everything

An apostle's authority does not cease when he begins to teach unpopular truths. We cannot be selective in our reading of the apostolic doctrine of the New Testament. We cannot, when we like what an apostle teaches, defer to him as an angel, and when we do not like what he teaches, hate him and reject him as an enemy. No, the apostles of Jesus Christ have authority in everything they teach, whether we happen to like it or not.

(1968c:115)

674. The beginnings of pastoral oversight

Although no fixed ministerial order is laid down in the New Testament, some form of pastoral oversight (*episkopē*), doubt-less adapted to local needs, is regarded as indispensable to the welfare of the church. We notice that it was both local and plural – local in that the elders were chosen from within the congregation, not imposed from without, and plural in that the familiar modern pattern of 'one pastor one church' was simply unknown. Instead, there was a pastoral team, which is likely to have included (depending on the size of the church) full-time and part-time ministers, paid and voluntary workers, presby-ters, deacons and deaconesses. Their qualifications Paul laid down in writing later (1 Tim. 3; Tit. 1). These were mostly matters of moral integrity, but loyalty to the apostles' teaching and a gift for teaching it were also essential (Tit. 1:9; 1 Tim. 3:2). Thus the shepherds would tend Christ's sheep by feeding them, in other words care for them by teaching them.

(1990b:236)

675. Gift and office

Ordination to the pastoral ministry of any church should signify at least (1) the public recognition that God has called and gifted the person concerned, and (2) the public authoriza-tion of this person to obey the call and exercise the gift, with prayer for the enabling grace of the Holy Spirit. So we must not separate what God has united. On the one hand, the church should acknowledge the gifts which God has given people, and should publicly authorize them and encourage their exercise in ministry. On the other, the New Testament never interpolates the grotesque situation in which the church commissions and authorizes people to exercise a ministry for which they lack both the divine call and the divine equipment. No, gift and office, divine enabling and ecclesiastical commissioning, belong together. **(1979e:165)**

676. The Christian pastor

The pastor is primarily a teacher. This is the reason for two qualifications for the presbyterate which are singled out in the Pastoral Epistles. First, the candidate must be 'able to teach' (1 Tim. 3:2). Secondly, he must 'hold firmly to the trustworthy message as it has been taught, so that he can encourage others by sound doctrine and refute those who oppose it' (Tit. 1:9). These two qualifications go together. Pastors must both be loyal to the apostolic teaching (the *didachē*) and have a gift for teaching it (*didaktikos*). And whether they are teaching a crowd or congregation, a group or an individual (Jesus himself taught in all three contexts), what distinguishes their pastoral work is that it is always a ministry of the Word. **(1992b:286)**

677. A double duty

The shepherds of Christ's flock have a double duty: to feed the sheep (by teaching the truth) and to protect them from wolves (by warning of error). As Paul put it to Titus, elders must hold firm the sure word according to apostolic teaching, so that they would be able both 'to give instruction in sound doctrine and also to confute those who contradict it' (Tit. 1:9). This emphasis is unpopular today. We are frequently told always to be positive in our teaching, and never negative. But those who say this have either not read the New Testament or, having read it, they disagree with it. For the Lord Jesus and his apostles refuted error themselves and urged us to do the same. One wonders if it is the neglect of this obligation which is a major cause of today's theological confusion. If, when false teaching arises, Christian leaders sit idly by and do nothing, or turn tail and flee, they will earn the terrible epithet 'hirelings' who care nothing for Christ's flock (Jn. 10:12ff.). Then too it will be said of believers, as it was of Israel, that 'they were scattered, because there was no shepherd, and . . . they became food for all the wild animals' (Ezk. 34:5). **(1990b:328)**

678. Loyalty to the apostolic message

A congregation's attitude to their minister should be determined by his loyalty to the apostolic message. No minister, however exalted his rank in the visible church, is an apostle of Jesus Christ. Nevertheless, if he is faithful in teaching what the apostles taught, a godly congregation will humbly receive his message and submit to it. They will neither resent nor reject it. Rather, they will welcome it, even with the deference which they would give to an angel of God, to Christ Jesus himself, because they recognize that the minister's message is not the minister's message, but the message of Jesus Christ.

(1968c:118)

679. The very first priority

The very first thing which needs to be said about Christian ministers of all kinds is that they are 'under' people (as their servants) rather than 'over' them (as their leaders, let alone their lords). Jesus made this absolutely plain. The chief characteristic of Christian leaders, he insisted, is humility not authority, and gentleness not power. **(1991c:120)**

680. The true model

'Ministry' means 'service' – lowly, menial service; it is, therefore, peculiarly perverse to turn it into an occasion for boasting. Jesus specifically distinguished between 'rule' and 'service', 'authority' and 'ministry', and added that though the former was characteristic of pagans, the latter was to characterize his followers: 'You know that those who are supposed to rule over the Gentiles lord it over them, and their great men exercise authority over them. But it shall not be so among you; but whoever would be great among you must be your servant, and whoever would be first among you must be slave of all. For the Son of man also came not to be served but to serve, and to give his life as a ransom for many' (Mk. 10:42–45). Thus the Christian minister is to take as his model, not the Gentiles (or the Pharisees) who preferred to be lords, but the Christ who came to serve.

This is not to deny that some authority attaches to the ministry, but rather to define and circumscribe it. It is the authority which inheres in sound teaching and consistent example. **(1970b:195)**

681. The best teachers
There is no doubt that the best teachers in any field of knowledge are those who remain students all their lives.

(1982a:180)

682. Christian counselling
The true pastor is always a good theologian, and what makes a pastoral counsellor 'Christian' is his or her skilled application of the Word of God. **(1991c:115)**

683. Episcopacy: more than one form
Whatever case may be made out *historically* for a distinctive monarchical episcopate, there is no express *biblical* warrant for it. The furthest we can go is to say that there are adumbrations of it in the New Testament – of the office without the title – in the wider oversight exercised by some resident apostles like James (if he was an apostle) in Palestine and John in Asia, and by apostolic delegates like Timothy in Ephesus and Titus in Crete. As a result, the later development of the monarchical episcopate may certainly be recognized as a flower which grew from a biblical seed. But it is only one form of *episkopē* and cannot claim to be the only one. The normal *episkopē* of the New Testament was congregational, not diocesan; plural, not monarchical. **(1966a:12)**

684. The historic episcopate
Anglican evangelicals may regard the historic episcopate as an acceptably biblical form of *episkopē* (though it has by no means always conformed to the scriptural ideas of pastoral oversight). They may also value it as a symbol of continuity and a focus of unity in the church. But to acknowledge its potential value as a domestic institution is one thing; to insist upon it as a non-negotiable condition of union with all other churches is quite another. Those who do this are not only hindering the church's advance to unity but infringing a principle which the church's Lord laid down. They are teaching as a doctrine a precept of men. They are failing to subordinate tradition to Scripture.

(1970b:89)

685. Priest or pastor?
It would be helpful to recover the New Testament designation

'pastor'. 'Minister' is a misleading term because it is generic rather than specific, and always therefore requires a qualifying adjective to indicate what kind of ministry is in mind. 'Priest' is unfortunately ambiguous. Those with knowledge of the etymology of English words are aware that 'priest' is simply a contraction of 'presbyter', meaning 'elder'. But it is also used to translate the Greek word *hiereus*, a sacrificing priest, which is never used of Christian ministers in the New Testament. To call clergy 'priests' (common as the practice is in Roman Catholic, Lutheran and Anglican circles) gives the false impression that their ministry is primarily directed towards God, whereas the New Testament portrays it as primarily directed towards the church. So 'pastor' remains the most accurate term. The objection that it means 'shepherd', and that sheep and shepherds are irrelevant in the bustling cities of the twentieth century, can best be met by recalling that the Lord Jesus called himself 'the good Shepherd', that even city-dwelling Christians will always think of him as such, and that his pastoral ministry (with its characteristics of intimate knowledge, sacrifice, leadership, protection and care) remains the permanent model for all pastors. **(1982a:117)**

686. Priest or presbyter?

It may be asked why in the sixteenth century some Reformed churches retained the word 'priest' as a designation of their ministers, including the Church of England. The answer is primarily one of etymology. The English word 'priest' was known to be derived from, and a contraction of, 'presbyter'. It therefore translated *presbyteros* ('elder'), not *hiereus* ('priest'). So 'priest' was kept only because its meaning was theologically unexceptionable and because 'presbyter' was not yet a word of common English currency. At the same time, there is evidence that the Reformers would have preferred the unambiguous word 'presbyter', for 'even in matter of nomenclature', wrote Professor Norman Sykes, 'there was considerable agreement' among them.[1] For instance, Calvin complained in the *Institutes* that the Roman bishops by their ordination created 'not presbyters to lead and feed the people, but priests to perform sacrifices'.[2] In England Richard Hooker, answering the Puritans who criticized the retention of 'priest' in the Prayer Book, expressed a plain preference for 'presbyter', since 'in truth the word *presbyter* doth seem more fit, and in propriety of speech more agreeable than *priest* with the drift of the whole gospel of Jesus Christ'.[3] If this was so at the end of the sixteenth century, it is much more so at the end of the twentieth. For today few people know that 'priest' is a contraction of 'presbyter', and even fewer are able to perform the mental gymnastic of saying 'priest' and thinking 'presbyter'. It would therefore be conducive to both theological clarity and biblical faithfulness to drop the word 'priest' altogether from our vocabulary. We could then follow the wisdom of such united churches as those of South India, North India and Pakistan, and refer to the three orders of ordained ministry as 'bishops, presbyters and deacons'. **(1992b:274)**

[1] Norman Sykes, *Old Priest, New Presbyter* (Cambridge University Press, 1956), p. 43.
[2] Calvin, *Institutes*, IV.v.4.
[3] Richard Hooker, *Laws of Ecclesiastical Polity* (1593–97), Book V.lxxviii.3.

687. Shepherds of Christ's flock

In Acts 20, the leaders addressed are called 'elders' (verse 17), 'pastors' (28a) and 'overseers' (28b), and it is evident that these terms denote the same people. 'Pastors' is the generic term which describes their role. In our day, in which there is much confusion about the nature and purpose of the pastoral ministry, and much questioning whether clergy are primarily social workers, psychotherapists, educators, facilitators or administrators, it is important to rehabilitate the noble word 'pastors', who are shepherds of Christ's sheep, called to tend, feed and protect them. This pastoral responsibility over the local congregation seems to have been shared by both deacons (though in a supportive role) and those who are called either *presbyteroi* (elders), a word borrowed from the Jewish synagogue, or *episkopoi* (overseers), a word borrowed from Greek contexts. These are often – and rightly – referred to as 'presbyter-bishops', in order to indicate that during the apostolic period the two titles referred to the same office. In those days there were only 'presbyter-bishops and deacons'. Those of us who belong to episcopally ordered churches, and believe that a threefold order (bishops, presbyters and deacons) can be defended and commended from Scripture, do not base our argument on the word *episkopoi*, but on people like

Timothy and Titus who, though not called 'bishops', were nevertheless given an oversight and jurisdiction over several churches, with authority to select and ordain their presbyter-bishops and deacons. **(1990b:323)**

688. The accountability of ministry

No secret of Christian ministry is more important than its fundamental God-centredness. The stewards of the gospel are primarily responsible neither to the church, nor to its synods or leaders, but to God himself. On the one hand, this is a disconcerting fact, because God scrutinizes our hearts and their secrets, and his standards are very high. On the other hand, it is marvellously liberating, since God is a more knowledgeable, impartial and merciful judge than any human being or ecclesiastical court or committee. To be accountable to him is to be delivered from the tyranny of human criticism.

(1991c:50)

689. The challenge of false teachers

Both our Lord and his apostles did not shrink when necessary from the task of exposing and overthrowing false teaching. Distasteful and even dangerous as it is, we cannot conscientiously avoid the same task ourselves. Indeed, in today's church, ravaged by many grievous wolves, there is a great need for good and faithful shepherds, who will not only feed the sheep but rout the wolves. **(1966a:15)**

690. The distinctiveness of ministry

Christian ministers are pastors, shepherds of Christ's flock. This is their only essential distinctiveness. Of course they are themselves also Christ's sheep. But they are called to be shepherds. The church is a universal priesthood; and also a universal diaconate, for all God's people are called to *diakonia*. But the church is not a universal pastorate. All God's people are priests; all are ministers or servants; but 'he gave *some . . .* pastors and teachers' (Eph. 4:11). **(1969b:45)**

691. The layman's part

There are three pragmatic reasons for the greater participation of laymen in the life and work of the church – need, fear and the spirit of the age. They are sound reasons too, so far as they go, but inadequate. The real reason for expecting the laity to be responsible, active and constructive church members is biblical not pragmatic, grounded on theological principle, not on expediency. It is neither because the clergy need the laity to help them, nor because the laity want to be of use, nor because the world now thinks this way, but because God himself has revealed it as his will. Moreover, the only way in which the laity will come to see and accept their inalienable rights and duties in the church is that they come to recognize them in the Word of God as the will of God for the people of God.

(1969b:12)

692. *Sheep, wolves and shepherds*

One must not follow the unbiblical tendency to despise the office and work of a pastor or to declare clergy to be redundant . . . pastoral oversight is a permanent feature of the church. Though the New Testament gives no detailed blueprint for the pastorate, yet the ascended Christ still gives pastors and teachers to his church.

And they are greatly needed today. As the sheep multiply in many parts of the world, there is an urgent need for more pastors to feed or teach them. And as the wolves multiply, there is an equally urgent need for more pastors to rout them by giving their minds to the refutation of error. So the more sheep there are, and the more wolves there are, the more shepherds are needed to feed and protect the flock. **(1989b:10)**

693. *Church and clergy*

Too low a view of laity is due to too high a view of clergy, and too high a view of clergy is due to too low a view of the church.

(1969b:13)

694. *The scandal of clericalism*

It is only against the background of the equality and unity of the people of God that the real scandal of clericalism may be seen. What clericalism also does, by concentrating power and privilege in the hands of the clergy, is at least to obscure and at worst to annul the essential oneness of the people of God. Extreme forms of clericalism dare to reintroduce the notion of privilege into the only human community in which it has been abolished. Where Christ has made out of two one, the clerical mind makes two again, the one higher and the other lower, the one active and the other passive, the one really important because vital to the life of the church, the other not vital and therefore less important. I do not hesitate to say that to interpret the church in terms of a privileged clerical caste or hierarchical structure is to destroy the New Testament doctrine of the church. **(1969b:19)**

695. An enabling ministry

The New Testament concept of the pastor is not of a person who jealously guards all ministry in his own hands, and successfully squashes all lay initiatives, but of one who helps and encourages all God's people to discover, develop and exercise their gifts. His teaching and training are directed to this end, to enable the people of God to be a servant people, ministering actively but humbly according to their gifts in a world of alienation and pain. Thus, instead of monopolizing all ministry himself, he actually multiplies ministries. **(1979e:167)**

696. A sturdy independence

There is a constant danger of clergy tying people to their apron strings, instead of encouraging them to develop a certain sturdy and healthy independence, as they rely more and more upon God himself. It is surely to this that Jesus referred when he warned us to call no man our 'father', 'teacher', or 'lord' on earth (Mt. 23:8–12). We are to adopt towards no-one in the church, nor require anyone to adopt towards us, the dependent attitude implied in the child–parent, pupil–teacher, servant–lord relationships. We are all brethren. We are to depend on God as our Father, Christ as our Lord, and the Holy Spirit as our Teacher. The ambition of every minister for his congregation should be so to warn every man and teach every man in all wisdom as to 'present every man' not dependent on his minister but 'full-grown, mature in Christ' (Col. 1:28). Although occasional consultations can indeed do good, I cannot see that frequent visits to the parson, whether for 'confession' or for 'conference', are productive of true spiritual maturity. **(1964:82)**

697. Every believer a bishop?

It is a mistake to suppose that God commits the oversight of his people to ministers only, and that the laity have no share in it. Hebrews 12:15 contains the exhortation: 'see to it that no-one fails to obtain the grace of God'. The words 'see to it' translate *episkopountes*. This is a general exhortation to members of the local church to accept spiritual responsibility for each other and to care for each other. Moulton and Milligan quote papyrus examples of the use of the verb as a common salutation at the end of letters, as we might say 'look after yourself' or 'look after so and so'. In this sense . . . every believer is a bishop also! **(1966a:13)**

698. 'Entering the ministry'

We do a disservice to the church whenever we refer to the pastorate as 'the ministry', for example when we speak of ordination in terms of 'entering the ministry'. This use of the definite article implies that the ordained pastorate is the only ministry there is. But *diakonia* is a generic word for service; it lacks specificity until a descriptive adjective is added, whether 'pastoral', 'social', 'political', 'medical' or another. All Christians without exception, being followers of him who came 'not to be served but to serve', are themselves called to ministry, indeed to give their lives in ministry. But the expression 'full-time Christian ministry' is not to be restricted to church work and missionary service; it can also be exercised in government, the media, the professions, business, industry and the home. We need to recover this vision of the wide diversity of ministries to which God calls his people. **(1990b:122)**

699. No ungifted Christian

The fact that every Christian has a gift and therefore a responsibility, and that no Christian is passed by and left without endowment, is fundamental to the New Testament doctrine of the church. **(1975b:105)**

700. The purpose of gifts

Much misunderstanding surrounds the purpose for which God distributes spiritual gifts in the church. Some speak of them as 'love gifts', as if their main purpose is to enrich the recipient and we are to use them for our own benefit. Others think of them as 'worship gifts', as if their main purpose is the worship of God and their main sphere of operation is the conduct of public worship. But Scripture asserts that they are 'service gifts', whose primary purpose is to 'edify' or build up the church. **(1975b:111)**

701. The ministry of letter-writing

I do not know any Christian leader of modern days who shared, as he did, the apostle Paul's conviction about the value of letter-writing. Bash [the Rev. E. J. H. Nash] was never separated from his writing materials, especially on his 'missionary journeys'. During the war he continued to travel, sometimes driving many miles to visit a small group or even only one boy, or using the erratic war-time train service. One of my most characteristic memories of him is to see him on an ill-lit railway platform during the blackout, with his attaché case on his knees and his writing pad on it, 'redeeming the time' by writing letters. **(1992e:84)**

51. THE UNITY OF THE CHURCH

702. One Father, one family

The fundamental spiritual unity of the church is as indestructible as the fundamental unity of the Godhead. You can no more divide the unity of the church than you can divide the unity of the Godhead. The one Father creates the one family; the one Lord Jesus creates the one faith, hope and baptism; and the one Holy Spirit creates the one body. **(1972c:209)**

703. What kind of Christianity?

In my own conviction, the visible unity of the church (in each region or country) is both biblically right and practically desirable, and we should be actively seeking it. At the same time, we should ask ourselves a simple but searching question. If we are to meet the enemies of Christ with a united Christian front, with what kind of Christianity are we going to face them? The only weapon with which the opponents of the gospel can be overthrown is the gospel itself. It would be a tragedy if, in our desire for their overthrow, the only effective weapon in our armoury were to drop from our hands. United Christianity which is not true Christianity will not gain the victory over non-Christian forces, but will itself succumb to them. **(1970b:20)**

704. A common truth and life

The Christian unity for which Christ prayed in John 17:20–23 was not primarily unity with each other, but unity with the apostles (a common truth) and unity with the Father and the Son (a common life). The visible, structural unity of the church is a proper goal. Yet it will be pleasing to God only if it is the visible expression of something deeper, namely unity in truth and in life. In our ecumenical concern, therefore, nothing is more important than the quest for more apostolic truth and more divine life through the Holy Spirit. As William Temple put it, 'the way to the union of Christendom does not lie through committee-rooms, though there is a task of formulation to be done there. It lies through personal union with the Lord so deep and real as to be comparable with his union with the Father.'[1] **(1992b:267)**

[1] William Temple, *Readings in St John's Gospel* (first published in two volumes, 1939 and 1940; Macmillan, 1947), p. 327.

705. Loyalty to the gospel

Only loyalty to the gospel can secure unity in the church.

(1994:25)

706. Unity in truth

Evangelicals hold different views regarding the nature of Christian unity and whether the visible, organic union of churches is a desirable goal. But all would agree that no movement towards reunion can be pleasing to God or beneficial to the church which is not at the same time a movement towards reformation. True unity will always be unity in truth, and truth means biblical truth. If only church leaders would sit down with their Bibles, would distinguish clearly between apostolic traditions (which are biblical) and ecclesiastical traditions (which are not), and would agree to subordinate the latter to the former by requiring the former of each other but giving each other liberty over the latter, immediate and solid advance could be made. **(1970b:87)**

707. Founded on truth

Since Christian love is founded upon Christian truth, we shall not increase the love which exists between us by diminishing the truth which we hold in common. In contemporary movements towards church unity we must never compromise the very truth on which alone true love and unity depend.

(1988g:206)

708. True apostolic succession

Almost deafened by the babel of voices in the contemporary church, how are we to decide whom to follow? The answer is: we must test them all by the teaching of the apostles of Jesus Christ. 'Peace and mercy' will be on the church when it 'walks by this rule' (Gal. 6:16). Indeed, this is the only kind of apostolic succession we can accept – not a line of bishops stretching back to the apostles and claiming to be their successors (for the apostles were unique in both authorization and inspiration, and they have no successors), but loyalty to the apostolic doctrine of the New Testament. The teaching of the apostles, now permanently preserved in the New Testament, is to regulate the beliefs and practices of the church of every generation. This is why the Bible is over the church and not *vice versa*. The apostolic authors of the New Testament were commissioned by Christ, not by the church, and wrote with the authority of Christ, not of the church. 'To that authority (*sc.* of the apostles),' as the Anglican bishops said at the 1958 Lambeth Conference, 'the Church must ever bow.' Would that it did! The only church union schemes which can be pleasing to God and beneficial to the church are those which first distinguish between apostolic traditions and ecclesiastical traditions and then subject the latter to the former. **(1968c:186)**

709. The way forward

If only we could agree that Scripture is 'God's Word written' (Anglican Article XX), that it is supreme in its authority over all human traditions however venerable, and that it must be allowed to reform and renew the church, we would take an immediate leap forward in ecumenical relationships. Reformation according to the Word of God is indispensable to reunion.
(1992b:182)

710. The Lord of the church

If the church is in the end to be united under the headship of Christ (Eph. 1:10), it will not in the meantime be united in any other way. Is the continuing fragmentation of the church due ultimately to this one thing, its failure to 'hold fast to the Head' (Col. 2:19)? No doubt many would dismiss this as a ludicrous over-simplification. But I am not so easily shifted from my ground. The stubborn obstacle to the uniting of churches is either the cherishing of traditions which are not in the Bible (the characteristic of the Roman Catholic church), or the abandoning of doctrines which are (the characteristic of liberal Protestantism). I keep returning to this simple question: is Jesus Christ the Lord of the church, so that it submits to his teaching however unpalatable, or is the church the lord of Jesus Christ so that it manipulates his teaching in order to make it palatable? Will the church listen humbly and obediently to Jesus Christ, or will it behave like the brash adolescent it often seems to be, contradicting its master and putting him right where he has gone wrong? Is the church 'over' or 'under' Christ? **(1991b:58)**

THE UNITY OF THE CHURCH

711. Fresh unity through fresh understanding

We must come to the biblical text with a recognition of our cultural prejudices and with a willingness to have them challenged and changed. If we come to Scripture with the proud presupposition that all our inherited beliefs and practices are correct, then of course we shall find in the Bible only what we want to find, namely the comfortable confirmation of the *status quo*. As a result, we shall also find ourselves in sharp disagreement with people who come to Scripture from different backgrounds and with different convictions, and find these confirmed. There is probably no commoner source of discord than this. It is only when we are brave and humble enough to allow the Spirit of God through the Word of God radically to call in question our most cherished opinions, that we are likely to find fresh unity through fresh understanding.

(1982b:50)

712. One holy, catholic and apostolic church

In one sense the church is not divided and cannot be. Even our outward divisions do not tear it asunder, since the one Spirit indwells it. Piers in a harbour may divide it into sections, so that boats are cut off from each other, but the same sea flows and swells underneath. Our man-made denominations also separate us outwardly and visibly, but inwardly and invisibly the tide of the Spirit unites us. The Nicene Creed characterizes the church as 'one, holy, catholic and apostolic', which are the four classical 'marks' or 'notes' of the church. And they are true. The church is both one and holy because the Holy Spirit has united and sanctified it, setting it apart to belong to God, even though in practice it is often disunited and unholy. The church is also catholic (embracing all believers and all truth) and apostolic (affirming the teaching of the apostles and engaging in mission), even though in practice it often denies the faith it should profess and the mission it should pursue.

(1991d:83)

713. Protestants and Roman Catholics

The proper activity of professing Christians who disagree with one another is neither to ignore, nor to conceal, nor even to minimize their differences, but to debate them. Take the Church of Rome as an example. I find it distressing to see

Protestants and Roman Catholics united in some common act of worship or witness. Why? Because it gives the onlooker the impression that their disagreements are now virtually over. 'See,' the unsophisticated spectator might say, 'they can now engage in prayer and proclamation together; what remains to divide them?'

But such a public display of unity is a game of let's pretend; it is not living in the real world. Certainly we can be very thankful for the signs of a loosening rigidity and of a greater biblical awareness in the Roman Church. In consequence, many individual Roman Catholics have come to embrace more biblical truth than they had previously grasped, and some for conscience' sake have left their church. Vatican II has so let Scripture loose in the church that no man can guess what the final result may be . . .

In the light of these things, what is needed today between Protestants and Roman Catholics is not a premature outward show of unity, but a candid and serious 'dialogue'. Some Protestants regard such conversation with Roman Catholics as compromising, but it need not be so. The Greek verb from which it is derived is used in the Acts for reasoning with people out of the Scriptures. Its purpose (for the Protestant) is twofold: first, that by careful listening he may understand what the Roman Catholic is saying, and thereby avoid mere shadow-boxing, and secondly, that he may witness plainly and firmly to scriptural truth as he has been given to see it. **(1970b:22, 23)**

714. The need for diligence

The fact of the church's indestructible unity is no excuse for acquiescing in the tragedy of its actual disunity. On the contrary, the apostle tells us to be *eager to maintain the unity of the Spirit* (Eph. 4:3). The Greek verb for 'eager' (*spoudazontes*) is emphatic. It means that we are to 'spare no effort' (NEB), and being a present participle, it is a call for continuous, diligent activity. **(1979e:153)**

52. REFORMING THE CHURCH

715. Mature adoration

The Divine Lover still sorrows when his love is unrequited, and pines for our continuing, deepening, maturing adoration. Love, then, is the first mark of a true and living church. Indeed, it is not a living church at all unless it is a loving church. The Christian life is essentially a love-relationship to Jesus Christ. 'Jesus captured me,' wrote Wilson Carlile, founder and 'chief' of the Church Army. 'For me to know Jesus is a love affair.'

(1990c:23)

716. The church's failings

We need to get the failures of the church on our conscience, to feel the offence to Christ and the world which these failures are, to weep over the credibility gap between the church's talk and the church's walk, to repent of our readiness to excuse and even condone our failures, and to determine to do something about it. I wonder if anything is more urgent today, for the honour of Christ and for the spread of the gospel, than what the church should be, and should be seen to be, what by God's purpose and Christ's achievement it already is – a single new humanity, a model of human community, a family of reconciled brothers and sisters who love their Father and love each other, the evident dwelling place of God by his Spirit. Only then will the world believe in Christ as Peacemaker. Only then will God receive the glory due to his name. **(1979e:111)**

717. Authentic relationships

Young people hunger for the authentic relationships of love. Hobart Mowrer, emeritus professor of psychiatry in the University of Illinois and well-known critic of Freud, though by his own profession neither a Christian nor a theist, once described himself as having 'a lover's quarrel with the church'. Asked what he meant by this, he replied that the church had failed him when he was a teenager and continued to fail his patients today. How? 'Because the church has never learned the secret of community,' he said. Unfair perhaps, because some churches *are* genuine communities. But it was his opinion, which was born no doubt of bitter experience. I think

301

it is the most damaging criticism of the church I have ever
heard. **(1977a)**

718. Jesus and the young

The young, with their strong loathing for the unauthentic,
quickly detect any dichotomy between the church and its
founder. Jesus has never ceased to attract them. They see him
as the radical he was, impatient with the traditions of the elders
and the conventions of society, a merciless critic of the religious
Establishment. They like that. But the church? Somehow it
seems to them to have lost the 'smell' of Christ. So many vote –
with their feet. They get out. **(1977a)**

719. Ideal and reality

What do you think of the church? Your answer will probably
depend on whether you are thinking about the ideal or the
reality. In the ideal, the church is the most marvellous new
creation of God. It is the new community of Jesus, enjoying a
multi-racial, multi-national and multi-cultural harmony which
is unique in history and in contemporary society. The church
is even the 'new humanity', the vanguard of a redeemed and
renewed human race. It is a people who spend their earthly
lives (as they will also spend eternity) in the loving service of
God and of others. What a noble and beautiful ideal! In
reality, however, the church is us (if you will pardon the bad
grammar) – a dishevelled rabble of sinful, fallible, bickering,
squabbling, stupid, shallow Christians, who constantly fall
short of God's ideal, and often fail even to approximate to it.
(1982b:53)

720. A contradiction of identity

Insofar as the church is conformed to the world, and the two
communities appear to the onlooker to be merely two versions
of the same thing, the church is contradicting its true identity.
No comment could be more hurtful to the Christian than the
words, 'But you are no different from anybody else.' **(1978f:17)**

721. Not to be abandoned

Some people construct a Christianity which consists entirely of
a personal relationship to Jesus Christ and has virtually
nothing to do with the church. Others make a grudging
concession to the need for church membership, but add that

they have given up the ecclesiastical institution as hopeless. Now it is understandable, even inevitable, that we are critical of many of the church's inherited structures and traditions. Every church in every place at every time is in need of reform and renewal. But we need to beware lest we despise the church of God, and are blind to his work in history. We may safely say that God has not abandoned his church, however displeased with it he may be. He is still building and refining it. And if God has not abandoned it, how can we? **(1979e:126)**

722. Patient biblical reform

The way of the Holy Spirit with the institutional church is more the way of patient biblical reform than of impatient rejection.
(1977g:163)

723. The church and the Word

The dependence of the church on the Word is not a doctrine readily acceptable to all. In former days of Roman Catholic polemic, for example, its champions would insist that 'the church wrote the Bible' and therefore has authority over it. Still today one sometimes hears this rather simplistic argument. Now it is true, of course, that both Testaments were written within the context of the believing community, and that the substance of the New Testament in God's providence . . . was to some extent determined by the needs of the local Christian congregations. In consequence, the Bible can neither be detached from the milieu in which it originated, nor be understood in isolation from it. Nevertheless, as Protestants have always emphasized, it is misleading to the point of inaccuracy to say that 'the church wrote the Bible'; the truth is almost the opposite, namely that 'God's Word created the church'. For the people of God may be said to have come into existence when his Word came to Abraham, calling him and making a covenant with him. Similarly, it was through the apostolic preaching of God's Word in the power of the Holy Spirit on the Day of Pentecost that the people of God became the Spirit-filled body of Christ. **(1982a:109)**

724. A deaf church

A deaf church is a dead church: that is an unalterable principle. God quickens, feeds, inspires and guides his people by his Word. For whenever the Bible is truly and systematically

303

expounded, God uses it to give his people the vision without which they perish. **(1982a:113)**

725. *Church and Bible*

One of the perennial questions facing the church in every age and place concerns its relationship to the Bible. How do the people of God and the Word of God relate to one another? Did the Word create the church or the church the Word? Is the church over the Bible or under it? Roman Catholic, Orthodox and Protestant churches answer these questions differently, and our division at this point is arguably deeper and wider than at any other.

2 Thessalonians 3 throws a bright light on this controversy, since it gives pre-eminence to the Word. Its opening prayer that 'the word of the Lord may speed on and triumph' puts all parochialism to shame and challenges us to develop a global vision and a commitment to world evangelization. And Paul's repeated commands, with their expectation of obedience, also condemn those churches whose attitude to the Word of God appears to be subjective and selective. They wander at random through Scripture, choosing a verse here and discarding a verse there, like a gardener picking flowers in a herbaceous border. They have no concept of a thorough study of the Bible, or of a conscientious submission to its teaching. Let not such a church imagine that it will receive the blessing of the Lord! For to despise the Word of the Lord is to despise the Lord of the Word, to distrust his faithfulness and to disregard his authority. **(1991c:198)**

726. *An adolescent church*

If the Christian church has one obvious characteristic today, I would suggest it is uncertainty, a lack of assurance. Indeed I think it is true to say that the nominal visible Christian church manifests an insecurity which is positively adolescent. Churches today are what adolescents are – unsure of themselves, insecure, not knowing who they are, what they are here for or where they are going. **(1971d:4)**

727. *The root of dissension*

Self-love vitiates all relationships . . . Personal vanity lies at the root of most dissensions in every local church today.
(1988g:231)

728. A heterogeneous church

It is of course a fact that people like to worship with their own kith and kin, and with their own kind, as experts in church growth remind us; and it may be necessary to acquiesce in different congregations according to language, which is the most formidable barrier of all. But heterogeneity is of the essence of the church, since it is the one and only community in the world in which Christ has broken down all dividing walls. The vision we have been given of the church triumphant is of a company drawn from 'every nation, tribe, people and language', who are all singing God's praises in unison (Rev. 7:19ff.). So we must declare that a homogeneous church is a defective church, which must work penitently and perseveringly towards heterogeneity.[1] (1994:397)

[1] See *The Pasadena Consultation on the Homogeneous Unit Principle* (Lausanne Occasional Paper no. 1, 1978).

729. How the church decides

If a local church desires to be a sign of the kingdom, and give evidence that Christ rules, this will be reflected also in the mundane matter of the decision-making processes it employs. Each local church ought to be able to say (not in feigned piety but in humble reality) 'it seemed good to the Holy Spirit and to us'. How then does the King guide his people? I mention as necessary conditions only prayer and patience. But often it is nothing but a formal and only partly sincere recognition that we desire to discover the will of God. What about a period of prayer instead? Can a Christian committee discuss together if it has not learned to pray together? Do we ever stop a committee in midstream, when it has reached an impasse, in order to pray again for light and wisdom. Secondly, patience. A truly Christian group will determine never to trample on minority opinions. To foreclose a debate by taking a snap vote and to decide issues by a bare majority, while minds are still confused and consciences troubled, is a worldly way to conduct the business of the church. It expresses a distrust in God and a disrespect for dissidents. Do we not believe in the Holy Spirit of unity? Then we must wait patiently, listen to each other, and strive to understand each other's concerns and scruples, until the Spirit brings us to a common mind. The local church is both a theocracy (not in the special sense that Israel was but in the general sense of submitting to God as King) and a brotherhood. Every attempt to crush the disagreement of fellow believers violates these truths and is therefore incompatible with the nature of the church. It is to use power like the world and to forget 'the meekness and the gentleness of Christ' (2 Cor. 10:1). **(1979b)**

730. Church and gospel

What is of particular interest, because it applies to Christian communities in every age and place, is the interaction which the apostle Paul portrays between the church and the gospel. He shows how the gospel creates the church and the church spreads the gospel, and how the gospel shapes the church, as the church seeks to live a life that is worthy of the gospel. **(1991c:20)**

731. A resurrection religion

The church of Jesus Christ is today facing a major crisis of faith. What is at stake is nothing less than the essential character of Christianity: is the Christian religion natural or supernatural? Various attempts are being made to rid Christianity of its supernaturalism, to reconstruct it without its embarrassing miracles. But these efforts will be as fruitless as they are misguided. You cannot reconstruct something by first destroying it.

Authentic Christianity – the Christianity of Christ and his apostles – is supernatural Christianity. It is not a tame and harmless ethic, consisting of a few moral platitudes, spiced with a dash of religion. It is rather a resurrection religion, a life lived by the power of God. **(1970b:63)**

732. Holy worldliness

All down history the church has tended to go to extremes . . . Sometimes, in its proper determination to be holy, it has withdrawn from the world and lost contact with it. At other times, in its equally proper determination not to lose contact, it has conformed to the world and become virtually indistinguishable from it. But Christ's vision for the church's holiness is neither withdrawal nor conformity. **(1992b:262)**

733. Reformation, revival and renewal

We need . . . a holistic or integrated vision of renewal in every dimension of the church's life.

The Roman Catholic word for this, at least since Vatican II (1963–65), has been *aggiornamento*, the process of bringing the church up to date in order to meet the challenges of the modern world. It implies that the world is changing rapidly and that, if the church is to survive, it must keep pace with this change, although without either compromising its own standards or conforming to the world's.

Protestants use a different vocabulary to describe the continuously needed restoring and refreshing of the church. Our two favourite words are 'reform', indicating the kind of reformation of faith and life according to Scripture which took place in the sixteenth century, and 'revival', denoting an altogether supernatural visitation of a church or community by God, bringing conviction, repentance, confession, the conversion of sinners and the recovery of backsliders. 'Reformation' usually stresses the power of the Word of God, and 'revival' the power of the Spirit of God, in his work of restoring the church. Perhaps we should keep the word 'renewal' to describe a movement which combines revival by God's Spirit with reformation by his Word. Since the Word is the Spirit's sword, there is bound to be something lopsided about contemplating either without the other. **(1992b:258)**

53. THE EVANGELICAL TRADITION

734. *The historic Christian faith*

At the risk of oversimplification and of the charge of arrogance, I want to argue that the evangelical faith is nothing other than the historic Christian faith. The evangelical Christian is not a deviationist, but a loyalist who seeks by the grace of God to be faithful to the revelation which God has given of himself in Christ and in Scripture. The evangelical faith is not a peculiar or esoteric version of the Christian faith – it *is* the Christian faith. It is not a recent innovation. The evangelical faith is original, biblical, apostolic Christianity. **(1983b:3)**

735. *Committed in advance*

The hallmark of evangelicals is not so much an impeccable set of words as a submissive spirit, namely their *a priori* resolve to believe and obey whatever Scripture may be shown to teach. They are committed to Scripture in advance, whatever it may later be found to say. They claim no liberty to lay down their own terms for belief and behaviour. They see this humble and obedient stance as an essential implication of Christ's lordship over them. **(1988d:104)**

736. *The catholic and liberal traditions*

Both the Catholic and the Liberal traditions have tended to exalt human intelligence and goodness and therefore to expect human beings to contribute something towards their enlightenment and their salvation. Evangelicals, on the other hand, while strongly affirming the divine image which our humanity bears, have tended to emphasize our human finitude and fallenness and therefore to insist that without revelation we cannot know God and without redemption we cannot reach him.

That is why evangelical essentials focus on the Bible and the cross, and on their indispensability, since it is through these that God's word to us has been spoken and God's work for us has been done. Indeed, his grace bears a trinitarian shape. First, in both spheres the Father took the initiative, teaching us what we could not otherwise know, and giving us what we could not otherwise have. Secondly, in both the Son has played a unique role as the one mediator through whom the Father's initiative was taken. He is the Word made flesh, through whom the Father's glory was manifested. He is the sinless one made sin for us that the Father might reconcile us to himself. Moreover, the word God spoke through Christ and the work God did through Christ were both *hapax*, completed once and for all. Nothing can be added to either without derogating from the perfection of God's word and work through Christ. Then thirdly, in both revelation and redemption the ministry of the Holy Spirit is essential. It is he who illumines our minds to understand what God has revealed in Christ, and he who moves our hearts to receive what God has achieved through Christ. Thus in both spheres the Father has acted through the Son and acts through the Spirit. **(1988d:336)**

737. Mainline Christianity

Evangelicals regard it as essential to believe not just 'the gospel revealed in the Bible', but the full revelation of the Bible; not just that 'Christ died for us' but that he died 'for our sins', in some sense 'bearing' them objectively in our place, so that in holy love God can forgive penitent believers; not just that we receive the Spirit, but that he does a supernatural work in us, variously portrayed in the New Testament as 'regeneration', 'resurrection' and 're-creation'.

Here are three aspects of the divine initiative – God revealing himself in Christ and in the total biblical witness to Christ, God redeeming the world through Christ, who became sin and a curse for us, and God radically transforming sinners by the inward operation of his Spirit. Thus stated, the evangelical faith is historic, mainline, trinitarian Christianity, not an eccentric deviation from it. For we do not see ourselves as offering a new Christianity, but as recalling the church to original Christianity. **(1988d:39)**

738. An Anglican evangelical Christian

First and foremost, by God's sheer mercy, I am a Christian seeking to follow Jesus Christ. Next, I am an evangelical Christian because of my conviction that evangelical principles (especially *sola scriptura* and *sola gratia*) are integral to authentic Christianity, and that to be an evangelical Christian is to be a new Testament Christian, and *vice versa*. Thirdly, I am an Anglican evangelical Christian, since the Church of England is the particular historical tradition or denomination to which I belong. But I am not an Anglican first, since denominationalism is hard to defend. It seems to me correct to call oneself an Anglican evangelical (in which evangelical is the noun and Anglican the descriptive adjective) rather than an evangelical Anglican (in which Anglican is the noun and evangelical the adjective). **(1986d:17)**

739. Evangelical theology

If 'evangelical' describes a theology, that theology is biblical theology. It is the contention of evangelicals that they are plain Bible Christians, and that in order to be a biblical Christian it is necessary to be an evangelical Christian. Put that way, it may sound arrogant and exclusive, but this is a sincerely held belief. Certainly it is the earnest desire of evangelicals to be neither more nor less than biblical Christians. Their intention is not to be partisan. That is, they do not cling to certain tenets for the sake of maintaining their identity as a 'party'. On the contrary, they have always expressed their readiness to modify, even abandon, any or all of their cherished beliefs if they can be shown to be unbiblical.

Evangelicals therefore regard as the only possible road to the reunion of churches the road of biblical reformation. In their view the only solid hope for churches which desire to unite is a common willingness to sit down together under the authority of God's Word, in order to be judged and reformed by it.

(1970b:32)

740. The nominal church

The persecution of the true church, of Christian believers who trace their spiritual descent from Abraham, is not always by the world, who are strangers unrelated to us, but by our half-brothers, religious people, the nominal church. It has always been so. The Lord Jesus was bitterly opposed, rejected, mocked and condemned by his own nation. The fiercest opponents of the apostle Paul, who dogged his footsteps and stirred up strife against him, were the official church, the Jews. The monolithic structure of the medieval papacy persecuted all Protestant minorities with ruthless, unremitting ferocity. And the greatest enemies of the evangelical faith today are not unbelievers, who when they hear the gospel often embrace it, but the church, the establishment, the hierarchy. **(1968c:127)**

310

741. 'Doing the truth'

We evangelicals tend to be strong in piety and weak in praxis
. . . All of us will agree that theological reflection is indispensable; I hope we agree that it is equally indispensable to
translate our theology into action. Knowledge of Scripture can
never be an end in itself. We are called not only to 'believe' the
truth, but to 'do' or 'obey' it.   **(1978c:181)**

742. Scholars or thinkers?

One of the best aimed of James Barr's poisoned arrows in his
Fundamentalism is directed at our evangelical lack of theology.
We have a stale tradition, he suggests, not a fresh theology.
'Fundamentalism (from which he scarcely seems to distinguish
evangelicalism) is a theologyless movement.' If we have a
theology at all, he continues, it is either 'formalized' or
'fossilized'. This criticism is a broad generalization, as inaccurate as all generalizations are bound to be. Yet it contains an
uncomfortable degree of truth. The resurgent evangelical
movement has produced biblical scholars rather than creative
thinkers.   **(1978c:180)**

743. The whole of life

We [evangelicals] have tended to have a good doctrine of
redemption, and a bad doctrine of creation. Of course we have
paid lip-service to the truth that God is the Creator of all things,
but we seem to have been blind to its implications. Our God
has been too 'religious', as if his main interests were worship
services and prayer meetings attended by church members.
Don't misunderstand me: God *does* take a delight in the prayers
and praises of his people. But now we begin to see him also (as
the Bible has always portrayed him) as the Creator, who is
concerned for the secular world as well as the church, who
loves all men and not Christians only, and who is interested in
the whole of life and not merely in religion.   **(1975a:45)**

744. 'Conservative' evangelicals

The proper use of the word 'conservative', when applied to
evangelicals, is that we hold tenaciously to the teaching of
Christ and the apostles as given to us in the New Testament,
and are determined to 'conserve' the whole biblical faith. This
was the apostle's charge to Timothy: 'keep the deposit',

conserve it, preserve it, never relax your hold upon it, nor let it drop from your hands. **(1967a)**

745. Impoverished discipleship

I am not saying that it is impossible to be a disciple of Jesus without a high view of Scripture, for this is manifestly not the case. There are genuine followers of Jesus Christ who are not 'evangelical', whose confidence in Scripture is small, even minimal, and who put more faith in the past traditions and present teaching of the church, or in their own reason or experience. I have no desire to deny the authenticity of their Christian profession. Yet I venture to add that their discipleship is bound to be impoverished on account of their attitude to the Bible. A full, balanced and mature Christian discipleship is impossible whenever disciples do not submit to their Lord's teaching authority as it is mediated through Scripture.

(1992b:173)

746. Evangelicalism and evangelism

It is not unusual to hear people use the term 'evangelical' as if it were a synonym for 'evangelistic'. One of my colleagues recently received a letter of instructions about a speaking engagement he had soon to fulfil. His correspondent informed him that, because they were all Christians in their group, they did 'not want anything evangelical'! He meant, of course, that they were not asking for an evangelistic address. But the words 'evangelical' and 'evangelistic' should not be confused. The adjective 'evangelistic' describes an activity, that of spreading the gospel, so that we speak of evangelistic campaigns and evangelistic services. 'Evangelical', on the other hand, describes a theology, what the apostle Paul called 'the truth of the gospel' (Gal. 2:5, 14). **(1970b:27)**

747. What finally matters

In the end what matters most of all to an evangelical is not a label, nor an epithet. It is not a party ticket; it is not even in the end the Bible and the gospel. It is the honour and glory of Jesus Christ. **(1977i:14)**

X. INTO ALL THE WORLD

54. Christian mission
55. A servant church
56. The call to evangelize
57. Proclaiming the gospel

54. CHRISTIAN MISSION

748. A God who sends

'Mission' is an activity of God arising out of the very nature of God. The living God of the Bible is a sending God, which is what 'mission' means. He sent the prophets to Israel. He sent his Son into the world. His son sent out the apostles, and the seventy, and the church. He also sent the Spirit to the church and sends him into our hearts today. **(1975e:66)**

749. The basis for mission

Monotheism remains the essential basis for mission. The supreme reason why God 'desires *all men* to be saved and come to the knowledge of the [same] truth' is that 'there is *one God*, and there is one mediator between God and men, the man Christ Jesus, who gave himself as a ransom for all . . .' (1 Tim. 2:4–6). The logic of this passage rests on the relation between 'all men' and 'one God'. Our warrant for seeking the allegiance of 'all men' is that there is only 'one God', and only 'one mediator' between him and them. Without the unity of God and the uniqueness of Christ there could be no Christian mission. **(1967e:23)**

750. A missionary religion

There are the five parts of the Bible. The God of the Old Testament is a missionary God, calling one family in order to bless all the families of the earth. The Christ of the gospels is a missionary Christ; he sent the church out to witness. The Spirit of the Acts is a missionary Spirit; he drove the church out from Jerusalem to Rome. The church of the epistles is a missionary church, a worldwide community with a world-wide vocation. The end of the Revelation is a missionary End, a countless throng from every nation. So I think we have to say that the religion of the Bible is a missionary religion. The evidence is overwhelming and irrefutable. Mission cannot be regarded as a regrettable lapse from tolerance or decency. Mission cannot be regarded as the hobby of a few fanatical eccentrics in the church. Mission lies at the very heart of God and therefore at the very heart of the church. A church without mission is no longer a church. It is contradicting an essential part of its identity. The church *is* mission. **(1980g:46)**

751. *The church's mandate*

Our mandate for world evangelization is the whole Bible. It is to be found in the creation of God (because of which all human beings are responsible to him), in the character of God (as outgoing, loving, compassionate, not willing that any should perish, desiring that all should come to repentance), in the promises of God (that all nations will be blessed through Abraham's seed and will become the Messiah's inheritance), in the Christ of God (now exalted with universal authority, to receive universal acclaim), in the Spirit of God (who convicts of sin, witnesses to Christ, and impels the church to evangelize) and in the church of God (which is a multinational, missionary community, under orders to evangelize until Christ returns).

(1981h:4)

752. *Jesus is for all*

Jesus is the light of the *world*. We cannot therefore keep him to ourselves. We dare not attempt to monopolize him. Christianity is inescapable and unashamedly a missionary faith.

(1966b:54)

753. *Christ's universal authority*

The fundamental basis of all Christian missionary enterprise is the universal authority of Jesus Christ, 'in heaven and on earth'. If the authority of Jesus were circumscribed on earth, if he were but one of many religious teachers, one of many Jewish prophets, one of many divine incarnations, we would have no mandate to present him to the nations as the Lord and Saviour of the world. If the authority of Jesus were limited in heaven, if he had not decisively overthrown the principalities and powers, we might still proclaim him to the nations, but we would never be able to 'turn them from darkness to light, and from the power of Satan unto God' (Acts 26:18).

Only because all authority on earth belongs to Christ dare we go to all nations. And only because all authority in heaven as well is his have we any hope of success. It must have seemed ridiculous to send that tiny nucleus of Palestinian peasants to win the world for Christ. For Christ's church today, so hopelessly outnumbered by hundreds of millions who neither know nor acknowledge him, the task is equally gigantic. It is the unique, the universal authority of Jesus Christ which gives us both the right and the confidence to seek to make disciples of all the nations. Before his authority on earth the nations must bow; before his authority in heaven no demon can stop them.

(1967d:46)

754. The Spirit and the church

It is the Holy Spirit who convicts sinners of their sin and guilt, opens their eyes to see Christ, draws them to him, enables them to repent and believe, and implants life in their dead souls. Before Christ sent the church into the world, he sent the Spirit to the church. **(1967d:56)**

755. The Spirit's witness

In the Upper Room Jesus emphasized that the distinctive work of the Spirit whom the Father was going to send would be in relation to himself, the Son; that the Spirit would delight above all else to glorify or manifest the Son (Jn. 16:14); and that therefore in the spread of the gospel the Holy Spirit would be the chief witness. 'He will bear witness to me.' Only after saying this did Jesus add to his apostles, 'and you also are witnesses' (Jn. 15:26–27). Once we have grasped the significance of this order, we shall have no difficulty in agreeing that *without his witness ours is futile.* **(1975d:34)**

756. A Christian lifestyle

Mission is our human response to the divine commission. It is a whole Christian lifestyle, including both evangelism and social responsibility, dominated by the conviction that Christ sends us out into the world as the Father sent him into the world, and that into the world we must therefore go – to live and work for him. **(1990a:15)**

757. Sharing God's mission

The call of God is to share in his own mission in the world. First, he sent his Son. Then he sent his Spirit. Now he sends his church, that is, us. He sends us out by his Spirit into his world to announce his Son's salvation. He worked through his Son to achieve it; he works through us to make it known. **(1967e:18)**

317

758. God's name and glory

If God desires every knee to bow to Jesus and every tongue to confess him, so should we. We should be 'jealous' (as Scripture sometimes puts it) for the honour of his name – troubled when it remains unknown, hurt when it is ignored, indignant when it is blasphemed, and all the time anxious and determined that it shall be given the honour and glory which are due to it. The highest of all missionary motives is neither obedience to the Great Commission (important as that is), nor love for sinners who are alienated and perishing (strong as that incentive is, especially when we contemplate the wrath of God) but rather zeal – burning and passionate zeal – for the glory of Jesus Christ.

Some evangelism, to be sure, is no better than a thinly disguised form of imperialism, whenever our real ambition is for the honour of our nation, church, organization, or ourselves. Only one imperialism is Christian, however, and that is concern for His Imperial Majesty Jesus Christ, and for the glory of his empire or kingdom. The earliest Christians, John tells us, went out 'for the sake of the Name' (3 Jn. 7). He does not even specify to which name he is referring. But we know. And Paul tells us. It is the incomparable name of Jesus. Before this supreme goal of the Christian mission, all unworthy motives wither and die. **(1994:53)**

759. God's church and Word

When Paul and Barnabas set out into the unknown on the first missionary journey, they found (as Abraham, Joseph and Moses had found before them) that God was with them. That is exactly what they reported on their return (Acts 14:27; 15:12). Indeed, this assurance is indispensable tᴐ mission. Change is painful to us all, especially when it affects our cherished buildings and customs, and we should not seek change merely for the sake of change. Yet true Christian radicalism is open to change. It knows that God has bound himself to his church (promising that he will never leave it) and to his Word (promising that it will never pass away). But God's church means people not buildings, and God's Word means Scripture not traditions. So long as these essentials are preserved, the buildings and the traditions can if necessary go. We must not allow them to imprison the living God or to impede his mission in the world. **(1990b:143)**

CHRISTIAN MISSION

760. The call to mission

The Christian calling is at one and the same time to worldliness (in the sense of living in the world), to holiness (in the sense of being kept from the world's evil) and to mission (in the sense of going into the world in the name of Christ as servants and witnesses). **(1971b:81)**

761. Authentic mission

The Son of God did not stay in the safe immunity of his heaven, remote from human sin and tragedy. He actually entered our world. He emptied himself of his glory and humbled himself to serve. He took our nature, lived our life, endured our temptations, experienced our sorrows, felt our hurts, bore our sins and died our death. He penetrated deeply into our humanness. He never stayed aloof from the people he might have been expected to avoid. He made friends with the dropouts of society. He even touched untouchables. He could not have become more one with us than he did. It was the total identification of love . . .

Yet when Christ identified with us, he did not surrender or in any way alter his own identity. For in becoming one of us, he yet remained himself. He became human, but without ceasing to be God.

Now he sends us into the world, as the Father sent him into the world. In other words, our mission is to be modelled on his. Indeed, all authentic mission is incarnational mission. It demands identification without loss of identity. It means entering other people's worlds, as he entered ours, though without compromising our Christian convictions, values or standards. **(1992b:357)**

762. The context of mission

To go 'into the world' does not necessarily mean to travel to a distant country or primitive tribe. 'The world' is secular, godless society; it is all round us. Christ sends us 'into the world' when he puts us into any group which does not know or honour him. It might be in our own street, or in an office or shop, school, hospital or factory, or even in our own family. And here in the world we are called to love, to serve and to offer genuine, sacrificial friendship. Paradoxically stated, the only truly Christian context in which to witness is the world. **(1967e:67)**

55. A SERVANT CHURCH

763. Authentic evangelism

When God spoke to us in Scripture he used human language, and when he spoke to us in Christ he assumed human flesh. In order to reveal himself, he both emptied and humbled himself. That is the model of . . . evangelism which the Bible supplies. There is self-emptying and self-humbling in all authentic evangelism; without it we contradict the gospel and misrepresent the Christ we proclaim. **(1981h:7)**

764. The mission of Jesus

The mission of Jesus was a mission of compassion. The words *mission* and *compassion* should always be bracketed, indeed almost hyphenated, so closely do they belong to one another. Again and again we read in the gospels that Jesus 'was moved with compassion' – now by the leaderless or hungry crowds, now by the sick, now by a single leprosy sufferer, now by a widow who had lost her only child. What aroused his compassion was always human need, in whatever form he encountered it. And out of compassion for people in need he acted. He preached the gospel, he taught the people, he fed the hungry, he cleansed the leper, he healed the sick, he raised the dead. All this was part of his mission. He had not come to be served, he said, but to serve (Mk. 10:45). Of course the climax of his self-giving service was his atoning death, by which he secured our salvation. Nevertheless, his mission of compassion was not limited to this, because human need is not limited to this. He was sent to serve, and his service was adapted with compassionate sensitivity to human need. **(1977d:54)**

765. The love that serves

Jesus sends us, he says, as the Father had sent him. Therefore our mission, like his, is to be one of service. He emptied himself of status and took the form of a servant, and his humble mind is to be in us (Phil. 2:5–8). He supplies us with the perfect model of service, and sends his church into the world to be a servant church. Is it not essential for us to recover this biblical emphasis? In many of our Christian attitudes and enterprises we have tended (especially those of us who live in Europe and

North America) to be rather bosses than servants. Yet it seems that it is in our servant role that we can find the right synthesis of evangelism and social action. For both should be for us, as they undoubtedly were for Christ, authentic expressions of the love that serves. **(1975c:25)**

766. Two instructions

I venture to say that sometimes, perhaps because it was the last instruction Jesus gave us before returning to the Father, we give the Great Commission too prominent a place in our Christian thinking. Please do not misunderstand me. I firmly believe that the whole church is under obligation to obey its Lord's commission to take the gospel to all nations. But I am also concerned that we should not regard this as the only instruction which Jesus left us. He also quoted Leviticus 19:18, 'you shall love your neighbour as yourself', called it 'the second and great commandment' (second in importance only to the supreme command to love God with all our being), and elaborated it in the Sermon on the Mount. There he insisted that in God's vocabulary our neighbour includes our enemy, and that to love means to 'do good', that is, to give ourselves actively and constructively to serve our neighbour's welfare.

Here then are two instructions of Jesus – a great commandment, 'love your neighbour' and a great commission, 'go and make disciples'. **(1975c:29)**

767. True incentives

Incentives are important in every sphere. Being rational human beings, we need to know not only what we should be doing, but why we should be doing it. And motivation for mission is specially important, not least in our day in which the comparative study of religions has led many to deny finality and uniqueness to Jesus Christ and to reject the very concept of evangelizing and converting people. How then, in the face of growing opposition to it, can Christians justify the continuance of world evangelization? The commonest answer is to point to the Great Commission, and indeed obedience to it provides a strong stimulus. Compassion is higher than obedience, however, namely love for people who do not know Jesus Christ, and who on that account are alienated, disorientated, and indeed lost. But the highest incentive of all is zeal or jealousy for the glory of Jesus Christ. God has promoted him to the supreme place of honour, in order that every knee and tongue should acknowledge his lordship. Whenever he is denied his rightful place in people's lives, therefore, we should feel inwardly wounded, and jealous for his name.   **(1990b:279)**

768. Service and suffering

The place of suffering in service and of passion in mission is hardly ever taught today. But the greatest single secret of evangelistic or missionary effectiveness is the willingness to suffer and die. It may be a death to popularity (by faithfully preaching the unpopular biblical gospel), or to pride (by the use of modest methods in reliance on the Holy Spirit), or to racial and national prejudice (by identification with another culture), or to material comfort (by adopting a simple lifestyle). But the servant must suffer if he is to bring light to the nations, and the seed must die if it is to multiply.   **(1986a:322)**

769. The primacy of evangelism

I think we should agree with the statement of the Lausanne Covenant that 'in the church's mission of sacrificial service evangelism is primary' (para. 6, *The Church and Evangelism*). Christians should feel an acute pain of conscience and compassion when human beings are oppressed or neglected in any way, whether what is being denied them is civil liberty, racial respect, education, medicine, employment, or adequate food, clothing and shelter. Anything which undermines human dignity should be an offence to us. But is anything so destructive of human dignity as alienation from God through ignorance or rejection of the gospel? And how can we seriously maintain that political and economic liberation is just as important as eternal salvation?   **(1975c:35)**

770. Evangelism and social action

If pressed . . . *if one has to choose*, eternal salvation is more important than temporal welfare. This seems to me indisputable. But I want immediately to add that one should not normally have to choose. As William Temple put it, 'if we have to choose between making men Christian and making the social order more Christian, we must make the former. But there is no such antithesis'.   **(1979c:21)**

771. Motive and source

Evangelism is born of love.   **(1967f:5)**

56. THE CALL TO EVANGELIZE

772. *God's Word to God's world*

I believe we are called to the difficult and even painful task of 'double listening'. That is, we are to listen carefully (although of course with differing degrees of respect) both to the ancient Word and to the modern world, in order to relate the one to the other with a combination of fidelity and sensitivity. . . It is my firm conviction that, only if we can develop our capacity for double listening, will we avoid the opposite pitfalls of unfaithfulness and irrelevance, and be able to speak God's Word to God's world with effectiveness today.　　**(1992b:13)**

773. *The essence of the gospel*

The English word 'evangelism' is derived from a Greek term meaning literally 'to bring or to spread good news'. It is impossible, therefore, to talk about evangelism without talking about the content of the good news. What is it? At its very simplest, it is *Jesus*. Jesus Christ himself is the essence of the gospel.　　**(1975d:12)**

774. *Fact, doctrine and gospel*

It is not enough to 'proclaim Jesus'. For there are many different Jesuses being presented today. According to the New Testament gospel, however, he is *historical* (he really lived, died, rose and ascended in the arena of history), *theological* (his life, death, resurrection and ascension all have saving significance) and *contemporary* (he lives and reigns to bestow salvation on those who respond to him). Thus the apostles told the same story of Jesus at three levels – as historical event (witnessed by their own eyes), as having theological significance (interpreted by the Scriptures), and as contemporary message (confronting men and women with the necessity of decision). We have the same responsibility today to tell the story of Jesus as fact, doctrine and gospel.　　**(1990b:81)**

775. *Evangelism defined*

Evangelism is neither to convert people, nor to win them, nor to bring them to Christ, though this is indeed the first goal of evangelism. Evangelism is to preach the gospel.　　**(1975c:39)**

776. *The honour due*

The greatest incentive in all evangelism is not the need of human beings but the glory of God; not that they shall receive salvation, but that they shall give to God the honour that is due to his name, acknowledging and adoring him for ever.

(1988e:69)

777. *Let God be God*

Our greatest need in evangelism today is the humility to let God be God. Far from impoverishing our evangelism, nothing else is so much calculated to enrich, deepen and empower it.

Our motive must be concern for the glory of God, not the glory of the church or our own glory.

Our message must be the gospel of God, as given by Christ and his apostles, not the traditions of men or our own opinions.

Our manpower must be the church of God, and every member of it, not a privileged few who want to retain evangelism as their own prerogative.

Our dynamic must be the Spirit of God, not the power of human personality, organization or eloquence.

Without these priorities we shall be silent when we ought to be vocal. **(1967e:117)**

778. *Keeping our distance*

Close contact with people involves an uncomfortable exposure of ourselves to them. It is much easier, in both fellowship and witness, to keep our distance. We are more likely to win the admiration of other people if we do. It is only at close quarters that idols are seen to have feet of clay. Are we willing to let people come close enough to us to find out what we are really like and to know us as we really are? True witness, born of friendship, requires a great degree of holiness in us as well as love. The nearer we get to people the harder it is to speak for Christ. Is not this the reason why the hardest people of all to whom to witness are members of our own family? They know us too well. **(1962g:16)**

779. *'No-one can . . .'*

It is grievously mistaken to suggest that the purpose of evangelism is to cajole sinners into doing what they can perfectly well do if only they put their minds to it and pull themselves together. This the Bible emphatically denies. Consider these two statements: 'No one can say "Jesus is Lord" except by the Holy Spirit' (1 Cor. 12:3). 'No one can come to me unless the Father . . . draws him' (Jn. 6:44). We need to hear much more in the church of this 'no-one can', this natural inability of men to believe in Christ or to come to Christ. Only the Spirit can reveal Christ to men; only the Father can draw men to Christ. And without this double work of the Father and the Spirit no-one can reach the Son. It is quite true that Jesus also said 'you are not willing to come to me that you may have life' (Jn. 5:40, lit.), and that the human mind finds it impossible neatly to resolve the tension between this 'cannot' and this 'will not'. But both are true, and man's refusal to come does not cancel out his inability without grace to do so.   **(1967e:113)**

780. The chief evangelist

Now who is to be the messenger?

The first and fundamental answer to this question is 'God himself'. The gospel is God's gospel. He conceived it. He gave it its content. He publishes it. The fact that he has committed to us both 'the ministry of reconciliation' and 'the message of reconciliation' (1 Cor. 5:18–19) does not alter this. He acted 'through Christ' to achieve the reconciliation and now acts 'through us' to announce it. But he still remains himself both reconciler and preacher.

He has used other and more exalted agencies through whom to publish salvation before partially delegating the work to the church. Apart from Old Testament prophets, the first herald of the gospel was an angel, and the first announcement of it was accompanied by a display of the glory of the Lord and greeted by the worship of the heavenly host.

Next, God sent his Son, who was himself both the messenger and the message. For God sent a 'word . . . to Israel, preaching good news of peace by Jesus Christ' (Acts 10:36). So Jesus not only 'made peace' between God and man, Jew and Gentile, but also 'preached peace' (Eph. 2:14–17). He went about Palestine announcing the good news of the kingdom.

Next, God sent his Spirit to bear witness to Christ. So the Father himself witnesses to the Son through the Spirit. And only now does he give the church a privileged share in the testimony: 'and you also will bear witness' (Jn. 15:27, lit.).

It is essential to remember these humbling truths. The chief evangelist is God the Father, and he proclaimed the evangel through his angel, his Son and his Spirit before he entrusted any part of the task to men. This was the order. The church comes at the bottom of the list. And the church's witness will always be subordinate to the Spirit's. **(1967e:57)**

781. *Paul the persuader*

Paul's presentation of the gospel was serious, well reasoned and persuasive. Because he believed the gospel to be true, he was not afraid to engage the minds of his hearers. He did not simply proclaim his message in a 'take it or leave it' fashion; instead, he marshalled arguments to support and demonstrate his case. He was seeking to convince in order to convert, and in fact, as Luke makes plain, many were 'persuaded'. Luke indicates, moreover, that this was Paul's method even in Corinth. What he renounced in Corinth (see 1 Cor. 1 – 2) was the wisdom of the world, not the wisdom of God, and the rhetoric of the Greeks, not the use of arguments. Arguments of course are no substitute for the work of the Holy Spirit. But then trust in the Holy Spirit is no substitute for arguments either. We must never set them over against each other as alternatives. No, the Holy Spirit is the Spirit of truth, and he brings people to faith in Jesus not in spite of the evidence, but because of the evidence, when he opens their minds to attend to it. **(1990b:312)**

782. *The consent of the mind*

Evangelistic preaching has too often consisted of a prolonged appeal for decision when the congregation have been given no substance upon which the decision is to be made. But the gospel is not fundamentally an invitation to men to do anything. It is a declaration of what God has done in Christ on the cross for their salvation. The invitation cannot properly be given before the declaration has been made. Men must grasp the truth before they are asked to respond to it. It is true that man's intellect is finite and fallen, but he must never be asked to murder it. If he comes to Jesus Christ in repentance and faith, it must be with the full consent of his mind. Much of the leakage of converts after evangelistic campaigns is due to the evangelist's disregard of this. If it be said that we cannot consider man's mind in our evangelistic preaching because it is darkened, I can only reply that the apostles were of a different opinion. **(1961:48)**

783. Jesus on trial

Jesus Christ stands on trial, not now before the Sanhedrin, before Pontius Pilate the procurator or Herod Antipas, but at the bar of world opinion. The 'world', which in biblical language means secular, godless, non-Christian society, now uncommitted, now hostile, is in the rôle of judge. The world is judging Jesus Christ continuously, passing its various verdicts upon him. The devil accuses him with many ugly lies and musters his false witnesses by the hundred. The Holy Spirit is the *Paraklētos*, the counsel for the defence, and he calls us to be witnesses to substantiate his case. Christian preachers are privileged to testify to and for Jesus Christ, defending him, commending him, bringing before the court evidence which they must hear and consider before they return their verdict.

(1961:54)

784. True testimony

So much so-called 'testimony' today is really autobiography and even sometimes thinly disguised self-advertisement, that we need to regain a proper biblical perspective. All true testimony is testimony to Jesus Christ, as he stands on trial before the world. **(1961:57)**

785. Testimony to Christ

The words 'witness' and testimony' have been much devalued, and are sometimes employed to describe what is little more than an essay in religious autobiography. But Christian witness is witness to Christ. And the Christ to whom we have a responsibility to witness is not merely the Christ of our personal experience, but the historic Christ, the Christ of the apostolic testimony. There is no other Christ. So if Scripture leads to witness, witness also depends on Scripture.

(1984d:191)

786. Our guilty silence

Again and again an opportunity presents itself to speak for our Lord Jesus Christ, but we hold our peace. And what is true of us as individual believers seems to characterize and paralyse the whole church.

What are the causes of our guilty silence?

No doubt any answer to this question would tend to be an

over-simplification, because the reasons are legion. But I believe there are four major causes. Either we have no compelling incentive even to try to speak, or we do not know what to say, or we are not convinced that it is our job, or we do not believe we shall do any good, because we have forgotten the source of power. **(1967e:14)**

787. God's purpose

The New Testament makes every believer, however young and immature, a witness and a soul-winner . . . God's purpose is that every local Christian congregation should be organized for witness as well as for worship, and that every single Christian should have a share in the work. **(1954b:xiv)**

788. Evangelism and the Bible

It is an observable fact of history, both past and contemporary, that the degree of the church's commitment to world evangelization is commensurate with the degree of its conviction about the authority of the Bible. Whenever Christians lose their confidence in the Bible, they also lose their zeal for evangelism. Conversely, whenever they are convinced about the Bible, then they are determined about evangelism. **(1981b)**

789. Dialogue evangelism

Dialogue is neither a synonym nor a substitute for evangelism. Dialogue is a serious conversation in which we are prepared to listen and learn as well as to speak and teach. It is therefore an exercise in integrity. **(1992b:111)**

790. To give the word

The early church understood its task to be the diligent and systematic proclamation of a message. If God's part was to give the power, their part was to give the word. **(1973a:4)**

791. United evangelism

Since evangelism, at its simplest and most basic, is the sharing of the good news, united evangelism is impossible without prior agreement about the good news to be shared. **(1980f)**

792. God's will to save

Let no-one say that the doctrine of election by the sovereign will and mercy of God, mysterious as it is, makes either evangelism or faith unnecessary. The opposite is the case. It is only because of God's gracious will to save that evangelism has any hope of success and faith becomes possible. The preaching of the gospel is the very means that God has appointed by which he delivers from blindness and bondage those whom he chose in Christ before the foundation of the world, sets them free to believe in Jesus, and so causes his will to be done.

(1979e:48)

793. *Evangelism and election*

The doctrine of election, far from making evangelism unnecessary, makes it indispensable. For it is only through the preaching and receiving of the gospel that God's secret purpose comes to be revealed and known. **(1991c:31)**

794. *Evangelism in Ephesus*

All the roads of Asia converged on Ephesus, and all the inhabitants of Asia visited Ephesus from time to time, to buy or sell, visit a relative, frequent the baths, attend the games in the stadium, watch a drama in the theatre, or worship the goddess. And while they were in Ephesus, they heard of this Christian lecturer named Paul, who was both speaking and answering questions for five hours in the middle of every day. Evidently many dropped in, listened and were converted. They then returned to their towns and villages as born-again believers. Thus the gospel must have spread to the Lycus valley and to its chief towns Colosse, Laodicea and Hierapolis, which Epaphras had visited but Paul had not, and perhaps to the remaining five of the seven churches of Revelation 2 and 3, namely Smyrna, Pergamum, Thyatira, Sardis and Philadelphia. This is a fine strategy for the great university and capital cities of the world. If the gospel is reasonably, systematically and thoroughly unfolded in the city centre, visitors will hear it, embrace it and take it back with them to their homes.

When we contrast much contemporary evangelism with Paul's, its shallowness is immediately shown up. Our evangelism tends to be too ecclesiastical (inviting people to church), whereas Paul also took the gospel out into the secular world; too emotional (appeals for decision without an adequate basis of understanding), whereas Paul taught, reasoned and tried to persuade; and too superficial (making brief encounters and expecting quick results), whereas Paul stayed in Corinth and

Ephesus for five years, faithfully sowing gospel seed and in due time reaping a harvest. **(1990b:314)**

795. The need for faithfulness

God intends every church to be like a sounding board, bouncing off the vibrations of the gospel, or like a telecommunications satellite which first receives and then transmits messages. In fact, this is God's simplest plan for world evangelization. If every church had been faithful, the world would long ago have been evangelized. **(1991c:43)**

796. 'Holy gossip'

We are a very media-conscious generation. We know the power of the mass media on the public mind. Consequently, we want to use the media in evangelism. By print and tape, by audio and video cassettes, by radio and television we would like to saturate the world with the good news. And rightly so. In principle nobody should quarrel with this ambition. We should harness to the service of the gospel every modern medium of communication which is available to us.

Nevertheless there is another way, which (if we must compare them) is still more effective. It requires no complicated electronic gadgetry; it is very simple. It is neither organized nor computerized; it is spontaneous. And it is not expensive; it costs precisely nothing. We might call it 'holy gossip'. It is the excited transmission from mouth to mouth of the impact which the good news is making on people. 'Have you heard what has happened to so and so? Did you know that such and such a person has come to believe in God and has been completely transformed? Something extraordinary is going on . . .'

(1991c:37)

797. A loss of faith

The principal reason in my judgment why there is so little effective evangelism to-day is that we clergy have, in many cases, ceased to believe in it. We are no longer expecting to see moral miracles. **(1952:4)**

798. The greatest hindrance

We claim to know, to love and to follow Jesus Christ. We say that he is our Saviour, our Lord, and our Friend. 'What difference does he make to these Christians?' the world asks searchingly. 'Where is their God?' It may be said without fear of contradiction that the greatest hindrance to evangelism in the world today is the failure of the church to supply evidence in her own life and work of the saving power of God.

(1988e:68)

799. The risen Lord

The greatest single reason for the church's evangelistic disobedience centres in the church's doubts. We are not sure if our own sins are forgiven. We are not sure if the gospel is true. And so, because we doubt, we are dumb. We need to hear again Christ's word of peace, and see again his hands and his side. Once we are glad that we have seen the Lord, and once we have clearly recognized him as our crucified and risen Saviour, then nothing and no-one will be able to silence us.

(1967d:39)

57. PROCLAIMING THE GOSPEL

800. The power of Jesus Christ

Jesus himself illustrated human lostness by the language of physical disability. By ourselves we are blind to God's truth and deaf to his voice. Lame, we cannot walk in his ways. Dumb, we can neither sing to him nor speak for him. We are even dead in our trespasses and sins. Moreover, we are the dupes and slaves of demonic forces. Of course, if we think this exaggerated or 'mythical' or frankly false, then we shall see no need for supernatural power; we shall consider our own resources adequate. But if human beings are in reality spiritually and morally blind, deaf, dumb, lame and even dead, not to mention the prisoners of Satan, then it is ridiculous in the extreme to suppose that by ourselves and our merely human preaching we can reach or rescue people in such a plight . . . Only Jesus Christ by his Holy Spirit can open blind eyes and deaf ears, make the lame walk and the dumb speak, prick the conscience, enlighten the mind, fire the heart, move the will, give life to the dead and rescue slaves from Satanic bondage. And all this he can and does, as the preacher should know from his own experience.   **(1982a:329)**

801. A doctrine of God

Behind the concept and the act of preaching there lies a doctrine of God, a conviction about his being, his action and his purpose. The kind of God we believe in determines the kind of sermons we preach.   **(1982a:93)**

802. The Word made flesh

True evangelism, evangelism that is modelled on the ministry of Jesus, is not proclamation without identification any more than it is identification without proclamation. Evangelism involves both together. Jesus Christ is the Word of God, the proclamation of God; in order to be proclaimed, however, the Word was made flesh.   **(1967d:41)**

803. Across the cultures

Let us imagine an American who is sent as a missionary to an African country. He will have to ask himself this question: How can I, who am the product of an Anglo-Saxon culture, take the gospel from the Bible, which was written in the cultures of Judaism and the Greco-Roman world, and communicate it to Africans who belong to a third culture, whether of Islam or of an African traditional religion, without either falsifying the message or rendering it unintelligible? It is this interplay between three cultures – the cultures of the Bible, of the missionary and of his or her hearers – which constitutes the exciting, yet exacting, discipline of cross-cultural communication. **(1981g:40)**

804. Meaning and message

To discover the text's *meaning* is of purely academic interest unless we go on to discern its *message* for today, or (as some theologians prefer to say) its 'significance'. But to search for its contemporary message without first wrestling with its original meaning is to attempt a forbidden short cut. It dishonours God (disregarding his chosen way of revealing himself in particular historical and cultural contexts), it misuses his Word (treating it like an almanac or book of magic spells) and it misleads his people (confusing them about how to interpret Scripture).

(1982a:221)

805. Words matter

We must not acquiesce in the contemporary disenchantment with words. Words matter. They are the building blocks of sentences by which we communicate with one another. And the gospel has a specific content. That is why it must be articulated, verbalized. Of course it can and must be dramatized too. For images are sometimes more powerful than words. Yet images also have to be interpreted by words. So in all our evangelism, whether in public preaching or in private witnessing, we need to take trouble with our choice of words. **(1991c:33)**

806. Sensitivity in preaching

Biblical preaching demands sensitivity to the modern world. Although God spoke to the ancient world in its own languages and cultures, he intends his Word to be for everybody. This means that the expositor is more than an exegete. The exegete explains the original meaning of the text; the expositor goes further and applies it to the contemporary world. We have then to struggle to understand the rapidly changing world in which

God has called us to live; to grasp the main movements of thought which have shaped it; to listen to its many discordant voices, its questions, its protests and its cries of pain; and to feel a measure of its disorientation and despair. For all this is part of our Christian sensitivity. **(1992b:213)**

807. Stewards and heralds

We are stewards of what God has said, but heralds of what God has done. Our stewardship is of an accomplished revelation; but an accomplished redemption is the good news which we proclaim as heralds. **(1961:30)**

808. Preaching and election

The doctrine of election does not dispense with the necessity of preaching. On the contrary, it makes it essential. For Paul preaches and suffers for it (literally) 'in order that' they 'may obtain the salvation in Christ Jesus with its eternal glory' (2 Tim. 2:11). The elect obtain salvation in Christ not apart from the preaching of Christ but by means of it. **(1973b:62)**

809. The price of preaching

It seems that the only preaching God honours, through which his wisdom and power are expressed, is the preaching of a man who is willing in himself to be both a weakling and a fool. God not only chooses weak and foolish people to save, but weak and foolish preachers through whom to save them, or at least preachers who are content to be weak and seem foolish in the eyes of the world. We are not always willing to pay this price. **(1961:109)**

810. Preaching the law

Before we preach the gospel we must preach the law. Indeed this has never been more necessary than it is today when we are witnessing a widespread revolt against authority. The gospel can only justify those whom the law condemns. These are the respective functions of law and gospel; as Luther put it, it is the work of the law to 'terrify', and the work of the gospel to 'justify'.[1] Thus every man's spiritual history becomes a microcosm of God's dealings with the human race. God did not immediately send his Son; nor can we immediately preach him. A long programme of education and preparation came first, in particular the giving of the law to expose the fact and gravity of sin. And the law still performs the same function. 'It is only when one submits to the law', wrote Dietrich Bonhoeffer in prison, 'that one can speak of grace . . . I don't think it is Christian to want to get to the New Testament too soon or too directly.'[2] To bypass the law is to cheapen the gospel. We must meet Moses before we are ready to meet Christ.   **(1967e:98)**

[1] *Commentary on the Epistle to the Galatians* (Clarke, 1953), p. 423.
[2] *Letters and Papers from Prison* (ET SCM Press, 1959), p. 50.

811. Law and conscience

It is often said that we should address ourselves to people's conscious needs, and not try to induce in them feelings of guilt which they do not have. This is a misconception, however. Human beings are moral beings by creation. That is to say, not only do we experience an inner urge to do what we believe to be right, but we also have a sense of guilt and remorse when we have done what we know to be wrong. This is an essential feature of our humanness. There is of course such a thing as false guilt. But guilt feelings which are aroused by wrongdoing are healthy. They rebuke us for betraying our humanity, and they impel us to seek forgiveness in Christ. Thus conscience is our ally. In all evangelism, I find it a constant encouragement to say to myself, 'The other person's conscience is on my side.'
(1994:88)

812. The preaching of the cross

Of this we are clear: man's salvation rests on the fact of the cross, and neither on the preacher's interpretation of it, nor on the hearers' understanding of it. Our desire is that men should believe that fact, not accept our explanations. 'Christ died for our sins' is enough without any further elucidation. Moreover, our appeal is never that men should accept a theory about the cross but that they should receive a Person who died for them. To this end we shall continue to preach Christ crucified, because what is folly to the intellectualist and a stumbling-block to the moralist, remains the wisdom and the power of God (1 Cor. 1:23–24).   **(1956a:37)**

813. Past history and present reality

It is by preaching that God makes past history a present reality. The cross was, and will always remain, a unique historical event of the past. And there it will remain, in the past, in the books, unless God himself makes it real and relevant to men today. It is by preaching, in which he makes his appeal to men through men, that God accomplishes this miracle. He opens their eyes to see its true meaning, its eternal value, and its abiding merit. **(1961:46)**

814. The offence of the cross

The 'stumbling block of the cross' remains. Sinners hate it because it tells them that they cannot save themselves. Preachers are tempted to avoid it because of its offensiveness to the proud. It is easier to preach man's merits than Christ's, because men greatly prefer it that way. **(1967e:40)**

815. The mark of true preaching

Persecution or opposition is a mark of every true Christian preacher . . . The Old Testament prophets found it so, men like Amos, Jeremiah, Ezekiel and Daniel. So did the New Testament apostles. And down the centuries of the Christian church, until and including today, Christian preachers who refuse to distort or dilute the gospel of grace have had to suffer for their faithfulness. The good news of Christ crucified is still a 'scandal' (Greek, *skandalon*, stumbling-block), grievously offensive to the pride of men. **(1968c:137)**

816. The gospel appeal

God finished the work of reconciliation at the cross, yet it is still necessary for sinners to repent and believe and so 'be reconciled to God'. Again, sinners need to 'be reconciled to God', yet we must not forget that on God's side the work of reconciliation has already been done. If these two things are to be kept distinct, they will also in all authentic gospel preaching be kept together. It is not enough to expound a thoroughly orthodox doctrine of reconciliation if we never beg people to come to Christ. **(1986a:201)**

817. No warmth within

Some preachers have a great horror of emotionalism. So have I, if this means the artificial stirring of the emotions by rhetorical tricks or other devices. But we should not fear genuine emotion. If we can preach Christ crucified and remain altogether unmoved, we must have a hard heart indeed. More to be feared than emotion is cold professionalism, the dry, detached utterance of a lecture which has neither heart nor soul in it. Do man's peril and Christ's salvation mean so little to us that we feel no warmth rise within us as we think about them?

(1961:51)

XI. CHRISTIAN THINKING ON SOCIAL ISSUES

58. Evangelism and social action
59. Christianity, religion and culture
60. Politics and the state
61. War, violence and peacemaking
62. Work, wealth, poverty and human rights
63. Gender, sexuality, marriage and divorce

58. EVANGELISM AND SOCIAL ACTION

818. An unbiblical dualism

The recent debate about the rival merits of evangelism and social responsibility was never necessary. It expressed an unbiblical dualism between body and soul, this world and the next. In any case we are called both to witness and to serve; both are part of our Christian ministry and mission.

(1991d:145)

819. Who is my neighbour?

Our evangelical neglect of social concern until recent years, and the whole argument about evangelism and social action, has been as unseemly as it has been unnecessary. Of course evangelical Christians have quite rightly rejected the so-called 'social gospel' (which replaces the good news of salvation with a message of social amelioration), but it is incredible that we should ever have set evangelistic and social work over against each other as alternatives. Both should be authentic expressions of neighbour-love. For who is my neighbour, whom I am to love? He is neither a bodyless soul, nor a soulless body, nor a private individual divorced from a social environment. God made man a physical, spiritual and social being. My neighbour is a body-soul-in-community. I cannot claim to love my neighbour if I'm really concerned for only one aspect of him, whether his soul or his body or his community. **(1975f:16)**

820. A partner in evangelism

There is a way of stating the relation between evangelism and social action, which I believe to be the truly Christian one, namely that social action is *a partner of evangelism*. As partners the two belong to each other and yet are independent of each other. Each stands on its own feet in its own right alongside the other. Neither is a means to the other, or even a manifestation of the other. For each is an end in itself. Both are expressions of unfeigned love. **(1975c:27)**

821. No 'social gospel'

The kingdom of God is not Christianized society. It is the divine rule in the lives of those who acknowledge Christ. It has to be 'received', 'entered' or 'inherited', he said, by humble and penitent faith in him. And without a new birth it is impossible to see it, let alone enter it. Those who do receive it like a child, however, find themselves members of the new community of the Messiah, which is called to exhibit the ideals of his rule in the world and so to present the world with an alternative social reality. This social challenge of the gospel of the kingdom is quite different from the 'social gospel'. When Rauschenbusch politicized the kingdom of God, it is understandable (if regrettable) that, in reaction to him, evangelicals concentrated on evangelism and personal philanthropy, and steered clear of socio-political action. **(1990a:7)**

822. *An aspect of conversion*

Social responsibility becomes an aspect not of Christian mission only, but also of Christian conversion. It is impossible to be truly converted to God without being thereby converted to our neighbour. **(1975c:53)**

823. *Love and justice*

The cross is a revelation of God's justice as well as of his love. That is why the community of the cross should concern itself with social justice as well as with loving philanthropy. It is never enough to have pity on the victims of injustice, if we do nothing to change the unjust situation itself. Good Samaritans will always be needed to succour those who are assaulted and robbed; yet it would be even better to rid the Jerusalem–Jericho road of brigands. **(1986a:292)**

824. *Uncomplicated compassion*

We are sent into the world, like Jesus, to serve. For this is the natural expression of our love for our neighbours. We love. We go. We serve. And in this we have (or should have) no ulterior motive. True, the gospel lacks visibility if we merely preach it, and lacks credibility if we who preach it are interested only in souls and have no concern about the welfare of people's bodies, situations and communities. Yet the reason for our acceptance of social responsibility is not primarily in order to give the gospel either a visibility or a credibility it would otherwise lack, but rather simple uncomplicated compassion. Love has no need to justify itself. It merely expresses itself in service wherever it sees need. **(1975c:30)**

825. Words and works

In the ministry of Jesus words and works, gospel preaching and compassionate service went hand in hand. His works expressed his words, and his words explained his works. It should be the same for us. Words are abstract, they need to be embodied in deeds of love. Works are ambiguous, they need to be interpreted by the proclamation of the gospel. Keep words and works together in the service and witness of the church.   **(1980i:23)**

826. The instrument of change

Evangelism is the major instrument of social change. For the gospel changes people, and changed people can change society.
(1990a:71)

827. No perfect society

The followers of Jesus are optimists, but not utopians. It is possible to improve society; but a perfect society awaits the return of Jesus Christ.   **(1989d)**

828. Church and community

In urging that we should avoid the rather naïve choice between evangelism and social action, I am not implying that every individual Christian must be equally involved in both. This would be impossible. Besides, we must recognize that God calls different people to different ministries and endows them with gifts appropriate to their calling . . .

Although every individual Christian must discover how God has called and gifted him, I venture to suggest that the local Christian church as a whole should be concerned for the local secular community as a whole.   **(1975a:46)**

829. Polarization and specialization

I suggest the need for a threefold recognition about evangelism and social action:

(a) A recognition that the two are partners in the Christian mission . . . 'distinct yet equal' partners. Neither is an excuse for the other, a cloak for the other, or a means to the other. Each exists in its own right as an expression of Christian love. Both should be included to some degree in every local church's programme.

(b) A recognition that both are also every individual Christian's responsibility. Every Christian is a witness, and must take whatever opportunities he is given. Every Christian is also a servant, and must respond to challenges to service, without regarding them as merely occasions for evangelism. Yet the existential situation will often assign priority to one or other of the two responsibilities. For example, the good Samaritan's ministry to the brigands' victim was not to stuff tracts into his pockets but to pour oil into his wounds. For this was what the situation demanded.

(c) A recognition that, although both are part of the church's and the Christian's duties, yet God calls different people to different ministries and endows them with appropriate gifts. This is a necessary deduction from the nature of the church as Christ's body. Although we should resist *polarization* between evangelism and social action, we should not resist *specialization*. Everybody cannot do everything. Some are called to be evangelists, others to be social workers, others to be political activists. Within each local church, which as the body of Christ in the locality is committed to both evangelism and social action, there is a proper place for individual specialists and for specialist groups. **(1979c:22)**

59. CHRISTIANITY, RELIGION AND CULTURE

830. Historical and experimental

Christianity is both a historical and an experimental religion. Indeed, one of its chief glories is this marriage between history and experience, between the past and the present. We must never attempt to divorce them. We cannot do without the work of Christ, nor can we do without the witness of Christ's apostles, if we want to enjoy Christ's grace and peace today.

(1968c:19)

831. Old and new

Christianity is old, and is getting older every year. Yet it is also new, new every morning. As John put it: 'Beloved, I am writing you no new commandment, but an old commandment which you had from the beginning . . . Yet I am writing you a new commandment, which is true in him and in you, because the darkness is passing away and the true light is already shining' (1 Jn. 2:7–8). What he wrote about the commandment is equally applicable to the whole of Christianity. It is both old and new at the same time . . . the Jesus of history is the Christ of faith, whom we know and love, trust and obey.

(1970b:37)

832. Twin foundations

The two foundation planks of the Christian religion are the grace of God and the death of Christ. The Christian gospel is the gospel of the grace of God. The Christian faith is the faith of Christ crucified.

(1968c:66)

833. Final and universal

If St Luke teaches the universality of the gospel, and St Paul its gratuity, the author of the epistle to the Hebrews teaches its finality. His great theme is that Jesus Christ is God's last word to the world, that he has fulfilled all the Old Testament foreshadowings, and that there is nothing more to follow. Christianity is the perfect religion; it can never be superseded. Christ, through his eternal priesthood and unique sacrifice, has brought us an 'eternal salvation' (Heb. 5:9).

(1954c:79)

834. Christianity is Christ

The word 'Christian' occurs only three times in the Bible. Because of its common misuse we could profitably dispense with it. Jesus Christ and the apostle Paul never used the word, or at least not in their recorded teaching. What distinguishes the true followers of Jesus is neither their creed, nor their code of ethics, nor their ceremonies, nor their culture, but Christ. What is often mistakenly called 'Christianity' is, in essence, neither a religion nor a system, but a person, Jesus of Nazareth.

(1983a)

835. A unique emphasis

Union with Christ is a unique emphasis among the world's religions. No other religion offers its adherents a personal union with its founder. The Buddhist does not claim to know the Buddha, nor the Confucianist Confucius, nor the Muslim Muhammad, nor the Marxist Karl Marx. But the Christian does claim – humbly, I hope, but nevertheless confidently – to know Jesus Christ. **(1991b:38)**

836. Three kinds of tolerance

How then are we to think of other religions? The word that immediately springs to most people's minds is 'tolerance', but they do not always stop to define what they mean by it. It may help if we distinguish between three kinds. The first may be called *legal* tolerance, which ensures that every minority's religious and political rights (usually summarized as the freedom to 'profess, practise and propagate') are adequately protected in law. This is obviously right. Another kind is *social* tolerance, which encourages respect for all persons, whatever views they may hold, and seeks to understand and appreciate their position. This too is a virtue which Christians wish to cultivate; it arises naturally from our recognition that all human beings are God's creation and bear his image, and that we are meant to live together in amity. But what about *intellectual* tolerance, which is the third kind? To cultivate a mind so broad that it can tolerate every opinion, without ever detecting anything in it to reject, is not a virtue; it is the vice of the feeble-minded. It can degenerate into an unprincipled confusion of truth with error and goodness with evil. Christians, who believe that truth and goodness have been

revealed in Christ, cannot possibly come to terms with it.
(1985:69)

837. Non-Christian religions

What, then, about those ignorant of the gospel? Are we to say that they are ignorant of God altogether, including those who adhere to non-Christian religions? No. *We recognize that all men have some knowledge of God.* This universal (though partial) knowledge is due to his self-revelation, what theologians call either *his general revelation* because it is made to all men, or his 'natural' revelation because it is made *in nature*, both externally in the universe and internally in the human conscience. Such knowledge of God is not saving knowledge, however. *We deny that this can save*, partly because it is a revelation of God's power, deity and holiness but not of his love for sinners or of his plan of salvation, and partly because men do not live up to the knowledge they have. **(1975d:10)**

838. Jesus the unparalleled

The world's religious situation has not greatly changed. True, the old gods of Greece and Rome have long since been discredited and discarded. But new gods have arisen in their place, and other ancient faiths have experienced a resurgence. As a result of modern communication media and ease of travel, many countries are increasingly pluralistic. What people want is an easygoing syncretism, a truce in inter-religious competition, a mishmash of the best from all religions. But we Christians cannot surrender either the finality or the uniqueness of Jesus Christ. There is simply nobody else like him; his incarnation, atonement and resurrection have no parallels. In consequence, he is the one and only mediator between God and the human race. This exclusive affirmation is strongly, even bitterly, resented. It is regarded by many as intolerably intolerant. Yet the claims of truth compel us to maintain it, however much offence it may cause. **(1992b:64)**

839. Alternative roads?

We do not therefore deny that there are elements of truth in non-Christian systems, vestiges of the general revelation of God in nature. What we do vehemently deny is that these are sufficient for salvation and (more vehemently still) that Christian faith and non-Christian faiths are alternative and equally valid roads to God. Although there is an important place for 'dialogue' with men of other faiths . . . there is also a need for 'encounter' with them, and even for 'confrontation', in which we seek both to disclose the inadequacies and falsities of non-Christian religion and to demonstrate the adequacy and truth, absoluteness and finality of the Lord Jesus Christ.

(1975c:69)

840. 'No other Mediator . . .'

To claim that Jesus Christ is unique is not to say that there is no truth in other religions and ideologies. Of course there is. For we believe in God's general revelation and common grace. The Logos of God is still 'the true light' coming into the world and enlightening every man (Jn. 1:9). All men know something of God's glory from creation and something of God's law from their own nature, as Paul argues in Romans 1 and 2. But how does this argument continue? Not that their knowledge of God saves them, but the very opposite! It condemns them because they suppress it. Indeed, 'they are without excuse, for although they knew God they did not honour him as God . . .'

It is against this dark background of the universal rebellion, guilt and judgment of mankind that the good news of Jesus Christ shines with such dazzling beauty. There is salvation in no other, for there is no other mediator between God and man but only Jesus Christ who died as a ransom for sinners (Acts 4:12; 1 Tim. 2:5–6).

Firmly to reject all syncretism in this way and to assert the uniqueness and finality of Jesus Christ is not 'doctrinal superiority' or imperialism, as it has been called. Conviction about revealed truth is not arrogance. Its proper name is 'stewardship', the humble and obedient stewardship of a church which knows it has been 'put in trust with the Gospel'.

(1976a)

841. New Age religion

It would be easy for Christians to dismiss New Age thinking as a naïve and harmless aberration. But it has to be taken seriously. From beginning to end the New Age movement expresses a preoccupation and even infatuation with self. More than that, I do not hesitate to say, its fundamental egocentricity is blasphemous. It puts the self in the place of God and even declares that we are God. New Agers have surrendered to the primeval temptation to be like God, as in the Garden of Eden. God is effectively dethroned. The New Age movement dispenses with the Trinity. First, it dispenses with God the Father, the transcendental creator, by identifying him with the universe. But it is essential for us to distinguish the creation from its creator and to affirm our creaturely dependence on him.

Secondly, the New Age movement dispenses with God the Son, our unique redeemer. Our human predicament is not ignorance, but sin. The solution to it lies not inside ourselves but outside. The true good news is not that I can awaken to my true self as being divine, but that Christ Jesus came into the world to save sinners.

New Agers sometimes speak of 'atonement'. But they twist its meaning out of recognition. They are correct in saying that atonement equals at-one-ment. But they then interpret this as 'oneness with the One', instead of as personal reconciliation with God through the Christ who died for us.

Thirdly, the New Age movement dispenses with God the Holy Spirit, our indwelling sanctifier. To New Agers 'transformation' has nothing to do with people's morality or behaviour. It refers rather to the transformation of their consciousness, the discovery and development of their own potential.

To followers of Jesus Christ, however, 'transformation' is not discovering ourselves but becoming like Christ. 'We are being transformed', wrote Paul, 'from one degree of glory to another into the image of Christ by the Spirit of Christ' (2 Cor. 3:18). Over and against the wild self-centred speculations of the New Age movement which dispenses with the Trinity, and so with creation, redemption and sanctification, it is a relief to re-confess the basic baptismal faith of Christians.

We have to choose between two incompatible gospels. On the one hand there is the false gospel of the New Age movement which centres on 'me', on my identity and my potentiality. On the other hand, there is the true gospel which centres on God – on the Father who loves us, the Son who died for us, and the Spirit who indwells and transforms us. There is no possibility of compromise between these two gospels. The true New Age was inaugurated by Jesus Christ at his first coming. The so-called 'New Age' movement is both a counterfeit and a fraud. **(1989a)**

842. Culture and religion

A respectful acceptance of the diversity of *cultures* does not imply an equal acceptance of the diversity of *religions*. The richness of each particular culture should be appreciated, but not the idolatry which may lie at its heart. For we cannot tolerate any rivals to Jesus Christ, believing as we do that God has spoken fully and finally through him, and that he is the only Saviour, who died, and rose again, and will one day come to be the world's Judge. **(1990a:224)**

843. The ambiguity of culture

Culture is ambiguous because man is ambiguous. Man is both noble (because made in God's image) and ignoble (because fallen and sinful). And his culture faithfully reflects these two aspects. **(1975d:26)**

844. Evaluating culture

Culture may be likened to a tapestry, intricate and often beautiful, which is woven by a given society to express its corporate identity. The colours and patterns of the tapestry are the community's common beliefs and common customs, inherited from the past, enriched by contemporary art and binding the community together. Each of us, without exception, has been born and bred in a particular culture. Being part of our upbringing and environment, it is also part of ourselves, and we find it very difficult to stand outside it and evaluate it Christianly. Yet this we must learn to do. For if Jesus Christ is to be Lord of all, our cultural heritage cannot be excluded from his lordship. And this applies to churches as well as individuals. **(1975d:26)**

60. POLITICS AND THE STATE

845. The state's authority

I confess that I find it extremely impressive that Paul writes of both the 'authority' and the 'ministry' of the state; that three times he affirms the state's authority to be God's authority; and that three times he describes the state and its ministers as God's ministers, using two words (*diakonos* and *leitourgos*) which elsewhere he applied to his own ministry as apostle and evangelist, and even to the ministry of Christ.[1] I do not think there is any way of wriggling out of this, for example by interpreting the paragraph as a grudging acquiescence in the realities of political power. No. In spite of the defects of Roman government, with which he was personally familiar, Paul emphatically declared its authority and ministry to be God's. It is the divine origin of the state's authority which makes Christian submission to it a matter of 'conscience' (Rom. 13:5).

Nevertheless, the fact that the state's authority has been delegated to it by God, and is therefore not intrinsic but derived, means that it must never be absolutized. Worship is due to God alone, and to his Christ, who is the lord of all rule and authority (Eph. 1:21–22) and 'the ruler of the kings of the earth' (Rev. 1:5; *cf.* 19:16). The state must be respected as a divine institution; but to give it our blind, unqualified allegiance would be idolatry. The early Christians refused to call Caesar 'lord'; that title belonged to Jesus alone.

(1986a:305)

[1] For *diakonos* applied to Christ see Rom. 15:8, and to Paul 2 Cor. 6:4. For *leitourgos* applied to Christ see Heb. 8:2, and to Paul Rom. 15:16.

846. The biblical concept

'Authority' in biblical usage is not a synonym for 'tyranny'. All those who occupy positions of authority in society are responsible both to the God who has entrusted it to them and to the person or persons for whose benefit they have been given it. In a word, the biblical concept of authority spells not tyranny but responsibility.
(1979e:219)

847. Models of church and state

Relations between church and state have been notoriously controversial throughout the Christian centuries. To over-simplify, four main models have been tried – Erastianism (the state controls the church), theocracy (the church controls the state), Constantinianism (the compromise in which the state favours the church and the church accommodates to the state in order to retain its favour), and partnership (church and state recognize and encourage each other's distinct God-given responsibilities in a spirit of constructive collaboration). The fourth seems to accord best with Paul's teaching in Romans 13.

(1994:339)

848. Ministers both of God and of the state

If we are seeking to develop a balanced biblical understanding of the state, central to it will be the truths that the state's authority and ministry are both given to it by God. Moreover, in writing about the ministry of the state, Paul twice uses the very same word which he has used elsewhere of the ministers of the church, namely *diakonoi* (although the third time he uses *leitourgoi*, a term which usually meant 'priests' but could mean 'public servants') . . . *diakonia* is a generic term which can embrace a wide variety of ministries. Those who serve the state as legislators, civil servants, magistrates, police, social workers or tax-collectors are just as much 'ministers of God' as those who serve the church as pastors, teachers, evangelists or administrators.

(1994:343)

849. Limits of authority

Whenever laws are enacted which contradict God's law, civil disobedience becomes a Christian duty. There are notable examples of it in Scripture. When Pharaoh ordered the Hebrew midwives to kill the newborn boys, they refused to obey. 'The midwives . . . feared God and did not do what the king of Egypt had told them to do; they let the boys live' (Ex. 1:17). When King Nebuchadnezzar issued an edict that all his subjects must fall down and worship his golden image, Shadrach, Meshach and Abednego refused to obey (Dn. 3). When King Darius made a decree that for thirty days nobody should pray 'to any god or man' except himself, Daniel refused to obey (Dn. 6). And when the Sanhedrin banned preaching in the name of Jesus, the apostles refused to obey (Acts 4:18ff.). All these were heroic refusals, in spite of the threats which accompanied the edicts. In each case civil disobedience involved great personal risk, including possible loss of life. In each case its purpose was 'to demonstrate their submissiveness to God, not their defiance of government'.[1]

(1994:342)

[1] Charles W. Colson, *Kingdoms in Conflict, An Insider's Challenging View of Politics, Power and the Pulpit* (William Morrow/Zondervan, 1987), p. 251.

850. God rather than men

The apostles' concern was not to defend themselves but to uplift Christ. *We must obey God rather than men!* they said (Acts 5:29), and in so doing laid down the principle of civil and ecclesiastical disobedience. To be sure, Christians are called to be conscientious citizens and generally speaking, to submit to human authorities. But if the authority concerned misuses its God-given power to command what he forbids or forbid what he commands, then the Christian's duty is to disobey the human authority in order to obey God's.

(1990b:116)

851. Christian civil disobedience

Discipleship sometimes calls for disobedience. Indeed, civil disobedience is a biblical doctrine, for there are four or five notable examples of it in Scripture. It arises naturally from the affirmation that Jesus is Lord. The principle is clear, even though its application may involve believers in agonies of conscience. It is this. We are to submit to the state, because its authority is derived from God and its officials are God's ministers, right up to the point where obedience to the state would involve us in disobedience to God. At that point our Christian duty is to disobey the state in order to obey God. For if the state misuses its God-given authority, and presumes either to command what God forbids or to forbid what God commands, we have to say 'no' to the state in order to say 'yes' to Christ. As Peter put it, 'we must obey God rather than men!' Or in Calvin's words, 'obedience to man must not become disobedience to God'. (1992b:96)

852. What God desires

God, because he is himself a righteous God, desires righteousness in every human community, not just in every Christian community. **(1978f:171)**

853. Forgiveness and punishment

In Romans 12 and 13 Paul draws a vital distinction between the duty of private citizens to love and serve the evildoer, and the duty of public servants, as official agents of God's wrath, to bring him to trial and, if convicted, to punish him. Far from being incompatible with each other, both principles are seen operating in Jesus at the cross. On the one hand, 'when they hurled their insults at him, he did not retaliate'. On the other, 'he entrusted himself to him who judges justly', in confidence that God's justice would prevail (1 Pet. 2:23; *cf.* Ps. 37:5ff.)

(1994:337)

854. Social righteousness

It would be a mistake to suppose that the biblical word 'righteousness' means only a right relationship with God on the one hand and a moral righteousness of character and conduct on the other. For biblical righteousness is more than a private and personal affair; it includes social righteousness as well. And social righteousness, as we learn from the law and the prophets, is concerned with seeking man's liberation from oppression, together with the promotion of civil rights, justice in the law courts, integrity in business dealings and honour in home and family affairs. Thus Christians are committed to hunger for righteousness in the whole human community as something pleasing to a righteous God. **(1978f:45)**

855. Democracy defined

Democracy is the political expression of persuasion by argument. If absolutism, being pessimistic, imposes law arbitrarily, and anarchy, being optimistic, dispenses with law altogether, then democracy, being realistic about human beings as both created and fallen, involves citizens in the framing of their own laws. At least this is the theory. In practice, especially in countries with a large number of illiterates, the media can too easily manipulate them. And in every democracy there is the constant danger of trampling on minorities. **(1990a:59)**

856. Jesus and politics

The words 'politics' and 'political' may be given either a broad or a narrow definition. Broadly speaking, 'politics' denotes the life of the city (*polis*) and the responsibilities of the citizen (*politēs*). It is concerned therefore with the whole of our life in human society. Politics is the art of living together in a community. According to its narrow definition, however, politics is the science of government. It is concerned with the development and adoption of specific policies with a view to their being enshrined in legislation. It is about gaining power for social change.

Once this distinction is clear, we may ask whether Jesus was involved in politics. In the latter and narrower sense, he clearly was not. He never formed a political party, adopted a political programme or organized a political protest. He took no steps to influence the policies of Caesar, Pilate or Herod. On the contrary, he renounced a political career. In the other and broader sense of the word, however, his whole ministry was political. For he had himself come into the world, in order to share in the life of the human community, and he sent his followers into the world to do the same.   **(1990a:11)**

857. Social reformers

The most influential leaders in history, the social reformers and pioneers, have been men and women of *action* because they have been men and women of *thought* and *passion*. **(1978c:182)**

858. Christian political influence

Although it is hardly the responsibility of a church or denomination as such to engage in direct political action, yet Christian individuals and Christian groups should be doing so, and should be encouraged from the pulpit to do so. For Christians should avoid the two opposite mistakes of *laissez faire* (making no Christian contribution to the nation's political well-being) and imposition (trying to force a minority view on an unwilling majority, as with the American liquor laws during the period of Prohibition). Instead, we remember that democracy means government with the consent of the governed, that 'consent' means majority public opinion, and that public opinion is a volatile thing, which is open to Christian influence. Pessimists will respond that human nature is depraved (which

355

it is), that Utopia is unattainable (which it is), and that socio-political activity is therefore a waste of time (which it is not). It is really absurd to say that social amelioration by Christian influence is impossible. For the historical record demonstrates the contrary. Wherever the Christian gospel has gone and triumphed, it has brought in its wake a new concern for education, a new willingness to listen to dissidents, new standards of impartiality in the administration of justice, a new stewardship of the natural environment, new attitudes to marriage and sex, a new respect for women and children, and a new compassionate resolve to relieve the poor, heal the sick, rehabilitate prisoners, and care for the aged and dying. Moreover, these new values become expressed, as Christian influence grows, not only in philanthropic enterprise but also in humane legislation.   **(1982a:166)**

859. *Compassion and justice*

Compassion needs moral guidelines; without the ingredient of justice it is bound to go astray.   **(1980d)**

61. WAR, VIOLENCE AND PEACEMAKING

860. Pacifism and nuclear weapons

Converted to Jesus Christ in my later teens, shortly before the outbreak of World War 2, I would describe myself at that time as an instinctive pacifist. Having read the Sermon on the Mount thoughtfully for the first time, it seemed to me self-evident that Jesus' prohibition of retaliation carried with it a ban on all participation in war. But as I learned to compare Scripture with Scripture, the issue became less clear-cut for me. It was a careful study of Romans 12:17 – 13:5 which convinced me of the state's God-given authority to punish evildoers, and to use force in doing so. This led me to resign from the Anglican Pacifist Fellowship. But then came the development and proliferation of nuclear weapons, which I found myself unable to fit into the categories of just-war thinking which I had accepted. My conscience condemned both the indiscriminate use of conventional weapons (as in the blanket bombing of German cities) and all use of indiscriminate weapons (chemical and biological as well as nuclear). For these things contradict Scripture, which forbids the shedding of innocent blood. They infringe the just-war principles of control and proportion, as well as of discrimination. And they have been outlawed by common consent in the Hague Convention and the Geneva Protocol. When Scripture, tradition and common sense are united in their condemnation of something, the case is overwhelming. **(1986b:xi)**

861. Morality and realism

I find myself in the personal dilemma of being both a nuclear pacifist and nevertheless, believing in a multilateralist approach to nuclear disarmament. Christian morality leads me to say that the use of nuclear weapons would be immoral, but Christian realism leads me to defend their conditional possession. Unilateralism (at least the kind which advocates the immediate, total dismantling of our nuclear arsenal) might well make nuclear war more likely. In that case the renunciation of one perceived evil (nuclear weaponry) would cause an even greater evil (nuclear holocaust). Therefore, the urgent search for balanced, multilateral and verifiable disarmament, together with what Pope John Paul II has called 'audacious gestures of peace' (*i.e.* unilateral gestures intended to break the log jam), seems a more prudent, and in this case a more moral, stance than unilateralism. **(1988f:46)**

862. Moral issues in modern war

The three weapons, atomic, biological and chemical, are sometimes referred to as 'ABC' weapons; they surely constitute the most gruesome alphabet ever conceived. The invention and refinement of ABC weapons, especially of nuclear devices, have radically changed the context in which one has to think about the morality of war; they challenge the relevance of the 'just war' theory. A war could still have a just cause and a just goal. But at least if macro-weapons were used ('strategic' or 'tactical'), there would be no reasonable prospect of attaining the goal (since nuclear wars are not winnable) and the means would not be just, since nuclear weapons are neither proportionate, nor discriminate, nor controlled. Millions of noncombatants would be killed. In a nuclear holocaust much innocent blood would be shed. Therefore the Christian conscience must declare the use of indiscriminate nuclear weapons, and also chemical and bacterial weapons, immoral. A nuclear war could never be a just war. **(1990a:95)**

863. Overcoming evil with good

Whenever an evil aggressor threatens the security of the state, Christians are likely to polarize. Just-war theorists concentrate on the need to resist and punish evil, and tend to forget the other biblical injunction to 'overcome' it. Pacifists, on the other hand, concentrate on the need to overcome evil with good, and tend to forget that according to Scripture evil deserves to be punished. Can these two biblical emphases be reconciled? At least we should be able to agree with this: if a nation believes it is justified in going to war, in order to resist and punish evil, Christians will stress the need to look beyond the defeat and surrender of the national enemy to its repentance and rehabilitation. The punishment of evil is an essential part of God's moral government of the world. But retributive and reformative justice go hand in hand. The highest and noblest of all attitudes to evil is to seek to overcome it with good.
(1984c:55)

864. Retaliation and revenge

Retaliation and revenge are absolutely forbidden to the followers of Jesus. He himself never hit back in either word or deed. And in spite of our inborn retributive tendency, ranging from the child's tit for tat to the adult's more sophisticated determination to get even with an opponent, Jesus calls us instead to imitate him. To be sure, there is a place for the punishment of evildoers in the law courts, and Paul teaches this in Romans 13. But in personal conduct we are never to get our own back by injuring those who have injured us. Non-retaliation was a very early feature of the Christian ethical tradition, going back to the teaching of Jesus, and beyond this to the Old Testament Wisdom literature.

The Christian ethic is never purely negative, however, and each of Paul's four negative imperatives in Romans 12 is accompanied by a positive counterpart. Thus, we are not to curse but to bless (verse 14); we are not to retaliate, but to do what is right and to live at peace (17–18); we are not to take revenge, but to leave this to God, and meanwhile to serve our enemies (19–20); and we are not to be overcome by evil, but to overcome evil with good (21).   **(1994:334)**

865. Violence and non-violence

The God of the Bible is a God of both salvation and judgment. But not equally so, as if these were parallel expressions of his nature. For Scripture called judgment his 'strange work'; his characteristic work, in which he delights, is salvation or peacemaking. Similarly, Jesus reacted to wilful perversity with anger, uttered scathing denunciations upon hypocrites, drove the moneychangers out of the temple and overturned their tables. But he also endured the humiliation and barbarities of flogging and crucifixion without resistance. Thus we see in the ministry of the same Jesus both violence and non-violence. Yet his resort to violence of word and deed was occasional, alien, uncharacteristic; his characteristic was non-violence; the symbol of his ministry is not the whip but the cross.   **(1983d:56)**

866. At any price?

'Peace at any price' is not biblical peace. For biblical peace is not appeasement, but peace with honour, peace with justice.

That is why peace has to be 'made' and why Jesus Christ came to make it. He broke down the barriers of partition, 'so making peace'. It is our privilege to share in this work of reconciliation, to announce to others the good news of peace through Jesus Christ, and so to be peacemakers. **(1970a:11)**

867. Called to be peacemakers

Every Christian is called to be a peacemaker. The Beatitudes are not a set of eight options, so that some may choose to be meek, others to be merciful, and yet others to make peace. Together they are Christ's description of the members of his kingdom. True, we shall not succeed in establishing Utopia on earth, nor will Christ's kingdom of righteousness and peace become universal within history. Not until Christ comes will swords be beaten into ploughshares and spears into pruninghooks. Yet this fact gives no possible warrant for the proliferation of factories for the manufacture of swords and spears. Does Christ's prediction of famine inhibit us from seeking a more equitable distribution of food? No more can his prediction of wars inhibit our pursuit of peace. God is a peacemaker. Jesus Christ is a peacemaker. So, if we want to be God's children and Christ's disciples, we must be peacemakers too.
(1990a:108)

868. A costly calling

The incentive to peacemaking is love, but it degenerates into appeasement whenever justice is ignored. To forgive and to ask for forgiveness are both costly exercises. All authentic Christian peacemaking exhibits the love and justice – and so the pain – of the cross. **(1986a:296)**

869. 'Cheap peace'

Other examples of peacemaking are the work of reunion and the work of evangelism, that is, seeking on the one hand to unite churches and on the other to bring sinners to Christ. In both these, true reconciliation can be degraded into cheap peace. The visible unity of the church is a proper Christian quest, but only if unity is not sought at the expense of doctrine. Jesus prayed for the oneness of his people. He also prayed that they might be kept from evil and in truth. We have no mandate from Christ to seek unity without purity, purity of both doctrine and conduct. If there is such a thing as 'cheap reunion', there is 'cheap evangelism' also, namely the proclamation of the gospel without the cost of discipleship, the demand for faith without repentance. These are forbidden short cuts. They turn the evangelist into a fraud. They cheapen the gospel and damage the cause of Christ. **(1978f:51)**

62. WORK, WEALTH, POVERTY AND HUMAN RIGHTS

870. *The origin of work*

Work is not a consequence of the fall, it is a consequence of creation. **(1980g:20)**

871. *Part of being human*

The two sentences of Genesis 1:26 belong together: 'let us make man in our image' and 'let them have dominion'. It is because we bear God's image that we share God's dominion. Therefore our potential for creative work is an essential part of our Godlike humanness. **(1979a)**

872. *The sin of Dives*

We are all tempted to use the enormous complexity of international economies as an excuse to do nothing. Yet this was the sin of Dives. There is no suggestion that Dives was responsible for the poverty of Lazarus either by robbing or by exploiting him. The reason for Dives's guilt is that he ignored the beggar at his gate and did precisely nothing to relieve his destitution. He acquiesced in a situation of gross economic inequality, which had rendered Lazarus less than fully human and which he could have relieved. The pariah dogs that licked Lazarus's sores showed more compassion than Dives did. Dives went to hell because of his indifference. **(1980b)**

873. *Our blind spot*

It is easy to criticize our Christian forebears for their blindness. It is much harder to discover our own. What will posterity see as the chief Christian blind spot of the last quarter of the twentieth century? I do not know. But I suspect it will have something to do with the economic oppression of the Third World and the readiness with which western Christians tolerate it, and even acquiesce in it. Only slowly is our Christian conscience being aroused to the gross economic inequalities between the countries of the North Atlantic and the southern world of Latin America, Africa and most parts of Asia. Total egalitarianism may not be a biblical ideal. But must we not roundly declare that luxury and extravagance are indefensible evils, while much of the world is undernourished and underprivileged? Many more Christians should gain the economic and political qualifications to join in the quest for justice in the world community. And meanwhile, the development of a less affluent lifestyle, in whatever terms we may define it, is surely an obligation that Scripture lays on us in compassionate solidarity with the poor. Of course we can resist these things and even use (misuse) the Bible to defend our resistance. The horror of the situation is that our affluent culture has drugged us; we no longer feel the pain of other people's deprivations. Yet the first step toward the recovery of our Christian integrity is to be aware that our culture blinds, deafens and dopes us. Then we shall begin to cry to God to open our eyes, unstop our ears and stab our dull consciences awake, until we see, hear and feel what through his Word he has been saying to us all the time. Then we shall take action.

(1981g:36)

874. The principle of simplicity

Materialism is an obsession with material things. Asceticism is the denial of the good gifts of the Creator. Pharisaism is binding ourselves and other people with rules. Instead, we should stick to principles. The principle of simplicity is clear. Simplicity is the first cousin of contentment. Its motto is, 'We brought nothing into this world, and we can certainly carry nothing out.' It recognizes that we are pilgrims.

It concentrates on what we *need*, and measures this by what we *use*. It rejoices in the good things of creation, but hates waste and greed and clutter. It knows how easily the seed of the Word is smothered by the 'cares and riches of this life'. It wants to be free of distractions, in order to love and serve God and others. **(1981a)**

875. Increasing injustice

The Old Testament recognizes that poverty is sometimes due to laziness, gluttony, or extravagance, but usually attributes it to the sins of others. Moreover, injustice tends to deteriorate because the poor are powerless to change it. **(1981e)**

876. Three approaches to poverty

How should Christians approach the harsh fact of poverty in the contemporary world?

First, we could approach the problem *rationally*, with cool statistical detachment. Indeed, this is where we must begin. There are over five billion inhabitants of planet Earth, one fifth of whom are destitute . . . Whereas one fifth of the world's population lack the basic necessities for survival, rather more than another one fifth live in affluence and consume about four fifths of the world's income. In 1988 the 'total disbursements' from these wealthy nations to the Third World 'amounted to $92 billion' (less than 10% of worldwide spending on armaments), 'but this was more than offset by the total debt service of $142 billion, resulting in a net negative transfer of some $50 billion' from the Third World to the developed countries.[1] The gross disparity between wealth and poverty constitutes a social injustice with which the Christian conscience cannot come to terms.

Secondly, we could approach the phenomenon of poverty *emotionally*, with the hot-blooded indignation aroused by the sights, sounds and smells of human need. When I last visited Calcutta airport, the sun had already set. Over the whole city hung a pall of malodorous smoke from the burning of cowdung on a myriad fires. Outside the airport an emaciated woman clutching an emaciated baby stretched out an emaciated hand for *baksheesh*. A man, whose legs had both been amputated above the knee, dragged himself along the pavement with his hands. I later learned that over a quarter of a million homeless people sleep in the streets at night, and during the day hang their blanket – often their only possession – on some convenient railing. My most poignant experience was to see men and women scavenging in the city garbage dumps like dogs. For extreme poverty is demeaning; it reduces human beings to the level of animals. To be sure, Christians should be provoked by the *idolatry* of a Hindu city, as Paul was by the idols in Athens, and moved to evangelism. But, like Jesus when he saw the hungry crowds, we should also be moved with compassion to feed them.

The third way, which should stimulate both our reason and our emotion simultaneously, is to approach the problem of poverty *biblically*. As we turn again to that book in which God has revealed himself and his will, we ask: how according to Scripture should we think about wealth and poverty? Is God on the side of the poor? Should we be? What does the Scripture say? Moreover, as we ask these questions, we have to resolve to listen attentively to God's Word, and not manipulate it. We have no liberty either to avoid its uncomfortable challenge, in order to retain our prejudices, or to acquiesce uncritically in the latest popular interpretations. **(1990a:230)**

[1] The World Bank Annual Report 1989, p. 27.

877. *The compassionate heart*

We have to feel what Jesus felt – the pangs of the hungry, the alienation of the powerless, and the indignities of the wretched of the earth. For ultimately, the unacceptable inequalities between North and South are neither political nor economic, but rather moral. Until we feel moral indignation about worldwide social injustice and strong compassion for world-wide human suffering, I seriously doubt if we shall be moved to take action. **(1980c)**

878. *A Christian lifestyle*

We should be thankful to God our Creator and Father for the good things he has given us to enjoy; a negative asceticism – self-denial as an end in itself – is a contradiction of the biblical doctrine of creation, for it overlooks the generosity of God 'who richly furnishes us with everything to enjoy' (1 Tim. 6:17). At the same time, we have to remember the numerous biblical warnings against the dangers of wealth (that it easily engenders pride, materialism, and a false sense of security), against the evils of covetousness, and against the injustice of condoning the inequalities of privilege . . . Most of us (for I include myself) ought to give more generously to aid and development, as well as to world evangelization. In order to do so, we ought further to develop a simple lifestyle. The two most discussed sentences in the Lausanne Covenant (1974) read: 'All of us are shocked by the poverty of millions and disturbed by the injustices which cause it. Those of us who live in affluent circumstances accept our duty to develop a simple lifestyle in order to contribute generously to both relief and evangelism.' **(1980c)**

879. *Humanity and race*

Consider these five bases of our common humanity. All of us, whatever our race or rank, whatever our creed, colour or culture, have the same Creator who made every nation from one man, the same Lord who disposes the history of every nation, the same God who is near and intends that we should grope after him and find him, the same Lifegiver who sustains us and the same Judge who will call us to account in the end.

So then, whether we look back to the beginning (the creation) or on to the end (the judgment), or whether we survey the intervening history of the world, our conclusion is the same. Whether we study anthropology (the origins of the human race), history, religion, physiology or medicine, these branches of human study all point in the same direction. Everything proclaims the unity of the human race – everything except sin, self, pride and prejudice . . . I dare to say that no man is altogether free from some taint of racial pride, because no man is free from sin. A sense of racial superiority is natural to us all, even if it is secret and undiscovered. Further, there is a black racism as well as a white. Everyone assumes that his race and colour are the norm, and that others are the abnorm, the deviation. This is simply the self-centredness of sin. But there is no norm in the colour of human skin, any more than there is in the colour of bird plumage. The norm is humanity: the races are variants of this.

This means that all forms of racism are wrong. They are an offence against God, the God of creation and history, of religion, nature and judgment. **(1968b)**

880. Revelation and race

Only a true theology, the biblical revelation of God, can deliver us from racial pride and prejudice. Because he is the God of Creation, we affirm the unity of the human race. Because he is the God of History, we affirm the diversity of ethnic cultures. Because he is the God of Revelation, we affirm the finality of Jesus Christ. And because he is the God of Redemption, we affirm the glory of the Christian church. Whatever policies for racial integration may be developed, we should try to ensure that they will reflect these doctrines. Because of the unity of humankind we demand equal rights and equal respect for racial minorities. Because of the diversity of ethnic groups we renounce cultural imperialism and seek to preserve all those riches of inter-racial culture which are compatible with Christ's lordship. Because of the finality of Christ, we affirm that religious freedom includes the right to propagate the gospel. Because of the glory of the church, we must seek to rid ourselves of any lingering racism and strive to make it a model of harmony between races, in which the multiracial dream comes true. **(1990a:225)**

881. A pointed parable

The main point of the parable of the good Samaritan is its racial twist. It is not just that neighbour-love ignores racial and national barriers, but that in Jesus' story a Samaritan did for a Jew what no Jew would ever have dreamed of doing for a Samaritan. **(1990a:140)**

882. The right to life

Since the life of the human fetus is a human life, with the potential of becoming a mature human being, we have to learn to think of mother and unborn child as two human beings at different stages of development. Doctors and nurses have to consider that they have two patients, not one, and must seek the well-being of both. Lawyers and politicians need to think similarly. As the United Nations' 'Declaration of the Rights of the Child' (1959) put it, the child 'needs special safeguards and care, including appropriate legal protection, before as well as after birth'. Christians would wish to add 'extra care before birth'. For the Bible has much to say about God's concern for the defenceless, and the most defenceless of all people are unborn children. They are speechless to plead their own cause and helpless to protect their own life. So it is our responsibility to do for them what they cannot do for themselves.**(1990a:327)**

883. The vocabulary of abortion

The popular euphemisms make it easier for us to conceal the truth from ourselves. The occupant of the mother's womb is not a 'product of conception' or 'gametic material', but an unborn child. Even 'pregnancy' tells us no more than that a woman has been 'impregnated', whereas the truth in old-fashioned language is that she is 'with child'. How can we speak of 'the termination of a pregnancy' when what is terminated is not just the mother's pregnancy but the child's life? And how can we describe the average abortion today as 'therapeutic' (a word originally used only when the mother's life was at stake), when pregnancy is not a disease needing therapy, and what abortion effects nowadays is not a cure but a killing? And how can people think of abortion as no more than a kind of contraceptive, when what it does is not prevent conception but destroy the conceptus? We need to have the courage to use accurate language. Induced abortion is feticide, the deliberate destruction of an unborn child, the shedding of innocent blood. **(1990a:328)**

884. Equality, not identity

The equality the Bible commends is not a total egalitarianism. It is not a situation in which all of us become identical, receiving identical incomes, living in identical homes, equipped with identical furniture, and wearing identical clothing. Equality is not identity. We know this from the doctrine of creation. For the God who has made us equal in dignity (all sharing his life and bearing his image) has made us unequal in ability (intellectually, physically, and psychologically). The new creation has even increased this disparity, bestowing on us who are 'one in Christ Jesus' different spiritual gifts or capacities for service.

How, then, can we put together this biblical unity and diversity, equality and inequality? Perhaps in this way: since all have equal worth, though unequal capacity, we must secure equal opportunity for each to develop his or her particular potential for the glory of God and the good of others. Inequality of privilege must be abolished in favour of equality of opportunity. At present, millions of people made in God's image are unable to develop their human potential because of illiteracy, hunger, poverty, or disease. It is, therefore, a fundamentally Christian quest to seek for all people equality of opportunity in education (universal education is arguably the principal means to social justice), in trade (equal access to the world's markets), and in power sharing (representation on the influential world bodies that determine international economic relations.) **(1980b)**

63. GENDER, SEXUALITY, MARRIAGE AND DIVORCE

885. Equal beneficiaries

It is essential to begin at the beginning, namely with the first chapter of Genesis:

> Then God said, 'Let us make man in our image, in our likeness, and let them rule over the fish of the sea and the birds of the air, over the livestock, over all the earth, and over all the creatures that move along the ground.'
>
> So God created man in his own image, in the image of God he created him; male and female he created them.
>
> God blessed them and said to them, 'Be fruitful and increase in number; fill the earth and subdue it. Rule over the fish of the sea and the birds of the air and over every living creature that moves on the ground' (1:26–28).

If we put together the divine resolve ('Let us make man . . . and let them rule . . .'), the divine creation ('So God created . . .') and the divine blessing ('Be fruitful . . . fill the earth and subdue it . . '), we see that the emphasis seems to be on three fundamental truths about human beings, namely that God made (and makes) them in his own image, that he made (and makes) them male and female, giving them the joyful task of reproducing, and that he gave (and gives) them dominion over the earth and its creatures. Thus from the beginning 'man' was 'male and female', and men and women were equal beneficiaries both of the divine image and of the earthly rule. There is no suggestion in the text that either sex is more like God than the other, or that either sex is more responsible for the earth than the other. No. Their resemblance to God and their stewardship of his earth (which must not be confused, although they are closely related) were from the beginning shared equally, since both sexes were equally created by God and like God. **(1990a:257)**

886. The gospel of womanhood

St Luke's gospel is the gospel of womanhood, and tells more than the others the gracious, courteous attitude of Jesus towards women, and the place he allowed them to occupy in his ministry. It is he who tells, with such delicate reserve, the story of the miraculous conception and birth of Jesus. Mary, the mother of Jesus, and Elizabeth, the mother of the Baptist, were kinswomen, and the story must have been derived directly or indirectly from Mary herself. The other evangelists tell the stories of the woman with the issue of blood, Jairus' daughter, Peter's sick mother-in-law, and the Bethany anointing, but only Luke writes of the prophetess Anna, of the widow of Nain, of the woman who was a sinner, of the ministering women, of Martha and Mary, of the woman whom Satan had bound for eighteen years, and of the daughters of Jerusalem who wept. Similarly, in the Acts he refers several times to the fact that 'multitudes both of men and women' embraced the gospel. He also tells of Tabitha, whom Peter brought back to life in Joppa, and of Lydia and the slave girl, who were converted during the mission in Philippi. **(1954c:32)**

887. A foundation principle

Since it is mainly on the facts of creation that Paul bases his case for the husband's headship (Eph. 5:22f.), his argument has permanent and universal validity, and is not to be dismissed as culturally limited. The cultural elements of his teaching are to be found in the applications of the principle, in the requirement of 'veiling' certainly, and I think also in the requirement of 'silence'. But the man's (and especially the husband's) 'headship' is not a cultural application of a principle; it is the foundation principle itself. This is not chauvinism, but creationism. The new creation in Christ frees us from the distortion of relations between the sexes caused by the fall (*e.g.* Gn. 3:16), but it establishes the original intention of the creation. It was to this 'beginning' that Jesus himself went back (*e.g.* Mt. 19:4–6). He confirmed the teaching of Genesis 1 and 2. So must we. What creation has established, no culture is able to destroy. **(1979e:221)**

888. Male headship

All attempts to get rid of Paul's teaching on [male] headship (on the grounds that it is mistaken, confusing, culture-bound or culture-specific) must be pronounced unsuccessful. It remains stubbornly there. It is rooted in divine revelation, not human opinion, and in divine creation, not human culture. In essence, therefore, it must be preserved as having permanent and universal authority. **(1990a:269)**

889. The husband's part

We picture the 'authoritative' husband as a domineering figure who makes all the decisions himself, issues commands and expects obedience, inhibits and suppresses his wife, and so prevents her from growing into a mature or fulfilled person. But this is not at all the kind of 'headship' which the apostle Paul describes, whose model is Jesus Christ. Certainly, 'headship' implies a degree of leadership and initiative, as when Christ came to woo and to win his bride. But more specifically it implies sacrifice, self-giving for the sake of the beloved, as when Christ gave himself for his bride. If 'headship' means 'power' in any sense, then it is power to care not to crush, power to serve not to dominate, power to facilitate self-fulfilment, not to frustrate or destroy it. And in all this the standard of the husband's love is to be the cross of Christ, on which he surrendered himself even to death in his selfless love for his bride. **(1979e:232)**

890. Headship and responsibility

On the one hand, headship must be compatible with equality. For if 'the head of the woman is man' as 'the head of Christ is God', then man and woman must be equal as the Father and the Son are equal. On the other hand, headship implies some degree of leadership, which, however, is expressed not in terms of 'authority' but of 'responsibility'. **(1990a:271)**

891. Submission and obedience

In my view the 1662 Prayer Book marriage service was wrong to include the word 'obey' in the bride's vows. The concept of a husband who issues commands and of a wife who gives him obedience is simply not found in the New Testament. The nearest approximation to it is the cited example of Sarah who 'obeyed Abraham, calling him lord'. But even in that passage the apostle Peter's actual instruction to wives is the same as Paul's, namely, 'Be submissive to your husbands' (1 Pet. 3:1–6). And . . . a wife's submission is something quite different from obedience. It is a voluntary self-giving to a lover whose responsibility is defined in terms of constructive care; it is love's response to love. **(1979e:238)**

371

892. Women's ministry

If God endows women with spiritual gifts (which he does), and thereby calls them to exercise their gifts for the common good (which he does), then the church must recognize God's gifts and calling, must make appropriate spheres of service available to women, and should 'ordain' (that is, commission and authorize) them to exercise their God-given ministry, at least in team situations. Our Christian doctrines of creation and redemption tell us that God wants his gifted people to be fulfilled not frustrated, and his church to be enriched by their service.   (1990a:280)

893. Some biblical principles

The Bible contains principles which are relevant to particular questions. Take marriage as an example. Scripture gives us general guidance and settles some issues in advance. It tells us that marriage is God's good purpose for human beings and that singleness is the exception, not the rule; that one of his primary purposes in instituting marriage is companionship, so that this is an important quality to look for in a spouse; that a Christian is at liberty to marry only a fellow-Christian; and that marriage (as a lifelong, loving, monogamous and heterosexual commitment) is the only God-ordained context for sexual intercourse. These general guidelines are clearly laid down in the Bible. But the Bible will not tell any individuals whether God is calling them to marriage or to remain single, or (if they should marry) who their spouse should be.

(1992b:130)

894. Marriage – God's invention

The Bible teaches that marriage is God's idea rather than ours, and his general loving provision for human beings; that it involves leaving parents (still of great importance psychologically, even if young people have physically 'left home' years previously); that it is a heterosexual, monogamous and ideally lifelong partnership, expressing love and companionship; and that it is the God-given context for sexual enjoyment and the procreation and nurture of children. These aspects of marriage are creational, not cultural.   (1988d:269)

895. *Four characteristics of marriage*

Genesis 2:24 implies that the marriage union has at least four characteristics. It is an exclusive relationship ('a man . . . his wife . . .'), which is publicly acknowledged at some social event ('leaves his parents'), permanent ('cleaves to his wife'), and consummated by sexual intercourse ('they will become one flesh'). A biblical definition of marriage might then be as follows: 'Marriage is an exclusive heterosexual covenant between one man and one woman, ordained and sealed by God, preceded by a public leaving of parents, consummated in sexual union, issuing in a permanent mutually supportive partnership, and normally crowned by the gift of children.'

(1990a:289)

896. *More than a human contract*

The marriage bond is more than a human contract: it is a divine yoke. And the way in which God lays this yoke upon a married couple is not by creating a kind of mystical union but by declaring his purpose in his Word. Marital breakdown, even the so-called 'death' of a relationship, cannot then be regarded as being in itself a ground for dissolution. For the basis of the union is not fluctuating human experience ('I love you, I love you not') but the divine will and Word (they 'become one flesh').

(1990a:292)

897. *Marriage, reconciliation and divorce*

Reconciliation lies at the very heart of Christianity. For some years now I have followed a simple rule, that whenever anybody asks me a question about divorce, I refuse to answer it until I have first talked about two other subjects, namely, marriage and reconciliation. This is a simple attempt to follow Jesus in his own priorities. When the Pharisees asked him about the grounds for divorce, he referred them instead to the original institution of marriage. If we allow ourselves to become preoccupied with divorce and its grounds, rather than with marriage and its ideals, we lapse into Pharisaism. For God's purpose is marriage not divorce, and his gospel is good news of reconciliation. We need to see Scripture as a whole, and not isolate the topic of divorce.

(1990a:303)

898. Jesus and divorce

Divorce for immorality is permissible, not mandatory. Jesus did not teach that the innocent party *must* divorce an unfaithful partner, still less that sexual unfaithfulness *ipso facto* dissolves the marriage. He did not even encourage or recommend divorce for unfaithfulness. On the contrary, his whole emphasis was on the permanence of marriage in God's purpose and on the inadmissibility of divorce and remarriage. His reason for adding the exceptive clause was to clarify that the only remarriage after divorce which is not tantamount to adultery is that of an innocent person whose partner has been sexually unfaithful, for in this case the infidelity has already been committed by the guilty partner. Jesus' purpose was emphatically not to encourage divorce for this reason, but rather to forbid it for all other reasons. **(1990a:294)**

899. Only people

We are all human beings. That is to say, there is no such phenomenon as 'a homosexual'. There are only people, human persons, made in the image and likeness of God, yet fallen, with all the glory and the tragedy which that paradox implies, including sexual potential and sexual problems. However strongly we may disapprove of homosexual practices, we have no liberty to dehumanize those who engage in them. **(1990a:336)**

900. The homosexual condition

Christians know that the homosexual condition, being a deviation from God's norm, is not a sign of created order but of fallen disorder. **(1990a:357)**

901. The call to singleness

Acceptance or tolerance of a same-sex partnership rests on the assumption that sexual intercourse is 'psychologically necessary'. That is certainly what our sex-obsessed contemporary culture says. But is it true? Christians must surely reply that it is a lie. There is such a thing as the call to singleness, in which authentic human fulfilment is possible without sexual experience. Our Christian witness is that Jesus himself, though unmarried, was perfect in his humanness. Same-sex friendships should of course be encouraged, which may be close, deep and affectionate. But sexual union, the 'one flesh' mystery, belongs to heterosexual marriage alone.   **(1988d:272)**

902. *Fully human*

If sex is for marriage, what does the Bible say about singleness? First, it reminds us that Jesus himself was single, although he is also set before us as God's model for humanness.

This should not lead us to glorify singleness (since marriage is God's general will for human beings, Gn. 2:18) but rather to affirm that it is possible to be single and fully human at the same time! The world may say that sexual experience is indispensable to being human; the Bible flatly disagrees.

Secondly, both Jesus and his apostle Paul refer to singleness as a divine vocation for some (Mt. 19:10–12; 1 Cor. 7:7). Paul adds that both marriage and singleness are a *charisma*, a gift of God's grace.

Thirdly, Paul indicates that one of the blessings of singleness is that it releases people to give their 'undivided devotion' to the Lord Jesus (1 Cor. 7:32–35).

The truth is: although unmarried people may find their singleness lonely (and at times acutely so), we will not end up in neurotic turmoil if we accept God's will for our lives. Unhappiness comes only if we rebel against his will.   **(1993a:3)**

XII. THINGS TEMPORAL AND THINGS ETERNAL

64. Time, history and prophecy
65. Miracles, healing and suffering
66. The reality of evil
67. The hope of glory

61. TIME, HISTORY AND PROPHECY

903. Christ at the centre

We have all studied history at school and may have found it (as I did) abominably dull. Perhaps we had to memorize lists of dates or of the kings and queens who ruled our country. But what is the point of history? Was Henry Ford right when in 1919, during his libel suit with the *Chicago Tribune*, he said, 'History is bunk'? Is history just the random succession of events, each effect having its cause and each cause its effect, yet the whole betraying no overall pattern but appearing rather as the meaningless development of the human story? Was Marx right in his dialectical understanding of the historical process? Or has history some other clue?

Christians affirm, in contrast to all other views, that history is 'his story', God's story. For God is at work, moving from a plan conceived in eternity, through a historical outworking and disclosure, to a climax within history, and then on beyond it to another eternity of the future. The Bible has this linear understanding of time. And it tells us that the centre of God's eternal-historical plan is Jesus Christ, together with his redeemed and reconciled people.   **(1979e:127)**

904. The God of history

Somebody once suggested that 'the most accurate chart of the meaning of history is the set of tracks made by a drunken fly with feet wet with ink, staggering across a piece of white paper. They lead nowhere and reflect no pattern of meaning'. Similarly, Rudolf Bultmann wrote that 'the question of meaning in history has become meaningless'.[1]

Christians who look to Scripture as their authority profoundly disagree with these gloomy assessments. For the God of the Bible is the God of history. He has entitled himself 'the God of Abraham, Isaac and Jacob'. He chose Israel out of the nations to be his covenant people and took about two thousand years to prepare them for the fulfilment of his promise to Abraham in the coming of their Messiah. Above all, he came to us in Jesus Christ when Augustus was emperor of Rome, and 'suffered under Pontius Pilate, was crucified, died and was buried'. Then on the third day he rose again and, having sent his Spirit, has for two further millennia been pushing his church out into the world to take the good news to its furthest extremities. One day (known only to the Father), when the gospel has been 'preached in the whole world as a testimony to all nations' (Mt. 24:13), the end will come. For Christ will return in glory, terminate the historical process and perfect his reign. **(1991c:139)**

[1] Quoted from Bultmann's *History and Eschatology* by George Eldon Ladd in *The Gospel of the Kingdom* (1959; Eerdmans, 1973), p. 131.

905. Church history

Church history is the story of God's incredible patience with his wayward people. **(1992b:388)**

906. The meaning of history

If we had to sum up in a single brief sentence what life is all about, why Jesus Christ came into this world to live and die and rise, and what God is up to in the long-drawn-out historical process both BC and AD, it would be difficult to find a more succinct explanation than this: *God is making human beings more human by making them more like Christ.* For God created us in his own image in the first place, which we then spoiled and skewed by our disobedience. Now he is busy restoring it. And he is doing it by making us like Christ, since Christ is both perfect man and perfect image of God (Col. 1:15; 2 Cor. 4:4). **(1991b:100)**

907. 'Salvation' history

We must never set theology and history over against each other, since Scripture refuses to do so. The history it records is 'salvation history', and the salvation it proclaims was achieved by means of historical events. **(1985:21)**

908. God's everlasting purpose

Some people seem to think of the Bible as a trackless jungle, full of contradictions, a tangled undergrowth of unrelated ideas. In fact, it is quite the opposite, for one of the chief glories of the Bible is its coherence. The whole Bible from Genesis to Revelation tells the story of God's sovereign purpose of grace, his master-plan of salvation through Christ.

The apostle Paul, with a breadth of vision which leaves us far behind, brings together Abraham, Moses and Jesus Christ. In eight short verses (Gal. 3:15–22) he spans about 2,000 years. He surveys practically the whole Old Testament landscape. He presents it like a mountain range, whose highest peaks are Abraham and Moses, and whose Everest is Jesus Christ. He shows how God's promise to Abraham was confirmed by Moses and fulfilled in Christ. He teaches the unity of the Bible, especially the Old and New Testaments.

There is a great need in the church today for a biblical, Christian philosophy of history. Most of us are short-sighted and narrow-minded. We are so preoccupied with current affairs in the twentieth century, that neither the past nor the future has any great interest for us. We cannot see the wood for the trees. We need to step back and try to take in the whole counsel of God, his everlasting purpose to redeem a people for himself through Jesus Christ. Our philosophy of history must make room not only for the centuries after Christ but for the centuries before him, not only for Abraham and Moses but for Adam, through whom sin and judgment entered the world, and for Christ, through whom salvation has come. If we include the beginning of history, we must include its consummation also, when Christ returns in power and great glory, to take his power and reign. The God revealed in the Bible is working to a plan. He 'accomplishes all things according to the counsel of his will' (Ephesians 1:11).   **(1968c:91)**

909. *The two ages*

The Bible divides history into two ages or 'aeons'. From the Old Testament perspective they were called 'the present age' (which was evil) and 'the age to come' (which would be the time of the Messiah). Moreover, the two ages were sometimes portrayed in terms of the night and the day. The present age was like a long dark night, but when the Messiah came, the sun would rise, the day would break, and the world would be flooded with light.

The Bible also teaches that Jesus Christ is that long-awaited Messiah, and that therefore the new age began when he came. He was the dawn of the new era. He ushered in the day. He proclaimed the break-in of the kingdom of God. At the same time, the old age has not yet come to an end. As John put it, 'the darkness is passing and the true light is already shining' (1 Jn.

2:8). So, for the time br ng, ᴜne two ᴜ ᵢ overᴜaᴜ. Unbelievers belong to the old age, and are stil¹ in ᴜ darkᴜ ᴣs. But those who belong to Jesus Christ have been transferred into the new age, into the light. Already in Christ we have 'tasted . . . the powers of the coming age' (Heb. 6:5). Already, God has brought us 'out of darkness into his wonderful light' (1 Pet. 2:9). Only when Christ comes in glory will the present overlap the end. The transition period will be over. The old age will finally vanish, and those who belong to it will be destroyed. The new age will be consummated, and those who belong to it will be fu¹ly and finally redeemed. **(1991c:111)**

910. Kingdom come and kingdom coming

The essence of the interim period between the 'now' and the 'not yet', between kingdom come and kingdom coming, is the presence of the Holy Spirit in the people of God. On the one hand, the gift of the Spirit is the distinctive blessing of the kingdom of God, and so the principal sign that the new age has dawned. On the other, because his indwelling is only the beginning of our kingdom inheritance, it is also the guarantee that the rest will one day be ours. The New Testament uses three metaphors to illustrate this. The Holy Spirit is the 'firstfruits', pledging that the full harvest will follow, the 'deposit' or first instalment, pledging that the full payment will be made, and the foretaste, pledging that the full feast will one day be enjoyed. In this way the Holy Spirit is 'both a fulfilment of the promise and the promise of fulfilment: he is the guarantee that the new world of God has already begun, as well as a sign that this new world is still to come'.[1]

(1992b:382)

[1] Johannes Blauw, *The Missionary Nature of the Church* (1962; Eerdmans, 1974), p. 89.

911. History is change

There has probably never been a generation more suspicious of the old and more confident in the new than the present generation. It is a generation in revolt against what it has inherited from the past (in many cases understandably and justifiably so). It hates tradition and loves revolution. Anything which savours of rigid institutionalism, of the *status quo* or of the establishment arouses its hot indignation.

Such a wholesale repudiation of what is old is, to say the least, extremely naïve. Nevertheless, the opposite tendency of resistance to all change is equally mistaken. Time does not stand still. History is change. Far from impeding progress, for example in scientific discovery and social justice, Christians should be in the vanguard of advance. **(1970b:36)**

912. The last days

When Paul refers to 'the last days' it may seem natural to apply this term to a future epoch, to the days immediately preceding the end when Christ returns. But biblical usage will not allow us to do this. For it is the conviction of the New Testament authors that the new age (promised in the Old Testament) arrived with Jesus Christ, and that therefore with his coming the old age had begun to pass away and the last days had dawned. Thus Peter on the day of Pentecost quoted Joel's prophecy that 'in the last days' God would pour out his Spirit upon all flesh, and declared that this prophecy has now been fulfilled. 'This is what was spoken by the prophet Joel,' he said. In other words, 'the last days' to which the prophecy referred had come (Acts 2:14–17). Similarly, the letter to the Hebrews begins with an assertion that the God who had spoken of old to the fathers through the prophets had 'in these last days' spoken to us through his Son (1:1–2). This being so, we are living in the last days. They were ushered in by Jesus Christ, God's Son.

(1973b:82)

913. The last of the 'last days'

The New Testament writers do not have an exact vocabulary to describe the chronology of the last time or the end, and it is not always easy to discern to what eschatological period or event they are alluding. What is clear is that they regarded the first coming of Christ as having inaugurated the new age and settled the doom of the old. 'The age to come' had come, and 'the present age' was therefore drawing to a close. It was not, of course, anticipated that this period would last for ever. It was a stage of transition called both the 'last days' and the 'last times'. The New Testament writers who describe its beginning are already looking forward to its consummation. The 'last days' will themselves have 'last days', a period of grievous moral and religious decadence. Similarly, the 'last times' will have a 'last time' in which ungodly scoffers will arise. Nor is

383

this all. The 'last time' of the 'last times' will have a culminating 'last time' when our eternal inheritance will be revealed. In the same way, 'the last days' of the 'last days' will themselves have a final 'last day' when Christ raises the dead and judges the world. **(1988g:112)**

914. God's programme

Now is the time of *restraint*, in which the secret power of lawlessness is being held in check. Next will come the time of *rebellion*, in which the control of law will be removed and the lawless one will be revealed. Finally will come the time of *retribution*, in which the Lord Christ will defeat and destroy the Antichrist, and those who have believed the Antichrist-lie will be condemned. This is God's programme. History is not a random series of meaningless events. It is rather a succession of periods and happenings which are under the sovereign rule of God, who is the God of history. **(1991c:173)**

915. The Judge of history

The God who is Lord of history is also the Judge of history. It is naïve to hail all revolutionary movements as signs of divine renewal. After the revolution the new *status quo* sometimes enshrines more injustice and oppression than the one it has displaced. **(1975c:18)**

916. The bedrock of Christ

Peter's message like Paul's focused on Jesus' death and resurrection. Both events were real, objective and historical. And surely the right response to the existential mood of today is not to create a parallel Christian existentialism which despises history in favour of experience, and demythologizes the resurrection into an inward encounter with reality, but rather to offer to the modern mind as it flounders in the quicksands of subjectivity the objective bedrock of Jesus Christ whose death and resurrection are solid historical events.
(1975c:45)

917. Three fulfilments of prophecy

The whole question of the fulfilment of Old Testament prophecy is a difficult one in which there is often misunderstanding and not a little disagreement. Of particular importance is the principle . . . that the New Testament writers themselves understood Old Testament prophecy to have not a *single* but usually a *triple* fulfilment – past, present and future. The past fulfilment was an immediate or historical fulfilment in the life of the nation of Israel. The present is an intermediate or gospel fulfilment in Christ and his church. The future will be an ultimate or eschatological fulfilment in the new heaven and the new earth.   **(1979f:24)**

918. *Spokesmen of God*

In the primary sense in which the Bible uses the word, a prophet was a person who 'stood in the council of God', who heard and even 'saw' his word, and who in consequence 'spoke from the mouth of the Lord' and spoke his word 'faithfully' (*cf.* Je. 23:16–32). In other words, a prophet was a mouthpiece or spokesman of God, a vehicle of his direct revelation. *In this sense* we must insist that there are no prophets today. Nobody can presume to claim an inspiration comparable to that of the canonical prophets, or use their introductory formula 'Thus says the Lord'. If this were possible, we would have to add their words to Scripture, and the whole church would need to listen and obey.   **(1979e:161)**

919. *The State of Israel*

There is some disagreement among biblical Christians as to whether we are to expect the Old Testament promises about Israel's future to be literally fulfilled, and whether the modern State of Israel in its occupation of the Holy Land is at least a partial fulfilment of them. Certainly God has a great future for the Jews, which is figuratively set forth by Paul as the grafting back into their own olive tree of the natural branches which had been broken off (Rom. 11:13–27). But there is no mention in the New Testament of any literal return of the Jews to the promised land. The overwhelming emphasis of the New Testament is that the Christian church is now 'the Israel of God', 'the circumcision', 'a chosen people, a royal priesthood, a holy nation, a people belonging to God', and that God's great promises to Abraham of both posterity and a land are fulfilled spiritually in Christ and his church.   **(1984d:181)**

65. MIRACLES, HEALING AND SUFFERING

920. God at work

There is an urgent need for all of us to grasp the biblical revelation of the living God who works primarily in nature not in supernature, in history not in miracle. He is the most high God who rules the kingdom of men (Dn. 4:32), with whom 'the nations are like a drop from a bucket' and who 'takes up the isles like fine dust' (Is. 40:15), who 'executes judgment, putting down one and lifting up another' (Ps. 75:7). It is he also who causes his sun to rise and sends the rain (Mt. 5:45), who maintains the regularity of the seasons (Gn. 8:22; Acts 14:17), who rules the raging of the sea (Ps. 89:9), who feeds the birds of the air and clothes the flowers of the field (Mt. 6:26, 30), and has the breath of man in his hand (Dn. 5:23).

Once we begin to see the living God ceaselessly at work through the processes of history and nature, we shall begin (for example) to recognize that *all* healing is divine healing, whether without the use of means or through the use of physical, psychological or surgical means. The former should probably be termed 'miraculous healing', while the latter is non-miraculous, but both are equally 'divine healing'.

(1975b:96)

921. Miracles in Scripture

The Bible is not primarily a book of miracles, since the God of the Bible is not primarily a God of miracles. Of course the Bible contains miracle stories, as we know, but they do not occur evenly throughout the books of the Bible, and whole tracts of biblical history are devoid of them. It is because they appear in significant clusters that it is possible to propose a biblical doctrine of miracles. For the clusters relate to the four major epochs of God's redemptive revelation, and are associated with the major figures of those epochs – first Moses, the exodus and the giving of the law; secondly, Elijah and Elisha, pioneers of the outburst of prophecy during the monarchy, and champions of the contest between Yahweh and the Canaanite deities, not to mention some of the later prophets; thirdly our Lord Jesus and his inauguration of the kingdom of God; and fourthly the apostles, whom he appointed and authorized to found and teach his church. That is why we refer to the Acts correctly as 'the Acts of the Apostles', and why Paul called his miracles 'the things that mark an apostle'. **(1988d:217)**

922. Special cases

The thrust of the Bible is that miracles clustered round the principal organs of revelation at fresh epochs of revelation, particularly Moses the lawgiver, the new prophetic witness spearheaded by Elijah and Elisha, the Messianic ministry of Jesus, and the apostles, so that Paul referred to his miracles as 'the things that mark an apostle' (2 Cor. 12:12). There may well be situations in which miracles are appropriate today, for example, on the frontiers of mission and in an atmosphere of pervasive unbelief which calls for a power encounter between Christ and Antichrist. But Scripture itself suggests that these will be special cases, rather than 'a part of daily life'.

(1990b:102)

923. Miracles in the gospels

The miracles of Jesus in the canonical gospels are sober, restrained, unsensational and spiritually significant . . . Moreover, they are evenly distributed through the four gospels and their sources, so that they are widely attested; the time elapsing between the public ministry of Jesus and the publication of the gospels was not long enough for the development of legends; and many eye-witnesses would have been still alive to refute (if the stories were not true), for example, the restoration to Malchus of his right ear and to Bartimaeus of his eyesight.

(1988d:221)

924. The 'already' and the 'not yet'

Is not the most helpful way to approach the gospel miracles to place them within the familiar and inescapable tension between the already and the not yet, kingdom come and kingdom coming, the new age inaugurated and the new age consummated? To the sceptical (who doubt all miracles) I want to say 'but *already* we have tasted the powers of the age to come'. To the credulous (who think that healing miracles are an everyday occurrence) I want to say 'but *not yet* have we been given resurrection bodies free from disease, pain, infirmity, handicap and death'. In this interim period between the beginning and the end we both look back to the outburst of miracles in the ministry of Jesus and his apostles, and on to the final resurrection of both body and universe.　　**(1988d:233)**

925. Miracles today?

There is much in the Acts of the Apostles which we shall probably not expect to witness in our day, as the apostles still lived and worked in an atmosphere of the miraculous. 'Signs and wonders' are frequently mentioned in its pages. Ananias and Sapphira die a dramatic death and Tabitha is raised from the dead. Prison doors are opened by an angel and prisoners' fetters unfastened by an earthquake. Handkerchiefs and aprons from Paul's body cure diseases and the sick are carried into the streets so that Peter's shadow may fall upon them. Peter sees a strange vision and hears God's voice on a housetop in Joppa, while Paul on the Damascus road is blinded by a light brighter than the sun and hears Christ's voice addressing him in Hebrew . . .

Two extreme positions are often taken, neither of which can establish itself from Scripture. The first is to assert that miracles either do not or cannot happen today, which denies freedom and sovereignty to God. The other is to assert that they take place with the same frequency as in the ministry of Christ and his apostles, which ignores the major purpose of miracles according to Scripture, namely to authenticate a fresh stage of revelation. Paul describes his miracles as 'the signs of a true apostle' (2 Cor. 12:12), because they confirmed his apostolic authority.　　**(1973a:1)**

926. Creation and miracle

The current controversy over signs and wonders should not lead us into a naïve polarization between those who are for them and those who are against. Instead, the place to begin is the wide area of agreement which exists among us. All biblical Christians believe that, although the Creator's faithfulness is revealed in the uniformity and regularities of his universe, which are the indispensable bases of the scientific enterprise, he has also sometimes deviated from the norms of nature into abnormal phenomena we call 'miracles'. But to think of them as 'deviations from nature' is not to dismiss them (as did the eighteenth-century deists), as 'violations of nature' which cannot happen, and therefore did not and do not happen. No, our biblical doctrine of the creation, that God has made everything out of an original nothing, precludes this kind of scepticism. As Campbell Morgan put it, 'granted the truth of the first verse in the Bible, and there is no difficulty with the miracles'. **(1990b:101)**

927. Open to God

If we take Scripture as our guide, we will avoid opposite extremes. We will neither describe miracles as 'never happening', nor as 'everyday occurrences', neither as 'impossible' nor as 'normal'. Instead, we will be entirely open to the God who works both through nature and through miracle. And when a healing miracle is claimed, we will expect it to resemble those in the Gospels and the Acts and so to be the instantaneous and complete cure of an organic condition, without the use of medical or surgical means, inviting investigation and persuading even unbelievers. **(1990b:104)**

928. Salvation today

I do not deny that disease and death are alien intrusions into God's good world; nor that God heals through natural means and sometimes supernaturally, for all healing is divine healing; nor that our new life in Christ can bring a new physical and emotional well-being as psychosomatic conditions due to stress, resentment, and anxiety are cured; nor that at the consummation when we are given new bodies and enter a new society we shall be rid of disease and death for ever. What I am saying is that the salvation offered in and through Jesus Christ today is not a complete psycho-physical wholeness; to maintain that it is is to anticipate the resurrection. **(1975e:73)**

929. Anticipating the resurrection

That the life of Jesus should be constantly revealed in our bodies; that God has put into the human body marvellous therapeutic processes which fight disease and restore health; that all healing is divine healing; that God can and sometimes does heal miraculously (without means, instantaneously and permanently) – these things we should joyfully and confidently affirm. But to expect the sick to be healed and the dead to be raised as regularly as we expect sinners to be forgiven, is to stress the 'already' at the expense of the 'not yet', for it is to anticipate the resurrection. Not till then will our bodies be entirely rid of disease and death. **(1986a:246)**

930. The new horizon

Complete healing of body, mind and spirit will not take place in this life. Some degree of deficit or disorder remains in each of us. But not for ever! For the Christian's horizons are not bounded by this world. Jesus is coming again; our bodies are going to be redeemed; sin, pain and death are going to be abolished; and both we and the universe are going to be transformed. Then we shall be finally liberated from everything which defiles or distorts our personality. And this Christian assurance helps us to bear whatever our present pain may be. For pain there is, in the midst of peace.

(1990a:359)

931. The God of the cross

There are limits to the sphere in which the finite mind of man can work. Men may indeed investigate the nature of disease, its causes, incidence, symptoms and cure, but no laboratory will ever witness the discovery of its meaning or its purpose. I would even believe that one of the reasons why God has not revealed this mystery is to keep us proud mortals humble. Our broad horizons are so narrow to God. Our vast knowledge is so small to him. Our great brain is so limited in his sight. He says to us as he said to Job: 'Where were you when I laid the foundation of the earth? Have you entered the storehouses of the snow? Can you bind the chains of the Pleiades, or loose the cords of Orion? Can you send forth lightnings, that they may go and say to you, Here we are?' (Jb. 38:4, 22, 31, 35).

The only right attitude towards suffering is worship, or humble self-surrender. This is not a grovelling humiliation but a sober humility. This is not to commit intellectual and moral suicide; this is to acknowledge the limits of our finite minds. This is in a word to let God be God and to be content ourselves to remain mere men. This is reasonable too when we have had a revelation of God like Job's. 'But', says a critic, 'we have not'. Wait a moment! We have, you know. We have had a better and a fuller one. We are much more favoured than Job. He only knew the God of nature; we know the God of grace. He only knew the God of the earth and the sky and the sea; we know the God of Jesus Christ. He only knew the God of the crocodile; we know the God of the cross. If it was right and reasonable for Job to worship, it is much more reasonable for us. We have seen the cross. Heaven is neither silent nor sullen. Heaven has been opened, and Christ has descended, and God has revealed himself in the Christ of the cross. The cross is the pledge of God's love. **(1956b:10)**

932. The essential perspective

We have to learn to climb the hill called Calvary, and from that vantage-ground survey all life's tragedies. The cross does not solve the problem of suffering, but it supplies the essential perspective from which to look at it. Since God has demonstrated his holy love and loving justice in a historical event (the cross), no other historical event (whether personal or global) can override or disprove it. This must surely be why the scroll (the book of history and destiny) is now in the hands of the slain Lamb, and why only he is worthy to break its seals, reveal its contents and control the flow of the future.

(1986a:329)

933. Holiness and suffering

Biblical teaching and personal experience combine to teach that suffering is the path to holiness or maturity. There is always an indefinable something about people who have suffered. They have a fragrance which others lack. They exhibit the meekness and gentleness of Christ. One of the most remarkable statements Peter makes in his first letter is that 'he who has suffered in his body is done with sin' (4:1). Physical affliction, he seems to be saying, actually has the effect of making us stop sinning. This being so, I sometimes wonder if the real test of our hunger for holiness is our willingness to experience any degree of suffering if only thereby God will make us holy.

(1986a:319)

934. 'Jesus wept'

On seven separate occasions in the Gospels Jesus was 'moved with compassion', for example towards the hungry and leaderless crowds, the widow of Nain, leprosy sufferers and a blind beggar. And in John 11 we read that 'Jesus wept' (verse 35) – not now tears of anger in the face of death but tears of sympathy for the bereaved sisters. Is it not beautiful to see Jesus, when confronted by death and bereavement, so deeply moved? He felt indignation in the face of death, and compassion towards its victims. **(1992b:124)**

935. *Christ with his people*

There is good biblical evidence that God not only suffered in Christ, but that God in Christ suffers with his people still. Is it not written of God, during the early days of Israel's bitter bondage in Egypt, not just that he saw their plight and 'heard their groaning', but that 'in all their distress he too was distressed'? Did Jesus not ask Saul of Tarsus why he was persecuting him, thus disclosing his solidarity with his church? It is wonderful that we may share in Christ's sufferings; it is more wonderful still that he shares in ours. **(1986a:335)**

66. THE REALITY OF EVIL

936. Our human predicament

'Death' is the one word which summarizes our human predicament as a result of sin. For death is the 'wage' sin pays, its grim penalty (Rom. 6:23). And this is true of each form which death takes. For Scripture speaks of death in three ways. There is physical death, the separation of the soul from the body. There is spiritual death, the separation of the soul from God. And there is eternal death, the separation of both soul and body from God for ever. All are due to sin; they are sin's terrible though just reward. **(1973b:37)**

937. Death as a penal event

The Bible everywhere views human death not as a *natural* but as a *penal* event. It is an alien intrusion into God's good world, and not part of his original intention for humankind. To be sure, the fossil record indicates that predation and death existed in the animal kingdom before the creation of man. But God seems to have intended for his human image-bearers a more noble end, akin perhaps to the 'translation' which Enoch and Elijah experienced, and to the 'transformation' which will take place in those who are alive when Jesus comes. Throughout Scripture, then, death (both physical and spiritual) is seen as a divine judgment on human disobedience. Hence the expressions of horror in relation to death, the sense of anomaly that man should have become 'like the beasts that perish', since 'the same fate awaits them both'. Hence too the violent 'snorting' of indignation which Jesus experienced in his confrontation with death at the graveside of Lazarus. Death was a foreign body. Jesus resisted it; he could not come to terms with it. **(1986a:65)**

938. Nothingness and death

Nothing baffles us human beings more than nothingness and death. The 'angst' of twentieth-century existentialists, is, at its most acute, their dread of the abyss of nothingness. And death is the one event over which (in the end) we have no control, and from which we cannot escape . . . But nothingness and death are no problem to God. On the contrary, it is out of nothing, that he created the universe, and out of death that he raised Jesus. The creation and the resurrection were and remain the two major manifestations of the power of God.   **(1994:133)**

939. Spiritualism forbidden

The Christian's attitude to spiritualistic activities is not necessarily to deny their validity, but to forbid their practice. No doubt some spiritualistic phenomena are fraudulent, and others may be explained by telepathy, thought transference or impersonation by evil spirits, but there is no need for Christians to assert that all spiritualistic claims are nonsense. If they were, why would the Scriptures forbid them?**(1977c:24)**

940. Deserving to perish

Some are too inclined, I think, to praise the good they see in others, and I may be too inclined to blame the evil. But the reason in my case is that I believe I know myself. To be sure, I welcome and affirm all those noble gifts of God which are part of his image in me (rationality and curiosity, moral aspirations, the primacy of love, artistic creativity, the urge to worship), but it is this very glory which highlights the shame – the vanity, obstinacy, selfishness, envy, impatience, malice, and lack of self-control. My perceptions of God and of myself, however distorted, convince me that in myself I am completely unfit to spend eternity in his presence. I need to be 'made fit' to share in the saints' inheritance in light. Without those white robes made clean in the blood of the Lamb, I could never stand before God's throne. 'Hell-deserving sinner' sounds an absurdly antiquated phrase, but I believe it is the sober truth. Without Christ I am 'perishing', and deserve to perish.   **(1988d:322)**

941. Scripture and universalism

It is impossible to be a biblical Christian and a universalist simultaneously.   **(1975e:76)**

942. Not without tears . . .

The gospel brings warnings as well as promise, of the retention of sins as well as the remission of sins. 'Beware, therefore', warned the apostle Paul, 'lest there comes upon you what is said in the prophets: "Behold, you scoffers, and wonder, and perish . . ."' (Acts 13:40–41). 'Perish' is a terrible word. So is 'hell'. We may, and I think we should, preserve a certain reverent and humble agnosticism about the precise nature of hell, as about the precise nature of heaven. Both are beyond our understanding. But clear and definite we must be that hell is an awful, eternal reality. It is not dogmatism that is unbecoming in speaking about the fact of hell; it is glibness and frivolity. How can we think about hell without tears?   **(1975c:113)**

943. The expectation of Antichrist

How should we react to what F. W. Farrar [in reference to attempts to identify the Antichrist] called 'that vast limbo of exploded exegesis'?[1] Certainly not by a contemptuous dismissal of prophecy, of the 'legend' of Antichrist, which 'is now to be found only among the lower classes of the Christian community, among sects, eccentric individuals and fanatics'.[2] If that were the case, I for one would be happy to be numbered among the 'lower classes' of eccentrics and fanatics! Instead, we should take careful note of the development of the Antichrist expectation within Scripture itself, how Daniel referred to Antiochus Epiphanes, how Jesus, Paul and John in Revelation reapplied the prophecy of Daniel, that is, how they recognized successive embodiments of godlessness and lawlessness, and how John in his letters saw the false teachers as 'many antichrists', spreading their heresy around, much as Jesus had talked about 'pseudo-Christs'. As Hendriksen has put it, 'history . . . repeats itself. Better, prophecy attains multiple fulfilment'.[3] Yet all these, together with other evil leaders down the centuries, have been forerunners or anticipations of the final 'man of lawlessness', an eschatological yet historical person, the decisive manifestation of lawlessness and godlessness, the leader of the ultimate rebellion, the precursor of and signal for the parousia. I agree with Geerhardus Vos that 'we may take for granted . . . that the Antichrist will be a human person'.[4] And whether we still believe in the coming of Antichrist will depend largely on whether we still believe in the coming of Christ.   **(1991c:166, 167)**

[1] F. W. Farrar, *The Life and Work of St Paul* (Cassell, popular edition, 1891), p. 350.

[2] W. Bousset, article 'Antichrist', in *The Encyclopaedia of Religion and Ethics*, vol. I, ed. James Hastings (T. and T. Clark, 1908).

[3] W. Hendriksen, *Exposition of I and II Thessalonians* (Baker, 1955), p. 177. G. C. Berkouwer, in *The Return of Christ* (ET Eerdmans, 1972), develops the concept of '*continuous reinterpretation*, in which

nothing of the eschatological promise is sacrificed' and by which 'the continuing actuality of the eschatological promise' is preserved (pp. 246–252).
[4] G. Vos, *The Pauline Eschatology* (1930; Baker, 1979), p. 113.

944. The secret power of lawlessness

Meanwhile, even during the period of restraint, and before the lawless one is revealed, *the secret power of lawlessness is already at work* (2 Thes. 2:7a). 'The secret power' translates *to mystērion*. It cannot here bear its usual meaning in Paul's writings of 'a truth once hidden but now revealed', since it is still secret and is contrasted with the coming 'revelation' of the man of lawlessness. Before he is revealed openly, however, the lawlessness he embodies is operating secretly. His antisocial, anti-law, anti-God movement is at present largely underground. We detect its subversive influence around us today – in the atheistic stance of secular humanism, in the totalitarian tendencies of extreme left-wing and right-wing ideologies, in the materialism of the consumer society which puts things in the place of God, in those so-called 'theologies' which proclaim the death of God and the end of moral absolutes, and in the social permissiveness which cheapens the sanctity of human life, sex, marriage and family, all of which God created or instituted.

Were it not for some remaining restraints (which preserve a measure of justice, freedom, order and decency) these things would break out much more virulently. And one day they will. For when the restraint is removed, then secret subversion will become open rebellion under the unscrupulous leadership of *the lawless one who will be revealed* (verse 8a). Then we can expect a period (mercifully short) of political, social and moral chaos, in which both God and Law are impudently flouted, until suddenly *the Lord Jesus* will come and *overthrow* him *with the breath of his mouth and destroy* him *by the splendour of his coming* (8). **(1991c:170)**

945. The plain teaching of Jesus

It is unfashionable nowadays in the church (even while satanism flourishes outside it) to believe either in a personal devil or in personal demonic intelligences under his command. But there is no obvious reason why church fashion should be the director of theology, whereas the plain teaching of Jesus and his apostles (not to mention the church of the subsequent centuries) endorsed their malevolent existence.   **(1979e:73)**

946. A dark kingdom

We need to rid our minds of the medieval caricature of Satan. Dispensing with the horns, the hooves and the tail, we are left with the biblical portrait of a spiritual being, highly intelligent, immensely powerful and utterly unscrupulous. Jesus himself not only believed in his existence, but warned us of his power. He called him 'the prince of this world', much as Paul called him 'the ruler of the kingdom of the air'. He has therefore a throne and a kingdom, and under his command is an army of malignant spirits who are described in Scripture as 'the powers of this dark world', and 'the spiritual forces of evil in the heavenly realms' (Jn. 12:31; Eph. 6:12).   **(1990c:50)**

947. The wiles of the devil

The 'wiles of the devil' take many forms, but he is at his wiliest when he succeeds in persuading people that he does not exist. To deny his reality is to expose ourselves the more to his subtlety.   **(1979e:265)**

948. Satanic opposition

The world's opposition is strong and subtle. And behind these things stands the devil, bent on 'taking men alive' and keeping them prisoner. For the devil hates the gospel and uses all his strength and cunning to obstruct its progress, now by perverting it in the mouths of those who preach it, now by frightening them into silence through persecution or ridicule, now by persuading them to advance beyond it into some fancy novelty, now by making them so busy with defending the gospel that they have no time to proclaim it.   **(1973b:126)**

949. Judgment now

Like eternal life, judgment begins now. As we respond to Christ, so we are being judged. The final judgment will be but the public declaration of a destiny already reaped.   **(1951:8)**

67. THE HOPE OF GLORY

950. *The return of Christ in glory*

The reason we believe that Jesus Christ is coming back is that
he said so. Some people maintain that he expected his *parousia*
('coming') to take place within the lifetime of his contemporaries, and that he was mistaken. But since he confessed that he
did not himself know the date of his return, it is extremely
unlikely that he would have taught when it would take place.
What he surely intended by his urgent predictions was to
persuade his followers to 'watch', because they did not know
when the time would come. As we look forward to the
parousia, we should neither 'demythologize' it (denying that
it will be an event of history) nor 'embroider' it (decorating it
with our own speculative fancies). Instead, if we are wise and
humble, we will acknowledge that much remains mysterious,
and we will be careful not to go beyond the plain teaching of
Scripture. While refusing to dogmatize over details, we can
then affirm at least that the Lord's coming will be personal
('this same Jesus', 'the Lord himself' – Acts 1:11; 1 Thes. 4:16),
visible ('every eye will see him' – Rev. 1:7), universal and
undisputed ('like the lightning' – Lk. 17:24), and glorious (in
'the majesty of his power' – 2 Thes. 1:9). 'He will come again in
glory', says the Nicene Creed; his second coming will be as
spectacular as his first was lowly and obscure.   **(1991d:73)**

951. *A defeated enemy*

What should be the Christian's attitude to death? It is still an
enemy, unnatural, unpleasant and undignified – in fact 'the last
enemy to be destroyed'. Yet, it is a defeated enemy. Because
Christ has taken away our sins, death has lost its power to
harm and therefore to terrify. Jesus summed it up in one of his
greatest affirmations: 'I am the resurrection and the life. He
who believes in me will live, even though he dies; and whoever
lives and believes in me will never die' (Jn. 11:25–26). That is,
Jesus is the resurrection of believers who die, and the life of
believers who live. His promise to the former is 'you will live',
meaning not just that you will survive, but that you will be
resurrected. His promise to the latter is 'you will never die',
meaning not that you will escape death, but that death will

prove to be a trivial episode, a transition to fullness of life.

(1986a:244)

952. Words of comfort

Nothing comforts and sustains the bereaved like words of Christian truth. In saying this, we must not forget one of the lessons of the book of Job. Job's already appalling condition was aggravated, not ameliorated, by his mindless and heartless so-called 'comforters'. They began well, in that for seven days they sat beside him in silent sympathy. One wishes that, when this first week was over, they had kept their mouths shut. Instead, they drowned poor Job in a torrent of cold, conventional, false verbiage to the effect that he was being punished for his sins, until in the end God himself contradicted them in anger, and accused them of not speaking about him what was right (Jb. 42:7–8). Their mistake, however, was not that they had talked, but that they had talked 'folly'. Generally speaking, words can and do comfort, if they are true and gentle, and if they are spoken at the right time. **(1991c:106)**

953. Triumph and tears

To be sure, it is appropriate at Christian funerals joyfully to celebrate Christ's decisive victory over death, but we do so only through tears of personal sorrow. If Jesus wept at the graveside of his beloved friend Lazarus, his disciples are surely at liberty to do the same. **(1991c:94)**

954. The intermediate state

In biblical thought death consists of the separation of the soul from the body. At death the body ceases to be the home of the human spirit, and so begins to decay or 'return to the dust'. But the soul or spirit survives this crisis and lives on in a disembodied condition until the day of resurrection when Christ returns. For this reason the period between death and resurrection is called by theologians 'the intermediate state' – not because it is a third alternative, intermediate between heaven and hell, but because it is a temporary state, intermediate between death and the resurrection. **(1977c:22)**

955. Christ abolished death

One of the most searching tests to apply to any religion concerns its attitude to death. And measured by this test much so-called Christianity is found wanting with its black clothes, its mournful chants and its requiem masses. Of course dying can be very unpleasant, and bereavement can bring bitter sorrow. But death itself has been overthrown, and 'blessed are the dead who die in the Lord' (Rev. 14:13). The proper epitaph to write for a Christian believer is not a dismal and uncertain petition, 'R.I.P.' (*requiescat in pace*, 'may he rest in peace'), but a joyful and certain affirmation 'C.A.D.' ('Christ abolished death'). **(1973b:39)**

956. On the last day

As at the creation God 'spoke and it came to be', and as at the tomb Jesus called in a loud voice 'Lazarus, come out!' and he came out, so on the last day the dead will hear the creative, commanding voice of God and will obey. **(1991c:102)**

957. 'A body of glory'

Resurrection is not the same as resuscitation. Those whom Jesus raised from death during his earthly ministry were resuscitated. They came back from death, resumed their former way of life, and then later died a second time. Resurrection, however, means the beginning of a new, a different, and immortal life. So our resurrected bodies, though retaining some kind of continuity with our present bodies, will also be changed. They will be as different, Paul says, as the plant is from the seed out of which it grows. They will be set free both from decay and from 'the flesh', the fallen nature which in some sense belongs to them. They will also have new powers. In fact our resurrection body will be a 'body of glory', like Christ's. **(1984d:134)**

958. What is and what will be

Already the kingdom of God has been inaugurated and is advancing; not yet has it been consummated. Already the new age (the age to come) has come, so that we have 'tasted . . . the powers of the coming age'; not yet has the old age completely passed away. Already we are God's sons and daughters, and no longer slaves; not yet have we entered 'the glorious freedom of the children of God'. An overemphasis on the 'already' leads to triumphalism, the claim to perfection – either moral (sinlessness) or physical (complete health) – which belongs only to the consummated kingdom, the 'not yet'. An overemphasis on the 'not yet' leads to defeatism, an acquiescence in continuing evil which is incompatible with the 'already' of Christ's victory.   **(1986a:240)**

959. Fears for the future

As we face the end of the second millennium since Christ, the hearts of most people around us are failing them for fear. It is not the lack of natural resources which is the chief problem, however, but the lack of spiritual and moral resources. Thinking people know that the problems facing us – bewildering in their number, magnitude and complexity – are beyond us. Only a return to the living God who created us, sustains us and can re-make us through Christ, and a recovery of the authentic Christian faith in its biblical fullness and contemporary relevance, can enable us, with confidence and without fear, to look forward to the Year 2000 AD.   **(1983e:viii)**

960. The resurrection of the body

The Christian hope is not the immortality of the soul (a shadowy, disembodied existence), but the resurrection of the body (a perfect instrument for the expression of our new life).

(1985:51)

961. Our Christian confidence

Christians are confident about the future, and our Christian 'hope' (which is a sure expectation) is both individual and cosmic. Individually, apart from Christ, the fear of personal death and dissolution is almost universal. For us in the West Woody Allen typifies this terror. It has become an obsession with him. True, he can still joke about it. 'It's not that I'm afraid to die,' he quips; 'I just don't want to be there when it happens.'[1] But mostly he is filled with dread. In a 1977 article in *Esquire* he said: 'The fundamental thing behind *all* motivation and *all* activity is the constant struggle against annihilation and against death. It's absolutely stupefying in its terror, and it renders anyone's accomplishments meaningless.'

Jesus Christ, however, rescues his disciples from this horror. We will not only survive death, but be raised from it. We are to be given new bodies like his resurrection body, with new and undreamed-of powers. For he is called both the 'firstfruits' of the harvest and 'the firstborn from the dead'. Both metaphors give the same assurance. He was the first to rise; all his people will follow. We will have a body like his. 'Just as we have borne the likeness of the earthly man (Adam) so shall we bear the likeness of the man from heaven (Christ)' (1 Cor. 15:49).

Our hope for the future, however, is also cosmic. We believe that Jesus Christ is going to return in spectacular magnificence, in order to bring history to its fulfilment in eternity. He will not only raise the dead, but regenerate the universe; he will make all things new. We are persuaded that the whole creation is going to be set free from its present bondage to decay and death; that the groans of nature are the labour pains which promise the birth of a new world; and that there is going to be a new heaven and a new earth, which will be the home of righteousness. **(1992b:83)**

[1] Graham McCann, *Woody Allen, New Yorker* (Polity Press, 1990), pp. 43 and 83.

962. Nature's bondage and future hope

Paul teaches in Romans 8 that creation will be *liberated from its bondage to decay* (verse 21b). *Phthora* (*decay*) seems to denote not only that the universe is running down (as we would say), but that nature is also enslaved, locked into an unending cycle, so that conception, birth and growth are relentlessly followed by decline, decay, death and decomposition. In addition, there may be a passing reference to predation and pain, especially the latter which is mentioned in the next verse. So futility, bondage, decay and pain are the words the apostle uses to indicate that creation is out of joint because under judgment. It still works, for the mechanisms of nature are fine-tuned and delicately balanced. And much of it is breathtakingly beautiful, revealing the Creator's hand. But it is also in bondage to disintegration and frustration. In the end, however, it will be 'freed from the shackles of mortality' (REB), 'rescued from the tyranny of change and decay' (JBP) . . . The creation's subjection to frustration was *in hope* (20). The bondage to decay will give place to the freedom of glory (21). The pains of labour will be followed by the joys of birth (22). There is therefore going to be both continuity and discontinuity in the regeneration of the world, as in the resurrection of the body. The universe is not going to be destroyed, but rather liberated, transformed and suffused with the glory of God.

(1994:239, 241)

963. *Forwards and backwards*

The reason we look forward with confidence to the consummation of all things is that we look back with confidence to the
resurrection. The Christian hope has already begun to be
fulfilled.   **(1985:49)**

964. *With Christ and like Christ*

It is enough for us to know that on the last day and through
eternity we shall be both with Christ and like Christ; for the
fuller revelation of what we are going to be we are content to
wait.   **(1988g:124)**

965. *What more do we need to know?*

There is no need for us to speculate about the precise nature of
heaven. We are assured on the authority of Jesus Christ that it
is the house and home of his Father and ours (there are twenty-
two references to the Father in John 14), that this home is a
prepared place containing many rooms or resting places, and
that he himself will be there. What more do we need to know?
To be certain that where he is, there we shall be also should be
enough to satisfy our curiosity and allay our fears.   **(1971b:34)**

966. *Not only negative joys*

Popular Christian devotion has perhaps concentrated too
much on the negative joys of heaven, that is, on the promises
of the Revelation that there will be no more hunger or thirst, no
more scorching heat or sunstroke, no more tears or pain, no
more night, no more curse, no more death. Thank God for
these absences. But thank God even more for their cause,
namely the presence – the central, dominating presence – of the
throne of God!   **(1984d:135)**

967. *Responsibility and rule*

Scripture contains many indications that the new heaven and
the new earth will be for the believer a place not only of
privilege but of responsibility. The 'good and faithful servant',
who has been 'faithful with a few things', will be put 'in charge
of many things' and will 'share [his] master's happiness' (Mt.
25:21, 23). Similarly, to the good servant in the parable of the
ten minas the nobleman says: 'Because you have been
trustworthy in a very small matter, take charge of ten cities'

(Lk. 19:17). And Paul adds to the Corinthians: 'Do you not know that the saints will judge the world?' (1 Cor. 6:2). It seems fitting that it should be so. Those who have learned to do Christ's works in this life will continue to do them in the next. Those who have come to rule their own passions on earth will rule over people in heaven. **(1990c:72)**

968. Love in heaven

The new age will be peopled by new beings living a new life under new conditions. Humans will be like angels. Mortals will have become immortal. Borrowing a phrase from the apostle Paul, they will have been 'raised imperishable' (1 Cor. 15:52–54). Consequently, the need to propagate the race will no longer exist. The creation command to 'be fruitful and multiply, and fill the earth' (Gn. 1:28) will be rescinded. And in so far as reproduction is one of the chief purposes of marriage, humans will no longer marry. Not that love will cease, for 'love never ends' (1 Cor. 13:8). But sexuality will be transcended, and personal relationships will be neither exclusive in their character nor physical in their expression. **(1970b:56)**

969. A countless throng

I have always derived much comfort from the statement of Revelation 7:9 that the company of the redeemed in heaven will be 'a great multitude which no man could number'. I do not profess to know how this can be, since Christians have always seemed to be a rather small minority. But Scripture states it for our comfort. Although no biblical Christian can be a universalist (believing that all mankind will ultimately be saved), since Scripture teaches the awful reality and eternity of hell, yet a biblical Christian can – even must – assert that the redeemed will somehow be an international throng so immense as to be countless. For God's promise is going to be fulfilled, and Abraham's seed is going to be as innumerable as the dust of the earth, the stars of the sky and the sand on the seashore. **(1979f:31)**

970. Eternal security

At the centre of the universe is a throne. From it the wheeling planets receive their orders. To it gigantic galaxies give their allegiance. In it the tiniest living organism finds its life. Before it angels and human beings and all created things in heaven above and earth beneath bow down and humbly worship. Encircling the throne is the rainbow of God's covenant, and surrounding it are twenty-four other thrones, occupied by twenty-four elders, who doubtless represent the twelve tribes of the Old Testament and the twelve apostles of the New, and so the completed and perfected church . . .

These chapters of the book of Revelation (4 to 7) leave us in no doubt about the security of the people of God. The Eternal Father sits on his throne, surrounded by the worshipping host of heaven. The Book of Destiny is in the hand of Christ, and no calamity can befall humankind unless he breaks the seals of the book. Moreover the winds of judgment are not permitted to blow upon those who have been sealed by the Holy Spirit. These are the symbols of divine sovereignty. The church's security is guaranteed by the Holy Trinity. **(1990c:126)**

LIST OF SOURCES

1951
'The coming Judge' (sermon on Jn. 12:48), in *All Souls Church Magazine* (February 1951).

1952
Parochial Evangelism by the Laity (London: Church Information Board, 1952) (Central Board of Finance of the Church of England).

1954
a. 'The Exaltation of Jesus' (sermon on Phil. 2:9–11), in *All Souls Church Magazine* (July 1954).
b. Foreword to *John Sung*, by Leslie T. Lyall (London: China Inland Mission, 1954).
c. *Men with a Message* (London: Longmans, 1954) = *Basic Introduction to the New Testament* (Grand Rapids: Eerdmans; Downers Grove: IVP, 1965). Illustrated edition, revised by Stephen Motyer (Grand Rapids: Eerdmans, 1994). Extracts are taken from the first edition.

1956
a. *Fundamentalism and Evangelism* (London: Crusade Booklets, 1956; Grand Rapids: Eerdmans, 1959).
b. *Why do the Innocent Suffer?* (London: Crusade Booklets, 1956). Also published in *Crusade* (January 1956).

1959
a. *The Doctor – a Person* (Cape Town: Medical Christian Fellowship, 1959).
b. 'Must Christ be Lord and Savior?' *Eternity* (September 1959) (Evangelical Ministries, Inc.).

1961
The Preacher's Portrait (London: Tyndale Press; Grand Rapids: Eerdmans, 1961).

1962

a. *Father and Creator.*

b. *He Shall Come to Judge.*

c. *I Believe in God.*

d. *Suffered under Pontius Pilate.*

The above are from the Episcopal Series (Atlanta: The Episcopal Radio–TV Foundation, 1962); transcripts of radio broadcasts on the Apostles' Creed.

e. 'The Calling of the Church': Studies in 1 Corinthians 1–6', in *The Keswick Week 1962*, ed. H. F. Stevenson (London: Marshall, Morgan and Scott, 1962).

f. 'The Meat of the Gospel', *Decision* (January 1962) (Billy Graham Evangelistic Association).

g. *Motives and Methods in Evangelism* (London: IVF, 1962) = *Evangelism: Why and How* (slightly adapted: Downers Grove: IVP, 1967).

1963

'The Evangelical Doctrine of Baptism', in *The Anglican Synthesis*, ed. W. R. F. Browning (Derby: Peter Smith, 1963).

1964

Confess your Sins (London: Hodder and Stoughton; Waco: Word, 1964).

1965

'Teacher and Lord', *Decision* (March 1965) (Billy Graham Evangelistic Association). Reprinted in *His* (January 1966).

1966

a. 'The New Testament Concept of Episkope: An Exposition of Acts 20:17–38', in *Bishops in the Church*, ed. R. P. Johnston (London: Church Book Room Press, 1966).

b. *The Canticles and Selected Psalms* (London: Hodder and Stoughton, 1966). See also 1988e.

c. *Men Made New* (London: IVF; Downers Grove: IVP, 1966. Reissued Grand Rapids: Baker, 1984).

1967

a. 'That Word "Radical"', *Church of England Newspaper* (24 February 1967).

b. 'Jesus Christ Our Teacher and Lord', in *Guidelines*, ed. J. I.

Packer (London: Falcon, 1967).

c. 'Was it Necessary for Jesus to Die on the Cross?' in *Hard Questions*, ed. Frank Colquhoun (London: Falcon, 1967).

d. 'The Great Commission', in *One Race, One Gospel, One Task*, ed. C. F. Henry and W. S. Mooneyham (Minneapolis: World Wide Publications, 1967).

e. *Our Guilty Silence* (London: Hodder and Stoughton, 1967; Grand Rapids: Eerdmans, 1969).

f. Foreword to *You in Your Small Corner*, by Ralph Capenerhurst (London: IVF, 1967).

1968

a. *The Call to Preach* (London: London Baptist Preachers' Association, 1968).

b. 'Racialism v. Our Common Humanity', in *Church of England Newspaper* (10 May 1968). Reprinted in *InterVarsity* (Autumn 1968).

c. *The Message of Galatians* (The Bible Speaks Today series: London and Downers Grove: IVP, 1968). Sometime title *Only One Way*.

1969

a. 'God's Man: Studies in 2 Timothy', in *The Keswick Week 1969*, ed. H. F. Stevenson (London: Marshall, Morgan and Scott, 1969).

b. *One People* (London: Falcon 1969; Downers Grove: IVP, 1970; rev. edn. Old Tappan: Revell, 1982).

1970

a. 'Genuine Peace' (sermon on Acts 10:36), in *All Souls Church Magazine* (May 1970).

b. *Christ the Controversialist* (London: Tyndale Press; Downers Grove: IVP, 1970).

1971

a. *Basic Christianity* (rev. edn. London: IVP; Grand Rapids: Eerdmans, and Downers Grove: IVP, 1971). First published 1958.

b. 'The Upper Room Discourse', in *Christ the Liberator*, by John Stott and others (Downers Grove: IVP, 1971; London: Hodder and Stoughton, 1972).

c. 'Reverence for Human Life', *Church of England Newspaper* (29 October and 5 November 1971), later published as *Reverence for*

Human Life (Fellowship Paper 278, London: Church Pastoral Aid Society, 1972).

d. *Following Christ in the Seventies* (Singapore: James Wong, 1971; Homebush West, NSW: Anzea, 1972).

1972

a. *Becoming a Christian* (rev. edn. London and Downers Grove: IVP, 1972). First published 1950.

b. *The Bible and the Crisis of Authority* (London: Falcon, 1972).

c. 'Christ's Portrait of a Christian: Studies in Matthew 5, 6 and 7', in *The Keswick Week 1972*, ed. H. F. Stevenson (London: Marshall, Morgan and Scott, 1972).

d. *Your Mind Matters* (London: IVF, 1972; Downers Grove: IVP, 1973. Reissued Brisbane: Australian Fellowship of Evangelical Students, 1994).

1973

a. *The Meaning of Evangelism* (rev. edn. London: Falcon, 1973). First published in *Christian Graduate* (June 1956).

b. *The Message of 2 Timothy* (The Bible Speaks Today series: London and Downers Grove: IVP, 1973). Original title *Guard the Gospel*.

1975

a. *Balanced Christianity* (London: Hodder and Stoughton; Downers Grove: IVP, 1975).

b. *Baptism and Fullness* (London: IVP, 1975; Downers Grove: IVP, 1976). Revised and enlarged edition of *The Baptism and Fullness of the Holy Spirit* (1964).

c. *Christian Mission in the Modern World* (London: Falcon; Downers Grove: IVP, 1975. Reissued Eastbourne: Kingsway, 1986).

d. *The Lausanne Covenant: An Exposition and Commentary* (Minneapolis: World Wide Publications; Charlotte: Worldwide Publications, 1975). Also published, under the same title, as Lausanne Occasional Paper 3 (Charlotte: Lausanne Committee for World Evangelization, 1975), from which the extracts are cited, and as *Explaining the Lausanne Covenant* (London: Scripture Union, 1975).

e. 'The Biblical Basis of Evangelism', in *Let the Earth Hear His Voice*, ed. J. D. Douglas (Minneapolis: World Wide Publications, 1975).

f. *Walk in His Shoes* (London: IVP, 1975) = *Who is My Neighbor?* (Downers Grove: IVP, 1976).

1976

a. 'Response to Bishop Mortimer Arias', *International Review of Mission* (January 1976).
b. 'The Authority and Power of the Bible', in *The New Face of Evangelicalism*, ed. R. Padilla (London: Hodder and Stoughton; Downers Grove: IVP, 1976).

1977

a. 'Unhooked Christians', *Christianity Today* (7 October 1977).
b. 'Is the Incarnation a Myth?' *Christianity Today* (4 November 1977).
c. 'Beyond the Divide', in *Death: Jesus Made it All Different*, ed. M. G. Meran (New Canaan: Keats Publishing, Inc., 1977). From a sermon at All Souls (February 1964).
d. 'The Biblical Basis for Declaring God's Glory', in *Declare His Glory Among the Nations*, ed. D. M. Howard (Downers Grove: IVP, 1977).
e. 'The Living God is a Missionary God', in *Declare His Glory Among the Nations* (see preceding entry).
f. 'Obeying Christ in a Changing World', in *Obeying Christ in a Changing World*, vol. 1: *The Lord Christ*, ed. and with a general introduction by John Stott (London: Collins, 1977). Used by permission of HarperCollins Publishers Limited.
g. 'The Sovereign God and the Church', in *Our Sovereign God*, ed. J. M. Boice (Grand Rapids: Baker, 1977).
h. 'The Sovereignty of God the Son', in *Our Sovereign God* (see preceding entry).
i. *What is an Evangelical?* (London: Falcon, 1977).

1978

a. 'Truth, Heresy and Discipline in the Church', *Christianity Today* (10 March 1978).
b. 'Must I Really Love Myself?' *Christianity Today* (5 May 1978).
c. 'Tasks Which Await Us', epilogue to *Essays in Evangelical Social Ethics*, ed. D. F. Wright (Exeter: Paternoster, 1978).
d. *Essentials for Tomorrow's Christians* (London: Scripture Union, 1978).
e. 'Biblical Preaching is Expository Preaching', in *Evangelical*

Roots, ed. K. S. Kantzer (Nashville: Thomas Nelson, 1978).

f. *The Message of the Sermon on the Mount* (The Bible Speaks Today series: Leicester and Downers Grove: IVP, 1978). Original title *Christian Counter-Culture*.

g. *The Uniqueness of Jesus Christ* (Chicago: Chicago Sunday Evening TV Club, 1978), Transcript of TV broadcast.

1979

a. 'Reclaiming the Biblical Doctrine of Work', *Christianity Today* (4 May 1979).

b. 'The Kingdom and Community: Can the Kingdom of God Satisfy Man's Search for Love?' *Crux* (September 1979).

c. *Evangelism, Salvation and Social Justice*, by R. J. Sider with a response by John Stott (2nd edn. Nottingham: Grove Books, 1979). First published in this form 1977.

d. Preface to *The Gospel and Culture* (the papers of the Willowbank Consultation, 1978: Pasadena: William Carey Library, 1979).

e. *The Message of Ephesians* (The Bible Speaks Today series: Leicester: IVP, 1979; Downers Grove: IVP, 1980). Original title *God's New Society*.

f. 'The Living God is a Missionary God', in *You Can Tell the World*, ed. J. E. Berney (Downers Grove: IVP, 1979).

1980

a. 'The Messenger and God: Studies in Romans 1–5', in *Believing and Obeying Jesus Christ*, ed. J. W. Alexander (Downers Grove: IVP, 1980).

b. 'Economic Equality Among Nations: A Christian Concern?' *Christianity Today* (2 May 1980).

c. 'The Just Demands of Economic Inequality', *Christianity Today* (23 May 1980).

d. 'Does Life Begin Before Birth?' *Christianity Today* (5 September 1980).

e. 'Saving Souls and Serving Bread', *Christianity Today* (7 November 1980).

f. 'Reviving Evangelism in Britain', *Christianity Today* (12 December 1980).

g. 'The Whole Christian', *Proceedings of the International Conference of Christian Medical Students*, ed. Lee Moy Ng (London: ICCMS and Christian Medical Fellowship, 1980).

h. 'The Gospel', *Southern Cross* (May 1980).

i. 'Evangelism and Social Responsibility', *Southern Cross* (October 1980).

1981

a. *The Christian and the Poor* (All Souls Paper: London: All Souls Church, 16 February 1981).
b. 'Scripture: The Light and Heat for Evangelism', *Christianity Today* (6 February 1981).
c. 'Seminarians are not Tadpoles', *Christianity Today* (6 February 1981).
d. 'Paralyzed Speakers and Hearers', *Christianity Today* (13 March 1981).
e. 'Who, Then, Are the Poor?' *Christianity Today* (8 May 1981).
f. 'Jesus is Lord! Has Wide Ramifications', *Christianity Today* (12 June 1981).
g. *The Authority and Relevance of the Bible in the Modern World* (Canberra: The Bible Society in Australia, 1979) = *Culture and the Bible* (Downers Grove: IVP, 1981), from which the extracts are cited. Also published in *The Bible in Perspective* (London: Bible Society, 1981).
h. 'The Bible in World Evangelization', in *Perspectives on the World Christian Movement*, ed. R. D. Winter and S. C. Hawthorne (Pasadena: William Carey Library, 1981). Adapted and condensed from 'The Living God is a Missionary God', in *Declare His Glory Among the Nations* (see 1977d).

1982

a. *I Believe in Preaching* (London: Hodder and Stoughton, 1982) = *Between Two Worlds* (Grand Rapids: Eerdmans, 1981).
b. *The Bible: Book for Today* (Leicester: IVP, 1982) = *God's Book for God's People* (Downers Grove: IVP, 1983), reissued as *You Can Trust the Bible* (Grand Rapids: Discovery House, 1991).
c. *True Wisdom* (Chicago: Chicago Sunday Evening TV Club, 1982). Transcript of TV broadcast.

1983

a. *In Christ* (Washington: National Prayer Breakfast, 1983).
b. *Make the Truth Known* (Leicester: IVP, 1983).
c. Foreword to *Masters of the English Reformation*, by M. L. Loane (2nd edn. London: Hodder and Stoughton, 1983).
d. 'John R. W. Stott: An Anglican Clergyman', in *Peacemakers*, ed. J. Wallis (New York: Harper and Row; Toronto: Fitzhenry

and Whiteside, 1983).

e. *The Year 2000 AD,* ed. and with a foreword by John Stott (London: Marshalls, 1983) = *The Year 2000* (Downers Grove: IVP, 1983).

1984

a. 'Am I Supposed to Love Myself or Hate Myself?' *Christianity Today* (20 April 1984).

b. *Free to Be Different,* ed. and with a foreword by John Stott (London: Marshalls, 1984).

c. 'Christian Responses to Good and Evil: A Study of Romans 12:9 – 13:10', in *Perspectives on Peacemaking,* ed. J. A. Bernbaum (Ventura: Regal Books, 1984).

d. *Understanding the Bible* (rev. edn. London: Scripture Union, 1976, 1984; Grand Rapids: Zondervan, 1980). First published 1972.

1985

The Authentic Jesus (London: Marshalls; Downers Grove: IVP, 1985). Used by permission of HarperCollins Publishers Limited.

1986

a. *The Cross of Christ* (Leicester and Downers Grove: IVP, 1986).

b. Foreword to *Decide for Peace,* ed. D. Mills-Powell (London: Marshall Pickering, 1986).

c. Introduction to *Evangelical Preaching* (sermons of Charles Simeon) (Portland: Multnomah, 1986).

d. 'I Believe in the Church of England', in *Hope for the Church of England?* ed. Gavin Reid (Eastbourne: Kingsway, 1986).

1988

a. 'The World's Challenge to the Church', *Bibliotheca Sacra* (April/June 1988).

b. 'Biblical Meditation: God in Christ', in *Christian Faith and Practice in the Modern World,* ed. M. A. Noll and D. F. Wells (Grand Rapids: Eerdmans, 1988).

c. 'Biblical Meditation: True Wisdom', in *Christian Faith and Practice in the Modern World* (see preceding entry).

d. *Essentials,* by David L. Edwards and John Stott (London: Hodder and Stoughton, 1988) = *Evangelical Essentials* (Downers Grove: IVP, 1989).

e. *Favourite Psalms* (Milton Keynes: Word UK; Chicago: Moody;

Willowdale, Ontario: R. G. Mitchell Family Books, 1988). Revised and illustrated edition of *The Canticles and Selected Psalms* (see 1966b).

f. 'Nuclear Weapons Change the Possibility of War', in *Handling Problems of Peace and War*, ed. A. Kirk (London: Marshall Pickering, 1988).

g. *The Letters of John* (Tyndale New Testament Commentaries: rev. edn. Leicester: IVP; Grand Rapids: Eerdmans, 1988). First published in 1964 as *The Epistles of John*.

1989

a. 'Conflicting Gospels', *Church of England Newspaper* (8 December 1989), reprinted as 'New Age', *All Souls Yearbook* (= *All Souls Church Magazine*, August 1990), from which the extract is cited.

b. 'Ideals of Pastoral Ministry', *Bibliotheca Sacra* (January/ March 1989).

c. *God's Word for Our Time* (London: Hodder and Stoughton, 1989).

d. *What is Man?* (London: National Prayer Breakfast Committee, 1989). Also published as 'The Glory and the Shame', *Third Way* (December 1990/January 1991).

1990

a. *Issues Facing Christians Today* (revised and enlarged edn. London: Collins/Marshall Pickering, 1990). Used by permission of HarperCollins Publishers Limited. = *Decisive Issues Facing Christians Today* (Old Tappan: Revell, 1990). First published 1984 (UK) and 1985 (USA).

b. *The Message of Acts* (The Bible Speaks Today series: Leicester: IVP, 1990) = *The Spirit, The Church and The World* (Downers Grove: IVP, 1990).

c. *What Christ Thinks of the Church* (revised and illustrated edn. Milton Keynes: Word UK; Wheaton: Harold Shaw, 1990). First published 1958 (UK) and 1959 (USA).

1991

a. Foreword to *For Christ and the University*, by K. and G. Hunt (Downers Grove: IVP, 1991).

b. *Life in Christ* (Eastbourne: Kingsway; Wheaton: Tyndale House, 1991). Revised and illustrated edition of *Focus on Christ* (London and Cleveland, Ohio: Collins, 1979) = *Understanding*

Christ (Grand Rapids: Zondervan, 1981).

c. *The Message of Thessalonians* (The Bible Speaks Today series: Leicester: IVP, 1991) = *The Gospel and the End of Time* (Downers Grove: IVP, 1991).

d. *Your Confirmation* (rev. edn. London: Hodder and Stoughton (1991) = *Christian Basics* (adapted for interdenominational US readership: Grand Rapids: Baker, 1991). First published 1958.

1992

a. 'Pride, Humility and God', in *Alive to God*, ed. J. I. Packer and L. Wilkinson (Downers Grove: IVP, 1992).

b. *The Contemporary Christian* (Leicester and Downers Grove, 1992).

c. 'Manufacturing Truth', *In Touch* (1992, no. 2).

d. 'Maintaining Spiritual Freshness', *InterVarsity's Student Leadership* (Winter 1992).

e. 'The Counsellor and Friend', in *A Study in Spiritual Power*, ed. J. Eddison (rev. edn. Guildford: Highland, 1992). First published as *'Bash': A Study in Spiritual Power* (London: Marshalls, 1983).

1993

a. 'Let's Talk About Sex', *In Touch* (1993, no. 2).

b. Foreword to *Under the Bright Wings*, by Peter Harris (London: Hodder and Stoughton, 1993).

1994

The Message of Romans (The Bible Speaks Today series: Leicester: IVP, 1994) = *Romans: God's Good News for the World* (Downers Grove: IVP, 1994).

For fuller details of all John Stott's writings see Timothy Dudley-Smith, *John R. W. Stott: A Comprehensive Bibliography* (Leicester and Downers Grove: IVP, 1995).

ACKNOWLEDGMENTS

Every effort has been made to secure permission for the use of copyrighted material in this book. Any errors or omissions will gladly be corrected in future printings. Grateful acknowledgment is made to the following for the use of extracts:

From *Christian Basics*, ©1991. Used by permission of Hodder & Stoughton Limited, London, England.

From *Christian Faith and Practice in the Modern World*, edited by Mark A. Noll and David F. Wells, ©1988. Used by permission of Wm. B. Eerdmans Publishing Co., Grand Rapids, Mich.

From *Confess Your Sins*, John Stott, ©1974, Word, Inc., Dallas, Tex. All rights reserved.

From *Decisive Issues Facing Christians Today*, ©1990. Used by permission of Fleming H. Revell Company, Grand Rapids, Mich.

From *Evangelical Roots*, edited by Kenneth S. Kantzer, ©1978. Used by permission of Thomas Nelson Inc., Nashville, Tenn.

From *Favourite Psalms*, ©1966, 1988. Used by permission of Three's Company, London, England.

From *Fundamentalism and Evangelism*, ©1959. Used by permission of Wm. B. Eerdmans Publishing Co., Grand Rapids, Mich.

From *Life in Christ*, ©1991. Used by permission of Tyndale House, Wheaton, Ill.

From *One People*, ©1982. Used by permission of Fleming H. Revell Company, Grand Rapids, Mich.

ACKNOWLEDGMENTS

From *One Race, One Gospel, One Task*, ed. C. F. H. Henry and W. S. Mooneyham, ©1967. Used by permission of Lausanne Committee for World Evangelism, Edinburgh, Scotland.

From *Peacemakers: Christian Voices from the New Abolitionist Movement*, edited by Jim Wallis, copyright 1983 by Sojourners. Used by permission of HarperCollins Publishers, New York, N.Y.

From *Perspectives on Peacemaking*, edited by John A. Bernbaum, ©1984. Used by permission of Regal Books, Ventura, Calif.

From *The Preacher's Portrait*, ©1961. Used by permission of Wm. B. Eerdmans Publishing Co., Grand Rapids, Mich.

From "Saving Souls and Serving Bread", printed in Christianity Today, November 7, 1980. Used by permission of Christianity Today, Carol Stream, Ill.

Taken from the book *Understanding the Bible*, by John Stott, copyright ©1972, 1976 by John Stott. Used by permission of Zondervan Publishing House.

Reprinted from *What Christ Thinks of the Church*, by John Stott, ©1990. Used by permission of Harold Shaw Publishers, Wheaton, Ill.

INDEX

Figures refer to extract numbers, not page numbers.

abortion, 882, 883
Abraham, 22, 58, 169, 192, 224, 385,
    412, 433, 451, 612, 723, 891,
    904, 908, 919, 969
acceptance, 614, 842
accountability, 294, 558, 602, 688
Adam, 286, 325, 395, 908
    and Eve, 225, 297
alienation, 288, 362, 877
ambition, 581, 582
analogy, 115, 202, 223, 542
Anglicanism, 231, 463, 684, 738
Antichrist, 914, 922, 943, 944
apostles, 132, 179, 180, 191, 200,
    204, 231, 235, 241, 351, 421,
    667–674, 678, 689, 708, 712,
    731, 744, 774, 782, 815, 830,
    921, 922, 924, 925, 945, 970
    witness of, 65, 113, 132, 140, 183,
    212, 241, 253, 255
assurance, 106, 173, 433, 437, 469–
    472, 474, 478, 726, 930
atonement, 36, 70, 72, 95, 368, 841
authority, 207, 216, 344, 366, 590,
    594–596, 623, 642, 680, 845–
    848, 850, 851, 888, 890; see also
    under God; Jesus Christ;
    Scripture

balance, 255, 257, 520, 618
baptism (water), 8, 134, 355, 371,
    377, 381, 419, 432, 451, 461,
    463, 464, 474, 485, 652, 655–
    658; see also Holy Spirit,
    baptism with
behaviourism, 290
Bible, 9, 18, 22, 169, 170, 179, 191,
    195, 199, 202, 203, 207, 211,
    215, 218, 239, 240, 242–245,
    257, 276, 277, 279–282, 299,
    338, 512, 515, 646, 723, 725,
    736, 737, 739, 750, 751, 788,

882, 893, 902, 908, 920–922; see
    also Scripture; Word of God
    'errors'/problems in, 222, 226

calling, see election; vocation
Calvin, John, 329, 400, 686, 851
Christian, characteristics of, 419,
    420, 425, 431, 432, 440, 489,
    492, 508, 528, 557, 559, 586
Christianity, 830–834
    nominal, 438
Christlikeness, 162, 367, 380, 517,
    537, 575, 906, 964; see also
    image of Christ
Christmas, 42, 132
church, 2, 133, 137, 169, 217, 233,
    242, 248, 252, 262, 264, 280,
    319, 419, 454, 568, 569, 574,
    611, 613–620, 622–626, 630,
    666, 685, 690, 693, 699, 715–
    726, 728–733, 740, 750, 751,
    759, 777, 780, 790, 795, 798,
    828, 829, 880, 892, 919, 970
    history, 217, 247, 905
    marks of, 712
    reformation of, 706, 709, 721,
    722, 733, 739
    renewal of, 733
    and state, 847
    unity of, 702–714, 739, 869
civil disobedience, 849–851
clergy, 691–694, 696
community, 66, 129, 284, 300, 315,
    615, 716, 717, 750, 819, 821,
    828, 852, 854, 856
compassion, 45, 764, 767, 769, 824,
    859, 876, 877, 934
confession, 319, 320
conscience, 67, 99, 217, 281, 298,
    300, 310–312, 369, 445, 530,
    619, 769, 811, 837, 845, 851,
    860, 862, 873, 876

conservatism (theological), 229, 252, 744

conversion, 49, 255, 380, 421, 426, 430, 443, 444, 446, 448, 453, 454, 458, 459, 485, 598, 822

covenant, 2, 22, 58, 134, 277, 278, 451, 970

creation, 2, 109, 167, 186, 225, 277, 285, 286, 293, 302, 307, 310, 315, 405, 583, 743, 840, 870, 874, 878–880, 884, 887, 888, 892, 894, 926, 938, 956, 961, 962, 968; see also God, creator

cross, 36, 38, 78–102, 316, 348, 355, 360, 368, 374, 402, 431, 441, 443, 538, 645, 736, 782, 812–815, 823, 853, 865, 868, 889, 931, 932; see also Jesus Christ, death of

cults, 130, 269

culture, 212–217, 219, 280, 300, 711, 803, 842–844, 873, 880, 887, 888, 894

death, 24, 86, 225, 325, 362, 369, 377, 403, 928, 934, 936–939, 951, 953–957, 961, 962; see also Jesus Christ, death of
  spiritual, 321, 325, 393, 936, 937
  to self, 538
  to sin, 90, 324, 486, 542, 605

'death of God', 19, 944

dehumanization, 288, 305

democracy, 855, 858

depression, 394

devil, 197, 252, 257, 261, 285, 649, 783, 945, 947, 948; see also Satan

dialogue, 713, 789, 839

discipleship, 170, 491, 555, 745

discipline, 162, 495, 545, 625

disease, 924, 925, 928, 929, 931

Dives and Lazarus, 872

divorce, 897

dominion, 296–298, 871, 885

'double listening', 772

doubt, 394, 398, 471, 472, 597, 799

Easter, 42, 132, 272

economics, 872, 873, 884

election, 422, 433–437, 439, 792, 793, 808

environment, 18, 217, 315, 858

episcopacy, episcopate, 683, 684, 687

equality, 884, 885, 890

error, 251, 252, 255, 265, 268, 677, 836

evangelicalism, evangelicals, 206, 208, 219, 235, 246, 367, 657, 684, 706, 734–747, 819

evangelism, evangelization, 8, 137, 412, 458, 624, 746, 751, 756, 763, 767, 769, 771, 773, 775–779, 782, 788, 791–799, 802, 805, 811, 818–821, 826, 828, 829, 869, 876, 878

evil, 33, 34, 36, 38, 95, 225, 251, 252, 261, 285, 300, 308, 320, 323, 362, 519, 649, 863, 864

evolution, 17

existentialism, 183, 187, 290, 916, 938

experience, 29, 40, 67, 105, 142, 143, 151, 157, 270, 272, 277, 378, 537, 610, 638, 639, 745, 785, 830, 916, 933

faith, 2, 10, 20, 170, 226, 266, 271, 348, 355, 360, 373, 377, 386–397, 400, 406, 444, 464, 467, 482, 488, 495, 498, 557, 607, 619, 655, 657, 662, 832, 839, 959

fall, 277, 286, 293, 315

family, 60, 562, 778, 944

fellowship, 27, 99, 137, 263, 305, 379, 507, 602, 624

flesh, 541

forgiveness, 79, 85, 134, 278, 317, 350, 367, 371, 373, 381, 403, 443, 463, 474, 483, 519, 868

freedom, 258, 266, 324, 334, 369, 371, 377, 413, 416, 427–429, 436, 587–590, 592–596, 648, 649

Freud, Sigmund, 308

fundamentalism, 206

God, 1–36, 278, 345, 356, 361, 378,

477, 558, 628, 653, 748, 751,
    757, 779, 780, 813, 880, 890,
    903–905, 920, 921, 931, 935,
    959, 966
acts of, 3, 186, 736
authority of, 165, 196, 725, 845,
    850
being of, 37, 169
consistency of, 13, 16, 28, 218
creator, 7, 10, 15, 17, 20, 169, 171,
    238, 288, 297, 298, 562, 593,
    743, 841; *see also* creation
fatherhood of, 20, 21, 521, 623
glory of, 167, 581, 776, 777, 962
holiness of, 26, 322
initiative of, 1, 19, 36, 88, 406,
    434, 436, 440, 736, 737
jealousy of, 23
judge, 32, 354, 383, 418, 688, 865,
    915; *see also* judgment
justice of, 823, 853, 932
love of, 29–31, 35, 36, 98, 102,
    129, 226, 290, 354, 402, 476,
    478, 497, 614, 823, 837, 931,
    932
mercy of, 31, 354
omnipotence of, 28, 354
power of, 2, 24, 28, 61, 98, 104,
    107, 109, 182, 434
righteousness of, 25, 30, 169, 354,
    374, 465, 852
sovereignty of, 5, 301, 914
transcendence of, 39
unity of, 8, 749
vision of, 2, 250, 457
will of, 17, 434, 522, 575, 729, 792
wrath of, 30, 31, 33–36, 318, 354,
    853
'God of the gaps', 19
gospel, 80, 87, 89, 243, 345, 347–
    353, 355, 358, 365, 371, 373,
    401, 404, 412, 415, 442, 615,
    616, 667, 703, 705, 730, 773,
    775, 777, 780–782, 792–796,
    810, 824, 826, 832, 833, 841,
    858, 869, 904, 942, 948
gospels, 37, 191, 211, 219, 221, 279,
    923
grace, 96, 147, 277, 348, 360, 361,
    372–374, 384, 390, 401–410,

412, 430, 434, 437, 454, 473,
    475, 517, 662, 736, 779, 832,
    840, 931
Great Commission, 758, 766, 767
growth, Christian, 480–482, 488,
    512, 513, 596
guidance, 576, 577
guilt, 83, 129, 277, 311, 369, 371,
    442, 447, 754, 811, 840

headship, 887–890
healing, 920, 927–930
heaven, 561, 931, 942, 954, 961,
    965–970
hell, 940, 942, 954, 969
heresy, 247, 248, 268
Hinduism, 68, 69, 259
history, 2, 7, 41, 105, 129, 774, 813,
    830, 831, 879, 903–909, 911–
    916, 920, 932; *see also* church,
    history
holiness, 148, 380, 433, 439, 494,
    532, 537–541, 543, 546, 547,
    557, 605, 645, 732, 760, 778,
    933; *see also* God, holiness of
holy communion, 95, 419, 474, 655,
    658, 661, 662, 664
Holy Spirit, 8, 10, 78, 114, 117, 132–
    163, 166, 169, 188, 200, 203,
    227, 233, 255, 277, 280, 345,
    371, 414, 415, 421, 458–460,
    463, 464, 471, 622, 637, 645,
    648, 650, 670, 723, 733, 736,
    737, 748, 750, 751, 754, 755,
    777, 779, 781, 841, 910, 970
    baptism with, 134, 151–153, 155
    fruit of, 150, 159, 162, 163, 493,
    494, 498, 546
    fullness of, 152–155, 158, 493,
    521, 603
    gifts of, 146, 147, 579, 700, 892;
    see also prophecy; tongues
    witness of, 65, 140, 143, 345, 471,
    521, 755
home, 60, 129, 528, 568
homosexuality, 899–901
human beings, humanity, 284–287,
    290–293, 295–299, 306, 307,
    309, 310, 314, 315, 328, 329,
    340, 584, 719, 800, 811, 843,

855, 871, 879, 880, 885, 899,
902, 937; *see also* image of God
humility, 223, 326, 437, 468, 522,
528, 548–553, 642, 645, 679,
777, 931

idolatry, 3, 7, 23, 43, 169, 250, 842,
845, 876
image of Christ, 99, 367; *see also*
Christlikeness
image of God, 171, 277, 285, 290,
292, 293, 295, 297, 298, 315,
325, 468, 836, 843, 871, 884,
885, 899, 906, 940
immortality, 367, 369, 960, 968
initiation, Christian, 134, 463, 464
integrity, 559, 602, 606, 789, 873
Islam, 68, 79, 217, 443, 835

James (apostle), 210, 385
Jesus Christ, 37–131, 169, 236, 272,
276, 284, 285, 289, 315, 318,
343, 345, 364, 371, 381, 384,
398, 430, 432, 442, 449, 568,
580, 692, 747, 750, 752, 756,
773, 774, 779, 780, 783–786,
799, 800, 831, 834, 841, 853,
864, 866, 867, 880, 889, 898,
903, 904, 906, 909, 933, 934,
937, 965; *see also* Messiah;
Word of God
appearances of, 111
ascension of, 115–118, 121, 122
attitude to, 77
authority of, 49, 50, 188, 189, 207,
208, 283, 598, 753
birth of, 44, 70, 116
controversialist, 51
death of, 36, 38, 39, 103, 105, 107,
110, 116, 129, 277, 324, 325,
355, 359, 361, 392, 404, 415,
447, 542, 832, 916, 938; *see also*
cross
deity/divinity of, 46, 63, 127,
130, 140, 202
exaltation of, 70, 116, 131, 277
humanity of, 74, 126, 127, 140,
202, 901
in the OT, 224
in other religions, 68

incarnation of, 2, 43, 47, 72, 126,
167, 202, 238, 248, 761
inerrancy of, 73
lordship of, 49, 50, 55, 56, 118,
128, 458, 559, 564, 596, 609,
710, 735, 767, 844, 845, 851,
914
love of, 45, 584, 641
mediation of, 39, 72, 88, 96, 134,
736, 749, 838, 840
ministry of, 44, 63, 78, 132, 141,
192, 685, 825, 856, 865, 886,
922, 924, 925
mission of, 761, 764, 765
name of, 131, 758
person of, 40, 43, 72
presence of, 139
priesthood of, 833
radical and conservative, 53
reign/rule of, 60, 129
resurrection of, 70, 87, 103–118,
129, 916, 938, 963
return of, 119–123, 129, 172, 323,
467, 586, 827, 842, 904, 930,
943, 944, 950, 961
revealer of God, 6, 172, 184, 280,
405
righteousness of, 74, 392
saviour, 75, 96, 118, 125, 277, 316,
358, 360, 458, 842
sinlessness of, 73, 356
source of goodness, 71, 405
suffering of, 45, 95, 278, 935
teaching of, 191, 192, 235, 273,
306, 308, 500, 550, 945
timelessness of, 124
transfiguration of, 325
union with, 355, 377, 380, 432,
447, 451, 452, 485, 486, 542,
610, 656, 704, 835
uniqueness of, 69, 70, 72, 342,
660, 749, 838, 840
victory of, 108, 128, 953, 958
words and works of, 54
work of, 10, 72, 359, 366, 470,
471, 736, 830

Jews, 68, 83, 740, 919
Job, 931, 952
John (apostle), 141, 172, 211, 263,

472, 489, 758
joy, 369, 505, 506
judgment, 13, 19, 30, 34, 91, 98, 104,
    277, 322, 348, 355, 369, 373,
    383, 412, 417, 840, 879, 913,
    937, 949, 962, 970
justification, 225, 368, 372–385, 390,
    395, 400, 406, 411, 412, 417,
    459, 474, 527, 661

kingdom, 2, 57–62, 64, 66, 550, 729,
    821, 867, 909, 910, 921, 924,
    958
knowledge, 38, 387, 501, 539, 600,
    840

laity, 691, 693, 697
last days, 912, 913
law, 377, 849, 855, 944
    God's, 24, 85, 195, 278, 299, 300,
    324, 358, 411–415, 499, 527,
    536, 810, 840, 849, 921
    moral, 287, 299, 531
    natural, 15, 16
leaders, leadership, 679, 687, 857,
    890
legalism, 413, 535
liberalism (theological), 206, 229,
    246, 249, 710, 736
liberation, 370, 406, 591, 769, 854,
    930, 962
lifestyle, 60, 560, 563, 756, 768, 873,
    878
Lord's supper, see holy communion
love, 44, 45, 81, 95, 100, 141, 213,
    286, 291, 292, 298, 300, 315,
    334, 336, 369, 433, 467, 482,
    493, 495–502, 504–506, 527,
    528, 534, 554, 556, 557, 579,
    608, 615, 618, 619, 641, 766,
    771, 819, 820, 824, 829, 869,
    891, 968; see also under God;
    Jesus Christ
Luke, 211, 781, 886
Luther, Martin, 385, 400, 474, 810

marriage, 60, 129, 462, 608, 858,
    887, 889, 891, 893–898, 902,
    944, 968
Marx, Karl, 284, 288, 835, 903

Mary, Virgin, 230, 249, 886
materialism, 562, 874, 944
meaningless, 289, 369
media, 573, 601, 796, 855
Messiah, 135, 192, 224, 272, 278,
    821, 909, 922
mind, 174, 178, 181, 184, 312, 326,
    533, 545, 553, 564, 576, 594,
    597–599, 605–609, 651, 781,
    782, 931
ministers, ministry, 574, 654, 667,
    674, 675, 679, 680, 685, 688,
    695, 697, 698, 845, 848, 892
miracles, 63, 115, 249, 670, 731, 797,
    920–927
mission, 138, 217, 488, 665, 748–
    753, 756–762, 764–769, 822
moral sense, 310, 315
morality, 60, 339, 392, 401, 526, 527,
    555
Moses, 22, 172, 192, 195, 224, 384,
    412, 810, 908, 921, 922

nature, 7, 15, 18, 39, 104, 184, 229,
    307, 446, 837, 839, 920, 926,
    927, 931
New Age, 841
new birth, 157, 456–462, 465–468,
    737, 821

obedience, 2, 6, 64, 77, 170, 176,
    209, 300, 348, 396, 415, 480,
    487, 525, 527, 556, 735, 767,
    851, 891
objective and subjective, 29, 40,
    165, 183, 255, 378, 916
Old Testament, 189, 191–193, 208,
    211, 219, 224, 360, 612, 750,
    833, 864, 908, 909, 970

pacifism, 860, 861, 863
pain, 369, 930, 962
parables, 61
pardon, 354, 379
pastors, 674–677, 682, 685, 687, 690,
    692, 698
Paul, 7, 84, 87, 97, 134, 172, 193,
    211, 225, 269, 307, 345, 355,
    384, 385, 413, 430, 489, 580,
    592, 625, 667, 740, 758, 759,

781, 794, 845, 853, 889, 908, 916, 925
peace, 506, 780, 869
  with God, 95, 378, 407, 408, 437
  world, 518, 861, 866–868
Pentecost, 132, 136–138, 723
persecution, 740, 815, 948
Peter, 134, 141, 211, 269, 916, 925
pluralism, 342, 531, 838
politics, 564, 856, 858, 882
poverty, 875, 876, 878, 884
praise, 511, 649
prayer, 26, 511, 514, 516–525, 577, 624, 729
preachers, preaching, 97, 624, 632–647, 783, 801, 805, 806, 808–810, 812–817, 825
prejudice, 14, 768, 880
pride, 85, 174, 326, 327, 335, 340, 382, 398, 433, 768, 815, 879, 880
priesthood, 319, 660, 685, 686, 690
promise, 22, 58, 135, 138, 145, 224, 394, 412, 516, 612, 655, 751, 910, 919
property, 562, 563, 627
prophecy, prophets, biblical, 50, 53, 120, 179, 192, 195, 199, 200, 219, 224, 233, 267, 338, 464, 815, 917, 918, 921, 922, 943
  contemporary, 146, 147, 267
  false, 260, 262, 269, 643
propitiation, 35, 36, 368
Protestantism, 230, 710, 713, 723, 725, 740
Psalms, 278
punishment, 863, 864

race, racism, 217, 225, 879–881
reason, rationality, 4, 174, 184, 188, 227–237, 298, 315, 386–388, 576, 599, 745, 876
reconciliation, 95, 96, 305, 368, 378, 736, 780, 816, 866, 897
redemption, 18, 74, 285, 293, 315, 368, 583, 736, 743, 807, 841, 880, 892, 909, 930
Reformation, Reformers, 242, 366, 384, 400, 461, 661, 662, 686
regeneration, see new birth

relationships, 288, 462, 503, 717, 727
religion, 6, 337–342, 344, 346, 366, 373, 426, 526, 629, 731, 743, 830, 833–840, 842, 955
remembrance, 445, 473, 490
repentance, 7, 58, 163, 350, 444, 445, 463, 464
responsibility, 22, 176, 292, 301, 334, 480, 488, 569, 588, 590, 699, 890, 967
resurrection, 377, 731, 737, 913, 924, 928, 929, 951, 954, 956, 957, 960–962; see also Jesus Christ, resurrection of
retaliation, 860, 864
revelation, 2, 7, 11, 12, 18, 26, 30, 37, 40, 67, 76, 164–187, 228–249, 264, 267, 277, 347, 389, 736, 737, 837, 839, 840, 880, 888, 921, 922, 925
revival, 132, 733
righteousness, 25, 26, 287, 414, 465, 481, 496, 526, 536, 554, 590, 852, 854, 961; see also under God; Jesus Christ
rights, 292, 302, 854, 880, 882
Roman Catholicism, 230, 400, 710, 713, 723, 725, 736

sacraments, 97, 474, 652–655, 657, 658, 662; see also baptism; holy communion
sacrifice, 500, 659, 660, 889
  Christ's, 97, 351, 660, 833, 889
  of the mass, 661
salvation, 85, 86, 102, 186, 260, 277, 305, 357–361, 363–371, 390, 393, 401, 406–408, 434, 435, 479, 510, 589, 769, 812, 833, 839, 840, 865, 907, 908, 928
sanctification, 380, 403, 404, 406, 411, 413, 458, 459, 462, 527, 841
Satan, 261, 625, 800, 946; see also devil
scholarship, 602, 604
science, 4, 16, 18, 19, 40, 171, 226, 229, 277, 296, 594, 911, 926
Scripture, 13, 52, 67, 160, 183, 184,

187, 190, 192, 193, 205, 209,
216, 226, 227, 229–232, 234,
237–239, 250, 265, 267, 274,
280, 402, 575, 577, 711, 734,
735, 745, 804, 927; *see also*
Bible; Word of God
authority of, 50, 53, 182, 188, 189,
204, 207, 208, 216, 217, 231,
283, 549, 594, 709, 739
canon of, 204, 205, 231
exposition of, 210, 634–636, 806
inspiration of, 50, 167, 179, 189,
195, 198–203
interpretation of, 206, 212, 218,
220, 227, 229, 234, 643
witness of, 9, 37, 86, 192, 229,
279, 388, 737
search for God, 14, 287
self-centredness, 330, 332, 334, 340,
369, 371, 430, 582, 628, 659,
841
self-control, 159, 493, 545
self-denial, 286, 315
self-image, 286, 293, 468
self-indulgence, 101, 332
self-love, 331, 336, 727
self-righteousness, 101, 340
self-will, 14, 332
sin, 19, 23, 24, 26, 58, 85, 90, 91, 102,
145, 148, 252, 278, 287, 306,
309, 310, 313, 316–325, 330,
331, 333, 335, 336, 350, 354,
356, 357, 359, 377, 398, 399,
412, 436, 442, 447, 458, 466,
483, 625, 754, 841, 933, 936
singleness, 893, 901, 902
service, 415, 561, 564–568, 571, 572,
579, 580, 583–586, 596, 680,
698, 764, 765, 818, 824, 829,
892
sex, sexuality, 858, 893–895, 901,
902, 944, 968; *see also*
homosexuality
social concern, *etc.*, 370, 756, 770,
818–824, 828, 829, 857, 858
social gospel, 819, 821
social justice, 323, 823, 854, 884, 911
society, 119, 293, 298, 300, 309, 323,
601, 621, 827, 844, 846, 856
sonship, 142, 483, 507

spiritualism, 939
state, 845–851, 860, 863
stewardship, 18, 175, 292, 315, 807,
840, 858, 885
subjective, *see* objective and
subjective
substitution, 9–95, 357, 368, 377, 542
suffering, 478, 649, 768, 877, 931–
933, 935

teachers, teaching, 137, 531, 624,
674, 676–678, 680, 681, 692
false, 41, 235, 248, 260, 262, 268,
269, 677, 689
temptation, 484
testimony, 784, 785
thanksgiving, 521
theology, 18, 226, 229, 238–250, 253,
497, 602, 606, 682, 739, 741,
742, 746, 774, 880, 907, 944
Third World, 873, 876
tolerance, 251, 259, 836
tongues, 138, 147, 464, 511
total depravity, 312
tradition, 52, 53, 113, 188, 227, 230–
237, 366, 684, 706, 710, 745
Trinity, 8–10, 471, 519, 633, 736,
737, 841, 970
truth, 10, 14, 175, 243, 247, 248, 254,
255, 257, 261, 262, 265, 266,
270–273, 280, 421, 579, 590,
594, 603, 618, 706, 707, 741,
782, 836, 838, 840

union with Christ, *see* Jesus Christ,
union with

violence, 865
vocation, 565, 566, 572, 574, 630,
750, 757, 828, 829, 902

war, 860–863, 867
wholeheartedness, 570
will (human), 398, 522, 523
wisdom, 38, 98, 174
witness (of church/Christians), 50,
60, 113, 129, 132, 169, 433, 561,
571, 624, 630, 755, 762, 778,
780, 785, 787, 805, 818, 825,
829

INDEX

women, 886, 892
  and men, 304, 885, 890
Word of God (Jesus Christ), 39, 180,
    181, 207, 736, 802
  (Scripture), 53, 144, 170, 171, 179,
    181, 182, 184, 186–188, 195,
    199, 202, 203, 207, 209, 216,
    218, 226, 227, 230, 232, 255,
    274, 281–283, 366, 513, 645,
    647, 652, 654, 723–725, 733,
    739, 759, 772, 873, 874, 876,
    896; *see also* Bible; Scripture

words, 805, 825
world, 362, 453, 454, 547, 561, 567,
    620, 621, 628, 720, 732, 740,
    760, 762, 772, 783, 806, 821
work, 128, 293, 462, 567, 568, 870,
    871
works, 361, 373, 384, 407, 417, 510,
    825
worship, 6, 42, 43, 84, 137, 169, 250,
    299, 338, 434, 468, 629–632,
    647, 648, 650, 651, 653, 665,
    728, 845, 931, 970